EMPIRES IN THE SUN

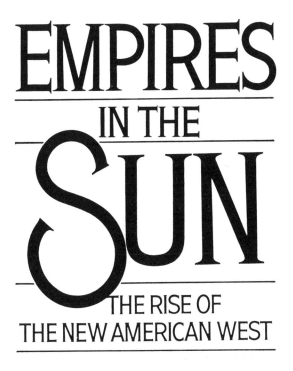

EMPIRES
IN THE
SUN

THE RISE OF
THE NEW AMERICAN WEST

PETER WILEY &
ROBERT GOTTLIEB

THE UNIVERSITY OF ARIZONA PRESS
Tucson, Arizona

About the Authors

PETER WILEY and ROBERT GOTTLIEB are working
journalists whose "Points West," a syndicated
column covering Western politics and resource issues,
is published in a number of major newspapers.
Mr. Wiley is a former editor with Pacific News Service.
Mr. Gottlieb is a director of the Southern California
Metropolitan Water District. *Empires in the Sun* is their
first book. A second, *America's Saints: The Rise of
Mormon Power*, was published in the summer of 1984.

THE UNIVERSITY OF ARIZONA PRESS
First printing 1985
Manufactured in the U.S.A.

Library of Congress Cataloging in Publication Data

Wiley, Peter.
  Empires in the sun.

  Reprint. Originally published: New York : Putnam,
c1982.
  Bibliography: p.
  Includes index.
  1. Southwest, New—Economic conditions. 2. Southwest,
New—Politics and government. 3. Minorities—Southwest,
New.   I. Gottlieb, Robert.   II. Title.
HC107.A165W53   1985   330.978'033   84-23945

ISBN 0-8165-0911-5

For our parents, Brad and Esther Wiley, and Sara Gottlieb
and for Carey McWilliams

CONTENTS

Acknowledgments

To work on a book of this scope required an enormous amount of help from people who guided us through their communities and institutions, helped us grasp a wealth of information, and told us about their lives in places like Bluff, Cedar City, Cortes, Ft. McDowell, Lukachukai, Provo, Picacho, Shungopavi, St. Johns, San Bernardino, and Trona. We especially want to thank Joseph Jorgensen, Carolina Butler, Adolfo Aguilar Zinser, Jeff Fox, Kay Kosow, Ed Dunn, Jonathan Olom, Gerald Kinghorn, Christopher McLeod, Ann and Richard Schmidt, who made us feel at home, read our manuscript, gave time and effort, advice and criticism, or tied us into their various networks where we might have functioned instead as hit and miss journalists.

We also want to thank Al Delugach, Barbara West, Ruth Galanter, Kathy Ferris, Michael Lacey, Michael Locker, George Ballis, Michael Bradley, Howard Mathews, George Baker, Lydia Lopez, Biliana Cicin-sain, Danny Beagle, Tim Brick, Steve Tullberg, and Richard Clemmer for taking the time to read parts of the manuscript and thoughtfully following our request to be ruthless in their criticism, but lavish in their praise.

There were many people who helped us in countless ways. We would especially like to thank: Colleen Colson, Sonia Johnson, Jerry Cahill, Jana Bommersbach, John MacFarlane, Debbie MacFarlane, Dennis Jolley, Rebecca Kuzins, Deedee Corridini, Gerry Pond, Kim Nelson, Don Devereux, Paul Swenson, William Reitz, Tom Kuhn, Parker Nielsen, Kathy Collard, Paul Van Dam, Lynne Van Dam, Renee Rampton, Steve Holbrooke, Dennis Gomes, Ned Day, Chester Hartmann, John Dombrink, Athia Hardt, Jim Larsen, Twinkle Chisolm, Ron Wolf, Ron Little, Judith Little, Carol Moss, Don Villarejo, Earl Warner, Barbara Hoenig, Myram Borders, Ray Toman, Lowell Bergmann, Leland Lubinsky, Richie Wassam, Richard Hall, Doris Ruiz, José Najera, Peter Carlson, Dee Jackson, John Wester, and Diane Rennert.

Peter Wiley's work on the book was inspired by working with Professor Franz Schurmann's Third Century America Project, which was funded in part by the Ford Foundation, and by close collaboration with Sandy Close and Jon Stewart from Pacific News Service.

To get this book through the intricate web of the publishing business, we want to thank Howard Bray and the Fund for Investigative Journalism, Bob Cornfield (and his bicycle), and Diane Reverand and Melissa Pierson for their support. Bob, who loves and understands books, became our real-life agent while Diane, our editor, supported our work with warmth and enthusiasm.

We would also like to thank those we live with who have persevered, loved, and tolerated us: Marge Pearson, the Yale Street Coop members, Julie Wiley, Celia Wiley, Jesse Wiley, and Nathaniel Wiley.

Preface

In February 1980 a Pacific storm devastated the Southwest. Mud slides swamped dozens of posh houses belonging to the wealthy residents of Pacific Palisades, Malibu, Topanga, and other communities on the west side of Los Angeles. As the governor declared a state of emergency, residents contacted their insurance brokers looking for funds to help rebuild their hilltop houses. Some of their fears were allayed by the knowledge that federal funds were available because of legislation originally passed in the wake of the 1965 Watts riots to assist poor residents made homeless by the destruction in the ghetto. Despite the recurring problems of fires, floods, and mud slides brought about by development in the hilly and mountainous areas on the wealthy west side, the Los Angeles supervisors and council members had more often than not allowed the necessary zoning variances.

To the north, flooding had also caused problems, particularly to the agricultural valleys of central California. Farm roads were awash, and when a levee collapsed flooding thousands of acres in the Sacramento River delta, the area's rich farmlands were threatened.

The storm intensified as it made its way eastward, regathering over the Sierra Nevada, where ski resorts had to shut down because of high winds and power failures. At first, many of the ski operators, part of the Southwest's burgeoning "leisure" industry, were ecstatic over the storm. "Look at this lovely, powdery snow we're getting," one proclaimed, anticipating the arrival of city dwellers unhappy with the flooding and mud slides.

Over the Sierra Nevada, back into the mountainous desert of the Great Basin, the storm followed the same path that a group of dam builders from the Six Companies and a couple of mobsters from the Lower East Side of New York had traveled in days past. In Las Vegas, the storm created havoc, closing thoroughfares and flooding casino parking lots.

Farther south in Arizona, the storm came close to causing a catastrophe, a man-made catastrophe. The water levels behind the dams of the Salt River Project were dangerously high and could at any moment spill over and rampage through downtown Phoenix. The flood threat resulted from a water development policy that favored big farmers and urban developers rather than flood control. There had been huge water projects in the past in this arid region. Instead of eliminating problems, the projects seemed to compound them, creating the demand for yet more water projects. Now the floods were wiping out bridges and major arteries, leading to massive traffic jams and colossal confusion.

Crossing the Great Basin to the north, the storm gathered intensity. In Utah, the flooding was the worst in a decade. In Salt Lake City, the Mormon Church, as it had in years past, readied its disciplined and highly motivated organizational apparatus to deal with any natural disaster.

Past Salt Lake City, the storm rose over the Wasatch Front and the Colorado Plateau, where the Colorado River has dug a mile-deep trench. Then the storm rose once again into the majestic Rockies. Here, ski operators in the chic Colorado mining-turned-resort towns of Aspen, Crested Butte, and Telluride welcomed the snow, anticipating an extended season and more skiers from Denver and other cities in the West. In Denver, there was more flooding, causing the usual blocked highways, traffic jams, and one big western headache.

In the end, the storm was not exceptionally heavy, yet for the arid West it had approached a catastrophe. The big urban centers of the region had been ill-equipped to handle the storm. With the exception of Salt Lake City, the cities had been poorly planned and hastily designed—instant cities that created problems as they grew. The residents of these cities, not prepared for the devastation caused by the storm, felt that things were somehow not right. How could a slight shift in nature create such monstrous problems?

The February 1980 storm seemed like a warning, a foreboding of future crisis. Instead of creating the opportunity to reassess the postwar western boom, to ask how much rapid growth can a desert environment sustain, the empire builders of the Southwest continued to push for more of the same: large-scale energy development, bigger water projects, greater cities in the desert. If the big plans continued to get bigger, then unforeseen consequences, similar to the storm, could affect this new urban civilization, where earlier civilizations had come and passed.

In the 1970s the term *Sun Belt* entered the vocabulary, describing the country stretching from Florida to central California. But the term is a misnomer, linking regions with different geographic, economic, and political features. The Southeast and Texas, both key parts of the Sun Belt, share only superficial similarities with the Southwest. In general the Sun Belt concept has worked against efforts to understand the true makeup of its constituent regions.

Empires in the Sun is about one of these regions, a region that has come to play an increasingly greater role in both the national economy and national politics since World War II. Our book is an interpretive analysis of the Southwest or arid West, a region that shares not only common geographic characteristics but is linked through a common history and a complex set of power relations.

When we use the term *Southwest*, we are talking about the arc of arid lands where annual rainfall hovers near ten inches, the lands that lie in a band which begins in southern California and the Mexican state of Baja California and sweeps north and east into the Great Basin of Utah and Nevada and then to the Rockies. This region includes the major metropolitan areas of California and the major urban centers of the interior West, including Denver, Salt Lake City, Phoenix, and Las Vegas. We have included San Francisco because, though average rainfall is about twenty inches and its source of water is the Sierras, the city historically has played a major role in the development of both the Colorado River and the Southwest.

The region is marked by the farthest reaches of the elaborate water systems developed to tap the Colorado River. For 1,450 miles, the Colorado River winds and twists its way from the highest peaks of the Rockies, drawing its water from mountains to the east and west, through the majestic canyons of Colorado, Utah, and Arizona, along the California-Arizona border into Mexico, where today it runs dry before reaching the Sea of Cortez between Baja and the Mexican mainland.

In 1857 a party of Anglo explorers led by Joseph Ives attempted to navigate the Colorado River to explore this new country of huge mountain ranges, long stretches of desert, and brilliant plateaus and canyons. "Ours was the first and doubtless will be the last party of whites to visit this profitless locality," Ives reported from his steamboat at Vegas Wash, near what became the site of Hoover Dam. "It seems intended by nature that the Colorado River along the greater portion of its long and majestic way shall be forever unvisited and unmolested."

Ives's party, in fact, passed along a stretch of the river that runs near the oldest continuously inhabited townsite in the United States, in the land of the Hopis, Zunis, and their Anasazi ancestors, located high on the sandstone mesas of the Four Corners region, where Arizona, Utah, Colorado, and New Mexico meet. Four Corners is a wild, lunar landscape, touched with a hundred shades of red and brown and the illusion of endless space, a panorama against which people seem closer to the insects than the gods. To Ives and later settlers, the Colorado bore little resemblance to the Hudson, the James, the Ohio, the Potomac, or the Mississippi—the rivers that had become the main arteries of civilization in the commercial-agrarian society of the Atlantic Coast and the Mississippi Valley. But the ancient peoples of central Arizona and the Colorado Plateau knew how to use the waters of the Colorado and its many tributaries to build their own fragile civilization. In time, the Anglo settlers would learn the same lessons.

Today, this spectral world is becoming the resource-producing heartland for the urban Southwest and the entire nation. Huge dams collect the river waters, colossal strip mines scar the landscape, and giant power plants project their looming stacks against the sky, pouring tons of noxious waste into the air. This land of the great Anasazi Indian civilization has become the pivot of a booming region.

The history of the Southwest is frequently described in terms of westward movement, the Anglo migration that pushed across the Great Plains, through the mountains, over the desert, and to the coast. To most Americans, the region is defined in terms of this migration. The history of Indian civilizations, the Spanish conquest, and the mestizo Mexican culture is viewed as a preface to the Southwest's "real" history, from the Gold Rush through the repeated cycles of boom and bust that characterize the last 150 years of the area's history.

We look at the region in terms of the ancient north-south trails that connect Mexico and the United States and we consider how, in modern times, people have converged on this region from all over the world—many of them brought to provide cheap labor. The interpenetration of Anglo, Hispanic, Indian, and Asian cultures has made for a unique situation in the Southwest. The Mexican and Indian struggle for survival and for control of land and resources has meant that the border itself has been called into question. Despite the boundary line that was drawn by Anglo conquest across the desert from Tijuana to El Paso, many Mexican-Americans still view parts of the Southwest as lost territories taken from them by the Yankees since 1848. To Indians, the Southwest remains a collection of sovereign principalities continually encroached upon by the white world.

Our southwestern region is also the territory of the state of Deseret and the Mormon Corridor, which extends from Salt Lake City to the Pacific Ocean at San Diego, as a result of the colonizing efforts of Brigham Young. It is the territory of the railroads that passed through the region on their way to the two great centers of power on the coast at Los Angeles and San Francisco. It is the territory of the upper and lower basins of the Colorado River, where control of water has been a dominant issue since the Ives party complained of this "profitless locality." This Southwest is also a region rich in energy resources such as coal, uranium, oil, and natural gas. It is an area coveted by the huge energy multinationals and mining companies who have focused on this land in recent decades in a manner reminiscent of the great resource raids on the West in the latter half of the nineteenth century.

Empires in the Sun is divided into three parts: a contemporary historical overview from the New Deal to Ronald Reagan's 1980 electoral triumph; a look at the major centers of power in the region; and a description of the constituent groups and areas of conflict in this region.

The key issues of the region—control over resources; control over land; the conflicting tendencies toward cultural diversity, homogenization, and balkanization; the emergence of new centers of power in the West that challenge the traditional centers of New York and Washington; the growth of the Pacific basin, and the Mexican connection, as crucial to the country's continuing international geopolitical designs—all have become prominent national issues. With the election of a second Californian to the presidency within a decade the importance of these issues has been heightened.

Our book, then, will shed light in a new and more rigorous way on the question of the location of national and international centers of power. Who has the power: Wall Street, the Washington bureaucracy, the energy multinationals, California, the interior West? Does a President Ronald Reagan signify the ultimate triumph of the West over the East?

In *All the President's Men*, Deep Throat tells Woodward to "follow the money." For the Southwest, it is a question of following the water, the resources, and the migratory trails. Where they lead tells us not only about the Southwest but about the future direction of the United States.

EMPIRES IN THE SUN

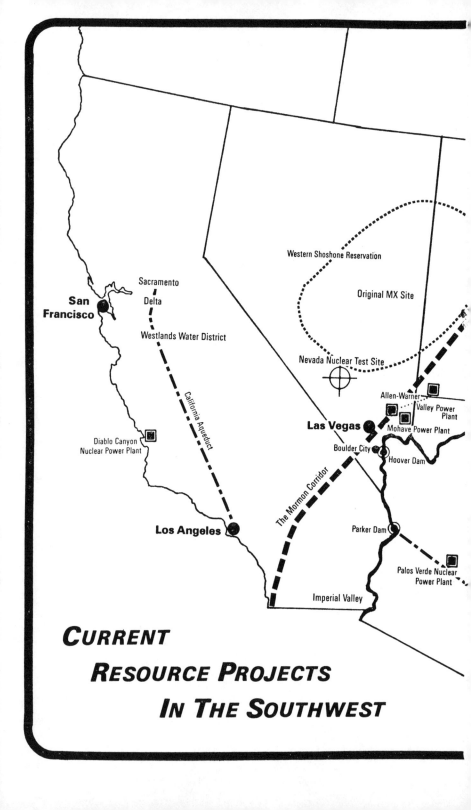

CURRENT
RESOURCE PROJECTS
IN THE SOUTHWEST

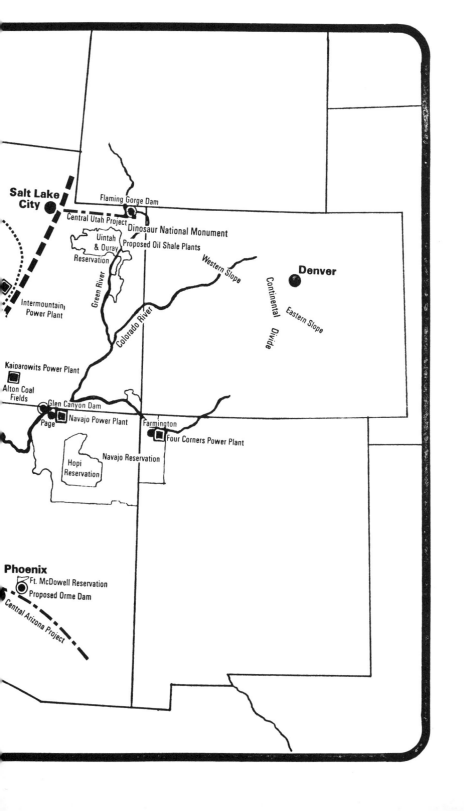

PART ONE
SUBSIDIZING THE WEST

At the start of the Great Depression, the federal government awarded an obscure consortium of western construction and engineering companies a massive contract for the construction of Hoover Dam. It was a pivotal moment for the West. The emergence of the Six Companies, which included regional corporate powers such as Bechtel, Kaiser, and Utah International, and the growth of the Bank of America coincided with the beginnings of an indigenous, resource-based, heavily subsidized southwestern capitalism. After World War II, the rise of this new regional power was also linked to the emergence of the Pacific basin as the newest and most important area of expansion for an aggressive, internationally oriented America. Simultaneously, the energy companies, at the height of their exploits in the Arab world, began in the 1950s and 1960s to lock up western resources, such as coal, uranium, oil, and gas, as part of their own international strategy.

In this section, the story of geopolitical design and the relation between corporate and political power unfolds through the Democratic administrations of John F. Kennedy and Lyndon B. Johnson, when the western utility companies devised their grand plan for resource development on the Colorado Plateau. During the administrations of Richard Nixon and Gerald Ford the Pacific basin came sharply into focus. The conflict over western resources produced a stand-off between the corporations, environmentalists, and Indian activists. The environmentalists and Indian activists gained a degree of access to the presidency in the Jimmy Carter years, but the president's blunders only produced a new corporate offensive. This is the story of massive energy plays and huge water projects in which political control of water, land, and energy became central to the development of a new urban civilization in the desert.

1 The Six Companies and the Rise of the West

On September 30, 1935, President Franklin D. Roosevelt left his crutches leaning against his folding chair and grabbed the podium with his powerful hands. Although only eleven o'clock in the morning, it was already 102°. The hot Nevada sun was beating down on the awning over the temporary pavilion built for the dedication ceremony near the Nevada end of the massive Hoover Dam.

Earlier the president and his party had been awakened in their special ten-car train by an army bugler from the Utah-based troops assigned to protect them. By 6:00 A.M. curious onlookers had gathered along the Union Pacific siding in the small Mormon oasis town of Las Vegas to stare at the train and await the president's appearance. By the time the president's party—including Mrs. Roosevelt dressed in white for the desert heat—was ready to depart for the dam site on the Colorado River, thousands of cars were headed out of Vegas on the road to Boulder City.

President Roosevelt had come to this remote corner of the West to dedicate Hoover Dam, one of the centerpieces of his huge public works program. Gathered around him were a handful of men central to his political future in the western provinces, men who had come to witness one of the key events in the whole turbulent history of the water-dependent West.

Foremost among them was the Secretary of Interior Harold Ickes. Although not a westerner, Ickes served Roosevelt at Interior as "minister of western affairs without portfolio." His department ran the numerous Indian reservations, controlled the endless expanses of resource-rich public lands in the West, and administered the all-important government-funded water projects through the Reclamation Service.

Next to Ickes stood Marriner Eccles, the maverick Mormon banker and businessman, chairman of the Utah Construction Company, one of the six companies that had built this marvel. Eccles was also a staunch Roosevelt man, serving him faithfully as chairman of the Federal Reserve Board. Then came other members of the Six Companies consortium: Felix Kahn of MacDonald-

3

Kahn, the builders of the Mark Hopkins Hotel and other San Francisco skyscrapers; Paul Wattis of the Wattis family, founders of Utah Construction; Kenneth and Stephen Bechtel of the W. A. Bechtel Company; Harry Morrison and M. H. Knudsen of Idaho-based Morrison-Knudsen; and Charlie Shea of the Shea Company.

Near them sat Averell Harriman, chairman of the Union Pacific, and Heber J. Grant, president and prophet of the Mormon Church, and a host of politicians: Senators Pat McCarran and Keyes Pittman of Nevada, Lawrence Phipps from Colorado, and Governors Henry Blood of Utah and B. B. Moeur of Arizona.

Moeur was a bitter opponent of the dam. Attacking it as a California water-grab, he had come close to turning the project into another classic shoot-out at the water hole when he declared martial law on the Arizona side of the Colorado River in 1931 and dispatched the National Guard and two old ferryboats, dubbed the Arizona Navy, to halt one part of the project. But, today, he could not miss this key event in western history.

Thousands jammed together against the rock wall at the edge of the thousand-foot gorge on the Nevada side of the dam: Reclamation Service employees from all over the West; businessmen; politicians; a teachers' delegation; public employees from all levels of government; and dozens of foreign dignitaries, including some Mexican representatives who could only wonder what this huge water development project north of the border might mean for those Mexican peasants who lived where the lower Colorado ran out to the sea.

The Roosevelt party's trip west had been a gay one, almost a grand family outing, despite the unprecedented crisis facing the country. A wave of violent strikes had swept across the nation, culminating in a general strike in San Francisco. On the Great Plains, farmers had destroyed their crops and their animals, threatening sheriffs with the rope when they posted eviction notices. In Louisiana, Huey ("Kingfish") Long, preaching redistribution of wealth, was challenging Roosevelt for leadership of the Democratic party in the South. In California, socialist Upton Sinclair, who ran as a Democrat, was narrowly defeated in his bid to win the governorship. Roosevelt had survived by walking an ideological tightrope and balancing laborer against industrialist, farmer against the railroads and processors, small-town entrepreneur against big-city financier, and western debtors against Wall Street creditors.

Before Roosevelt set out from Washington, Alfred Sloan, the head of General Motors, announced that the Depression was over, but Roosevelt and his advisers knew differently. At first the economy had responded to Roosevelt's reform measures. Now it was faltering again. One out of every three workers—11 million people—was unemployed. In his 1935 State of the Union speech, Roosevelt embraced deficit spending and announced the biggest public works program ever. Just before his departure for the West, he again announced that the government would pour a billion dollars into the faltering spending stream.

When the president reached Salt Lake City, thousands of people who had gathered for the state fair jammed the Union Pacific station to catch a glimpse of Roosevelt even though Mormon leaders had warned the faithful about the twin evils of Roosevelt and Communism. With Eccles and the Utah governor aboard, the president's train traveled down the Union Pacific line along the old

Mormon Corridor toward Las Vegas. Along the route it passed numerous farm villages where poor but worthy Saints had built their homes and farms around cooperatively constructed irrigation systems, systems dwarfed by the huge project on the Colorado. In the spectacular red-rock canyon country of southern Utah, it rumbled by the sleeping ruins of numerous nineteenth-century mining towns with odd names like Pioche, Silver Reef, Frisco, Beryl, and Zane, finally arriving in Las Vegas in the middle of the night.

September was a critical month. Huey Long was assassinated in Louisiana. On the San Francisco waterfront Harry Bridges' longshomen squared off with the shipping companies in preparation for another bitter strike. In many of California's farm valleys, now harvest brown, Communist-led farmworkers were locked in a pitched battle with a paramilitary farmers organization that was imposing its own form of martial law in the countryside.

Dr. A. H. Giannini, of the San Francisco Bank of America Gianninis, returned to California from Europe to announce, "We are Americanizing the world through our motion pictures. You see platinum blondes on the streets of Rome, in Madrid, Cannes, and Piccadilly."

Fresh from a victory over the Morgan interests for control of their banks, the Gianninis were backing Roosevelt and his campaign, led by Eccles, to reform the banking structure. Referring to new powers assigned to the Federal Reserve Board, Amadeo Peter Giannini, founder of the bank, told a reporter, "Personally, I would rather that this power be exercised by a public body in the public interest than by the New York banking fraternity."

For Harold Ickes, September was a difficult month, beginning as it did with his wife's death. Before leaving for Hoover Dam, he was approached by a go-between for Andrew Mellon, the wealthy Pittsburgh banker and former Secretary of the Treasury. Mellon wanted Ickes to desert Roosevelt and run for president as a liberal Republican. Ickes turned down the offer. He could already see that he was leaving a major mark on the Roosevelt administration despite his Republican background. He was supervising the expenditure of billions through the Public Works Administration. Hoover Dam, the largest public-funded project up till then, was awesome in its scope. Besides providing for flood control and water for both irrigation and urban use, hydroelectric plants at the dam would provide enough cheap public power to weaken the grip of the private utilities and to supply a whole new generation of homes, factories, and farms.

At the dam, the president and his entourage marveled at the spectacle, a massive water project that by all accounts was the greatest engineering feat in history. The Six Companies, a consortium of little-known western construction companies, had plugged the mighty and destructive Colorado by anchoring a giant wedge—4.5 billion cubic feet of concrete—in the volcanic breccia of the canyon walls where the red-brown water roared through a narrow gorge like a freight train.

Finally at 11:00 A.M. the president moved forward to address the crowd of ten thousand and the unseen others huddled over their radios. He called the massive dam and power stations "a twentieth-century marvel" and spoke of "altering the geography of a region." Mindful of the bitter disputes between the southwestern states that had marked the negotiation of the Colorado River Compact and the construction of the dam, he twice assured his audience that the dam represented "a just, safe, and permanent system of water rights" for the whole region.

The president knew that both he and Herbert Hoover had been criticized by many easterners and midwesterners for playing sectional favorites with this crucial project. The *Chicago Tribune* had called the signing of the dam contract in 1931 a raid on the national treasury. "It would save a lot of time, trouble, and train fares if Mr. Mellon would transfer his Treasury Department to the land of eternal sunshine," the *Tribune* sneered. "The money of Eastern taxpayers has to be shipped out there anyway." Today Roosevelt warned against sectionalism and explained that what helped one part of the country helped the other parts as well. Although he acknowledged the dam's importance to this young and dynamic region, the president focused on the national picture. He was eager to offer the olive branch to his opponents in the business community who associated his programs with creeping socialism. He would continue, he explained, to use public power as a yardstick to curb the monopolistic tendencies of the private utilities. Despite the millions being poured into public works, he saw the need for private enterprise to accept "the principal responsibility" for creating jobs in the future.

Roosevelt's words, enunciated in his eastern patrician tones, were cautious. He wanted to undercut the ever-present tendency toward sectionalism and political polarization. He knew that the California and Texas delegations, delivered to him at the 1932 convention by his one-time ally William Randolph Hearst, had secured him the nomination. He sensed now that the growing strength of California and Texas at the polls foreshadowed the new power of the western provinces.

Roosevelt knew that the role of the government was going to expand. That was clear in this region where the federal government was the largest landowner and was now preparing to make a major contribution to the economic infrastructure by providing cheap water and power. Here in this God-awful desert, Roosevelt was proposing a partnership, not an adversarial relationship. He wanted the New Deal to reflect a new spirit of cooperation between business and progressive government, not the growth of one at the expense of the other or at the expense of the common man.

Roosevelt's cautious approach contrasted sharply with the more grandiose visions of those westerners who celebrated the mighty dam project. Harry Chandler, owner of the *Los Angeles Times*, epitomized in the eyes of nonwesterners the bombastic, slightly demented, and grossly exaggerated vision of the typical western boomer. The *Times* celebrated the dam as typical of the southwestern pioneers "who have laughed at logic and driven their destiny over obstacles that rational minds deemed insuperable." Chandler ballyhooed the prospect of water for irrigation of another 650,000 acres and another 8 million newcomers in the desert valleys of southern California.

A NEW JERUSALEM IN THE DESERT

In retrospect the western boomers' seemingly exaggerated vision of future empire turned out to be uncannily accurate. By 1935 it was the Utah banker Marriner Eccles, not the California boomers, who had arrived at the seat of power in Washington and best represented the emergence of a whole new generation of western leaders. Eccles was born in 1890 in Huntsville, Utah, a small town in the mountainous canyons west of the railroad town of Ogden. His father, David, one of the foremost Utah businessmen of his day, had been born in the slums of Glasgow. In the 1850s the Eccles family became converts to Mormonism, a new inspirational religion then being preached in northern Europe and Great Britain by itinerant missionaries who spoke in glowing terms of the coming of heaven on earth in the new Zion in the mountains of the faraway American West. Soon after, the family joined one of the well-organized Mormon emigrant parties. After crossing the Atlantic in steerage, the family traveled by train to Omaha and from there by ox cart to Salt Lake City, where they arrived at the height of the Mormon immigration.

Salt Lake City in 1863 was the third new city to have been built by the followers of the martyred prophet Joseph Smith as they were driven along the western edge of the frontier, persecuted by other settlers and hounded by the federal government. Smith was a compelling, hypnotic, and controversial figure, a visionary who displayed both great charisma and the dubious skills of the confidence man. At the age of fourteen, Smith, whose family had wandered to New York from Vermont, claimed he was visited in the woods by Moroni, a messenger from God. In a second vision Moroni told him of a book written on golden tablets that gave "an account of the former inhabitants of this continent and the sources whence they sprang." Through these writings, God called on Joseph to ignore the squabbling of the various frontier sects, found a new church, and gather his people in the new Jerusalem where harmony would prevail under the leadership of a single patriarch (i.e., Smith) and all material possessions would be owned through the church.

To his followers in the new Church of Jesus Christ of Latter-Day Saints (Mormons), Joseph was the True Prophet, a man who would restore the gospel in the Americas. To others Smith and his disciples were anathema. Smith and his followers were forced to leave New York and then Kirtland, Ohio, where they had built a town and a temple. Once in Missouri, now proclaimed the new Zion by Smith, they were again greeted by violence because of their reputation as New England abolitionists, their unity as a voting bloc, their efforts to convert the Indians, and their material success as a cooperating community. The Saints, now numbering twelve thousand to fifteen thousand, were driven out of Missouri and into Illinois after a mob killed fifteen of their number and sacked and burned their houses. Smith was seized to be tried for treason but soon escaped with the help of his jailers. In Illinois, the Mormons built Nauvoo, the largest commercial center on the upper Mississippi, and they became a growing independent political force on the frontier. When Smith ran for the presidency in 1844, he and his brother were assassinated after his followers destroyed a non-Mormon newspaper. After Smith's death, leadership of the church passed into the hands of Brigham Young.

An organizational genius, Young took up the task of getting his followers to the Promised Land, now defined as somewhere beyond the prairies and as far as possible from the anarchy of the middle border. Young, characterized by Bernard De Voto as "the first American who learned to colonize the desert," rallied the fleeing Mormons, organized them into disciplined companies, and led them along the Platte River over the Rockies and into the valley of the Great Salt Lake.

By now, the Mormons were practiced community builders, but they had emerged from the eastern woodlands, crossed the vast plains, and were in a land of little rain. With no previous knowledge of dry farming, the Saints began to master the magic of irrigation. "The brethren immediately rigged three plows," wrote one of the party, "and went to plowing a little northeast of camp; another party went with spades, etc., to make a dam on one of the creeks to irrigate the land in case rain should not come sufficiently." The Saints were on their way to solving the riddle of survival in a hostile land.

Young acknowledged that the Mormons were a peculiar people, and this peculiarity made them want to keep well away from other more settled areas, such as California, and the possibility of future confrontations with the mob. Having laid out Salt Lake City as a great metropolis, they also claimed all the land between the Rio Grande and the Sierra Nevada for their newly formed state of Deseret. They pushed their settlements in a southwesterly direction with the goal of establishing a line of towns stretching through Saint George, Utah, and Las Vegas, past San Bernardino, a Mormon community east of Los Angeles, to San Diego, which, they hoped, would serve as a port at the end of the Mormon Corridor to the sea.

The Saints' expansionism and the practice of polygamy, which Smith introduced at Nauvoo, soon drew the attention of Washington. When non-Mormons reported that the Saints were in "a constant state of rebellion," soldiers were dispatched to Utah in 1857, two years after Deseret became the Territory of Utah under Governor Brigham Young. Intercepting the small force of government soldiers as it moved westward through Wyoming, Mormon guerrillas scattered their stock and burned their supply wagons. When the army reached Salt Lake City, Young and his followers abandoned the city, prepared to burn their latest home to the ground. Soon the government in Washington became preoccupied with the Civil War. The siege was lifted, but the federal government continued to intervene in the affairs of Deseret.

With the Mormon church engaged in a struggle for survival with Washington and the gentile world, Young at first emphasized the need for the Saints to build a self-sustaining agricultural economy. Commerce, Young argued, was less than righteous. "Gold and silver," Young told his followers, "will ruin any nation." As more and more miners passed through Salt Lake City, the Mormons began to engage in a wide range of economic activity with the exception of mining precious metals, which they left to the gentiles.

On their trek westward, the Saints experimented with forms of cooperative enterprise based on the communistic principles revealed to the prophet in 1832, although Smith, Young, and the church elders also seemed to oscillate between good works, real estate speculation, and profiteering from various enterprises in the church community. Late in his life, Young showed renewed interest in communalism by encouraging the establishment of experimental communities in the southern part of the state. Although he hoped these communities would become the economic and ideological heartland of a Mormon empire, Salt Lake, located along the ever-busy immigrant trail, was destined to outgrow the small towns in Mormon Dixie and become the hub of the new mountain empire.

By the end of the Civil War, Salt Lake was already the second largest city in the West and perhaps the only fully planned American city outside of

Washington. San Francisco, swelled by the forty-niners and more recently by the incredible fortunes being made on the Comstock lode, outstripped all rivals in size and grandeur. By 1880 Salt Lake City was still twice as large as Los Angeles, which was just a cow town on the verge of its first real estate boom. Above all, the Mormons' enterprise was designed to prevent their new homeland from being overwhelmed by the more powerful forces of the gentile world, represented by the mining companies and the railroads. The Saints' greatest thrust toward economic self-determination came just as the railroads were busy laying the groundwork for the modern western economy. These new links with the outside world spurred the Mormons' plans to direct their own economy.

In a poor community with little hope of attracting outside capital for anything but mining, the church played a role designed to aid capital formation similar to a central government in a modern emerging nation. Organizations like Zion's Cooperative Mercantile Institution, the School of Prophets, and Zion's Board of Trade were set up to plan production, control trade, build railroads, and encourage manufacturing. In time, communistic experiments gave way to church-owned enterprise under the control of church leaders. The Saints used tithing funds (10 percent of a member's income) to move into business after business. The Order of Enoch, set up by the Prophet Joseph to bring the Christian community of goods to the world of economics, was forgotten.

In the end, Brigham Young sounded more like a Bismarck of the desert than the prophet as he sang the praises of "iron and coal, good hard work, plenty to eat, good schools, and good doctrine." To Joseph Smith, the semiliterate field hand, the messenger of the Lord appeared in great flashes of white light, the frenzy of his religious experience serving as a counterpoint to the terrible bleakness of the westward migration. To Young, God was the "author of sciences," "the great mechanic," "the systematizer of all things." Unlike Smith, Young never claimed constant communication with God or his angels. An occasional revelation sufficed. "Prayer is good," he explained in one sermon, "but when baked potatoes and milk are needed, prayer will not supply their place."

Young turned out to be the first great western geopolitician to understand the link between environment and community building. As such, he was the most important forerunner of the great visionary planners and social engineers like John Wesley Powell, William Mulholland, and Arthur Powell Davis—the men whose works led to the construction of Hoover Dam and the takeoff of the western economy.

Despite the constant intervention of the federal government, Young used his diplomatic skills to avoid confrontations with the gentile world. With the arrival of the railroads, he demonstrated his ability to work closely and skillfully with the powerful new economic forces that would shape Utah's and the West's future. After the church constructed a number of intrastate railroad lines, Young sold them to the Union Pacific, an arrangement "favored by the church because it gave 'the Mormon roads' a powerful advocate in Washington," according to church historian Leonard Arrington.

During the years of fragmentation before the Civil War, Young had to deal with Washington's fear that a new nation, based on its own set of beliefs and social organization, was being built by the Saints on the western frontier. After

his death, the federal government intensified its attacks on polygamy, imprison-
ing many church leaders, driving others into exile, and ultimately bankrupting
the church. Finally, at the turn of the century, the church and the federal
government reached an accommodation.

A HEAD-SPLITTING AWAKENING

The Eccles family arrived in Salt Lake City in 1863, in the waning years of
the federal siege, known as the Utah War. Troops fresh from a bloody skirmish
with the Shoshone Indians were still camped on the East Bench, overlooking
downtown Salt Lake City. The church sent the Eccles family to Huntsville,
where it survived by digging potatoes for neighboring farmers for fifty cents a
day.

Marriner's father soon set out for the forests of Oregon, where he built a vast
business empire, starting with sawmills and logging railroads in Oregon and
then a lumber company in Ogden, Utah, north of Salt Lake City. In 1885
David Eccles took a second wife, who bore him eighteen children, including
Marriner, bringing his progeny to twenty-one. In 1890, the year of Marriner's
birth, David invested, at the insistence of the church hierarchy and against his
better judgment, in one of the country's first sugar beet factories. The factory
became the Utah-Idaho Sugar Company, which today is known as U and I,
Inc., the most powerful agribusiness firm in the Great Basin. U and I is now
controlled by the Mormon church.

Marriner wrote that his father "took special pride in the fact that unlike most
other men, he never had to look to the East for capital. He produced his own
capital for all his ventures, saying that a business, like an individual, could
remain free only if it kept out of debt, and that the West itself could remain free
only if it kept out of debt to the East."

Marriner Eccles went to work at the age of eight even though his father was
by this time a millionaire. After graduating from Brigham Young College and
spending two years in Scotland as a missionary, Marriner was sent by his father
to manage the funds for construction of a hydroelectric dam in a nearby
canyon. While Marriner was on the job, his father died, leaving a $7 million
estate built on a wide range of businesses that included lumber operations, sugar
factories, coal mines, heavy construction, banking, and utilities. After his
father's death, Marriner went immediately into the banking business, becoming
president of a small local bank at the age of twenty-five.

By then Ogden was a railroad town. Bernard De Voto, who was born there,
described it as a confluence of the Mormon and gentile worlds, where the
descendants of Irish railroad workers fought the Mormons for political control; a
famous madam known as Gentile Kate cruised the streets in an elaborate
carriage once owned by Brigham Young; and "gamblers, settlers, bartenders,
Mexicans, Chinks, and remittance men" jostled each other in the streets.

Using Ogden as a base, Marriner built an elaborate financial structure on the
solid foundation laid by his father. His efforts eventually led to the creation of
First Security Corporation, one of the country's first bank holding companies.
He also represented his family's substantial investment in companies like Utah-
Idaho Sugar by serving on their boards of directors.

When the stock market collapsed in 1929, Marriner was forced to scramble to forestall runs on several banks, including one owned by the Mormon church. The great crash proved to be "a head-splitting awakening" for Eccles, who became aware of "the dangers inherent in the concentration of productive forces in fewer and fewer hands." From his ten years in banking, Eccles was familiar with the process by which banks "withdrew funds from the hinterland and concentrated them in New York and other large cities [and] hastened the collapse of countless country banks." Eccles's observation of national banking practices forced him to reevaluate his father's devotion to laissez-faire and finally to abandon the notion of an economy that regulated itself without the intervention of the government. "I saw at this time," he wrote, "that men with great economic power had an undue influence in making the rules of the economic game, in shaping the actions of government that enforced those rules, and in conditioning the attitude taken by people as a whole toward those rules."

By examining the creditor-debtor relationship between the eastern centers of finance and industry and the western provinces of farming and resource production, Eccles came to the startling conclusion that "the only way we could get out of the depression was through government action in placing purchasing power in the hands of people who were in need of it." Years before the emergence of John Maynard Keynes as an influential economist, Eccles, operating out of an Ogden backwater, had discovered the essence of Roosevelt's New Deal. "My conceptions were based on naked-eye observation and experience in the intermountain region," he wrote later.

His missionary zeal fired, Eccles began to preach what he called "logical radicalism," the necessity for government action to spend the economy back to prosperity. When he addressed the Senate Finance Committee in 1932, he felt overawed by the men from the eastern business community, whom he regarded as "still our intellectual elite." Not surprisingly his call for government action fell on deaf ears. Even Roosevelt supported a balanced budget by reducing government spending through 1934.

But Roosevelt began to realize that the canny westerner's alternative to cutting the budget might be worth trying in those dog days of the Great Depression. With his trusted aide Rexford Tugwell backing the Utah banker, Roosevelt appointed Eccles a governor of the Federal Reserve Board in November 1934. The next year *Fortune* magazine pointed out that Roosevelt's new policies forced one to conclude that "M. S. Eccles of Ogden, Utah, was not only a Mormon but a prophet."

RECLAMATION AND THE WEST

While Eccles was settling in Washington, bringing a western perspective to national politics, a chance investment by his father was pyramiding into a major venture that helped build the foundation for the modern economy in the arc of arid lands. In 1900, two brothers named Wattis had approached David Eccles for a loan. They had been working for a railroad contractor who had gone bust and were looking for investors to allow them to finish the job themselves. Eccles and the Wattis brothers brought together three other Utah families, the Christensens, the Dees, and the Brownings, and raised the grand sum of $24,000.

With new funds, the Wattis brothers went on to finish the job and then embarked on construction of the Western Pacific Railroad, which linked Salt Lake City with Oroville, California, by way of the Feather River Gorge. The new Utah Construction Company, having entered the railroad business, soon branched out into other forms of construction, including the government-financed dam-building business.

In 1902 the federal government, with the passage of the National Reclamation Act, launched a new program to encourage the settlement of the arid West. The law, which created the Reclamation Service in the Department of the Interior, called for the government to build a series of dams to provide irrigation for desert lands in seventeen western states.

The reclamation program grew out of the work of Major John Wesley Powell. After navigating the Colorado River in an open boat and exploring the Colorado Plateau, Powell wrote his famous *Report on the Arid Region of the United States*. Powell reached a number of conclusions, which, although startling in their simplicity, corrected certain misunderstandings about the arc of arid lands. He pointed out that the southwestern provinces were fundamentally different from the East or even from his own birthplace in the Mississippi Valley. The difference came from the fact that beyond a north-south line that conformed roughly with the hundredth meridian the annual rainfall fell below twenty inches.

In order to make the land arable, Powell argued, irrigation works would have to be developed because "the rapid development of these mining industries [gold, silver, iron, coal, etc.] will demand *pari passu* a rapid development of agriculture." After studying the irrigation systems in numerous Mormon communities, Powell concluded that the development of water sources, at first carried out by small diversion dams, would eventually lead to the construction of "great reservoirs in the highlands where lateral valleys may be dammed and the main streams conducted into them by canals." He suggested that these water projects be developed by cooperative efforts among the farmers themselves, a method he preferred to government participation in water development. Above all, he insisted that irrigated farming be developed in harmony with the peculiar characteristics of the arid lands of the Southwest.

Powell played a major role in the gradual development of the idea that the government could take more than a passive role in the face of rapacious private interests. Despite his own opposition to a government role in the development of irrigation, his work demonstrated for the next generation that the government could serve the public that paid for it. Powell's effort to get the government to conduct an irrigation survey also played a key role in triggering the fight by small farmers for public ownership and control of irrigation systems.

This struggle was most intense in California, where American occupation produced a different pattern of settlement from the Mormon communities of Deseret. American settlers began to acquire the huge ranchos granted to the original Spanish and Mexican settlers. Along with the large blocs of land transferred to the railroads, these grants became the basis of a pattern of large-scale land ownership that persists to the present day. Ultimately, control of vast acreage by a small number of individuals and corporations not only restricted settlement but also limited the development of irrigation.

The fight between the farmers, on the one side, and the railroads and big landed interests, on the other, finally provided the momentum for public ownership and control of irrigation. These warring interests came together in the 1890s to promote a series of National Irrigation Congresses financed by the railroads and western business associations. The railroads and land barons recognized that the necessary extensive irrigation works could not be financed privately.

When Theodore Roosevelt, who came to know the West as a dude rancher, became president, he put public irrigation at the top of his agenda. After Congress passed the Roosevelt-backed Reclamation Act in 1902, a whole new era in the development of the arid West began. The Reclamation Act provided that funds from the sale of public lands in seventeen states in the arid West, excluding Texas, would be used to finance irrigation works. Over time, the Reclamation Fund would be replenished by the farmers through delayed payment for water. No interest was charged for the cost of construction, and farmers had at least thirty years to pay back the cost of the project.

The most controversial feature of the new law was the 160-acre limit, which restricted the amount of acreage for which each farmer could receive federally subsidized water. In the long-standing struggle against land monopolists, the 160-acre limit was specifically inserted in the law to keep the railroads and the large landed interests from benefiting from this public subsidy for family farmers.

Over the next two decades, the Reclamation Service, led by Frederick Newell and John Wesley Powell's nephew, Arthur Powell Davis, drew up extensive plans for the construction of irrigation works throughout the arid West. The Reclamation Service soon became a powerful fiefdom within the Department of the Interior. Reclamation Service bureaucrats tapped a new, youthful engineering impulse, more orderly and disciplined than the earlier uncontrolled profit-seeking activities that had so plagued the West, but often as unwittingly destructive. Born of a tradition that passed from the Indians to the Mormons and to the later American settlers, these bureaucrats would eventually become proficient in the geopolitics of water, laying the groundwork for new centers of economic and political power in the West.

Although the first reclamation projects were scattered throughout the West, California's greater political muscle meant that the Reclamation Service became absorbed with the development of the lower Colorado and the problems of the Imperial Valley. The Imperial Valley, a furnace where less than three inches of rain fell a year, lay just north of the Mexican border in the Colorado desert. The first would-be farmers were brought to the valley in special Southern Pacific trains. From the railroad terminus, the farmers took stagecoaches to pick out land that they got "free" for the purchase of water scrip—hence the saying "Sell the water and throw the land in free."

After the first water was brought to the valley by a private irrigation company in 1901, a three-way fight between the farmers, the private water interests, and the Reclamation Service developed over who would control the water system. When disastrous floods tore through the valley in 1906, E. H. Harriman, owner of the Southern Pacific, financed attempts to save the valley at the personal urging of his friend President Theodore Roosevelt. In order to prevent a recurrence of flooding and to develop more water for irrigation, the valley's farmers formed the Imperial Irrigation District in 1911. The district became the principal advocate of damming the Colorado and capturing water headed for

Mexico by constructing the All-American canal—so named because, unlike earlier efforts, it would originate north of the border and cross the desert in American territory. Phil Swing, the irrigators' attorney, became the chief spokesman for the project. Swing represented the new water wizards. Masters of the complex water laws, they were astute politicians who replaced the promoters of private irrigation when the Reclamation Service was created. These water brokers welded lasting ties between Congress, the bureaucracy, and the new farm and real estate interests that stood to benefit from this new subsidy.

Swing worked with Reclamation Service head Arthur Powell Davis to move their plans through the bureaucratic maze in Washington. Meanwhile, the city of Los Angeles' Power Department, led by reform-minded public power advocates, began developing its own plans to benefit from a dam on the Colorado. Planners in the Los Angeles Power Department had already cast their eyes across the desert even before the arrival of the water taken from the Owens Valley.

The Los Angeles Power Department's hopes were buttressed by Reclamation's plans to develop a series of publicly owned hydroelectric power plants at a new dam site on the Colorado. The addition of hydroelectric power to the project initially brought the private utilities led by Southern California Edison into an alliance with public-power advocates.

As the different California interests took their campaign to Washington, the project drew the attention of the other Colorado basin states. Basic to western water law was the doctrine of prior appropriation, which meant "first in time, first in right" or "use it or lose it," as it was popularly known. The upper basin states (Colorado, Wyoming, Utah, and New Mexico) knew that if California, which was already far ahead in economic growth, got hold of the Colorado, they might, because of this law, never get it back.

Finally, after years of haggling between California and the Reclamation Service, on the one side, and Arizona, Colorado, and Utah, on the other, the Colorado River Commission was formed under Herbert Hoover, President Warren Harding's secretary of commerce.

For months, the commission met, but no state would agree to any solution that restricted its use of the river until Delph Carpenter, known as the Silver Fox from Colorado, suggested that the commission divide the waters of the Colorado between the upper and lower basins rather than by states. Eventually, all the states backed Carpenter's proposal and agreed to divide the river into two basins at Lee's Ferry, Arizona, just south of the Arizona-Utah border. Each basin would receive 7.5 million acre-feet of water. (An acre-foot is equivalent to an acre covered by a foot of water.) The compact, thanks to Carpenter's maneuvers, guaranteed the upper basin states full use of their half of the Colorado without endorsing California's plans for the lower basin.

Although Hoover's historic compromise was signed in 1922, it still had to be ratified by the legislatures of the seven states. Before the ink was dry, the proposed agreement produced a new controversy between California and Arizona over how to divide the 7.5 million acre-feet reserved for the lower basin. At the last minute during the compact negotiations, Arizona had made its own proviso to the agreement, reserving to itself the waters of the Gila River, estimated to equal 1 million acre-feet. When California failed to recognize this provision, Arizona refused to ratify the compact.

Without a fully ratified compact, the Imperial Valley farmers renewed their campaign in Washington. They were joined by the towns and cities of southern California, which, under the leadership of Los Angeles, had formed the Metropolitan Water District (MWD). The MWD wanted to build a 150-mile aqueduct from the Colorado to the Los Angeles area to bring another 1 million acre-feet into the area.

California's increasingly elaborate plans for the Colorado were doggedly opposed in Congress by Arizona and an association of private power companies backed by Harry Chandler's *Los Angeles Times*. Repeated attempts by Phil Swing, now representing the Imperial Valley in Congress, and California Senator Hiram Johnson to get through Congress what would become the Hoover Dam project were blocked by Arizonans with the support of Utah and Senator Lawrence Phipps of Colorado, who has been described as "practically an open representative of private power." Finally, after Arizona twice employed the filibuster to block the project, Swing conceived of a new strategy to split up the opposition.

Years later, Swing told writer Remi Nadeau that he went to the opening of the Union Pacific's new hotel on the northern rim of the Grand Canyon in Utah in pursuit of his new strategy. There he found himself seated in a bus next to Heber J. Grant, the head of the Mormon church. Swing launched into an enthusiastic description of the Hoover project, but Grant stopped him saying, "Mr. Swing, I'm only the spiritual head of the church. President Ivins is in charge of business affairs." Swing quickly changed busses and found a seat next to President A. W. Ivins. He had found the right man. After Swing explained what he wanted, Ivins answered, "Mr. Swing, you know Senator Smoot is a stubborn man. I can't promise you his vote, but I'll promise you Senator King's support. And I will try to get Senator Smoot not to vote against you."

When Swing returned to Washington, he agreed to an amendment that limited California's share of the river to 4.4 million acre-feet. On the final vote on the project itself, Senator William King voted yes and Senator Reed Smoot, seized by a sudden headache or perhaps a revelation, left the chamber before his name was called. The Hoover Dam project was ready for the bid of a new western consortium that called itself the Six Companies.

THE SIX COMPANIES

By the time the Boulder Canyon Act had been signed into law, Eccles and Wattis' Utah Construction had already built four dams for the Reclamation Service as well as the controversial dam for San Francisco's Hetch Hetchy water system, which backed up a reservoir into part of Yosemite Valley. In the process, Utah Construction became one of the leading western construction companies and formed a close working relationship with another Great Basin construction company, Morrison-Knudsen of Boise, Idaho.

In time, this successful new partnership attracted Reclamation Service engineer Frank ("Hurry Up") Crowe as engineer and field commander. As early as 1919, Crowe had visited Black Canyon on the Colorado River near Las Vegas to look into the possibility of damming the river in this narrow gorge. When the Hoover administration announced in 1929 that it would accept bids to dam the Colorado, the Wattis and Morrison companies began casting about for sufficient funding to take on the mammoth job. When Morrison approached some eastern financiers, his scheme was greeted with skepticism. Utah and Morrison-Knudsen might be major construction companies by western standards, but eastern financiers viewed them as too small to undertake such a major project. Rebuffed, Morrison began thinking in terms of a consortium of western companies. With a million dollars from Utah Construction and $500,000 from his own company, he then approached the J. F. Shea Company of Los Angeles, a tunnel and sewer construction company that had participated in the construction of water lines for San Francisco, Oakland, and Berkeley. Company head Frank Shea brought in the Pacific Bridge Company of Portland, Oregon, and the two companies put up another million dollars. At the same time, Morrison signed up the San Francisco firm of MacDonald and Kahn.

While Morrison was looking around for partners, Henry J. Kaiser, another little-known contractor, was also toying with the idea of bidding for the dam job. Kaiser had led a restless and itinerant life since his youth in upstate New York. He had started off operating a photography studio and supply business and moved into highway construction in Vancouver, British Columbia. In the 1920s, Kaiser's business took him to California, where he worked on a number of jobs with W. A. ("Dad") Bechtel. Bechtel had gotten his start in railroad construction in Oklahoma, and his single most remarkable achievement up to that time was the invention of a folding toothbrush that fit neatly into a vest pocket. Until the late 1920s, both Kaiser and Bechtel had worked mostly on dozens of small road jobs, including one worth $737, which turned a profit of $26. When word of the massive dam project and Morrison's plans reached Kaiser in Cuba, where he was putting the finishing touches on a highway job, Kaiser got in touch with Bechtel and the two companies pledged an additional $1.5 million.

With $5 million in hand, the new partners (Utah Construction, Bechtel, Kaiser, Morrison-Knudsen, J. F. Shea, MacDonald-Kahn, and Pacific Bridge, actually seven in number) met at the San Francisco Engineers Club in early 1931 and named their consortium the Six Companies after the organization that controlled San Francisco's Chinatown. In April they submitted their bid to the Reclamation Service. When the bids were opened in Washington, the Six Companies had come in lowest. Their bid of $48,890,995.50 was $5 million below the nearest competition, the largest civil contract ever let by the United States government.

"Western builders will build the Hoover-Boulder Dam, a Western project in the West for the West," crowed the *Pacific Builder*. The Six Companies were about to embark on a project that had been promoted, despite the opposition of Arizona and the skepticism of the other Colorado basin states, as a benefit to the whole region. The *San Francisco Chronicle*, however, editorialized that the dam project showed that "California, first of all, knows what it wants, and, second, knows how to get it." Felix Kahn was even blunter telling one reporter, "We are glad we have been able to get this contract virtually for San Francisco and northern California. . . . Why, the bank clearings will put San Francisco in the front ranks of the financial centers of the nation."

In a daring move, an obscure group of western businessmen, short on capital and lacking influential ties in Washington, had won a major prize for the West, a prize that marked the beginning of the growth of a new kind of western influence in national affairs and the rise of a resource-based western capitalism.

Meanwhile, out in the desert the tiny Mormon town of Las Vegas, a division point on the Union Pacific line, was already entering the third year of a boom triggered by talk of the dam project thirty miles to the south. Despite the government's plans for a model community for construction workers that would later be turned into a tourist facility, Vegas had already taken on all the earmarks of a classic western boomtown—here today with a gaudy and chaotic vengeance and gone tomorrow, leaving a trail of broken machinery, abandoned homes, rusted automobiles, and assorted litter. As early as 1929, small tent communities blossomed near the dam site despite the bleakness and unbearable heat. By 1931 the secretary of the interior was warning job-seekers that ten thousand people had already trooped into the desert, while the labor press was reporting that some of the penniless itinerants were leaving. An organizer from the carpenters' union found four hundred people living in tents in the brush along the river bottom. Hundreds threatened to riot when it was announced that hiring for the job would take place in Los Angeles.

Most of the real estate within fifty miles of town was bought up overnight and quickly platted for future subdivisions with fanciful names like Fairview Heights and Artesian Park Estates. Two operators from Chicago formed the Southern California Land Company and announced plans to build a new town. They sold lots that they had originally purchased for $15 an acre for $50 an acre plus additional charges for needed improvements like streets, sewers, and water lines. Some lots sold for as much as $500 an acre, with the promoters planning to carve up the desert into enough little rectangles to accommodate a city of four hundred thousand despite the limited water supply.

When the Six Companies finished construction of Boulder City—long, neat rows of 750 identical wooden family bungalows, 8 men's dormitories, dining halls, and even a company store all arranged on the desert in a fanlike pattern— a modicum of order was restored, at least for a time.

Boulder City never became "the epitome of perfect planning" nor the "temperance town" promised by Commissioner of Reclamation Elwood Mead. At first, near beer was served in the company clubhouse, but in a year the police chief was running a poker game in the same building, and the Six Companies were forced to serve real beer. In fact, according to occupants, Boulder City, owned by the government and run by the Six Companies, was more of a company town than a model city. While the men and their families objected to the company store's monopoly, the Six Companies were reporting that the store was "making very gratifying profits." The residents also complained about being paid in scrip; the excessive rents charged for the cottages and dormitories; the eighteen-minute lunch period; and the ten-cent-per-day fee for drinking water. Outside Boulder City, less fortunate families clustered in a camp of tents and shanties known as Rag Town, until the law moved in and cleared them out after liquor was found in the collection of hovels.

Gambling was partially legalized in Nevada in 1931, just in time for the first paychecks. Soon after two enterprising itinerants opened a couple of casinos adjacent to Boulder City. Others prospered in Las Vegas, where liquor flowed freely in spite of a raid in May 1931 that netted sixty-four delinquents and resulted in the destruction of three breweries and two stills. "Boulder Dam and

Las Vegas are cities with a unique Western quality," reported the *Portland* (Oregon) *Labor Press*, "where persons of all classes have come to be shipwrecked, partially salvaged, and then merged with the rugged atmosphere."

While Boulder City was being laid out and Las Vegas transformed into a speculators' haven, Charlie Shea, the Six Companies' field commander, and Frank Crowe, the hard-driving engineer, marshaled their troops for the attack on the river. More than two years after the first dynamite charge was set off to divert the river, construction on the dam itself began. With the dam site ready, Shea and Crowe faced an enormous task. They had to assemble 3.25 million cubic feet of concrete, 3 million board feet of lumber, 662 miles of copper tubing, and tons of other supplies. No less than 6.5 million tons of concrete had to be poured in at temperatures that sometimes soared as high as 140°.

Working conditions, if anything, were worse than living conditions, particularly in the long tunnels where Shea and Crowe drove their men and insisted on using gasoline-engine trucks despite the dangerous buildup of carbon monoxide fumes. Six days after the first charge was set against the canyon wall, the first two men were killed.

By June, temperatures had climbed to 140°. At least one worker had died because of the heat. In August, the worst month in the desert, the workers in the tunnels began a slowdown. On August 8, all 1,400 men on the job were idled when 125 laborers in the tunnels stopped work. The workers, a number of whom had been shifted from a higher- to a lower-paying job category, were demanding $5 a day, a dollar more than the basic wage of $4 a day.

In San Francisco, Wattis explained that the strike was the work of Communists and the dread Wobblies. He told the *Examiner*, "They will work under our conditions or they will not work at all." The next day Crowe gave the malcontents three days' pay and fired them. Strikers were expelled from the dorms but moved right into camps like Rag Town. Shea and Crowe threatened to call troops in from Salt Lake City. Sheriff's deputies claimed they confiscated five hundred guns from workers.

In a show of apparent evenhandedness, the United States attorney and marshal confiscated the small arsenal held by the Six Companies' private security force and halted efforts to deport the strikers. Within a few days, the strike was broken, and the men returned to work under semi-martial law. With thousands of men waiting to take any job available, the unions had almost no impact on the job.

In the end, 110 men lost their lives in Black Canyon. When the project was completed, Secretary Ickes charged the Six Companies with seventy thousand violations of the eight-hour-day law and fined them $350,000, later reduced to $100,000.

For twenty-two months, night and day, concrete buckets swung out from the canyon wall and dumped their load into the huge forms. In early 1935, the dam was finally finished. It rose—vertical on the upriver side and in a steep, majestic upward sweep on the downriver side—from a base 660 feet wide to a curving 45-foot-wide causeway at the top, the greatest engineering feat in history. The Six Companies completed the job two years and two months ahead of schedule. These were the days before the huge cost overruns and repeated delays that have more recently characterized work carried out under government contract by private corporations. Despite the enormousness of the task and the complexity and pioneering nature of the work involved, the Six Companies made a profit of more than $10 million.

"There is every reason to believe," wrote the *Las Vegas Nevada Age* at the height of the construction boom, "in the future greatness of Las Vegas." But Las Vegas, with the completion of the dam, slipped back into desert lethargy. When the dust settled at the dam site and the presidential visit had become a small, but significant, moment in history, most of the men abandoned the cottages and dormitories at Boulder City and the tents and shacks clustered along the river and resumed the endless trek of the western construction worker moving to the next big job.

A year after the dam's dedication, a year spent building the powerhouses and connecting them to the outside world, a switch was thrown at the dam, juice surged through the lines, and downtown Los Angeles, jammed by thousands of spectators, was filled with the bright glow of electric lights. Within a few more years, Los Angeles and the Imperial Valley farmers received their share of water and power from the Colorado through the All-American Canal and the Los Angeles Aqueduct. Despite the threat of a new and deeper depression, the West was ablaze with new energy and optimism.

Working with the Reclamation Service, the Six Companies had taken the great western engineering tradition almost beyond "the realm of reason." The Six Companies and the Reclamation Service had laughed at the logic of weather and geography and had set out to transform the western landscape by bringing water and electric power to the arid lands of southern California. With this job behind them, they barely paused to reflect before throwing themselves into new efforts which would guarantee that a new industrial empire would be built on the solid foundation of cheap, government-funded water and power.

THE HIGHER INDUSTRIALISM

A month before Roosevelt's western trip to Hoover Dam, Bernard De Voto wrote a bitter essay for *Harper's* magazine entitled "The West: A Plundered Province." De Voto lamented the popular eastern image of the westerner as "gaunt, ragged and wild-eyed," a kind of "radical nincompoop" who nevertheless was adept at tapping the congressional pork barrel. "Nearly always," he wrote about press coverage of the West, "a caption informs a reader how much Massachusetts paid in federal taxes and how many miles of concrete in Idaho were laid by the sum."

The reality of western development was quite the opposite, he argued. "From 1860 on, the Western mountains have poured into the national wealth an unending stream of gold and silver and copper, a stream which was one of the basic forces in the national expansion." This stream, De Voto concluded, has made the East, not the West wealthy; in exchange the West was sometimes "tipped a fractional percent of its annual tribute in the form of government works or social supervision."

Twelve years later De Voto looked on a very different scene. "The ancient Western dream of an advanced industrial economy," he wrote again in *Harper's* in 1946, "controlled at home and able to compete nationally is brighter now than it ever has been." Indeed, in a scant dozen years—years that marked the end of the Great Depression and the successful conclusion of World War II—the West witnessed one of those incredible economic leaps that characterize its whole history of boom and bust. As Henry J. Kaiser put it, the nation was finally witnessing "the phenomenon of the self-industrializing West." Kaiser knew the process well because he and his associates in the Six Companies played a major role in this modern-day miracle.

Henry Kaiser liked to think of himself as both prophet and champion of this new western industrialism. During the construction of Hoover Dam (or Boulder Dam, as it was known in the late 1930s and 40s), Kaiser had become the project's chief publicist, generating a steady flow of news stories, information kits, progress reports, and special briefings. At the dam, he constructed guest quarters for visiting dignitaries from Washington and became particularly adept at playing politics. He coaxed and manipulated, grandstanding his way toward successful appropriations, contracts, and loans.

From Hoover Dam on through Pearl Harbor, Kaiser and the other heads of the Six Companies—individually and in a variety of partnerships and consortia, sometimes competing, sometimes working together, and sometimes sub-contracting—pursued their lucrative alliance with the federal government in the dam-building and public-works business. Kaiser also demonstrated a bold ingenuity in pushing eagerly and relentlessly beyond the narrow confines of the construction business into new, but related, enterprises, most of which were supported by government funds. He became the symbol and substance of the new western and California industrialism. *Fortune* magazine declared in 1951, "Not since the rise of Henry Ford has an industrial figure successfully gone into so many and various projects."

By the end of the 1930s, the New Deal experiment, with its massive dams and other public works, was drawing to a close. The federal government began to turn its attention toward national defense. In 1939, the United States Maritime Commission announced plans to rebuild the nation's antiquated merchant fleet. By the following year, the British were looking for American shipyards to help them rebuild their own merchant fleet. Since most of the eastern shipbuilders were working at full capacity, some of the Six Companies, led by Kaiser and Bechtel, were brought into the business with a contract to construct thirty tramp steamers. The Six Companies leaped into this new enterprise by building shipyards in Oregon and Washington and around San Francisco Bay and by moving workers from their dam projects into this new line of work. Fortuitous circumstances had propelled Kaiser and his partners into the top ranks of a western business controlled by eastern companies—in this case Todd Shipyards of New York and Bethlehem Steel, which dominated San Francisco Bay shipbuilding operations.

Kaiser regarded the war as an ideal opportunity to branch off into what *Fortune* called "higher industrialism." Again he turned to Washington for financing, this time represented by Roosevelt insider Thomas ("The Cork") Corcoran. With Corcoran's help, Kaiser persuaded the Reconstruction Finance Corporation, for which Corcoran had worked as an attorney, to lend him $20 million to set up Permanente Metals, which would produce magnesium for incendiary bombs. Permanente was a partnership with Utah Construction, Morrison-Knudsen, and MacDonald-Kahn. Kaiser had entered another indus-try with no direct knowledge of its intricacies. Permanente, however, was merely a prelude to his most grandiose scheme of all—the construction of the first fully integrated steel works in the West.

At the outbreak of the war, a *San Francisco News* columnist called the West "a crown colony of steel empires of the East." As early as the Comstock lode in Virginia City, Nevada, a number of iron foundries had been built along San Francisco Bay to produce iron products for the mines and rails for the Southern Pacific and other railroads. The largest of these factories, the Union Iron Works, was eventually bought by Bethlehem Steel to produce iron products for its shipyards in the same area. United States Steel also had a small plant at Pittsburgh, California, in the Sacramento delta and had acquired a locally owned iron foundry in Utah during the 1920s. Before Pearl Harbor, eastern steel men, based in Chicago and the Ohio Valley and led by the Bethlehem, United States, and Republic steel companies, headed off efforts by the government to finance the expansion of steel production in the West. As late as 1941 an industry-influenced government report claimed that there was adequate steel production in the West to meet anticipated needs.

Throughout the war, the cost of steel to westerners was governed by the Pittsburgh-plus formula, also known as the basing-point system. Regardless of where steel was produced, the purchaser paid the price plus the cost of shipment from Pittsburgh, Pennsylvania, and other eastern points—a practice supposedly banned by the government in the 1920s. Indeed, the western economy labored under a double burden: the pricing formula increased the costs of a basic necessity, raising the cost of every product that used steel; and the lack of a large-scale steel industry adequate to the needs of the region also deprived the economy of all the other related forms of production that develop around concentrations of blast furnaces. For example, California, because of its extensive agriculture, produced more canned food than any other part of the country. Unfortunately, all the tin plate necessary for canning had to be bought from eastern steel companies at eastern prices.

"There has never been a question of the feasibility of an iron and steel industry in this area," a western steel executive testified before Congress in the early days of the war, "but on each occasion when the efforts have been made to establish an industry, the planning and work of those engaged in the project has been frustrated through connivance and intervention on the part of existing steel corporations and existing financial combinations."

Undaunted by the eastern steel powers, Kaiser, as always, picked just the right moment to unveil his plans in Washington. The massive shipbuilding program was then under way, and there were already increasing shortages of steel. So Kaiser proposed in 1941 that he and Republic Steel build a steel plant on the Pacific Coast north of Los Angeles. As collateral for yet another government loan, Kaiser pledged the earnings from his government-financed shipyards.

The response in Washington was equivocal. Eastern steel interests were a strong presence in Washington, particularly through the Office of Production Management (OPM), a new agency designed to organize the preparedness drive. OPM initially refused to authorize the construction of Kaiser's new plant. Instead, the government financed the construction of a steel plant at Geneva, Utah, by Utah Construction and leased the plant to Columbia Steel, United States Steel's western subsidiary. As the war intensified the steel shortage, the government in 1942 finally lent Kaiser the funds to open his own pig-iron plant in California. The pig iron was shipped east to be turned into steel. Soon after Kaiser built the iron works, A. P. Giannini, who had first introduced Kaiser in Washington, supported Kaiser's steel project before the Reconstruction Finance Corporation (RFC). The agency agreed to lend Kaiser $120 million for a fully integrated steel works, but only on two conditions. First, the plant would have to be located at Fontana, east of Los Angeles, rather than on the coast. The reason given was fear of Japanese attack. According to A. G. Mezerik, Kaiser was "forced into an uneconomic location" away from sea-lanes that would provide him with access to cheap overseas raw materials. The second condition was that Fontana be a one-product plant with a small capacity and no blooming mill. This condition forced Kaiser to use a more costly and old-fashioned process for steel production. Kaiser nevertheless agreed to the conditions. He opened an iron ore mine in California's Mojave Desert, tapped the rich underground coal deposits in central Utah, and signed up the Union Pacific to haul raw materials to the plant. In the end, the Fontana plant produced steel a year ahead of United States Steel's plant at Geneva, Utah.

When the war ended, the battle over western steel was renewed. On a trip to Salt Lake City before the end of the war, Benjamin Fairless, president of United States Steel, suggested a return to the prewar situation saying, "Abstract economic justice no more demands that the Pacific Coast have a great steel industry than that New York grow its own oranges." In response western governors and chambers of commerce began a campaign to push for the expansion of western steel. At first, Fairless told the government that his company was interested in purchasing both the Geneva plant, which it was then leasing, and the Fontana plant. Kaiser was incensed that Fairless was negotiating with the government to buy out his operation.

In November 1945, as the postwar recession deepened, United States Steel made the first move by closing down the Geneva plant and by announcing that it was planning to expand its operations at Pittsburgh, California. The company announced that it would produce high-profit items at Pittsburgh, California. The announcement was interpreted to mean that United States Steel was defying any other producer to reopen the Geneva plant and compete with United States Steel's other western operation. At the same time, Bethlehem Steel announced the formation of the Bethlehem Pacific Coast Steel Corporation to operate all its West Coast shops and expand their operation into areas that competed directly with Fontana. As westerners saw it, the squeeze was on.

Kaiser, meanwhile, was also busy. With his money men at the Bank of America, he explored the possibility of acquiring Colorado Fuel and Iron (once owned by the Rockefellers) and of leasing the Geneva plant. Kaiser also demonstrated his independence by breaking with the rest of the industry to reach an accommodation with the United Steelworkers after a strike in late 1945—a move that further antagonized the eastern steel men. Then, in 1948, United States Steel reopened the Geneva plant. Faced with a Federal Trade Commission investigation of pricing, the eastern steel industry dropped the basing-point pricing system.

By 1950, Kaiser had paid off all his government loans. His new ventures were now being financed by the Bank of America and Mellon's First Boston Corporation. In the fight for a western steel industry, Kaiser had won a prolonged struggle against the eastern steel men for what he called "the decentralization of power in industrial organization" and "the independent industrialization of the West." Kaiser had defeated the attempt by the easterners to control the development of the western economy by limiting industrialization in order to keep the West a resource-producing province of the East. Above all, Kaiser's fight had been a political fight directed at Washington.

THE POLITICS OF CAPITALIZATION

October 1945 was a momentous day at San Francisco's Bank of America. At a regular board meeting, a senior officer, under the impatient prompting of A. P. Giannini, the bank's seventy-five-year-old founder, announced that the bank had just passed New York's Chase National Bank to become the largest bank in the world. In a little more than four decades, old A. P., the patron saint of West Coast banking, had transformed the original Bank of Italy from what San Francisco's Montgomery Street bankers liked to call a "dago bank" serving the "foreign colony" in North Beach into one of the most powerful financial empires in the world. Giannini, perhaps more than any other western business leader, had fought a political battle to build his vast financial empire. Above all, he had gloried in the use of well-tested anti–Wall Street rhetoric in the consolidation of his power.

Giannini's use of the popular theme of breaking Wall Street's monopoly was bound to inspire a California and western audience nurtured on the image of western colonial dependency on the East. By the end of the war, California, unlike the interior West, had clearly developed the beginnings of a semi-autonomous economy and an influential new power base. According to Carey McWilliams in *California: The Great Exception*, the anticolonial rhetoric of those like Giannini and Kaiser, although based on real conflicts, could also be used by Californians "as a smokescreen to conceal certain important aspects of its relations with other Western states."

Although western banks such as First Security in Salt Lake City, the Bank of America, Crocker, and Wells Fargo in San Francisco played a big role in financing the rapid expansion of the western economy, the federal government, and particularly the RFC, played the central role in financing the takeoff of an industrialized western economy. From 1932 to 1945, the RFC poured an astounding $50 billion into the national economy, beginning with its efforts to bail out failing banks and the railroads. During these formative years, the RFC was synonymous with the name of its chairman, Houston businessman Jesse H. Jones. Jones, a Wilson Democrat and a wealthy land developer, had strong feelings, like most westerners, about the domination of the nation's economy by eastern financial institutions. When the RFC was being considered, he counseled that "if such a government agency is created, the directors should realize that most of the country lies west of the Hudson River, and none of it east of the Atlantic Coast."

When Jones launched a major effort to bail out the railroads, historically the main instrument of eastern control of the western economy, he locked horns with the East's leading bankers, including J. P. Morgan and Company, the Rockefellers' Chase National Bank, and Chicago's Continental Bank and Trust. Jones noted that the banks were not lending their own funds to the railroads but tended to dominate management on certain roads. When the Southern Pacific, which had once dominated California politics from its offices in San Francisco, approached the RFC for a loan in 1933, Jones imposed salary limitations on its three New York–based top executives and told them, "You live too far from the tracks."

Jones, like Marriner Eccles and Henry Kaiser, saw to it that part of the Roosevelt strategy was to distribute the largesse evenly around the country. He allied with regional business leaders, such as Giannini and Kaiser, one of the first to approach the RFC for funding, to offset the concentrated power of Wall Street and the eastern industrial centers.

Between 1940 and 1944 the government invested more than a billion dollars in California aircraft plants, shipyards, steel plants, synthetic-rubber plants, and other industries. In all the major cities of the West large investments were made in both industry and military installations. Utah got one of the West's first steel plants at Geneva. Las Vegas got the Basic Magnesium Company, a project coveted by Kaiser, but ultimately run by a Cleveland company. Denver obtained an armaments plant, while two military bases were built outside of Phoenix. In the end California, with its larger population, richer farmlands, ample resources, and excellent ports with ready access to the Pacific basin battlefields and markets, benefited the most from the government-financed wartime economic boom.

A. P. Giannini's Bank of America, of all the western and California financial powers, had the sophistication and reach to challenge the eastern money centers. The bank's founder was born in the Santa Clara Valley, at the south end of San Francisco Bay, the son of a Genovese couple who had migrated to California soon after the opening of the transcontinental railroad. At the age of fifteen, young Amadeo Peter went to work in the wholesale produce business in the Italian colony of San Francisco. In a short time he became a familiar figure along the waterfront and was making regular buying trips to the inland delta country, from which the farm produce moved down the Sacramento River to the big city. In those days it was common practice for the wholesalers to act as bankers for their farmer-customers, lending them money against their crops. In this way A. P. got some early experience with finance.

In 1904, with a handful of North Beach associates, he formed his own bank, the Bank of Italy. At the turn of the century, San Francisco was the money capital of the West Coast, serving as a source of capital for eager businessmen from Seattle to Los Angeles. Indeed, with its economy built on the mammoth wealth gleaned from the mining centers of the interior, San Francisco was a major financial center with ties extending from Europe to the Orient. "But in San Francisco," wrote Bessie R. and Marquis James in their authorized classic, *Biography of a Bank: The Story of Bank of America, N.T. and S.A.*, "it was hard for a man to borrow $100 from a bank, particularly if he was a foreigner." To fill this vacuum, Giannini decided to cultivate small investors in the Italian community, many of whom had never dealt with a bank before.

After the 1906 earthquake and fire, the Bank of Italy expanded rapidly. At first most of the bank's loans were made to small real estate investors. With the passage of a new banking law in 1909, Giannini became a pioneer in the field of branch banking. The 1909 law gave a state superintendent of banking the power to authorize the opening of new branches and banned the purchase of one bank's stock by another bank. The ingenious Giannini found a way to get around the law: he had "individuals representing the Bank of Italy" buy in their own names a controlling number of shares in new banks. As his operations grew, Giannini and his associates moved quickly to expand their operations throughout the state, acquiring two San Francisco banks, a Santa Clara Valley bank, and another in San Mateo. In 1913 Giannini moved into Los Angeles despite the opposition of the conservative Los Angeles financial community, which inveighed against "the Italians" taking over their banks.

Giannini was particularly eager to serve the small foreign-born farmers. His support for what he called "the little fellow" against the established gentry enhanced his image as a populist businessman. By 1921 there were thirty-five thousand immigrant-owned farms in California out of a total of one hundred thousand farms. Giannini had first made contact with these farmers as a commission agent. He turned to these farmers when he sought to build his bank in the rich agricultural valleys of the state. He expanded into the San Joaquin Valley, offering multilingual services to Swiss, Portuguese, Armenian, and Basque farmers and lower interest rates than the small local banks, which in many cases were tied to the large established farm interests. When the farm economy, overstimulated by wartime demand, collapsed in the early 1920s, Giannini went on another bank-buying spree and acquired numerous banks that were on the verge of closing their doors.

Giannini had started out by funding the little fellow, but as farm output grew, the bank poured more and more funds into land syndicates, marketing cooperatives, processing plants, and canning operations, all of which played a major role in the transformation of the farm economy into factorylike agribusiness. By 1929, Giannini's land subsidiary, California Lands Inc., operated eleven hundred farms, most of them in the San Joaquin Valley, totaling 216,000 acres and worth $14.5 million. In a decade and a half, Giannini had moved from the champion of the little fellow to one of the biggest farm operators in the state.

In time the rapid expansion of the Bank of Italy drew national attention. When Giannini decided to seek a charter for a new national bank, he met resistance from the San Francisco Federal Reserve District. The Federal Reserve had already received orders from Washington, where the influence of the New York financial community was strongest, to discourage the alarming growth of branch banking in California. Ignoring the new restrictions on acquiring branches outside the metropolitan area in which the bank was headquartered, Giannini continued to acquire banks in Los Angeles and elsewhere.

When Giannini applied in 1926 for permission from the state banking superintendent to consolidate the complex system of banks that he had organized to sidestep the branch-banking laws, the superintendent requested detailed information on Giannini's operations and asked, "Is it your intention, in cooperation with Bank of Italy, to thus attempt a monopoly of the banking business of the State of California?" Giannini and his lieutenants decided that their best response was to launch an all-out effort to elect a new governor who would support a bank superintendent friendly to the Bank of Italy. Overnight Giannini transformed his extensive network of employees into a political force. Ultimately Giannini's man was elected.

His victory in California and successful attempt to influence the McFadden Act, the latest national banking law, whetted Giannini's appetite for further expansion, this time in quest of a transcontinental bank anchored in New York. In 1927 he purchased the New York Bank of America, an old, prestigious bank with ties to the Morgan empire.

As his banking operations expanded in New York, Giannini consulted with the Morgan interests, known as the Corner because of the location of the Morgan office at 44 Wall Street. Giannini selected his new board and chairman with Morgan approval even though this meant relegating his Italian-American friends to an advisory board. At the last minute something went awry. When he applied to the Federal Reserve for national bank status, it told the Bancitaly Corporation that it would have to transfer its ownership of the Bank of America to individuals before it could approve full powers for the bank.

Giannini's highly publicized arrival in New York and his new plans created a burst of speculation in the stocks of all the Giannini institutions. When stock prices plummeted, Giannini decided that New York brokers were leading a bear raid on his financial empire. In response, Giannini formed Transamerica to remove the stocks of his other companies from active trading and to get around the continuing attempt by the Federal Reserve to weaken his control of Bank of America.

With Elisha Walker, a member of the New York banking community, in charge, Transamerica brought together the New York and California banks under the name Bank of America National Trust and Savings Association and branched out by buying a life insurance company and a controlling interest in General Foods.

Giannini had achieved his goal. He had constructed a nationwide banking operation that was now the third largest bank in the country, but his troubles had just begun. Ever suspicious of Wall Street, Giannini realized that there were people in the financial community who agreed with the statement of a Boston banker that "we simply can't have this Sicilian peasant fruit vendor at the head of this nation's banking."

In 1931, in the midst of the Great Depression, Giannini's worst fears were realized when Walker and his associates, in a move designed to save the hard-pressed Giannini banks, proposed splitting up the Bank of America financial empire by selling some of the banks, including the New York–based Bank of America. Seeing the fine hand of the Morgan people behind this move, Giannini wired one of his associates, "Corner never liked our substantial interest in leading companies, nor our going to Europe for business."

Not to be outdone, Giannini came out of semiretirement to launch the greatest campaign of his career, a California-wide crusade to win enough proxies to take back control of the Transamerica board from Walker and his associates. Throughout the state, Giannini's able young orators trumpeted the theme of defeating Wall Street and returning control of the Bank of America to California. Giannini sat on the platform, answered questions, and pressed the flesh among his faithful followers. More like a populist political campaign than a systematic effort to regain control of a bank, the Giannini road show ended up with a massive rally at the Dreamland Auditorium in San Francisco, where ten thousand people chanted, "Save the Bank of America from Wall Street racketeers." When the final count was completed, Giannini had won by a landslide.

Having regained control of his beloved banks, Giannini set out to preach against the fears that he felt had led to the Great Depression. This effort brought Giannini, who called himself an independent Democrat, into the Roosevelt camp by means of an introduction by Joseph Kennedy. Giannini, who met with Roosevelt numerous times and was close to Jesse Jones, was particularly interested in banking reform.

For a time Giannini found that the needs of his huge banking empire dovetailed nicely with New Deal financial reforms. The first reform measure, which followed on the heels of Roosevelt's famous threat to drive the money changers from the temple, gave national banks the right to practice branch banking in all states where branch banking was already legal. This allowed Giannini to expand his operations into western states such as Nevada and Oregon while consolidating his California empire. When Ferdinand Pecora, counsel for the Senate Committee on Banking and Currency, subjected Wall Street to a withering examination of its banking practices, Giannini escaped without a scratch. Then when Eccles launched his campaign in 1935 to concentrate greater control of the Federal Reserve in Washington, Giannini became an active supporter. In general, Giannini agreed wholeheartedly with the Eccles-Roosevelt strategy to spend the country back to prosperity. He and his associates shared a similar concern—how to get people to spend more and thereby increase the volume of loans at the bank.

During World War II the bank put special emphasis on participating in the financing of the region's rapidly expanding industrial base, particularly in the aircraft industry, a field dominated by eastern banks. Although Glenn Martin and Lockheed were building planes in southern California as early as 1916 and the major shift to the West Coast began during the 1930s, the Bank of America was not asked to participate in a bankers' pool for the aircraft industry until the beginning of the war. At this point, the Bank of America joined a pool organized by Chase National for a loan to Consolidated-Vultee Aircraft in San Diego. While the government played a major role in financing the Six Companies' shipbuilding activities, the Bank of America financed many of Kaiser's ventures. In both aircraft and building, the bank made a major effort to subcontract work to smaller operations in the interior West, an approach consistent with Giannini's bid to build his banking operations on a regional basis.

The bank's aircraft loans proved to be the prelude to participation in other major syndicated loans organized by eastern money-center banks including multimillion dollar loans to Allis-Chalmers, Bendix, Chrysler, Radio Corporation of America (RCA), and Westinghouse. When the bank joined in major expansion loans for corporations with assembly plants in California after the war, Marquis and Bessie James wrote, "For the first time to any considerable degree, the Bank of America broke the isolation, the sectionalism, that had characterized the past."

In fact, the bank's activities had become so extensive in the West that the Federal Reserve Board issued a formal complaint in 1945, charging that the acquisition of additional western banks "constituted a potential monopoly with the power to stifle competition." The board found that in the five states of California, Nevada, Arizona, Oregon, and Washington, financial institutions run by Transamerica-affiliated banks controlled 38.85 percent of all deposits and 49.97 percent of all loans. Eventually the fight over Transamerica's control of western finance became so bitter that Eccles thought that Truman had removed him from the chairmanship of the Federal Reserve because of pressure "from within the inner citadel of the Giannini banking interests." Others noted that Transamerica's aggressive expansionism was bringing the Giannini empire too close to the sphere of influence of the Eccles business domain centered in Utah.

The incredible burst of wartime economic activity played a greater role in setting the pattern of western economic development than any other period in western history. Two million workers streamed into California alone, creating urban boomtowns that overshadowed Boulder City and the settlements of the West's mining districts. Richmond, California, the location of a major Kaiser shipyard, grew from 23,000 to 115,000, while San Diego doubled in size. Los Angeles ended the war as the third largest city in the nation. Rapid expansion was not confined to California. Utah, locked in its own economic depression for the two decades prior to the war, added forty-nine thousand jobs in the early 1940s. After having the highest percentage of any statewide work force employed on public works projects, Utah ended up with a labor shortage.

California and the other western states had already made major contributions in mining, agribusiness, and new areas such as the film industry before the war. The war added steel, aircraft, and shipbuilding while spinning off new ventures such as high-technology industries geared to the war effort. From this impressive base the West would build a unique new industrialism in the years to come and experience what seemed like a permanent boom economy. While much of the struggle during the war focused on whether the West would be allowed to follow the eastern pattern of industrialization, what resulted was a whole new mix of economic activity, the evolution of a distinctly western economic identity.

After the war, Carey McWilliams noted "an amazing lack of intraregional exchange and communication." More than anything, the region was a collection of occasionally feuding city states, each an oasis dependent on elaborately engineered water projects and each with its own sphere of influence separated from the others by broad deserts and major mountain ranges. The railroads had laid the foundation for a regional economy, but the struggle over water resources had increased intraregional conflict. Efforts to form regional alliances like the Six Companies were the exception, not the rule. Hoover Dam gave a major boost to the economy of the whole region, but when it was completed, the greatest share of the water and power went to southern California. The other states of the Colorado basin would have to wait their turn.

The fight for an autonomous western economy had been substantially political in character, involving attempts to gain influence in Washington and to capture public subsidies offered by New Deal programs to lay the groundwork for new industries, new cities, and a new agriculture. Californians had been the most successful at this kind of politics. California emerged from the war a young Pacific republic with a greater degree of control than ever over its own destiny.

In the rest of the western drylands, dependence on outsiders for capital and, increasingly, on the federal government for expenditures remained the keys to the existence of these states. In the ensuing years, water continued to be the single most contentious issue dividing these states. The appearance of the energy crisis eventually led to a new battle royal over who would control the resources of the interior.

2 Geopolitics at Home and Abroad

THE ENGINEERING IMPULSE GOES INTERNATIONAL

In September 1967 the United States was fatally enmeshed in a no-win situation in Vietnam, fighting a determined guerrilla army with more than two decades of military experience and the support of two Communist superpowers. Two summers before, the Watts district of Los Angeles had exploded in rioting that resulted in thirty-five deaths and millions of dollars in damage. During the summer of 1967, the rioting spread to 150 communities across the nation. The massive disorders, added to the growing antiwar movement, took on all the elements of the early stages of a social insurrection.

On September 1, Marriner Eccles, still active at seventy-seven, addressed the prestigious Commonwealth Club in San Francisco on the question of Vietnam. A critic of American foreign policy since the defeat of Chiang Kai-shek by the Chinese Communists in 1949, he was in a bitter and pessimistic mood. Denouncing the American role in Vietnam, he linked the war to the tumultuous events of the past two summers: "While we've been spending tens of billions abroad, our cities are exploding in violent protest as a result of our injustice, neglect, and failure to meet the unfulfilled promises of the Great Society." In spite of the Southwest's miraculous postwar expansion, Eccles was expressing the deepest kind of pessimism about the future. Somehow the region's incredible success had become the basis of a profound crisis.

Many of the families of the young blacks rioting in Watts had originally come from the South to work in the war industries when the demand for manpower opened up better-paying jobs for nonwhites for the first time. The rioting, however, highlighted one of the central causes of the great boom, which was at the same time its greatest social weakness: the region's economy was built on a steady oversupply of cheap labor.

To an outsider, Watts and its neighboring black and Chicano communities seemed a far cry from the squalid urban ghettos in the older parts of the country. The farm workers' hovels, clustered in labor camps along the railroad tracks and highways of California's great agricultural belts, were a testament to the impoverishment of the region's underclass. In Watts the preponderance of single-family homes and the absence of endless tenements and public housing projects seemed to be convincing proof that all classes in western society had benefited from the boom. Thus, the explosive conditions in Watts were largely ignored by the Los Angeles newspapers and the city's business elite: unemployment was rampant and often permanent; schools were segregated and inadequate; housing was substandard and largely owned by absentee landlords; health conditions were poor. Contributing most to the riots were the deaths of sixty blacks at the hands of the police between 1963 and 1965.

The Watts riots exploded the myths about the pervasiveness of the California life-style and western middle-class prosperity, which, according to *Life* magazine, made the golden state "a laboratory for experiments in modern living." In other regions, ghetto life was clearly a dead end for all but a handful who escaped into the middle class. But the ghetto realities of Watts behind its middle-class appearance made the mythical road to success an even crueler hoax. The Watts riots were a by-product of the great boom, not the result of economic collapse like the Great Depression or the disintegration of the older eastern cities.

For westerners, the Vietnam crisis, too, was a product of the very successes achieved since World War II. During the war, the West, and particularly the Pacific Coast states, had become the staging area for the military's island-hopping victories in the Pacific basin. After the war, the same states became the springboard for America's remarkable economic expansion into the Pacific.

With the end of World War II, nationalist revolt swept the entire Asian rim of the Pacific basin with the exception of Japan. "For better or worse, the colonial empires were disintegrating," wrote Richard Nixon in his memoirs. "The great question in the 1950's was who would fill the vacuum." The United States, perceiving such discontent as an invitation to Chinese and Soviet intervention, moved to anchor its Pacific defense perimeter on the Asian mainland in Korea, with Japan and the Philippines as major new bases.

In a sense, the war in the Pacific never ended. The continued militarization of the region had a hothouse effect on the western economy as federal funds flowed into the western states. The great boom gained momentum, linking the West permanently to this Washington-funded military Keynesianism.

In this period, the careers of the leaders of the Six Companies exemplified the uninterrupted rise of western businessmen and civic leaders to positions of national and international influence. For a time, Henry Kaiser was the preeminent new western businessman. He was well connected in Washington, had access to a huge line of credit at the Bank of America, and refused to be confined to one or two lines of endeavor. Instead, he set out to build an economic empire based on raw materials such as aluminum but including autos, steel, housing, shipbuilding, broadcasting, engineering, and the health field. From his new Oakland headquarters, Kaiser was building what later became known as a multinational conglomerate.

Despite his successes, Kaiser was still considered an interloper after the war. His rise to the top was seen as somehow illegitimate because of his ready access to government funding. He was the man, according to *Fortune*, who "backed a truck up to the mint." As late as 1951 he still operated under a cloud. According to George Woods, his new "minister of finance" from the First Boston Corporation, "The problem was mainly to get these boys accepted in eastern banking and industrial circles."

Kaiser's attempt to build a mass-produced inexpensive car was his most ambitious project, but the attempt was soon plagued with problems. By the early 1950s his factories were losing millions. As a newcomer, he found himself a weak fourth in an industry increasingly dominated by three manufacturers. In 1956 Kaiser called it quits in Detroit, selling his factory to a subsidiary in Argentina and taking up the production of Willys jeeps in Latin America and India.

While his bid to enter the domestic auto industry ultimately turned out to be a failure, the aluminum business proved to be Kaiser's great money-maker. With the outbreak of the Korean War, the government sought a huge increase in aluminum production, guaranteeing to buy Kaiser's increased production for two and a half years. Through this arrangement Kaiser went overseas, operating a mine in Jamaica and a mine and processing plant in India. By 1956, Kaiser Aluminum was America's number three producer of aluminum, responsible for one-quarter of all output in an industry in which the top three produced 80 percent of the country's aluminum.

As Henry Kaiser's days as an active businessman waned in the late 1950s, control of the day-to-day activities of the company passed into the hands of his son, Edgar. Edgar continued to look overseas for new expansion. He consulted with Kwame Nkrumah about a new aluminum complex in Ghana to be powered by a dam on the Volta River and went to British Columbia to open a coal mine to supply the renascent Japanese steel industry.

Ironically, the new international thrust of the former Six Companies was helping to undermine the results of the creation of a western industrial base. As both Utah Construction and Kaiser moved to provide the Japanese steel industry with iron ore and coal from mines located around the Pacific basin, the Japanese steel industry began to undercut Kaiser's steel complex at Fontana. By 1963, Kaiser, still laboring under the burden of the unsuccessful auto venture, was also losing millions in the steel business. Imported Japanese steel had moved into the western market, and Kaiser's share of the market steadily declined. Kaiser's bid to join the industrial big leagues dominated by eastern manufacturers of steel and autos was never answered outside the aluminum industry. Kaiser's expansionary drive after the war had obscured the true nature of the emerging western economy.

The West's new industrialism developed from economic activities with peculiarly regional characteristics. These included the traditional resource-based activities combined with new high-technology industries introduced by postwar entrepreneurs. Business activities associated with the control of land and resources—which dated back to the nineteenth-century mining frontier, the huge western cattle ranches, and the giant wheat farms of California's San Joaquin Valley—remained fundamental to the western economy. The mining of metals like copper, iron ore, lead, silver, zinc, and uranium was still carried out in the remote boomtowns of Arizona, Colorado, Nevada, and Utah, while Tucson and Salt Lake City continued to be major smelting centers. California and the interior West still produced their share of vital fuels such as natural gas and oil.

At the same time, agribusiness had become the dominant form of agriculture in the irrigated valleys of Arizona, California, Colorado, and Utah. In some cases, the new agribusiness giants incorporated the traditional family farmer into new integrated forms of production and distribution. In others, as the average size of farms increased and the number of farms decreased, the family farmers were finally overwhelmed.

Huge landholding corporations such as the Southern Pacific, the Tejon Ranch, the Irvine Company, the J. G. Boswell Company, and Texas-based Tenneco developed what Tenneco calls "a multiple-purpose land-use operation." These corporations could choose on the basis of profit between mineral development, farming, and huge real estate ventures. Tenneco-West, based in Bakersfield, California, is heir to the Kern County Land Company, one of the state's great land empires, formed by George Hearst's partners, James Ben Ali Haggin and Will Tevis. With 250,000 acres in California, another 850,000 acres in Arizona, and ownership of Heggeblade-Marguelas (the largest wholesale marketing operation for fresh fruit and vegetables in the country), Tenneco controls all aspects of food production and distribution "from seedling to supermarket," while providing everything from tractors to fertilizer from its own subsidiaries.

Inspired by the permanent militarization of the economy, the demand for new technology, and the rapid rise in consumer spending, such entrepreneurs as William Hewlett and David Packard started new enterprises in electronics, military hardware, and aerospace. Hewlett-Packard, begun in a small garage in Palo Alto, California, is perhaps the best known of these new industries. Working closely with Stanford University graduates, Hewlett-Packard and numerous other entrepreneurs transformed agricultural Santa Clara County into one of the leading centers of high-technology industry. With an estimated 150,000 workers, Santa Clara's Silicon Valley has grown so fast that it has spawned numerous satellite operations near other western cities, including a whole new complex near Sacramento that will eventually employ twenty-five thousand people.

The growth of leisure-time industries became another central component of the western economy. During the 1920s the entertainment industry, although essentially controlled by the eastern banks, provided a certain allure for that extraordinary boomtown, Los Angeles. With the growth of commercial and cable television and other forms of mass entertainment, Hollywood became a potent economic force in its own right as some of its financing and corporate control shifted westward.

Tourism—the selling of the West to the rest of the country as a source of entertainment—became an important part of the western economy after World War II. The great parks established throughout the Colorado River basin became a magnet for visitors to the West. Las Vegas was built solely on the tourist dollar. By 1970 tourism had become the largest source of jobs in San Francisco and by 1980 the biggest industry in California. The creation of Disneyland in 1955 became the core attraction not just for southern California tourists but for the industries that helped to transform the Anaheim–Santa Ana area of Orange County into a regional center competitive with downtown Los Angeles.

As in the construction of Hoover Dam, government subsidies were crucial to the development of the West's new industrialism. Capturing the subsidy became the essence of western politics. Farming became agribusiness in part because of the reclamation subsidies, crop subsidies, set-aside programs, and the

Food for Peace program. Repeatedly, the largest share of these subsidies went to the biggest agribusiness corporations.

The oil and natural-gas industries were also widely subsidized through depletion allowances. Hard-rock mining companies were turned loose on public lands for minimal fees. Whole sectors of the western aerospace and electronics industries were totally dependent on massive defense spending in the region. The Defense Department, according to Pacific Studies Center, was spending $1 billion a year in Silicon Valley by 1970.

The Republican party in the West, the party of the big corporations and landowners since the days of the Southern Pacific political machine, saw the westerner as a prototypical entrepreneur or Anglo male homeowner, someone who resented the government's attempts to redistribute his income to the underclass. The Democrats, on the other hand, moved in the perpetual shadow of the New Deal, attempting time and again to reconstruct the Roosevelt coalition, which ranged from wealthy businessmen with a "populist" outlook to labor and the disadvantaged. While politicians on the right and left disagreed about social-welfare spending and government initiative in crucial areas like electric power development, there was no disagreement about the necessity of massive government spending to subsidize "free enterprise." Conservatives such as Arizona's Senator Barry Goldwater and Utah's Governor J. Bracken Lee were bitter opponents of government interference in welfare and the economy, but they stood firmly behind water subsidies. Ultimately the whole thrust of the western economy into the Pacific basin was an outgrowth of the policies of subsidization and militarization.

A PACIFIC RIM STRATEGY

The leaders of the Six Companies saw a link between the western drive to colonize the desert, by spanning it with huge water projects and by filling in the empty spaces with great cities and industrial and mining projects, and the expansion of American influence into the Pacific basin. During World War II, the Six Companies' Felix Kahn told Fortune, "A contractor has to set up a tremendous organization where nothing exists, house and feed thousands of workers, establish his own communications. That is what an army does. In both instances you have to move into the 'enemy's' territory, destroy him, then clear out and set yourself up somewhere else."

When the postwar foreign-aid program for underdeveloped countries put special emphasis on the construction of the economic infrastructure—highways, water projects, irrigation, and the like—in countries newly penetrated by American interests, the West's great construction companies were ready to step in. The new international thrust was the same that had led to the development of the West: build military outposts, conquer or wipe out those natives who did not understand or accept American beneficence while allying with those who did, then model a new society after the American benefactor.

Bechtel was the first of the Six Companies to undertake major projects overseas. In the late 1930s, young Stephen Bechtel formed a company with Los Angeles entrepreneurs John McCone and Ralph Parsons to build refineries and other facilities for the major oil companies including the San Francisco–based Standard Oil of California and the Los Angeles–based Union Oil Company.

World War II was crucial to the emergence of the Bechtel empire, an empire that eventually spanned four continents and engaged in business worth billions of dollars. As their enterprise grew, the Bechtels opened a revolving door between their own upper management and the highest levels of government. Bechtel executives included several future government officials: George Schultz, John McCone, and Caspar Weinberger. By the 1970s, Bechtel was the largest privately-held corporation in the world.

The Bechtel empire first moved overseas with the construction of the Pacific basin air bases after Congress appropriated $63 million in 1939 to ring Japan with military air bases from the Philippines to Guam. During the war, Bechtel built refineries in Curaçao, off the coast of Venezuela; in Saudi Arabia for Aramco; and in Bahrain, on the Persian Gulf. Bechtel, in particular, enjoyed a special relationship with the Saudis. The company had its hand in almost every major construction project in this oil-rich kingdom, including the construction of Aramco's headquarters city at Dhahran, major pipelines, port facilities, railroads, refineries, and highway systems. Bechtel also teamed up with Morrison-Knudsen and Utah Construction to build both domestic and overseas military bases. The companies made more money building military bases than they ever had in the dam-building business.

Several of the Six Companies members cashed in on major construction and engineering contracts abroad. With the beginning of the postwar foreign-aid program, Morrison-Knudsen became a key international contractor, with several Middle East projects, including water development in Iran and Afghanistan.

Like the Six Companies, the Bank of America put special emphasis on international expansion after World War II. Early in his banking career, A. P. Giannini became a student of European finance, making regular trips to the Continent's financial capitals. At the time he bought his first bank in New York, Giannini purchased a branch-banking system in Italy and became a particular friend of Mussolini's second finance minister, Giuseppe Volpi, Count di Misurata. By the thirties, he was heavily invested in many of the major European banks.

Giannini's interest in international finance came in part from his bank's role in the movement of California's farm produce into international markets. Although he thought that his entrance into European banking was one of the reasons that the Morgan interests opposed him, his foreign banking operations remained on a minor scale compared to those of the great banks of New York.

His bank's major international breakthrough came with the implementation of the Marshall Plan, which financed the reconstruction of the wartorn European economy. Again the bank's close ties with the Democratic administration paid off. In time, a bank vice-president became head of the Italian food and agriculture division of the Marshall Plan's Economic Cooperation Administration. By the end of the Marshall Plan, the bank ranked sixth in international loans.

The Pacific basin was the most logical area for the bank's expansion. With California controlling one-third of the trade with Asia before the war, the bank opened new offices in the Philippines, Bangkok, Shanghai, and Tokyo right after the war. "We were drawn into the Asian sphere much faster than Europe by the middle fifties," recalled former president Rudolph Peterson, a key figure in the bank's international expansion in the 1960s.

Marriner Eccles also moved his Utah Construction Company into the forefront of Pacific expansion. With the end of the war, earnings in the domestic construction business had reached a plateau. Since business was increasingly competitive, partnerships like the Six Companies were harder to put together. The new battle, Eccles argued, would be against the corrosive effects of inflation. At the center of his plans for Utah Construction, Eccles put "the acquisition of basic raw materials, the ownership of which would serve as a source of profits as well as a hedge against inflation." Eccles' strategy to transform Utah Construction into Utah Construction and Mining made perfect sense. The whole history of his native state was tied up with mining. Eccles correctly predicted that a growing scarcity of raw materials would be one of the essential characteristics of the postwar world.

A student of what he called "the underlying causes of worldwide revolution," Eccles set out to move Utah Construction into the turbulent world of foreign investment and world trade, particularly in the Pacific basin. First, the company bought a mine near Cedar City, Utah, tapping resources that Brigham Young had hoped would form the basis of an industrialized Mormon state. From here, Utah Construction shipped iron ore to Japan to be used in rebuilding the Japanese steel industry.

In 1953, Utah looked into the possibility of mining an iron ore deposit known as La Montaña del Iman ("the Magnetic Mountain") in Peru. When the Utah engineers discovered that the company was sitting on mammoth ore deposits sixteen by eighteen miles long, they formed a partnership called Marcona with the Los Angeles–based Cyprus Mines. In time, the company signed major contracts to provide iron ore from the Peruvian mine to the Japanese steel industry.

Marcona eventually built a fleet of convertible ore carriers that began to ply the Pacific in a modern variation of the old Atlantic-triangle trade. The ships carried ore to Japan and then sailed to Indonesia, where they picked up crude oil to be taken to West Coast refineries. Utah also played a major role in developing Australia into a resource-producing outpost in the Pacific in which American corporations had a major stake. In the early 1960s the company, in partnership with Japan's Mitsubishi Corporation, opened a huge, immensely profitable coal mine in Queensland and an iron ore mine in western Australia, to supply both the Japanese and European steel industries.

The Six Companies and other western businesses were becoming full-fledged multinationals by the middle sixties. Not only was political power shifting westward within the United States, but the Pacific basin was turning out to be the most important area of American expansion. With the wars in Korea and Vietnam, the United States was sending the bulk of its aid to Asia despite the original European orientation of its foreign-aid programs.

Trade with the Pacific was increasing faster than trade with Europe. Japan and Canada had become the United States' major trading partners. Bank of America's Rudolph Peterson reminded audiences in 1967 that "there is no more vast or rich area for resource development or trade growth in the world today than this immense region, and it is virtually our own front yard. . . . Were we California businessmen to play a more dynamic role in helping trade development in the Pacific Rim, we would have giant, hungry new markets for our produce and vast new profit potentials for our firms."

For a time, the United States had hoped that with the northern end of its defense perimeter anchored in South Korea, the southern end would be secured at a huge new base at Camranh Bay in Vietnam. In this way, the rich rice-growing areas of Vietnam would once again become a major supplier to the rest of Southeast Asia, buttressing the United States' effort to limit the influence of nationalist-Communist movements in the area. The United States was pouring aid into Thailand, seconded by dozens of American firms investing in what the United States called "the center of political and economic stability in Southeast Asia." Kaiser Aluminum and the Bank of America had investments in Thailand, and Utah Construction and Mining, despite Eccles' opposition to the war, built one of the major American air bases from which B-52s pounded Vietnam and Laos. Indonesia, a center of anti-American nationalism until Sukarno was ousted in a bloody coup, was opening its vast storehouse of resources to American investors, including Kaiser and the Bank of America.

Japan was the pivot of American strategy in the Pacific basin. Above all, the United States was concerned that a rebuilt Japan would reorient itself toward Russia and China. President Dwight Eisenhower had explained as early as 1954 that the loss of Indochina "would take away that region Japan must have as a trading area, or it would force Japan to turn toward China and Manchuria, or toward the Communist areas in order to live. The possible consequences of the loss of Japan to the free world are just incalculable."

While Eisenhower, Kennedy, and Johnson talked in terms of variations on the domino theory, the corporations in the forefront of Pacific economic expansion saw the development of a Pacific Rim strategy as the key to orienting Southeast Asia and Japan toward the West and integrating them into a market system under United States control. For Kaiser, the Bank of America, Bechtel, Utah Mining and Construction, and others, San Francisco was the financial and strategic capital of this effort, and the Stanford Research Institute (SRI) in Menlo Park, the major think tank.

The SRI, funded by a number of large corporations and the federal government, began to articulate a conscious strategy for the Pacific basin in 1967. It fused global geopolitics with the western engineering impulse, which resulted in a modern Pacific version of the old Atlantic-triangle trade policies, and projected a complex trade and investment hierarchy with the United States and Japan at the top; the less advanced, but semi-industrialized, nations of Australia, Canada, and New Zealand on a second tier; and the least developed nations of the Pacific Rim, particularly those of Southeast Asia and western Latin America, at the bottom. The integration of all these countries into a triangular set of economic relations would enable the richer, industrialized nations to find and utilize basic raw materials while expanding the potential markets of the less developed countries.

SRI's Pacific Rim strategy, however, amounted to nothing more than a sophisticated rephrasing of the domino theory. Thus, the implications of the Vietnam conflict for SRI were "much wider than the battlefield." The neighboring countries were continually faced with "the danger of hostilities erupting across their borders," and the whole Asian rim of the Pacific would "ultimately be affected by any outcome of the present hostilities." SRI emphasized, "The war in Vietnam, therefore, must be viewed as a struggle likely to determine the economic as well as the political future of the whole region."

As the American military effort bogged down in Vietnam, officials in the Johnson administration talked about "the light at the end of the tunnel." Western leaders saw a light too, but it was the eerie reflection of Watts burning and their whole system being undermined by an endless series of brush-fire wars in Asia.

In the midst of this unprecedented crisis, Richard Milhous Nixon was elected president, inheriting the complex web of relationships between the federal government and the western corporations. Born in the small town of Yorba Linda in the agricultural belt south of the San Gabriel Mountains between Los Angeles and San Bernardino, Nixon was the first president from the West since Herbert Hoover.

Like many ambitious Westerners, Nixon "dreamed of going to college in the East," but his family, plagued by the expenses of his brother's fatal tuberculosis, could not afford to send him. After a job in Washington and a tour of duty in the navy, Nixon was tapped by the manager of the local Bank of America to run for Congress. Supported by what he called representatives of southern California's middle class, Nixon was elected to the House of Representatives in 1946. He ran successfully for the Senate in 1950 in a campaign managed by Los Angeles power broker Asa Call. He had strong financial backing from independent oilmen and agribusiness interests who were hostile to his liberal opponent's stands on the offshore oil drilling and the 160-acre law.

In 1952 Eisenhower chose Nixon as his running mate. Nixon explained in his memoirs that since Eisenhower was the candidate of the eastern liberal establishment, Nixon's selection meant "recognition of the postwar power and influence of the western United States and particularly California."

Although both he and Eisenhower were preoccupied primarily with the state of the North Atlantic Treaty Organization (NATO), Eisenhower asked Nixon to make a trip to Asia and the Far East in 1953. While visiting a number of countries that had never received an American president or vice-president before, Nixon described how he "came face to face with the new kind of Communist warfare that was already threatening the stability of the entire region." After Nixon returned from Asia convinced that "three centuries of European colonialism" were on their deathbed, he embraced the domino theory, to which he remained wedded throughout his vice-presidency. As late as 1965, he called for escalation of the Vietnam War by extending United States bombing into Laos and North Vietnam.

In 1967, after another trip to Asia, Nixon began developing a new theme— first at the Bohemian Grove, a Bay Area retreat for the western elite, and then in an article in *Foreign Affairs* entitled "Asia after Vietnam." Nixon declared that most Americans did not understand the growing importance of the Pacific basin; the vital role of Japan; and, above all, how to deal with China, which, he believed, "posed the greatest threat to peace during the final third of the twentieth century." In his Asian travels, Nixon found that even some of the staunchest anti-Communist leaders were arguing for a new and direct relationship between the United States and the People's Republic of China. Thus, he argued that United States policy should move along two tracks simultaneously. In the short run, it was necessary to take steps to buttress the non-Communist states of Asia against the danger of Chinese aggression. In the long run, he advocated "pulling China back into the world community," but "not as the epicenter of world revolution."

Although Nixon appeared to be talking about the future, he began making gestures toward China as soon as he was elected. He also began preparing the public for his planned foreign-policy departure. In July 1969 he set out to visit South Vietnam, Thailand, and Indonesia, the principal American outposts in Southeast Asia. On the island of Guam, he announced the Nixon Doctrine, describing the United States as a Pacific power being propelled across the Pacific. In his memoirs, he recalls, "I stated that the United States is a Pacific power and should remain so. But I felt once the Vietnam war was settled, we would need a new Asian policy to ensure that there were no more Vietnams in the future." He also announced that in the future the United States would supply only military and economic assistance to countries willing to supply the manpower in the fight against foreign intervention. To Nixon, a Pacific policy was the key to world peace, since American military ventures had been tied so often in the past to events in the Pacific.

For the next four years, Nixon gradually escalated the air war in Vietnam while withdrawing ground troops in an attempt to undercut the increasingly powerful American antiwar movement. At the time, Nixon's critics bitterly denounced him for "changing the color of the corpses" in Southeast Asia. In retrospect, one can see that Nixon was beginning to establish the terms for a new balance of power in the western Pacific. As he put it later, "The Nixon Doctrine was not a formula for getting America out of Asia, but one that provided the only sound basis for America's staying in."

The Chinese were already getting the message. During 1971 Henry Kissinger made two secret trips to China for high-level talks with Zhou En-lai. Then Nixon went to China in February 1972. In discussions with Zhou and Mao Zedong, Nixon argued convincingly that if the United States were to reduce its military strength in the Pacific or withdraw from the area, "the dangers to the United States would be great—but the dangers to China would be greater." Nixon and Zhou, of course, were talking about limiting Russian influence in Asia.

At the end of Nixon's visit, he and Zhou signed the Shanghai Communiqué. The first part of the document described each country's position on Korea and Vietnam, the major fronts along which the two Pacific superpowers had fought each other since World War II. The communiqué also spelled out their respective positions on Taiwan and Japan. Nixon and Zhou agreed that neither nation "should seek hegemony in the Asian Pacific and each is opposed to efforts by any other country or group of countries to establish such hegemony."

In effect, Nixon was saying when the Vietnam conflict ended—and he clearly intended to end it, short of a war with China—the United States would maintain its present sphere of influence in the Pacific. This was precisely the kind of agreement that Stalin, supported by Churchill, tried to extract from the United States in 1944–1945. Now Nixon was ready to put his name on a spheres-of-influence agreement for the western Pacific in the interest of a new balance of power.

Nixon's opening to China came as the tides of nationalism, strengthened by the Vietnamese revolution, continued to run against the United States around the world. In 1969 after the rise of Muammar el-Qaddafi in Libya, the major oil-producing countries, led by Venezuela and Saudi Arabia, began a campaign to give the Organization of Petroleum Exporting Countries (OPEC) a voice along with the major oil companies in the international oil-pricing system. A number of countries, including Iran, Libya, and Saudi Arabia, insisted that the American oil companies also share control of production with local state oil companies.

Closer to home, in 1970 Salvador Allende was elected president of Chile. Allende immediately took steps to nationalize the American-owned copper companies. Two years later, the Peruvian military began to prepare for a new wave of nationalizations. Among its targets was Marcona's huge iron ore mine.

The United States was clearly on the defensive. Although the CIA intervened in Chile to help bring about Allende's downfall, the United States simply could not intervene in all the world's hotbeds of nationalism at once. Nixon's awareness of the limitations of the traditional American response to revolutions that threatened United States interests led to his dramatic diplomatic offensive in China, the greatest departure in American foreign policy in the postwar epoch. In a bold move, he discarded the domino theory, which he had played a major role in promoting. He opted instead to try to contain the nationalist revolt by leapfrogging over the conflict in Southeast Asia and achieving a major breakthrough with China.

Central to Nixon's foreign policy were his efforts to work with major American corporations to create an atmosphere in which a number of dramatic superdeals would bind both the principal antagonists of the United States and the newly rich oil-producing countries, particularly Iran and Saudi Arabia, to a United States–oriented world economy. The Soviet grain deal and Occidental Petroleum's plan to build a large-scale fertilizer complex in the Soviet Union were integral parts of Nixon's policy of seeking détente with the Soviet Union. The defense industry and construction companies with close political ties to Nixon, such as Bechtel, moved quickly in the Middle East through massive arms sales and huge construction projects to soak up the billions in American dollars that went to pay for the new OPEC prices of oil. In general, Nixon tried to undercut the increasing number of confrontations over American interests abroad by stressing negotiations in an effort to conciliate the economic demands of Third World countries.

After two decades in Washington, Nixon was a displaced figure, a westerner turned easterner. His very isolation made him a maverick, capable of breaking with the conventional wisdom emanating from the eastern foreign-policy establishment. Furthermore, as a westerner with close ties to the region's leading strategic thinkers in the corporate world, he understood the importance of long-range planning, something that was not given enough emphasis in a government absorbed with defensive crisis management. In the end, the spheres-of-influence arrangement with China in the western Pacific and the superdeal approach to diplomacy marked the transformation of Richard Nixon from his generation's leading anti-Communist to a master of realpolitik.

THE GRAND PLAN: THE DOMESTIC RESOURCE PLAY

While the country was preoccupied with Vietnam, a loose grouping of western utilities, railroads, mining, and construction companies, including Utah Construction and Mining, Bechtel, Morrison-Knudsen, and Kaiser, were moving ahead with plans to cover the Colorado Plateau with an elaborate complex of strip mines, power plants, and coal-gasification projects to feed the growing energy needs of the Southwest. After the war, as the western economy entered the permanent boom, many of these corporations looked overseas for the resources to feed the boom. Then as the boom continued, it became apparent that the rapidly growing cities of the West were quickly outstripping their original resource base.

New plans, linked with similar plans for the northern Great Plains, envisioned a new mining boom for the remote interior far beyond any experienced during the great booms of the nineteenth century. The impact would be profound, particularly for the Indian population, under whose land much of the coal and uranium was located. Throughout the western hinterland, spectacular mining projects had come and gone, leaving a scarred landscape and crumbling ghost towns. This new raid on western resources promised to turn a number of Indian reservations and some of the most beautiful scenic areas in the Southwest into a vast industrialized energy colony under the control of major corporations headquartered in cities hundreds of miles away.

The early explorers of the Colorado canyon lands, such as John Wesley Powell, noted rich outcroppings of coal in such places as the Kaiparowits Plateau in the Four Corners region where Arizona, Colorado, New Mexico, and Utah meet. As early as the 1920s, the Los Angeles Department of Water and Power, driven by visions of an eternally expanding city, began to study coal from the Four Corners region in their quest for new sources of energy. By the 1950s, California utilities—particularly the Los Angeles Department of Water and Power which relied on several oil-burning steam plants within the area—realized that they would soon have to go outside the region for new sources of energy. Smog attacks in Los Angeles had worsened. Air quality had deteriorated so badly in southern California that use of coal meant generating stations would have to be built well beyond the city limits. In effect, the department wanted to import electricity while exporting the smog.

Meanwhile, utilities in Phoenix and Tucson were also facing an energy crunch. Arizona Public Service, for example, drew its supply from a couple of oil- and gas-fired plants, small hydroelectric plants, and a number of plants that used wood chips and sawdust from nearby sawmills. The utility, which relied on natural gas from the El Paso Company, was informed that when its twenty-year contract ran out in 1955 there might be difficulties in obtaining future supplies. It feared that California utilities might preempt the Texas gas. When the Arizona utilities realized that they had to diversify their supplies to keep up with the incredible population growth in and around Phoenix and Tucson, they began to focus on the Colorado Plateau and particularly on coal reserves located on the Navajo and Hopi reservations.

A few years earlier, Utah Construction and Mining, in line with its postwar resource strategy, had also looked into Four Corners coal. "We had come up with the idea that natural gas and oil were just too precious to burn for electricity," recalled Utah's Edmund Wattis Littlefield. In 1957, Utah signed a contract with the Navajo Tribal Council to lease more than thirty-one thousand acres of Navajo coal for 15 cents a ton. For three years, Utah looked for customers for its coal. "We tried everything we could think of," said Littlefield. "And nobody sniffed at our bait." Finally, Utah persuaded Arizona Public Service to buy Navajo coal for about $2.50 a ton. With a ready source of cheap coal, the utility decided to construct the first unit of the Four Corners power plant near Farmington, New Mexico.

As plans for energy development on the Colorado Plateau progressed, Arizona Public Service and a number of California utilities began to argue that the time was right for a regionwide strategy for energy development. Arizona Public Service, although wary of California's ability to get what it wanted, was forced to conclude that the smaller southwestern utilities needed California as much as California needed them. In order to expand, it needed large-scale capital-intensive projects. Only the California utilities could muster the huge amounts of capital needed for these mammoth plants. The southwestern utilities had to link up with California, recalled the Arizona company's William Reilly, despite their great fear that "if California said 'frog,' somebody over here would have to jump." Nervous about the consequences, Arizona Public Service and Public Service of New Mexico decided to join the discussions about building a regional power grid with California at the center of the talks. The discussions, because of their regional character, were unique. For the first time, the utilities dealt with joint financing, construction, and sharing of power, in some cases involving both private and public utilities.

The major thrust of the early discussions, even before a coalition was formalized, centered around what James Mulloy of the Los Angeles Department of Water and Power called "the Grand Plan." The Grand Plan involved the construction of massive coal and nuclear power plants to provide an ample and inexpensive new energy source for the West's booming metropolises via economies of scale.

The idea, according to Mulloy, was that coal-fired plants would be built inland, while the California utilities would build nuclear plants on the coast. Plans for coastal nuclear plants, such as Southern California Edison's plant at San Onofre and the Los Angeles department's plant at Malibu (which was later scrapped), were already on the drawing boards. Ocean water could be used for cooling to eliminate the problem of water scarcity. Transmission lines, which would bring electricity from the coal-fired plants on the Colorado Plateau, could simply be reversed to carry some of the nuclear-generated power back to the interior West.

In 1964 the coalition became a formal entity called Western Energy Supply and Transmission (WEST) Associates. Within a short period of time, WEST included twenty-one utilities in Arizona, California, Colorado, Nevada, New Mexico, Utah, and Texas, including municipally owned utilities in California, Colorado, and Arizona. The formation of WEST Associates gave a major push to the utilities' plans for the Colorado Plateau. The Four Corners plant was expanded with the addition of three much larger units after El Paso Electric, Public Service of New Mexico, the Salt River Project, Southern California

Edison, and Tucson Gas and Electric joined the project. The utilities then turned their attention to a new source of coal on Black Mesa in the joint-use area controlled and fought over by the Hopi and Navajo tribes.

The private utilities' plans, however, faced greater and greater opposition as they collided with the Bureau of Reclamation's plans for the Colorado River and then became entangled in the fight between the bureau and environmentalists over building dams in the area's spectacular national parks.

The Bureau of Reclamation emerged from the New Deal dam-building era as one of the most powerful bureaucratic fiefdoms in Washington. In 1946 the agency prepared for a new period of expansion by publishing a dramatic program for massive water development on the Colorado. Citing overdevelopment of groundwater in the Phoenix area; the need for more power in Arizona, southern California, and Salt Lake City; and the need for more irrigation in Utah's Uintah Basin and the Grand Valley of Colorado, the bureau proposed building another 134 water projects, 100 in the upper Colorado basin and the rest in the lower basin, at a price of more than $2 billion. Noting the future importance of the huge deposits of coal, oil shale, and uranium in the basin, the bureau concluded that "tomorrow the Colorado River will be utilized to the very last drop."

Having devoted much of its energies to California's water needs, the Bureau of Reclamation recognized that the next big development schemes would take place in the other Colorado basin states, particularly Arizona. After the bureau's plans were revealed, Arizona water users led the charge to get their share of the Colorado. Their plan, the Central Arizona Project, was the largest multipurpose project ever proposed. It involved diverting 1.2 million acre-feet at Parker Dam on the Colorado, pumping it over the mountains using hydroelectric power generated at Bridge Canyon in the Grand Canyon, and distributing the water throughout central Arizona. Arizona finally ratified the Colorado River Compact in 1944 in preparation for the battle over the project.

In Congress, the fight for the project was led by Arizona Senators Ernest MacFarland and Carl Hayden, a close ally of the Bureau of Reclamation. While the bureau officials allied with Arizona, California, with a larger congressional delegation, continued to keep the Central Arizona Project bottled up in committee, leading Arizona in 1951 to drop the fight in Congress and challenge California in the federal courts.

While the courts took eleven years to reach a decision in *Arizona v. California*, the upper basin states mounted their own campaign for a series of projects known as the Colorado River Storage Project. This project called for the construction of dams in Dinosaur National Monument, at Flaming Gorge, across the San Juan River in New Mexico, and on the Gunnison River in Colorado, in part to divert water across the Rockies to Denver. The storage project also called for additional projects in Colorado as well as the Central Utah Project, Utah's answer to Arizona and California.

The backers of the Colorado River Storage Project included liberals like Wyoming Senator O'Mahoney, Utah's ultraconservative Governor J. Bracken Lee, and the Mormon church. The Mormon church aided the fight through the *Deseret News*, which denounced conservationists' opposition to the Dinosaur Monument dam as "romantic tripe." Backers also got the Navajo tribal government to support their project by promising to start a tribal irrigation project with water from the Navajo Dam on the San Juan River.

The main opposition to the storage project came from conservationists who felt that the plan to build a dam in Dinosaur National Monument threatened the future of the national park system. To strengthen their position, the conservationists argued that the dam to be built at Glen Canyon just south of the Arizona-Utah border could be enlarged.

In the Eisenhower years, anticonservationist sentiment ran high in the Department of the Interior, but conservation groups were able to work with sympathetic officials in the National Park Service to hold up legislation. A revised bill, including a provision for a Glen Canyon dam and a pledge not to tamper with the national parks, was finally passed in 1956 after conservationists agreed to the compromise. By the early 1960s, four of the Colorado River Storage Project dams had been built, including the massive Glen Canyon project.

In 1960, Arizona's chances for a massive water project were enhanced when President John Kennedy appointed Stewart Udall as Secretary of the Interior. Udall, the son of a conservative Arizona judge from a prominent Mormon family that had founded Saint John, Arizona, on the Colorado Plateau, was the first Arizonan to achieve cabinet status. Udall put the highest priority on getting a water project for Arizona. But, according to Udall, "I had to be conscious of California's size and power." When he heard that California's Governor Edmund ("Pat") Brown and Senator Clair Engle wanted an undersecretary from their state, he appointed James Carr, an Engle aide.

In 1963 the United States Supreme Court ruled in favor of Arizona in the twelve-year-old *Arizona* v. *California* case. Senator Hayden immediately introduced a Central Arizona Project bill in the Senate, while Morris Udall, Stewart's brother, provided important support in the House. The Arizonans immediately ran into opposition from the conservationists even though the Udalls were nominal environmentalists. The conservationists, led by David Brower from the Sierra Club, opposed the construction of dams that would back water up into the Grand Canyon. These dams were required by the project to provide hydroelectric power to bring water from the Colorado to central Arizona. Colorado's Congressman Wayne Aspinall, who, as chairman of the House Interior Committee, could block the project in a dozen different ways, also opposed the Central Arizona Project until Colorado got more of its share of the river.

With the project opposed by those very forces needed to get it through Congress, Stewart Udall moved to bring about a remarkable series of compromises. First, Aspinall got five projects for Colorado, a decision that Udall justified in part by mentioning that this water would be needed at some later date for the development of Colorado's oil-shale deposits. Then California got its guarantee of a minimum 4.4 million acre-feet delivered annually, regardless of the flow of the Colorado. To placate the environmentalists, Udall called in the utilities that had formed WEST Associates and convinced them to enlarge their coal-fired power plant adjacent to Glen Canyon Dam at Page, Arizona, which was to be fueled by coal taken from strip mines on Black Mesa. Udall's deal with the WEST utilities gave the Bureau of Reclamation 24 percent of the power from this plant, enough to power the Central Arizona Project's huge pumps. Udall also used his influence in Indian affairs to open up

Indian lands on Black Mesa for the new strip mines serving the coal-fired plant. The Grand Plan dovetailed nicely with his program to encourage major corporations to develop Indian resources.

In the early 1960s, Peabody Coal Company had signed two leases with the Navajo and Hopi tribal councils, one to mine forty thousand acres on the Navajo reservation and the second for twenty-five thousand acres in the joint-use area. The coal was eventually used for two more power plants. While the Navajo received a $100,000 fee, besides royalties, for assigning their rights to Peabody, the Hopi received a token fee of $10. The Southern Pacific, soon after, constructed the country's first slurry pipeline to bring the coal to the new power plant from Black Mesa, considered sacred ground by the Hopi. The first plant, the Mojave (a joint venture of Los Angeles Department of Water and Power, Southern California Edison, Nevada Power, and the Salt River Project) was to be built at Bullhead City, Nevada, on the Colorado River. The second, to be built at Page, was called the Navajo plant.

While this new power grid was planned and carried out by a coalition of private and public utilities, actual construction of the plants brought Bechtel, Morrison-Knudsen, and Utah Construction and Mining into the projects. At the same time, Utah held one of the major coal leases. Kaiser held an undeveloped lease north of the Navajo plant. In 1977 Bechtel joined a consortium of Newmont Mining, Williams Company, Boeing, Fluor, and Equitable Life Assurance Company to purchase Peabody, the country's number-one coal producer.

The construction of power plants on the Colorado Plateau brought rapid changes to the area. The plants generated a series of boomtowns reminiscent of Virginia City and Butte, Montana. Farmington, New Mexico, grew to a population of twenty thousand in less than ten years. Page, Arizona, with dirt streets that changed to bogs during the spring thaw and rows of barracklike homes for power-plant and dam workers, soon reached ten thousand, while Kayenta, on the Navajo reservation at the foot of Black Mesa, became a desert company town for the Peabody mines.

Soon the plants began to bring fundamental changes to the Colorado Plateau. The Navajo and Hopi, many of whom were still pursuing subsistence farming, were given a minimal number of jobs in the new plants and mines, but rapid changes soon threatened to overwhelm the local people. Although the utilities and the Department of the Interior, which held trust responsibility over all Indian tribes, had worked together to implement the Grand Plan, neither the Indians nor anyone outside a handful of Interior officials and the corporations involved was ever really informed about what was being planned for the Four Corners region or about the consequences of these developments. Writing in *Audubon* magazine, Alvin Josephy, Jr., called the negotiations a "classroom example of how serious has become the lack of accountability by government agencies working hand-in-glove with industry in the United States today."

Slowly, information about the extent of what was being planned for the Colorado Plateau began to leak out. In 1967 a Bureau of Reclamation official, after spotting the smoke from the Four Corners plant from a small plane, complained to his superiors. It was soon discovered that even though the utilities had signed a pollution-control agreement with the Department of the Interior, the plant was emitting 383 tons of fly ash, 1,032 tons of sulfur dioxide, and an unknown amount of nitrous oxide each day—an amount that surpassed the daily pollution in New York City.

At about the same time, Thomas Banyacya, a political leader and interpreter for a group calling themselves traditional Hopi, had gotten his hands on a report prepared for the Four Corners Commission by the Westinghouse Corporation. The report projected an industrial city of one hundred thousand in the area and declared that in order to attract new industries, the communities of the Four Corners region had to offer a package of inducements such as "an abundant, largely unskilled labor of undeveloped groups" (i.e., Indians), "prevailing wage rates below those in more specialized sectors of the country," and publicly funded job-training programs and facilities.

Banyacya and the rest of his traditional group were being aided by Richard Clemmer, an anthropology student from the University of Illinois. Through careful investigation, they outlined the scenario for development contained in the Grand Plan. In his account about how the traditionals mobilized support, "Black Mesa and the Hopi," Clemmer tells the story of mounting opposition from both Indians and environmentalists over the way in which the Grand Plan had been put together and its consequences. A defense fund was set up in Santa Fe and the Native American Rights Fund, supported by the Ford Foundation, filed a suit against Peabody and Secretary of the Interior Rogers Morton on behalf of the Navajo, the Apache, the Colorado River Indian tribes, the Sierra Club, Friends of the Earth, and the National Wildlife Federation.

The opposition to the Black Mesa strip mine—dubbed the Angel of Death—stirred up a hornet's nest in the bureaucracy in Washington. The environmentalists' victory over the Grand Canyon dams had already greatly strengthened that movement. Now the environmentalists had begun to diversify their points of attack. By the time Richard Nixon and his Interior Secretary Walter Hickel took office, the environmental movement had become a national force. With the passage of the National Environmental Policy Act in 1969, the movement developed new legal weapons in its fight with major corporations and the government. With the Grand Plan now center stage, the different forces girded up for confrontation over the fate of the Colorado Plateau and the Southwest.

GEOPOLITICS COMES HOME

Although Udall was a committed conservationist and a strong advocate of public power in the tradition of Harold Ickes, his eight years as Secretary of the Interior marked the biggest raid on public resources since the giant raids of the nineteenth century. The Grand Plan was part of a profound but quiet shift taking place in the United States' relationship to the world of fuels. The major oil companies had expanded and consolidated their holdings in foreign countries in the years after the war. The resulting flood of cheap oil had contributed greatly to the demise of the coal industry, for many years America's major source of energy. The coal industry, in effect, collapsed in the late 1950s and early 1960s, leaving the Appalachian mining communities, the original American energy colony, plagued by poverty and unemployment.

During this same period, numerous resource-based multinationals, including the oil companies, recognized that their control of oil and other resources was becoming the principal target of powerful nationalist forces rising out of the collapse of European colonialism. Through their experiences in such countries as Iran, these companies recognized that the supplies of oil and natural gas could not last forever and that with each encounter the forces of nationalism were growing stronger and more sophisticated. As a result, Exxon set out in the middle 1960s to undertake a massive exploration campaign in less politically volatile areas: Australia, the North Sea, the MacKenzie River basin in Canada, and Alaska.

After building a global strategy based on the Stanford Research Institute's premise that "the raw materials that enable the rich countries to grow richer must increasingly be bought from the poor," a number of corporations, many of them based in the West, realized that in an age of revolution the next big energy play would be within the United States. With the price of coal at rock bottom because of the influx of cheap oil, a number of major corporations moved during the 1960s to buy up the major coal companies at the same time that they were consolidating their control over the uranium industry.

This aggressive resource strategy, pursued overseas for many years, was now being brought to bear on the United States and its interior West, particularly the Four Corners region and the northern Great Plains. In the West, most of the best coal was under public and Indian lands. At the same time that Indian coal was being leased at bargain prices by the Department of the Interior, the new energy conglomerates leased public coal at incredibly low prices. The most intense period of leasing came under Udall from 1964 to 1967. The government received about 19 cents a ton for coal that would sell in the 1970s for more than $20 a ton. Within a short period, a group of oil, mining, and railroad companies, led by Conoco, Amax, Burlington Northern, and the Union Pacific, managed to buy up a huge share of the domestic coal reserves. Five companies, led by Exxon, obtained 31 percent of all federal coal leases during this period. In the great raid of the 1950s and 1960s, a handful of corporations, for ridiculously low prices, gained control of resources soon to be worth billions.

The arrangement between Udall and the utilities for joint control and financing of power generated at Glen Canyon and the Navajo plant furthered the Grand Plan and consolidated corporate influence in the Department of the Interior. That influence had been growing steadily since World War II. While the oil and mining companies were engineering a gradual shift in their energy strategy toward greater reliance on domestic fuels, Interior acted as if the low prices of coal would last forever. In time, Udall came to regret his role in the plundering of the Colorado Plateau and took an active role in efforts to undo its consequences.

To the Nixon administration, the Grand Plan was just another of those exciting geopolitical visions, like the Pacific Rim strategy, spun out of the fertile relationship developed between Washington and the largest private corporations. Under Nixon, the Department of the Interior dropped any reservation about all-out development of public resources and became a willing ally (some called it appendage) of the major resource companies. While the department worked closely with the promoters of the Grand Plan, both Nixon and his new Secretary of the Interior, Walter Hickel, focused most of their attention on the construction of the Alaska pipeline.

Hickel was the son of a Kansas tenant farmer, a youthful wanderer and amateur boxer who ended up in the construction business in Alaska, where he built and operated one of the state's first modern hotels. He came to Washington with a view of his department similar to that of many conservative westerners, particularly in those states where the federal government owned much of the land. "We were governed by the Department of Interior," Hickel wrote in his book *Who Owns America?* "But nobody in Washington appeared to know where or who we were." Hickel immediately embroiled himself in controversy by announcing at his first press conference, "I think we have had a policy of conservation for conservation's sake."

As soon as the controversy over his first press conference died down, Hickel went to work to lift the federal land freeze in Alaska imposed by Udall shortly before he left office. For years, Nixon had been a close associate of Charles Jones of Richfield Oil, the first company, along with Exxon, to make major discoveries in Alaska's Prudhoe Bay. After Richfield's merger with the Atlantic Company to form Arco, the company's new head, Robert O. Anderson, became a substantial Nixon backer, contributing $60,000 to Nixon's 1968 campaign.

The Nixon administration was able to force approval of the pipeline through Congress even though the project had been delayed by requirements of the new National Environmental Policy Act. Nixon, in fact, called approval of the pipeline his one significant energy measure passed by Congress. In general, the pipeline was consistent with the politics of the Nixon administration. It was a Pacific basin project. It was a big resource play involving both eastern and western corporations like Exxon, Los Angeles–based Arco, and Bechtel. And it was consistent with the new emphasis on development of domestic resources underlined by Nixon in his Project Independence speech in 1973.

Although a willing ally of the energy companies, Hickel, unlike other members of the Nixon administration, became increasingly concerned with how young people felt as antiwar sentiment grew. Hoping that a strong environmental message coming out of Washington would help rebuild confidence in public institutions, Hickel set out on a campaign to bring students back into the fold through a series of proposals designed to channel environmental activism.

Hickel's inflated view of his role in Washington ultimately led to a confrontation with Nixon. After using him in the 1970 campaign, the president ultimately forced Hickel to resign in early 1971, replacing him with Rogers Morton, chairman of the Republican party and Nixon's original choice for vice-president. After Hickel departed, Morton worked closely with the energy companies to promote the development of domestic energy resources such as the strip mines and power plants in the Four Corners region and the northern Great Plains. By the early 1970s, the plans of the energy companies and utilities had moved into high gear. In 1972 Morton announced plans for enough new power plants in the Southwest to produce an additional thirty thousand megawatts, beginning with a massive five-thousand-megawatt coal-fired plant on the Kaiparowits Plateau.

The Kaiparowits project was put together by a consortium of WEST utilities including Southern California Edison, Arizona Public Service, Salt River Project, and San Diego Gas and Electric. The group proposed to develop some of the coal resources on the plateau, where they held leases on more than

48,000 acres of coal lands. It would be the largest single power plant ever built. The California utilities would provide the largest share of the financing and planned to take more than half of the energy.

By the time Rogers Morton took office, the project was under strong attack from environmentalists. An April 1971 article in *Life* magazine entitled "Hello Energy, Goodbye Big Sky" and similar pieces in the *New York Times* and other publications demonstrated the growing national interest and controversy over the project. More than 25 percent of the country's national park land lay within a 250-mile radius—known as the Golden Circle—of the proposed plant. Environmentalists bitterly attacked the plant and the related coal mining as a potential eyesore and source of pollution.

With Kaiparowits under attack and subject to a series of delaying lawsuits, the controversy moved inside the Nixon administration, where the Bureau of Reclamation and the Bureau of Land Management were the major advocates of the utilities' plans. The Environmental Protection Agency (EPA) proposed that the project be scotched on environmental, rather than technical, grounds, an unprecedented action involving a federal prerogative over private utilities. Although both bureaus opposed the EPA's proposal, Morton decided in mid-1973 to veto the specific site suggested by the utilities. A second site, fourteen miles from the first one, was then proposed.

The utilities' public efforts to save Kaiparowits contrasted with their growing private reservations about the plant. Unresolved questions over transportation combined with escalating costs, thanks in part to the delaying tactics, had made the project far more expensive than originally estimated. More important, demand for energy in southern California had begun to decline, with Edison's growth rate slipping from 8 percent in 1971 to 4.5 percent in 1975. Although Edison still publicly dismissed the falling growth rate and continued to project future increases in demand, the issue of declining demand took on increasing importance through the later part of the decade. With a falling growth rate, there was no longer a reason for the Grand Plan.

In 1976, Edison formally called it quits on the Kaiparowits plant. Environmentalists immediately hailed the action as a great victory with tremendous significance for the future of the Southwest. The defeat of Kaiparowits, on the face of it, did seem like a monumental victory for the environmentalists and a critical defeat for the proponents of the Grand Plan. In the end, the utilities had offered little resistance because both Edison and Arizona Public Service were concerned with their major nuclear power plants at San Onofre, California, and Palo Verde, Arizona, and needed cooperation from the Department of the Interior in order to bring those plants on line.

The increased interest in the nuclear option, combined with other resources such as oil shale, kept the Grand Plan very much alive in the minds of the utilities and the energy companies. The promotion of domestic energy resources, such as oil shale and uranium, were given a big boost with Nixon's 1973 announcement of Project Independence, a program that simply gave the president's endorsement to the strategy of the energy multinationals.

With Nixon's blessing, the utilities in the early 1970s made a major move toward nuclear power as the single most comprehensive alternative to foreign oil. Energy giants such as Exxon, Arco, Kerr-McGee, Gulf Oil, Mobil, and Phillips Petroleum immediately began to buy up public leases and private lands containing uranium ore, in a manner reminiscent of the play for coal resources in the middle and late 1960s. The systematic locking up of uranium resources by the multinationals contrasted sharply with the earlier uranium boom of the late 1940s and early 1950s in the Southwest when, in gold-rush style, individual boomers and roustabouts wandered from mining area to mining area in search of "yellow gold."

Through the Nixon-Ford years, the plans for nuclear power proceeded rapidly. With more than 65 plants operating, the Republican administration estimated that an additional 100 reactors would be operating by the late 1980s. Domestic uranium output would continue to be centered in a hundred-mile stretch between New Mexico and Arizona known as the Grants Mineral Belt.

While the uranium boom gathered momentum in the early 1970s, the energy companies also began to focus attention on an area of western Colorado and eastern Utah known as the Piceance (or Piss Ants) basin. Located in this area were deposits of organic marlstone or shale in which a waxy substance known as kerogen was deeply embedded. When properly extracted and heated, the kerogen yields a relatively heavy oil that can be used for motor oil, heating oil, and even electric power generation.

There were three problems with producing oil from shale. First, the process of extracting the oil from the shale was complicated, was costly, and could create enormous problems for the environment, ranging from the disposition of the thousands of tons of crushed rock to possible effects on the area's water supply and air quality. Secondly, shale was subject to the maneuvers of the energy multinationals who had tried for three decades to gain control of all other sources of energy. Finally, the oil companies feared intervention by the federal government, which controlled most of the leases and which could play an active role in developing this new industry.

Over the years, the shale industry had experienced a series of booms and busts tied to the rise and fall of the price of oil. By the time Nixon announced Project Independence, another oil-shale boom seemed to be under way. Several oil companies, including Sohio, Shell, Arco, and Ashland Oil, had become involved in shale. Nixon's energy czar, William Simon, talked of shale and synthetic fuels as the country's answer to the Arab oil embargo. Legislation was introduced to grant shale companies a tax credit in order to make shale-derived oil more competitive. The tax credit, guaranteed purchase agreements, and large loan guarantees for front-end financing were essential industry demands, sought to insure high profit margins.

In his 1975 State of the Union address, Gerald Ford proposed that the federal government underwrite twenty privately owned synfuel productions plants. When utilities such as Southern California Edison considered financing the construction of a shale plant, when oil majors such as Gulf and Standard of Indiana bought major leases with long-term development in mind, and when the maverick Occidental Petroleum Company pushed a new in situ extraction process, the shale boom appeared to be imminent this time.

But the boom evaporated before it even started. After Ford's massive multibillion-dollar subsidy program was scaled down, the subsidy bill passed the Senate by a wide margin. A last-minute effort in the House spearheaded by oil lobbyists working in conjunction with environmentalists and conservative

Republicans, who feared "creeping socialism" because of government involvement, defeated the legislation.

By the 1976 election, the great resource play embodied in the Grand Plan and the activities around coal, uranium, domestic oil, and shale had reached a critical impasse. Led by the energy multinationals, a major effort had been made to lock up those resources in the form of outright acquisition of the land or lease arrangements with the federal government or Indian tribes. The energy companies had explored coal, shale, and uranium, pursuing and then retreating on each of these fronts.

In the case of shale, the energy companies were still interested although reluctant. With coal, the massive power plants had been crucial to the development of this resource. Although the defeat at Kaiparowits had hampered those developments, the issue was only postponed as new and only slightly more modest versions of Kaiparowits began to take shape. Even the nuclear option, which had been most successfully exploited in the early and middle 1970s, began to have difficulties, culminating a few years later in the accident at Three Mile Island and the collapse of the uranium boom in the Grants Mineral Belt.

The Grand Plan triggered widespread opposition. Congressmen, governors, local politicians, environmentalists, and Indian activists challenged the plans for development of the Colorado Plateau. The air was thick with the old charge that "outsiders" were tearing up the West, making it a resource-producing colony of the major urban centers. A series of environmental suits forced the suspension of coal-leasing on federal lands. All parties awaited the outcome of the 1976 presidential elections to see how they would affect the future of this great energy play.

The Grand Plan and the resource play of the energy companies had almost reached fruition under the Republicans' policy of stepping up the development of domestic energy as a response to the Arab oil boycott. Despite the widespread influence of the energy multinationals in the Nixon and Ford administrations, the plans of the utility, energy, and mining companies to launch an all-out assault on the resources of the interior West remained in flux.

The Grand Plan was still feasible, but the strategies continued to shift about. With the fall of the administration that had promoted a new Pacific basin strategy and a geopolitical strategy for the development of the resources of the interior West, the companies began to anticipate their own worst fears, including the possibility of abandoning their spectacular plans for the West.

THE SUN BELT STRATEGY

Richard Nixon, the Californian, made Washington his home after his election to Congress in 1946, but to the end of his political career, he saw himself as an outsider lacking ties to both his native state and his new home. He found Washington a city "run primarily by Democrats and liberals, dominated by like-minded newspapers and other media, convinced of its superiority to other cities and points of view." After returning to California to make his unsuccessful bid for governor against Pat Brown in 1962, Nixon concluded that "nothing tied me to California" and that "business opportunities would be much greater in New York."

Once elected to the presidency, Nixon was determined to make his mark in foreign policy. His breakthrough to China involved a major reevaluation of the direction of American foreign policy. Thus, he told reporters on Guam when he announced the Nixon Doctrine that "as we look over the historical perspective, while World War II began in Europe, for the United States it began in the Pacific. It came from Asia. The Korean War came from Asia. The Vietnamese War came from Asia." The realities of the United States' ties to the Pacific basin, many of them radiating from California, forced Nixon to focus much of his attention on this part of the world.

In domestic affairs, Nixon was a mixture of a western and a national politician. Although a friend of Arizona and California agribusiness, he was not a promoter of Bureau of Reclamation water projects. His administration looked critically at a number of projects from a cost standpoint. In 1969 his Water Resources Council criticized the common bureaucratic practice of doctoring up cost-benefit ratios to make projects economically justifiable. The Office of Management and Budget (OMB) took a particularly careful look at the Central Arizona Project and the Central Utah Project. In 1970 Nixon impounded the Arizona Project's first construction appropriations, saying, "There is too much pork in this barrel." The OMB also cut back funding on the Utah project.

The Nixon administration made an early decision to concentrate on western water projects that were developing municipal and industrial water rather than irrigation water. Nixon, through Secretary of Agriculture Earl Butz, was already attacking federal subsidies to farmers and crop reductions. He could hardly justify bringing more land under cultivation through subsidized irrigation.

Although Nixon was critical of big water projects, his domestic policies were extremely sympathetic to the plans of the energy companies, utilities, export-oriented industries of California, and large integrated agribusiness operations. In general, Nixon maintained the high level of government subsidization of the western economy. Nixon also signed a treaty with Mexico assigning to the United States responsibility for reducing the salt content of the overused Colorado River. To the president, this was more a foreign-policy matter than part of the geopolitics of water development in the arid West. In another area of western concern, Nixon delivered the first environmental message to Congress. This idea, which originated among his more environmentally attuned advisers, was a belated gesture to an increasingly effective political movement. In the midst of the greatest resurgence of Indian politics in modern time, Nixon called for self-determination for Indian tribes. This development came in part from efforts to reach an accommodation with Alaskan Indians over control of Alaskan lands so that the oil companies could move ahead with their plans to develop the state's oil.

In his memoirs Nixon blamed the liberal establishment's continued control over Washington for his inability to bring about significant domestic reforms. When he became president, he urged his cabinet members "to resist the Washington habit of recruiting their staffs solely from Eastern schools and companies and instead to branch out and get new blood from the South, the West, and the Midwest." The president decided at first, according to Nixon aide Patrick Buchanan, not to purge the lower levels of the predominantly Democratic bureaucracy nor to attack the Great Society domestic programs. In exchange, he hoped that his opponents would allow him time to achieve an end to the war in Vietnam. However, when antiwar sentiments spread through the bureaucracy, Nixon gave up his attempt to reach an accommodation. He pushed ahead instead with a plan by Litton Industries' Roy Ash to reorganize the executive branch—a plan that was never realized.

As the confrontation in Washington became more bitter, the coterie of conservative intellectuals, lawyers, and confidence men around the president began talking about a reelection strategy based on a new Republican majority. This strategy was spelled out in *The Emerging Republican Majority*, a book published in 1969 by Kevin Phillips, an aide to John Mitchell. Phillips claimed that "the new popular majority is white and conservative." The liberal establishment's support for the civil rights movement, Phillips argued, had driven white voters away from the Democratic party into a new insurgency. In the 1968 election the Republican party had tapped this new insurgency in the key areas of the South, the West, and on "the Catholic sidewalks of New York." Phillips concluded that, in general, "political power in America is slowly but surely drifting west with the restless millions of migrants to the Sun Belt." The Republicans stood to benefit the most from this power shift.

The 1972 election appeared to confirm Phillips' predictions about the growth of the Republican party. But by 1976 the talk about the Sun Belt as a center of antiestablishment insurgency seemed like so much empty rhetoric. The executive branch had been tightly interlocked with the corporate sector, especially the energy multinationals, many of them located in eastern centers of power. Nixon left Gerald Ford little in the way of a political base or a program. In the 1976 election, Ford retained control of the West but lost most of the South to Jimmy Carter, a strong regional candidate. Ford's strength in the West had little to do with new insurgencies. His showing in the West was based more on Carter's total unfamiliarity and lack of appeal in that part of the country.

With their one-time hero in disgrace and the Democrats back in power, conservative theoreticians like Kevin Phillips dropped the idea of a new regional political alignment, lamenting instead the political fragmentation that pitted interest group against interest group and region against region. The new Republican majority had evaporated.

3 The Money Supermarket

On the night of February 17, 1977, President Jimmy Carter called a meeting in the Cabinet Room to discuss water projects. Less than a month after his inauguration, Carter was looking for dramatic initiatives to demonstrate how he, as a little-known outsider, was going to fulfill his pledge to shake up Washington. Carter knew that he had no power base. He hoped that these initiatives would build the support he felt he lacked.

Before the inauguration, his pollster, Patrick Caddell, had laid out the plan of attack for the new administration, citing "the need for small sets of promises and projects that we can accomplish quickly to provide evidence that longer-term goals can be realized." Carter had already made two important gestures on his very first day in office—pardoning Vietnam draft violators and calling for a $31 billion recovery package, including a $50 rebate for each taxpayer to stimulate the faltering economy. Now the president considered trimming funds for water projects to demonstrate his commitment to budget-cutting.

The night's meeting brought together Vice-President Walter Mondale; Burt Lance, head of the OMB; Secretary of Defense Harold Brown; Secretary of the Army Clifford Alexander, Jr.; Secretary of the Interior Cecil Andrus; and representatives of the Army Corps of Engineers and the Bureau of Reclamation. They were discussing the federal dam-building program, a massive public-works program run by the Army Corps and Interior's Bureau of Reclamation.

About to send his first budget recommendations to Congress, Carter wanted to drop several dams from the recommended expenditures. If he cut some of these projects, he could demonstrate that he was serious about a frontal attack on the sacrosanct pork-barrel deals worked out annually between the Army Corps and Bureau of Reclamation bureaucrats, the western water lobby, and their friends in Congress.

The meeting came after three months of bureaucratic infighting between the Bureau of Reclamation, the Army Corps, OMB, and the Council on Environmental Quality over the funding of water projects. Officials from the first two complained that they had not had a chance to study the projected cuts while Vice-President Mondale warned of the possibility of a hostile congressional reaction to this presidential invasion of its turf. Both Mondale and Andrus suggested the number of project cuts be pared down and that there be further review before any final decision.

But it was Carter, not his aides, who directed the meeting. "I want to do it as a kind of campaign statement," the president declared as he prepared to make his move. From his own experience in Georgia, Carter knew something about the dam-building program. As governor, he had opposed the Army Corps' plans to dredge marshland along the Georgia coast and had forced the Army Corps to cancel plans for a dam on the Flint River. But he had had no contact with the Bureau of Reclamation's huge water-development projects in the arid West and knew little about the historical connection between these projects and the growth of the western urban centers. Carter saw all of the projects in terms of his own views about costs, environmental damage, and safety problems.

When Carter was governor, Joseph Browder, the youthful southern representative of the National Audubon Society, had met Carter and sized him up as "a brilliant politician" and "a sincere and committed conservationist." Browder eventually went on to Washington, and Carter began his long campaign for the presidency.

In Washington, Browder and a group of young activists organized the Environmental Policy Center to lobby on the issues of water and energy development. As early as 1974, while working on an energy paper for the Democratic National Committee, Browder began to work for Carter by preparing memos on resource and environmental issues. Advised by his aides to develop his expertise in environmental matters, Carter was open to people like Browder. Two years later Browder left the center and joined the Carter campaign.

Through Browder and other young advocates, Carter developed a connection to a carefully planned campaign against water projects, which had been building among the public interest and environmental establishment in Washington since the Bureau of Reclamation's attempt to dam the Colorado River in the Grand Canyon. In 1973 the National Water Commission, appointed by Lyndon Johnson, noted "a shift in national priorities from development of water resources to restoration and enhancement of water quality," concluding that "subsidization of new irrigation projects is not justified on either social or economic grounds." That same year, Ralph Nader's Center for Study of Responsive Law launched a broad-gauged attack on the Bureau of Reclamation in *Damming the West*. The conclusion of the Nader study paralleled the National Water Commission report. "The Bureau of Reclamation itself has outlasted its chief purpose," the Naderites argued. "No longer is there a need for more and bigger dams and irrigation canals to reclaim the arid lands of the West." In this period, the Environmental Policy Center also published its own attack on federal dam-building in a pamphlet entitled *Disasters in Water Development*.

Influenced by the growth of environmentalism, Carter took the time during the campaign to portray himself as a man of the soil and an outdoorsman who enjoyed fishing, rafting, and canoeing. As early as the New Hampshire primary, Carter raised the issue of water projects, saying, "We ought to get the Army Corps of Engineers out of the dam-building business." He pledged that as president he would be "extremely reluctant" to build any dams. The young environmentalists were pleased with Carter, an unknown quantity in Washington circles who had taken some of the activists into his confidence, used them in the campaign, and would later include environmentalists in the transition team.

While Carter was campaigning, Brent Blackwelder, the Environmental Policy Center's water expert, was working with a coalition of environmental organizations to prepare a list of actions "recommended for immediate or near-immediate implementation by the Chief Executive upon assuming office." At the top of the list was a call for "an instant moratorium" on funding for fourteen water projects, including the Central Arizona Project and the Central Utah Project.

After the election, Carter announced that he was appointing the former governor of Idaho, Cecil Andrus, as Secretary of the Interior. Andrus had been an early supporter of Carter, and their relationship, begun at governors' meetings, eventually grew into a friendship. Andrus was a self-made man who had worked in the timber industry right out of high school. At the age of twenty-nine, he ran successfully for state senator. As governor, he gained a reputation for dealing evenhandedly with environmentalists and the state's mining companies after he forced a mining company to abandon its plans to open a mine in a scenic area and opposed damming the Snake River. Despite his strong environmentalist stand, Andrus was reelected by an overwhelming majority in a traditionally conservative state. At this early stage of his presidency, Carter viewed Andrus as representative of the new environmental values ascendant in the West.

In Washington, Andrus worked closely with the Carter transition team and particularly with Katherine Fletcher, an environmental-oriented lawyer who served as liaison with the Department of the Interior. Although younger than the new secretary, the Carter environmentalists were in many ways more experienced with the intricacies of Washington insider politics and more familiar with Interior through several years of challenging this deeply entrenched bureaucracy. The environmentalists in the transition team produced a collection of confidential background papers for Andrus, describing Interior as "a feudal kingdom" in which the department's responsibilities to protect publicly owned resources had "in large part given way to efforts to promote rapid exploitation of resources under the agency's jurisdiction, particularly for energy."

The transition team recommended a number of actions "to establish secretarial leadership and tone for the new administration." Its recommendations included the suspension of construction of an irrigation project, a moratorium on coal-leasing on public lands, the suspension or revision of outer continental shelf oil-leasing schedules, and support for strip-mine regulation.

When the supposedly secret background papers on Interior were first seen at Andrus' office in Idaho by a reporter, the press described a list of Army Corps projects considered questionable by the transition team. By the inauguration, Blackwelder and others had told *San Francisco Examiner* reporters that the list had grown to some sixty-one projects considered of dubious value. As the story started circulating, the transition team was encouraged by a letter to Carter from seventy-three congressmen calling for an end to construction of "unnecessary and environmentally destructive dams" and a reduction in the "waste of taxpayers' dollars on unnecessary projects." Among the signers was Congressman Morris Udall, a longtime supporter of the Central Arizona Project, who would soon become chairman of the powerful House Interior Committee.

Facing a February 21 deadline for budget recommendations, the Domestic Council staff worked feverishly to put together a list of water projects to be reviewed and/or cut from the budget. It drew extensively on analyses of the projects compiled over the years by the project's opponents in the OMB and Council on Environmental Quality. Armed with the recommendations from the Domestic Council staff, Jimmy Carter decided to call the February 17 meeting to review his decision before the budget deadline four days hence. "We discussed some of these boondoggles, or what I call 'dogs,' projects that shouldn't have been authorized, the ones that were environmentally degrading," recalled Andrus. "We also talked about a lot of good projects and narrowed it eventually down to the dogs."

On the day after the meeting, Brent Blackwelder got a telephone call from the White House. Carter, he was informed, was going to cut eighteen water projects and could he help get some favorable press coverage. How naive, Blackwelder thought. There was no way he could drum up press coverage over a weekend. "They had jumped off the deep end," he concluded. Blackwelder was surprised that Carter had taken such a precipitous step, even though it was a step advocated by the Environmental Policy Center.

Over the weekend, the White House worked furiously to inform the congressmen in whose districts the projects were located. Then, on Monday, Carter announced in a letter to Congress that he was going to cut eighteen projects from the new budget because these projects were "unsupportable on economic, environmental, and/or safety grounds." The cuts, he explained, would lead to a total savings of $5.1 billion.

What came to be known as the Carter hit list proved to be an audacious and ultimately disastrous move for the new administration. No one, not even Andrus, anticipated the furor that would be caused by the hit list. One environmentalist called it "a bomb drop." Congressional leaders, wary of the new boy in town, took it as the beginning of a clumsy assault by outsiders on their jealously guarded power over the pork barrel. Udall, who had run for president as an environmentalist but had also been a major supporter of the Central Arizona Project, which would bring Colorado River water to Phoenix and his hometown of Tucson, called it "a Washington Day ambush."

Soon the western press, led by such water-project boosters as the *Denver Post*, the *Deseret News*, and the *Arizona Republic*, joined the attack, jumping all over Carter and his aides for their actions every chance they could get. By the time the press finished its campaign, the hit list had been transformed into Jimmy Carter's "War on the West." More than a year after that fateful February 17 meeting, the Interior secretary would complain that every time he set foot on western soil, reporters would inevitably ask, Is Jimmy Carter still against the West?

RAIDERS AND REFORMERS AT THE MINISTRY OF WESTERN AFFAIRS

When Cecil Andrus accepted the appointment as Secretary of the Interior, he became Carter's "minister for western affairs." He inherited one of the most impressive bureaucratic empires in Washington. The massive Interior building—a labyrinth of corridors that defies the navigational instincts of the most avid explorer—occupies an entire block just west of the White House. While the department's responsibilities range from administering the last vestiges of nineteenth century colonialism (the United States Trust Territories in the Pacific) to protecting the nation's miners, control of the greatest share of the nation's publicly owned resources is at the heart of the department's activities. Most of this resource-rich land is concentrated in the West, where the department controls 538 million acres. Beneath these acres lies the nation's last energy storehouse, an enormous concentration of coal, uranium, shale, oil, natural gas, and a host of other resources needed to sustain the United States as a world power in the aftermath of the Arab oil boycott.

The department supervises the huge Bureau of Reclamation network of dams and irrigation projects, which by the 1970s was bringing water to 17 million acres of land and one-third of the people in seventeen western states. Through hydroelectric and coal-fired power plants, the bureau also provides cheap electricity for many of the major metropolises of the West.

The department is the final arbiter of the fate of the country's Indian population through its trust responsibility over more than 270 Indian reservations and 51.6 million acres. The department is also charged with the care of the country's vast national park system, much of which is located in the West. Thus, at the heart of Interior's duties is the contradictory task of preserving the nation's parks and resources while providing for their development by private interests.

One of Washington's oldest agencies, the Department of the Interior was created in 1848 to deal with home affairs, including the sale and distribution of public lands and the supervision of Indian affairs. During its first two decades, Interior played a largely passive role in western development. A large portion of the land distributed to homesteaders ended up in the hands of bankers, land speculators, and large landed interests. During these years, most of the West was wide open and control of public resources fell to whoever got there first and could hold off other marauders.

The raid on public resources began in earnest with the gold rush of 1849, when thousands of miners illegally removed millions in gold from public lands. It culminated in the biggest of the great giveaways—Congress transferred 150 million acres to the railroads to promote the construction of the transcontinental railroad. While the purloined treasures of the West flowed into San Francisco, New York, Boston, and London, the consequences for the western environment were disastrous. In the span of one generation, the newcomers wiped out whole species of wildlife, leveled great forests, and ripped at the soil. In places like the Powder River basin in the northern Great Plains, overgrazing even brought about fundamental changes in the climate.

From frontier times, the Department of the Interior has been the scene of a seesaw battle between public and private interests over control of western resources. Secretary Carl Schurz, who served under President Rutherford B. Hayes, took the first steps toward public control of private exploiters by ordering a survey of the plunder in public forests. He dispatched Major John Wesley Powell to explore the Colorado Plateau. Theodore Roosevelt took dramatic steps toward conservation by creating the national park system and by promoting more orderly development of western resources through the Reclamation Service.

During the 1920s, Interior was rocked by the Teapot Dome scandal. Secretary Albert Fall, a former senator from New Mexico, eventually went to jail for leasing two publicly owned oil fields, one at Teapot Dome in Wyoming and the other in the Elk Hills of California, to oilmen Harry Sinclair and Edward Doheny without competitive bidding.

After Harold Ickes established a policy of water development linked to soil conservation, park development, and Indian reform, the Eisenhower administration reversed his policies by rebuilding the links between corporate interests and the Interior bureaucracy. Eisenhower's Secretary Douglas McKay, who liked to call conservationists punks, helped weaken the Bureau of Reclamation's 160-acre limit, turned vast amounts of uranium lands over to the nuclear industry, and aided the campaign to bring about the final elimination of Indian tribal government.

Under Kennedy, Secretary Udall formalized the ties between Interior and the private sector through deals like the Navajo power plant and the Black Mesa strip mines. Although Udall made major efforts to expand the park system and to protect public lands in Alaska, his term marked one of the great transfers of public resources to private hands in the history of the West. The Central Arizona Project was the keystone of Udall's work as secretary. The Central Arizona Project, the last of the big federal water projects, ended an era begun during the New Deal, an era that had been characterized by massive subsidies and giant engineering feats.

Under Presidents Nixon and Ford, the Interior Department, from Walter Hickel to prodevelopment Secretaries Rogers Morton and Thomas Kleppe, was wedded to industry's viewpoint. Hickel came into office talking about "trying to make a Fifth Avenue out of the Alaskan tundra." When he left, he wrote, "It is not fair to label the developing Interior-industry relationship as an unholy alliance. But as the twentieth century progressed the private interests called more and more shots. It began to appear that these interests owned America."

By the end of the Ford administration, the Department of the Interior had reached its lowest point since the infamous Teapot Dome scandal. Conflict of interest was a way of life, an outgrowth of the contradictory responsibilities of protecting and developing publicly owned resources. Under the Republican policy of stepping up development of domestic resources as a response to the Arab oil boycott, the department had come increasingly under the sway of private interests. By the end of 1976, the revolving door through which individuals shuttled back and forth between the public and private sectors was spinning furiously at Interior.

THE CAMPAIGN AGAINST THE THREE Rs

In January 1977, Cecil Andrus inherited a department in eclipse. Before he arrived in Washington, Andrus drew up a list of possible actions to be undertaken as secretary. Among them were passing a strip-mine reclamation bill, increasing the role of the states in leasing oil and gas on the outer continental shelf, revising the 1872 mining law, and expanding federal wilderness areas in Alaska. Above all, he wanted to reorganize Interior and end the era of what he called the Three Rs: "rape, ruin, and run."

He told the *New York Times,* "The policy has been for the grazing interests to have their chunk here, for coal to have another chunk; lumber, mining, all with their own part of the department." Andrus was eager to break up these "little fiefdoms" and end a situation in which "this place was like a centipede with each little pair of legs scuttling off in its own direction."

Andrus' plan was ambitious. Any one of his contemplated reforms would bring him toe to toe with Washington's well-organized, well-financed corporate lobbyists. But nowhere, despite his own opposition to damming the Snake River, did he mention taking on the federal dam-building program.

President Carter was still looking for a constituency in the West, where he had lost every state in the 1976 election. Although the Sun Belt analysts linked the South with the West as the new seat of national power, the southerner Carter's perceptions of the West were fuzzy. California in particular seemed an alien and threatening culture to Carter. At a cabinet discussion of drug abuse and welfare cheating, he remarked, "Whatever starts in California unfortunately has an inclination to spread."

Carter liked to refer to himself as a peanut farmer, but he was in fact a farm businessman involved in a whole range of farm activities from growing to warehousing. While Carter's agribusiness background could have been the basis for some kind of rapport with the powerful western agribusiness interests, he was instead incensed by the blatant way in which the bureaucracy doctored its figures to justify expenditures for water projects of doubtful value. He did not object to the subsidy for peanut farmers, but the strict accounting practices of a small businessman made him bridle at the way Washington bureaucrats played fast and loose with figures.

As a son of a region blessed with a high annual rainfall, he had little understanding of the central role of water projects in the rise of a new civilization in the arid West or the historical relationship between the rise of western agribusiness and federally funded irrigation. Andrus summed up the crucial difference between the South and the West for Carter by saying, "In Georgia the problem is getting water off the land. In the West the problem is getting water on the land."

When Carter brought environmentalists into his operation, he began receiving advice from two sources about how to proceed on western issues. On the one hand, Andrus was saying, go ahead, shake up the bureaucracy and embrace a number of environmental positions but proceed with caution. The youthful activists in the White House, on the other hand, were more aggressive, suggesting that Carter embrace the ongoing fight against water projects.

Seeing himself as an activist reformer, Carter in his first hundred days lunged forward, launching forays in a dozen different directions. Although lacking a coherent strategy, Carter was eager to build a program and a constituency in the shortest time possible. If he had known the ways of Washington better, Carter might have suspected that the hit list would raise a howl of protest.

Carter's proposal to cut funds for water projects from the 1978 budget was greeted in Congress with angry disapproval. Wary of discussing the projects' merits, congressional leaders focused instead on the lack of consultation between the White House and Congress before the cuts were announced. Carter had boldly interjected himself into areas considered the sole prerogative of Congress. In the process, he had antagonized some of the most powerful figures on Capitol Hill, including Senators Edmund Muskie, Russell Long, and John C. Stennis and House leaders James Wright and Morris Udall, all of whom had water projects in their districts on the hit list.

Although water-project reform was not Andrus' program, he was a loyal soldier and so set out boldly to declare the end of the era of big water projects and to defend the president's budget cuts. He and Mondale had warned the president in the crucial meeting on the night of February 17 that if the president did not move cautiously, a coalition would form to fight him. Now Andrus seemed to enjoy the opportunity to indulge in the rhetoric of populism and to take on the big interests behind the projects. Called before the House Interior Committee, chaired by Morris Udall, Andrus tore into the "dogs," as he now liked to call the projects. At the end of the session, he commented wryly, "The messsage I got . . . was that if a member had a project, he didn't want it canceled."

When the Senate responded by restoring funding for all water projects in a new funding bill, national environmental groups mobilized behind Carter. An environmental leader commented that "the president is in the process of destroying the cozy relationship among powerful governmental bureaucracies, pork-barrel congressional committees and water-development and -user interests."

On April 18, Carter announced the results of his review of all water projects. He recommended the deletion of funds for eighteen projects, modification of five projects, and the continuation of nine others without modification. Citing one project that "benefited only two companies" and another that "spent over $1 million per landowner," he called for a more "realistic assessment of both economic and environmental costs and benefits." In addition, the president demanded increased emphasis on safety and state contribution to the costs of the projects. Noting that "over half of the water delivered through Bureau of Reclamation irrigation systems is completely wasted," he called for a future water policy based on "wise management and conservation." Bureau projects with funding deleted included the Fruitland Mesa, Narrows, and Savery-Pot Hook projects in Colorado. The two major projects in the Colorado basin, the Central Arizona and Central Utah projects, were to be funded after modification, while the Dallas Creek and Dolores projects in Colorado were recommended for funding.

Carter concluded his statement by pointing out that jobs created by water projects were more expensive than those created by other forms of federal spending. He stressed that "the current pattern of water project distribution is contributing to the federal dollar drain out of the heavily populated Northeast, where economic stimulus is needed."

Congress responded quickly, fashioning a compromise that deleted funding for only half the recommended projects. The outcome was a classic deal. Among the projects restored were projects in the districts of the Appropriations Committee members, including five in Carter's own region the South, and the Central Utah Project. Others, according to one participant in the maneuvering, were "thrown to the wolves." In August, Carter signed the public-works appropriation bill, noting his continuing opposition to all of the projects on the original list.

Carter's environmental supporters were disappointed that Carter did not veto the appropriations bill. A House vote in June indicated that Carter would have the strength to prevent an override. According to Blackwelder, Carter "had devastated the water lobby," but with the compromise "he sawed the limb off on his supporters on Capitol Hill." Carter pressed on with his plans to reform federal water policy. Although the president promised a Denver audience in October 1977 that there would be "no federal preemption of state or private prerogatives in the use or management of water," Andrus had already engineered an unprecedented move in Arizona by threatening to hold up final water allocations for the Central Arizona Project until the Arizona legislature reformed the state's groundwater laws.

THE WESTLANDS FIGHT

By the summer of 1977 Carter and Andrus were embroiled in another aspect of the water-project fight, this time over the 160-acre limit and California's Westlands Water District, the largest reclamation district in the West. The Westlands district, part of the federally funded Central Valley Project, covered 600,000 acres lying along the western edge of the San Joaquin Valley between Fresno and Interstate 5. In the days when the Southern Pacific dominated the valley, Westlands was part of Henry Miller's ambitious scheme to divert the San Joaquin River for irrigation. Once a luxuriant swamp teeming with wildlife during the rainy season, the land had begun to crack and subside by the 1950s. By drawing down the water table through deep wells, farmers threatened to turn the area into an alkaline wasteland. The water having been drained from the land, the San Luis unit of the Central Valley Project began to bring irrigation water from the Sacramento delta to the district in 1967.

Since the passage of the reclamation law, controversy over the 160-acre limit had flared up from time to time, particularly in California, where two huge projects, the Central Valley and State Water projects, had become the basis of the most mechanized and energy-intensive agricultural system in the world. Originally, the law specified that farmers receiving federally subsidized water could only receive that water on 160 acres. Although the reclamation law was amended in 1926 to cut back on speculation in reclamation lands, it was never really enforced.

The 1926 amendment provided for the sale of excess land (i.e., acreage over 160 acres) receiving subsidized water and specified that the land must be sold according to its value without the water—a change meant to limit profiteering on the basis of public largesse. Further, the amendment made agreement to sell the excess land a precondition for signing a contract with the Reclamation Service for delivery of publicly funded water. The law was also changed by administrative decision to allow a farmer and his wife each to own 160 acres.

Before Hoover and Parker dams were completed, in part to deliver irrigation water to the Imperial Valley, President Hoover exempted the entire valley from the 160-acre limit. Next the Colorado–Big Thompson Project was exempted by Ickes with little notice taken. Then during World War II, when California and the federal government were fighting over control of the Central Valley Project, a furor arose when a Kern County congressman tried to slip through an amendment exempting the entire Central Valley Project.

In part, because of the lack of enforcement of the 160-acre limit throughout the West, the average size of farms grew. Corporate forms of agriculture became increasingly influential. In California, and to a lesser extent Arizona, Colorado, and Utah, corporate farming dominated agriculture, soaking up huge subsidies from a number of federal programs while undermining the western farm family. Production became concentrated in the irrigated desert valleys that the agribusiness giants controlled. By 1977, out of more than 10 million acres in the West irrigated by Bureau of Reclamation projects, approximately 1 million acres were excess lands, lands that the agribusiness giants were required to sell.

The fight to enforce the 160-acre limit was revived in the Westlands Water District in the early 1970s by the Fresno-based National Land for People (NLP), a loose coalition of small farmers, farm workers, and university-educated agricultural experts that was backed by the National Farmers Union and the California State Federation of Labor. A number of NLP members, eager to take advantage of the public subsidy in the Westlands district, tried to buy excess lands in the district but found that huge operators, led by the Southern Pacific, Standard Oil of California, Anderson-Clayton, and a number of large local farm corporations, had effectively blocked entrance into the district. The Southern Pacific, for example, owned 109,000 acres in the district, including 83,000 excess acres.

Some of these corporations appeared to have complied with the requirement to sell their excess land. When NLP researched the actual transactions, it found that through a complicated system of sales and lease-backs involving relatives, employees, and friends, the original owners had reconcentrated their holdings to retain control of the district or had sold to other large corporations.

In 1976, after NLP's lawyers challenged the Westlands owners in court, the court enjoined any further sales of excess lands in the Westlands district until the Department of the Interior drew up new rules governing the enforcement of the 160-acre limit.

After Carter's election, the Interior transition team drew attention to the Westlands controversy, since the new administration would be responsible for drawing up the regulations called for by the courts. In its briefing book, the transition team called the Westlands situation a "national disgrace." It described the district as "made up of corporate landowners whose federal subsidy already approaches $2 billion." After the inauguration, Andrus, having stepped into another imbroglio not of his own making, ordered all excess-land sales halted and called for an audit of the Central Valley Project and a review of the Westlands contract.

Then, in August 1977, Andrus announced a proposed set of new rules. The proposals called for a residency requirement but no limit on leasing and for a careful review of excess-land sales. Andrus' announcement came at the same time as the United States Appeals Court's decision that the Imperial Valley Irrigation District was not exempt from the 160-acre limit. With Andrus' announcement, the Carter administration found itself locked in a bitter confrontation with the single most powerful and well-organized corporate interest in California, whose fight for control of California's farmlands went back to the days of the Southern Pacific's domination of state politics.

Soon after Carter's election, supporters of the Westlands land-reform scheme in Governor Jerry Brown's administration greeted Andrus as a new ally in their fight against the San Joaquin Valley agribusiness interests. The year before, Brown appeared to have taken the side of the land reformers at congressional hearings in Fresno by calling for a cooperative effort between the state and the federal government to make excess land in Westlands available for new farmers. "The large corporate farms will finally be broken up," Brown aide Bill Press happily declared.

Andrus accordingly appointed the Westlands Task Force, which closely mirrored the reform coalition supporting NLP. When Andrus was accused of loading the panel with critics of Westlands, he added two state representatives with close ties to agribusiness.

Governor Brown, however, had already won one major confrontation with agribusiness over farm workers' right to organize and was not eager to take on the farm interests a second time. Instead of allying himself with Andrus, a development that everyone expected after his dramatic performance at the Fresno hearings, Brown refused to speak out publicly on the issue. He deferred to Richard Rominger, his new director of agriculture, whom he had appointed to appease the state's farm interests.

With Brown out of the way, California politicians with close ties to agribusiness, such as Senator Alan Cranston, called for a one-year moratorium on the release of new rules governing the 160-acre limit. A bloc of pro-agribusiness state legislators charged that Andrus' proposals "have outraged California's agricultural community." In November 1977, the Westlands Task Force came out with a draft report estimating that the subsidy in Westlands totaled $796 million, or an average of $2,200 an acre. The total Central Valley Project subsidy amounted to $2.7 billion. The task force estimated that it would take 270 years for the Westlands corporations to pay for the last part of the project. Rominger responded by calling for exemption of the Imperial Valley from the 160-acre limit.

As the year ended, reports were circulating that Carter had abandoned the 160-acre-limit fight in favor of the so-called Engle formula, which called for the recipients of federally subsidized water to buy out the government by paying the interest on the cost of irrigation. Already in deep trouble with his hit list, Carter had unwittingly extended the size and depth of the coalition of water and agribusiness interests opposed to his reforms.

THE CORPORATE COUNTEROFFENSIVE

While Richard Nixon "discovered" environmentalism in response to the post–Earth Day resurgence of the environmental movement, Jimmy Carter, despite his calculated vagueness, was the first postwar president who appeared to be committed to a conservation ethic. He had tapped young talent available from a wide range of public interest, environmental, and consumer organizations; brought them into the government; and then launched a series of bold initiatives that brought him head to head with the corporate lobbyists and their allies in the bureaucracy and Congress. After a year of pressing forward on several fronts, his advancing units encountered a well-entrenched, well-organized enemy and were easily turned aside. Now the president was scrambling to turn a rout into a more systematic retreat. After calling for the elimination of a number of questionable water projects, the president warned Congress that he was not in a mood to horse-trade votes on other measures for one of these projects. However, he had ended up accepting a typical deal and one that primarily favored politicians from his own region.

At first Washington insiders were thrown on the defensive by Carter's erratic behavior. The roads of access carefully constructed during the Nixon-Ford years ended outside the White House gates under Carter. By 1978 Washington had taken the measure of its new leader, and all agreed that he appeared to lack the power and finesse to get even minimal results from Congress and the bureaucracy. Before Carter, corporate lobbyists, in particular, had been paralyzed by the Watergate collapse and the attendant inquiries into a wide range of questionable activities at home and abroad involving bribes, payoffs, and intervention in the political affairs of other countries. But the Watergate scandal had not, as many had expected, been followed by another upsurge in popular unrest against the powers that be. Patrick Caddell had counseled Carter early in his campaign that "there would be a movement to socialist action except that the government is feared and disliked as much as big business." The social movements of the 1960s, with the exception of the late-blooming environmental movement, had largely faded. Many activists, abandoning the protest posture that placed them outside the established political process, had moved into organized politics. They ran for office, joined the entourages of liberal politicians, and built organized pressure groups in Washington and across the country.

In the West, a revitalized environmental movement and the protests of numerous Indian tribes had tied up the elaborate plans of the utilities and energy companies in the northern Great Plains and the Four Corners region. The old water lobby was also demoralized by the impact of the young environmentalists. NLP was making headway in the Westlands Water District; environmentalists were holding up further water development for Denver; and the whole issue of government water development for energy producers, rather than family farmers, was being challenged by many of the same people. In response, the water lobby seemed to be gradually accepting the idea that the era of the big project was over. The most important projects had already been authorized, if not funded. Although on the defensive, the old water lobby hoped to outmaneuver the opposition and finish those projects that were partially funded.

When Carter, not revolt or collapse, followed Nixon's demise, the corporate interests slowly got back on their feet and prepared for new campaigns. The insurgencies of the 1960s had produced new "activist" politicians such as Jerry Brown, Governor Richard Lamm and Senator Gary Hart of Colorado, and Governor Bruce Babbitt of Arizona. In a fearful mood, the corporations active in the West threw together a number of powerful new lobbying organizations. The California Business Roundtable was formed so that the heads of the fifty largest corporations could deal directly with the Brown administration and the legislature. In the interior West, Salt Lake businessman B. Z. ("Bud") Kastler, head of Mountain Fuel Supply; former governor Calvin Rampton; and executives from Kennecott pulled together a new coalition of corporate executives to contest the EPA's clean-air regulations in the wake of the 1976 decision to deny permits for the Kaiparowits plant in the canyon lands of southern Utah. The Utah group, the Western Regional Council, was soon joined by Denver banker Bruce Rockwell. He brought Colorado corporate interests into the council and forged a link through Governor Lamm with the newly organized Western Governors Policy Office (WESTPO). The shift to a regional organization was partially engineered by Bonneville Associates of Salt Lake City. These young policy-oriented professionals were concerned that the council start out with a progressive image, a possibility that they feared might be undermined by "the neanderthal approach" of the Salt Lake business leaders.

The Western Regional Council consisted of top executives from the largest corporations in the interior West, including the regional vice-presidents of the largest energy multinationals. The council identified itself as a regional equivalent of the national Business Roundtable. It was, in fact, dominated by corporations headquartered in major centers of power outside the interior West—the very corporations that had controlled the region's resources since the days of the railroads' land grab.

The key to the council's influence was its close relations with WESTPO and with the region's development-oriented congressional delegation. Together they hoped to shape Carter's policies. In regulatory matters like the EPA's enforcement of clean air laws, they sought "a regional-variation provision" that would allow for the development of their favorite industrial projects. In water matters, they hoped to effect the new national water policy, and in mineral leasing, they tried to pressure the Carter administration not to lock up resources in newly formed wilderness areas.

The fight to enforce the 160-acre limit also led to the creation of lobbying organizations. In 1976, Westlands operators formed California Westside Farmers, headed by John Weidert, a former aide to Earl Butz, Nixon's Secretary of Agriculture and a longtime advocate of corporate farming. When Congress began considering a number of bills to revise the reclamation law, California and Arizona agribusiness and banks, including the Bank of America and Southern Pacific, formed the Farm-Water Alliance to influence the new legislation.

When Carter turned out to be a bolder reformer than expected, the corporate lobbyists decided that the president had fallen captive to the numerous reform groups headquartered in Washington. The environmentalists have taken over, warned Standard Oil of Indiana. The Western Oil and Gas Association branded Carter's environmental message, which came six weeks after his energy speech, "an environmentalist's 'wish list.'" Each new Carter initiative reinvigorated the established lobbying networks to create the aggressive coalitions that Andrus and Mondale had warned Carter against at the fatal meeting in February 1977.

The impact of the corporate counteroffensive began to be felt as early as 1977. Central to the shift in attitude among the young, nominally liberal western politicians was their ambivalent response to the hit list. Right after its publication, Senator Hart, for example, attacked the manner in which the list had been developed and promised to work for the restoration of Colorado's Narrows and Dolores projects. Heartened by the collapse of the potential opposition even before the fight was started, the *Denver Post*, long an advocate of big water projects, lashed out at "the hatchet job engineered by Fletcher and other environmentalists." By mid-1977 Governor Lamm was telling *Forbes* magazine, "I wasn't elected by environmentalists," while Senator Hart declared, "They may have claimed me, but I'm not claiming them." Even Morris Udall, who welcomed the reforms proposed by Carter, including Andrus' effort to force Arizona to reform its groundwater laws, was calling for greater balance between the demands of environmentalists and prodevelopment forces.

Abandoned by his own allies and with a steady string of congressional losses behind him, in early 1978 Carter began to rethink his strategies on the water and energy issues that most affected the West. As all parties maneuvered to influence Carter's new water-policy statement, the *Washington Post* anticipated an "unconditional surrender" and "a retreat reminiscent of Carter's abandonment of the $50 tax rebate and his human rights stand." Andrus' remarks to the press before the announcement of Carter's new water policy revealed that the Carter administration had definitely retreated. At one point Andrus told reporters, "We put together a coalition that beat us."

In June 1978, Carter announced his new national water policy. In an attempt to conciliate the western water lobby, Carter noted that his policy would not affect any of the more than eight hundred projects with an estimated cost of $34 billion; projects that were already authorized but not funded. The policy also contained some reform measures. The heart of these reforms was the old National Water Commission proposal that the states pay from 5 percent to 10 percent of the cost of new projects. Carter also proposed a stringent set of new criteria to deal with safety, environmental impacts, and financing. An independent White House review process was to be carried out before construction on new projects. In effect, Carter's policy assigned a greater role to the executive branch in matters traditionally reserved for congressional wheeler-dealers. It also forced the states to face up to the realities of water subsidies.

Environmentalists considered the new water policy generally positive, although overly conciliatory toward western water interests and lacking mandatory conservation measures. They were nevertheless pleased that the president had staked out a permanent role for the executive branch through the independent review process. Western politicians, however, were far from satisfied. Most western governors boycotted a personal meeting with Carter to discuss the forthcoming reforms. After Carter announced his policy, Utah's Governor Scott Matheson attacked it, declaring his opposition to an independent review process that he called a source of further bureaucratic delays. Matheson was also fearful of the cost-sharing idea because it would work to the advantage of bigger, wealthier states. Behind his words lurked the old fear of California.

In an attempt to avoid a repeat of the hit-list controversy, Carter proposed twenty-six new projects for funding in the 1979 public-works authorization bill but warned Congress that he would veto any measure that attempted to restore projects already targeted for removal. Congress took Carter's conciliatory gestures as a sign of weakness and immediately beefed up the public-works bill by adding an additional twenty-seven projects and by restoring funding for six projects that Carter had opposed. More significantly, Congress moved to abolish the Water Resources Council, the agency charged with Carter's new review process. Outraged by the blatancy of the congressional response, Carter vetoed the public-works bill, the first such veto since the Eisenhower era.

Carter's supporters in the fight against water projects looked forward to 1979 and 1980, hoping that the momentum developed by Carter's veto would carry over. But Carter's dealings with Congress had fallen into a predictable pattern. When the president moved to eliminate funding for eighteen projects, including some of the old standbys, Congress restored the projects. In the end, Carter capitulated once again by trading votes on the water project for support for his Department of Education.

In 1980 the House rolled out one of the biggest pork barrels ever, which indicated that Congress would again try to undercut Carter by continuing to hold up funding for the independent review process. When the final legislation was signed in October 1980, only four of the original eighteen projects on the hit list had been eliminated. All three Bureau of Reclamation projects in Colorado from the original hit list were funded, one of them after being reevaluated for energy use as a favor to Senator Gary Hart.

The Carter administration's attempt to modify the Central Arizona Project and the Central Utah Project had also proved largely unsuccessful. In 1980 Congress funded a new study of the Central Arizona Project's Orme Dam, which was originally removed from the project as a gesture to environmentalists and the Yavapai Indians whose reservation would be flooded by the dam. While the administration minimized the importance of the new study, project supporters claimed that this was the first step in restoring the dam to the project. In Utah the Bureau of Reclamation was still engaged in searching for new methods to fund the Central Utah Project to meet its rapidly increasing costs. Despite the new Carter water policy, partial state funding was not one of the methods being considered.

While Carter was retreating on water policy, the administration appeared to be holding the line on reform efforts in the Westlands Water District. Gradually the California farm-water lobby developed access to the highest levels of the Carter administration. As early as the 1978 election, it became apparent that the administration's strategy would be shaped by the necessities of politics. George Baker of the *Sacramento Bee* reported in late October that at a Fresno breakfast meeting of farmers, including Westlands operators, Andrus told his audience to change the reclamation law so that he would not have to enforce it. Then Andrus gradually lifted the moratorium on the sale of excess lands except those halted by the courts in Westlands. He reserved to himself the right to approve all sales. After the 1978 elections, the Westlands district made a major bid to conclude negotiations for a new contract for Central Valley Project water. The district hired a Washington lawyer who was a former aide to Vice-President Mondale and a former member of the Carter transition team who had worked on the issues of water and agriculture. After months of negotiations, the contract was finally signed in August 1979. The new contract made a number of concessions on the price of water and the quantity delivered, concessions that some regarded as a defeat for the new Carter policy of getting recipients to pay the full cost of delivery.

In 1979 and 1980 the Farm-Water Alliance mounted a major campaign to gut the 160-acre law. But the bill was repeatedly bottled up in committee. Meanwhile, *Bee* reporter Baker revealed that President Carter would be attending a fund raiser at the home of a Modesto lobbyist who had worked to exempt from the 160-acre limit areas along the Kings River being farmed by corporate farmers. Carter's newly found lobbyist–supporter hoped to raise $150,000 for the Democratic National Committee.

Referring to the all-out effort to change the reclamation law, George Miller, a Democratic congressman from California and an opponent of Westlands, told reporter Baker: "This is a case study of money, politics, and influence against the public interest. Their power, the concentration of money was astounding—beyond anything I ever imagined. They even tried to hire my campaign manager and a former associate of mine to influence me."

Like the hit list, the attempts to reform the Westlands Water District through the 160-acre law had largely come to naught. Carter had moved toward an election-year accommodation with western water and agribusiness interests. The corporate farmers in the Westlands District were still receiving subsidized water. And Andrus had postponed the question of the 160-acre limit until next year.

THE MONEY SUPERMARKET

From the start, President Carter considered energy the most crucial issue facing his administration. The nature of Carter's energy policy was vital to the West's future, since greater and greater pressure was being placed on domestic, particularly western, resources. During the campaign, Carter had indulged in vague anti–oil company rhetoric about "vertical accountability" and the possibility of horizontal divestiture (i.e., ending oil-company control of other sources of energy, such as coal and uranium). At the same time, Carter, according to Clark Mollenhoff's *The President Who Failed*, was looking for campaign contributions, particularly from independent oil companies. Congressional critics also noted that Carter used the verbatim text of an Oklahoma oil-lobbyist's letter in his pledge to the governors of Texas, Louisiana, New Mexico, and Oklahoma to deregulate the price of natural gas.

In April 1977, in his famous "moral equivalent of war" speech, Carter laid out a national energy plan that placed heavy emphasis on conservation. Arguing that the availability of cheap energy had led to its inefficient use, Carter based his strategy on making the world price of oil, as set by the alliance between OPEC and the major oil companies, the basis for the price of all oil and gas. Saying that "the energy industries need adequate incentives to develop new resources and are entitled to sufficient profits for exploration for new discoveries," Carter argued that higher prices were the key to conservation. The energy producers also wanted an end to all government regulation of prices and production. Despite their commitment to "free enterprise," they also wanted to encourage new production, particularly in such areas as synthetic fuels. Carter at first parted with the energy industry by proposing the crude-oil equalization tax. Carter wanted a healthy chunk of the huge increase in profits awarded to the energy industry in the name of conservation through higher prices to be turned over to the government for the benefit of consumers and low-income people. Carter also mounted a campaign to pass a law calling for regulation of strip mining, which had been bottled up in Congress by the coal operators for years.

When Carter's first energy proposals reached the Senate, they faced the opposition of two key spokesmen of the energy industry, Senate Majority Leader

Robert Byrd from the coal-producing state of West Virginia and Senate Finance Committee Chairman Russell Long of Louisiana, the oil companies' most forceful representative on Capitol Hill. In hard bargaining with the White House, Long, who considered Carter's plan insufficiently production-oriented, won an agreement that some of the funds accumulated through the crude-oil equalization tax would be used to subsidize the oil producers. The oil companies had their foot in the door, and elements of the plan for a massive subsidization of the energy industry proposed by Ford's Vice-President Nelson Rockefeller began to reappear on the Hill.

Within a year, the administration had begun to retreat on its oil equalization tax, although advocating, and then implementing, the decontrol of oil prices. With Carter abandoning his conservation stance and becoming increasingly production-oriented, he began to seek an accommodation with the energy companies, an accommodation that he hoped to work out, in part, through Cecil Andrus by opening up additional resources on the Colorado Plateau.

Even though plans for the Kaiparowits plant had been dropped in 1976, the energy companies continued to push for a smaller number of projects in the Four Corners region. The Western Regional Council attacked the larger policy questions such as air-quality standards and coal-leasing regulations, which stood in the way of wide-open development. The Union Pacific, for instance, pushed for coal-leasing on public lands on the Kaiparowits Plateau, while other companies pushed for new leases on the Navajo and other Indian reservations and prepared to build a number of coal-gasification plants.

When Andrus arrived in Washington, he was confronted with a renewed effort by the energy companies to push through at least some of these projects. Instead of going along with any of the major projects proposed by the big energy producers, he began a review of coal-leasing regulations as ordered by the courts and then selected one project, the Intermountain Power Project, to be the largest coal-fired plant in the world, as a model of federal-state cooperation in the siting of power plants. Dubbed "Son of Kaiparowits" by environmentalists, the project was proposed by a group of Nevada and Utah electric cooperatives and six southern California municipal utilities. Intermountain, like Kaiparowits, was designed in large measure to meet the energy needs of California. The Los Angeles Department of Water and Power, one of the six California utilities, planned to take 50 percent of the power.

Working with Utah Governor Matheson, Andrus helped put together a task force to select a site. The group, under Joseph Browder, was composed of representatives of the Department of the Interior, California, and Utah. The task force recommended moving the Intermountain plant from the proposed site at Salt Wash, where the plant would have affected air quality in Capitol Reef National Park, to a new site in the small western Utah farming community of Lynndyl. In December 1979, Andrus gave the go-ahead for construction on the plant at a special celebration in the Grand Ballroom of the Mormon Church's Hotel Utah in Salt Lake City.

Next the secretary turned his attention to another major mine–power plant complex in Utah and Nevada, the Allen–Warner Valley System. The idea for this project originated with the Nevada Power Company in the 1960s and grew into a partnership with California utilities. The project involved two power plants, the Harry Allen plant north of Las Vegas and the Warner Valley plant near Saint George, Utah. The plan was to supply these plants with coal mined by Utah International (the new name for Utah Construction and Mining) at a strip mine in the Alton Hills and carried to the plants by a coal slurry line. The proposed location of the mine was immediately adjacent to Bryce Canyon National Park.

Using a fast-track approach to overcome delays caused by regulatory procedures, Andrus had the Bureau of Land Management prepare an environmental-impact report to evaluate all the different ways of handling the power complex. The report was to include the development of alternatives, such as cogeneration, that would make construction of the plants unnecessary. Andrus' instructions to the Bureau of Land Management to evaluate all alternatives was unique. For the first time, an alternative plan for energy development worked out by environmentalists would be contrasted head to head with the utilities' scenario for the Southwest. In general, the environmentalists had been arguing that the utilities' elaborate plans were based on inflated estimates of the energy needs of the Southwest. They also claimed that the utilities emphasized huge capital-intensive complexes like the Allen and Warner Valley plants rather than smaller, less environmentally destructive alternatives like cogeneration. By the late 1970s the environmentalists had developed a full-blown policy alternative based on renewable resources, conservation, scaled-down growth estimates, and smaller generating plants.

With their alternative scenario in hand, the Sierra Club, the Environmental Defense Fund, and Friends of the Earth, along with some local ranchers who worried about their water supply, filed a petition with the Office of Surface Mining to prevent strip mining in the area. Andrus had taken the position that he would follow the lead of the California Public Utilities Commission in determining whether the new power complex was needed. In the fall of 1980, the commission staff recommended eliminating the Warner Valley plant and the slurry pipeline, calling instead for coal to be shipped from the underground coal fields in central Utah. Soon after, the EPA denied Nevada Power's application for a permit to construct the Warner Valley plant, citing the threat to the air quality of Zion National Monument.

Andrus, however, gave way under pressure from the utilities and Utah International. Interior's Joseph Browder had already told Utah International, according to a company memo, that he had a mandate from the secretary "to make the Allen–Warner Valley System work." Andrus finally approved the Harry Allen plant in Nevada, some coal leases adjacent to Bryce Canyon National Park, and a coal slurry pipeline from the coal field to the Allen plant.

The energy producers were equally successful in their attempt to influence other aspects of Carter's energy program. One of the clearest signs of energy-company influence was the appointment of Lynn Coleman as counsel for the new Department of Energy, which had been created as part of Carter's 1977 energy package. Coleman, a lobbyist for natural-gas and coal-slurry pipeline interests, came from the Houston law firm of Vinson and Elkins, which included numerous oil and gas companies among its clients.

Coleman's role in the department drew attention during the uproar over long lines at gas stations in the winter of 1978–1979. The department was charged with investigating the reasons for a gasoline shortages during a period when there was a glut of crude oil. The investigation, which was ultimately controlled by Coleman, absolved the oil companies of any responsibility for the shortages. When Carter was ready to announce his second energy plan, Coleman was identified as one of its major architects.

Pressure on Carter for a new energy package had been building since the Iranian revolution and subsequent gasoline shortages in early 1979. In the face of the growing anger over the long lines at gas stations and mistrust of the oil companies, Carter proposed in April 1979 the first part of his second energy program based on the windfall-profits tax. By taxing the oil companies, Carter was staking out a major role for the government in his new energy program. The question was, Who would benefit from government intervention?

With great fanfare, Carter, in the summer of 1979, retreated to Camp David and stage-managed a series of meetings with various people who were called in to consult with and advise the president. When Carter emerged from his retreat, he called for the creation of an "energy security corporation" that would use funds from the windfall-profits tax—$88 billion over a ten-year period—on the development of synthetic fuels. Although Carter also called for increased funds for solar energy and a greater emphasis on mass transit, the bulk of his plan was production-oriented, favoring both synfuels and coal production. Grants and loans for public utilities were to be provided for the purpose of converting power plants to coal. As a boon to the energy producers, Carter also called for the creation of an energy-mobilization board that would have the power to override state and federal regulations that interfered with the rapid construction of vital energy facilities.

With the second energy plan, Carter abandoned his earlier emphasis on conservation and opted instead for massive subsidization of the energy companies through his synfuels program. Energy lobbyists called the Carter approach "the federal money supermarket," as they eagerly awaited funds for their "pet projects." An oil lobbyist told the *Wall Street Journal* that the program would produce an "energy-industrial complex" creating a "symbiotic relationship" between the energy companies and the federal government "like what you see between defense contractors and the Pentagon."

By the end of the Carter administration, the big energy play in the Southwest had shifted from plans for a string of power plants and strip mines to be built across the Colorado Plateau to the development of oil-shale areas in eastern Utah and western Colorado. When Congress passed the synfuels bills earmarking an initial $20 billion for the program, the oil-shalers readied their plans to build a whole new industry with federal funds. Carter then announced that his new synfuels board would be made up primarily of major corporate figures, although it also included Lane Kirkland from the AFL-CIO, and—for his next act in Washington—Cecil Andrus.

THE OLD SOLUTION

Andrus had come to the Department of the Interior committed to ending the cozy relationship between the department and private industry. In large measure, he succeeded in closing the revolving door between industry and government by bringing a new generation of public servants, including a small number from the environmental movement, into the department. Under Nixon and Ford, the environmental movement was treated as a fringe phenomenon, bothersome but inconsequential. Although environmental thinking had penetrated the bureaucracy in Washington, even affecting Nixon aides like John Ehrlichman, the environmental bureaucrats from agencies like Interior and the EPA were kept away from the center of action.

Andrus, who considered himself a member of the environmental community, took a new approach. "I took the position that I was going to have all sides inside and all sides considered," he said in a 1980 interview. As a result, conservation and fiscal restraint became major themes of the new administration for a time. Andrus became Carter's spokesman in the attack on subsidized water projects throughout the West and the main advocate of reform in the Westlands Water District. In this situation, Andrus played a major role in forcing Arizona to reform its groundwater laws and in making public the activities of the alliance between the water lobby, Congress, and the Bureau of Reclamation.

In the end, Carter's reform measures only revitalized the old water lobby, now strengthened by the addition of major energy companies seeking federal water for their new projects. The environmentalists, preoccupied with more elite forms of politics centered in Washington, failed to mobilize new forces to support Carter's reforms. They even saw their political influence wane in key states like Colorado.

Finding themselves isolated, Carter and Andrus made efforts to accommodate western corporate interests, although Andrus never countenanced a raid on public resources like that of the 1960s. In the Westlands controversy, NLP's George Ballis concluded that "Andrus never gave us a thing" when there were administrative decisions to be made that could have gone either in favor of agribusiness or the 160-acre limit. Andrus finally exempted important parts of the San Joaquin Valley from the limit at the eleventh hour. Besides soliciting funds through a Central Valley water lobbyist, first Carter and then his wife attended fund-raising events in the Bay Area organized by San Francisco real estate magnate Walter Shorenstein, a leading checkbook Democrat and a major backer of the campaign against the 160-acre limit.

When Carter became convinced that the MX missile had to be built in the Nevada-Utah desert to strengthen American defenses and reach an arms-limitation agreement with the Russians, his plans for the biggest public-works project in history colored all other policies in the interior West. Having originally proposed modification of the Central Utah Project, the White House reached an agreement with Congressman Gunn McKay to promote the project in exchange for support for the construction of the MX. When Teddy Kennedy delegates asked Andrus at the 1980 Democratic convention about a jobs program, he told them that the MX was the administration's jobs program.

After four years, Carter showed few signs of having developed an understanding of, or rapport with, the people of a region often paired with the South by facile Sun Belt analysts. The political realignment that first Nixon and then Carter sought continued to be elusive. The fact was that politicians in Carter's own party who shared the same general attitudes, such as Jerry Brown, Bruce Babbitt, Gary Hart, and Richard Lamm, were only too eager to disassociate themselves from Carter's actions when it was expedient to do so.

Carter had begun his administration as an advocate of the new politics of conservation and fiscal restraint and as an enemy of the congressional pork barrel. He ended up opting for yet another program of massive subsidies—the same old solution, now called the federal money supermarket, which had been the historical basis of the western boom. In the end, the campaign plotted by the president's young protégés failed to build mass support. Instead, they had only succeeded in reinvigorating the corporate interest groups and the old water lobby. The surviving members of the Six Companies, the oil-shalers, the oil companies, the defense contractors, the big mining companies, and the agribusiness giants were all ready by the 1980s to resume where they had left off.

For the 1980s and beyond, Exxon chairman Clifton Garvin, in a presentation before the Business Roundtable, delivered a breathtaking proposal for Exxon shale development. Garvin proposed the construction of six huge oil-shale pits, measuring a half-mile deep, 3.5 miles long, and 1.75 miles wide. The amount of rock excavated each day would be the equivalent of that excavated for the whole Panama Canal. Water requirements would be so monumental that another huge water transfer project—perhaps a revival of the long-discredited North American Water and Power Alliance (NAWAPA) plan to deliver water to the West from Canada and the Pacific Northwest—would have to be implemented.

The cost, according to Exxon: $500 billion over three decades for the shale and another $300 billion for the supplemental coal program. Each pit operation would require twenty-two thousand miners and eight thousand refinery workers. In three decades, the western Colorado region of small towns and rural farms would be transformed through this monstrous project, which would bring 1.5 million people to the region.

This extraordinary development was a risk, Garvin declared, but one well worth taking. The Colorado Plateau, once again, braced for the onslaught.

PART TWO
CENTERS OF POWER

The new regional power of the Southwest is preeminently urban, the mythology of the cowboy and rugged individualism notwithstanding. The six major metropolises of the region—Los Angeles, San Francisco, Denver, Salt Lake City, Phoenix, and Las Vegas—are the new centers of power. These cities exploit the resources of the interior, compete with each other (although the larger California cities exercise a dominant role), and challenge the traditional centers of power in the East.

California is the region's economic and geopolitical headquarters, evolving into what its governor, Jerry Brown, likes to call "the Pacific Republic of California." Los Angeles is the West's ultimate boomtown, turned now into a city with a nonwhite majority. San Francisco is the corporate headquarters city, the original financial center trying still to exercise control over the new round of resource development. Denver is the interior's energy capital, a hub city where the energy multinationals build their future. Salt Lake City is the headquarters of Mormon power, which still extends through the old territory of the State of Deseret, stretching from Idaho through Utah, Nevada, and Arizona into southern California. Phoenix is the quintessential Sun Belt boomtown, a real estate speculator's paradise and a planner's nightmare. Las Vegas is the end of the desert road, a gamblers' mecca, where fantasy blends with the region's ultimate quest for a new urban empire.

4 California: The Pacific Republic

The Hyatt Regency at the Los Angeles Airport in June 1978 was an incongruous place for an incongruous meeting. The executives of the California Business Roundtable were busy men, top officers in the very largest financial institutions and energy, aerospace, agricultural, electronics, engineering, and high-technology companies in California. They had been told about the meeting on less than twenty-four-hours' notice, but it was worth the effort to lay out their position and hear the response from California's unpredictable governor.

It would be a short meeting, with not even time for a quick cocktail. Jerry Brown whirled in a few minutes late and got down to business at once. He was already wired, probably on his tenth cup of coffee, and wasted little time.

The Roundtable's leaders had had problems in the past communicating with Jerry Brown. This was their third full session with the governor, and they wondered whether the earlier problems would recur. At first, the businessmen had been wary of some of Brown's appointments. They had decided that Brown's coterie was part of the massive drift to the left brought about by Vietnam and Watergate. These young, aggressive public-interest lawyers, environmentalists, and reform advocates who served as Brown's aides were, indeed, scornful of the Roundtable.

Jerry Brown's rhetoric had not helped either. His talk of "small is beautiful," "appropriate technology," and even his anti–big government statements made these business people fretful. Some of them wondered whether this ascetic politician was really just a wild-eyed new leftist pushing his own version of "participatory democracy." It had become a question, according to Roundtable leader Ben Biaggini, the head of Southern Pacific, of not just influencing one politician or another, or even getting Jerry Brown's ear, but "of heading off a move toward socialism."

Big issues were now on the horizon: the Peripheral Canal, coal and nuclear plants, the regulatory climate. The immediate cause of concern was how to interpret the passage of Proposition 13. Some businessmen feared that this big

77

property-tax cut, which turned out to be a $4 billion windfall for the state's largest landowners, would lead to rent control and an attempt to get back at the corporate "bad guys" with new taxes. What would Brown do, they wondered?

Brown liked being unpredictable. He particularly resented comparisons with his father, whose style was so different from his own. Yet, Jerry Brown had begun to feel the squeeze. The logic of his own rhetoric and all of his delicate balancing acts finally seemed to have caught up with him. For someone who had for so long detested the father-son connection, Jerry Brown, the critic of big New Deal–style government, was about to make the ultimate bid for big government expenditures.

Pat Brown was, indeed, very different from his son. A consummate politician whose ideas were formed in the aftermath of the New Deal, Pat Brown came to power as governor in 1958 through the efforts of a revived New Deal coalition led by the grass-roots California Democratic clubs. Brown's victory had broken a Republican grip on the statehouse that had lasted sixteen years through the Earl Warren and Goodwin Knight periods.

Both Warren and Knight were politicians of the permanent California boom that had favored business expansion, inmigration, and the growth of publicly funded services such as the state's massive highway construction program. Although strongly anti-labor on agricultural matters, Warren and Knight tended to minimize and even neutralize labor opposition by their tacit support of the top-down unionization of California industry that began during World War II.

The 1958 election undercut the boom politics of the Republicans. A faction had become increasingly disenchanted with the party's accommodation to parts of the New Deal program, particularly the acceptance of unionism. This conservative faction promoted a right-to-work law designed to outlaw closed-shop agreements. After being rebuffed in the legislature, they got the right-to-work question placed on the 1958 ballot as an initiative measure. This deepened the division within the Republican party.

The Republicans also found themselves in a weakened position because conservative Senator William Knowland switched roles with Governor Goodwin Knight. The senator's running for governor forced the governor to run for the Senate, with resulting confusion. Brown easily swept to victory as a more moderate, less ideological version of his liberal Democratic-club champions.

Brown immediately set out to recreate a California version of the New Deal partnership between the public and private sectors. Given the size and diversity of the state, Brown knew he had to create a coalition along both class and geographic lines. The key issue for such a coalition was water. Through a redistribution of water resources from north to south, Brown would not only be able to help sustain the California boom, but he could put together a distributive alliance led by Los Angeles and Central Valley agribusiness.

Since the turn of the century the California economy had been tied to the transportation of water supplies from areas where water was abundant to areas where water was not. In terms of rainfall, California is dramatically divided between water-surplus and water-deficit areas. Two-thirds of the rainfall occurs north of the Sacramento delta. The northern coastal area, with less than 5 percent of the state's population, receives nearly 40 percent of all the surface water, while the Los Angeles basin, with 40 percent of the population, receives about 2 percent of the state's surface water. Two of the largest agricultural areas, the San Joaquin Valley and the Imperial Valley, are, like southern California, extremely water-deficient.

Agriculture in California has been primarily irrigated farming. The availability of subsidized water through the federally funded Central Valley Project has been an essential feature of the growth of corporate-style farming. The agribusiness operator, wrote Erwin Cooper, "was the power peer of the California Club tycoon in Los Angeles and the Montgomery Street magnate in San Francisco. In fact, he was frequently the same person."

After the war, the Central Valley also experienced growing urbanization side by side with thousands of acres of newly irrigated cropland. By Pat Brown's ascendancy to power, this integration of farm and city and the nature of farm production had created a fully urbanized agribusiness that completely overshadowed the isolated, although surviving, small farmer.

The major danger to the stability of large-scale agribusiness operations was the threat that the big farms might be broken up to comply with the Reclamation Act's 160-acre limit. Even though the 160-acre provision had never been enforced in California, a substantial campaign in the 1940s had been launched by academics, small farmers, and the trade union movement to "break up the big farms."

In addition to agribusiness fears about the 160-acre limit, the southern California water lobby, led by the Metropolitan Water District, opposed new Bureau of Reclamation plans in Arizona, which included reducing Greater Los Angeles' share of both the Colorado River and Owens Valley water. Increasingly suspicious of the bureau's postwar schemes, the district decided to explore new ways of funding interbasin water transfers, such as importation from the Snake and Eel rivers and the Columbia River basin in the Pacific Northwest.

Both the southern California water interests and the San Joaquin farmers were ready by the early 1950s to utilize California's own resources instead of going the usual route of federal subsidization and control. During the Great Depression, the Bureau of Reclamation had taken over the Central Valley Project, originally conceived as a state project, because its size, cost, and complexity were beyond the means of the state. The expanding California of the 1950s, with its boom-oriented economy and sense of itself as a separate nation-state, was another matter.

The idea of a large state-run water project gathered momentum in the mid-1950s when a special legislative session called by Governor Knight established the Department of Water Resources. The new department united several different water agencies and created the bureaucratic apparatus needed to undertake a large intrastate project. A proposal by state engineer A. D. Edmonston and a further study by the Bechtel Corporation had already begun to make the rounds of the state capitol. The Edmonston-Bechtel package called for diverting water from northern California's Feather River into a multipurpose dam and aqueduct system. That system would provide power and storage facilities and would be able to transfer water southward through the farmlands of the Central Valley over the Tehachapi Mountains to the industries and consumers of southern California.

Although strongly backed by some key interests, such as the big Central Valley farmers, the Edmonston-Bechtel proposal also faced innumerable hurdles. North-south hostilities were then at their height. Some of the southern California water lobbyists feared that even with contracts to deliver water to the southland, future northern California opposition in the legislature could ultimately overturn such deliveries. Neither the Warren nor the Knight administration had been able to overcome the hostilities and generate the necessary coalition to get a state water project through the legislature. When Pat Brown took office, he overcame the difficulties preventing coalition through the fine art of distributive pork-barrel politics.

Carefully and systematically Brown tied together the different components of his geographical and class-based coalition. Trying to confine opposition to San Francisco, he put together a legislative package of different water projects for various other northern California areas, such as the Santa Clara Valley and the northern Sierra Nevada. He then mollified southern California's suspicions by writing contract-delivery guarantees into the proposed State Water Project legislation. The Central Valley farmers backed the project when the 160-acre limit was eliminated and when the cost structure of the project promised yet another round of subsidized water supplies. Brown also managed to obtain union backing from the operating engineers, teamsters, and construction trades, who coveted the jobs the project would create. The governor, however, failed to obtain support from the California State Federation of Labor because of its longstanding hostility to the antiunion agribusiness interests.

Brown succeeded in pulling together a coalition and getting the legislature to pass a bond measure that would have to be approved through the initiative process by the state's voters. Some elements of the coalition did not hold, but ultimately, enough of Brown's alliance held together to pass the measure in November 1960 by a few thousand votes. California had entered the realm of big-league water projects.

Shortly after the passage of the State Water Project initiative, California celebrated its emergence as the most populous state in the country. All during 1962, the media riveted attention on the state's continuing growth, anticipating that California would surpass New York in size. The boom was then at its peak, and the growth patterns seemed invincible and permanent.

Through the early 1960s, Pat Brown remained the focal point of the vision of California as a nation-state. He had managed to hold together the old New Deal Democratic coalition even while undercutting principal liberal demands, such as the 160-acre limit. In his 1962 election campaign Brown was able to isolate opponent Richard Nixon as a "me-too" candidate.

Although Brown defeated Nixon handily, he never quite maintained his early popularity nor held together his tenuous coalition of so many disparate elements. During his first term, he had managed to neutralize opposition from the state's business forces, who had long been oriented toward the Republican party. The 1958 Democratic sweep had laid the groundwork for a more permanent Democratic majority in the state. The state's Republican business backers had only gradually begun to recognize this new state of affairs when they considered supporting fiscally responsible incumbent Democrats with a probusiness track record in the early 1960s. Despite this new approach, the California business community remained wary of Pat Brown's distributive politics and his concept of an alliance of business, labor, and the public sector, an alliance grounded in large-scale projects designed to stimulate the boom.

By 1965 Pat Brown's middle-ground position was in serious trouble. His policies and the overall approach of the Democrats had fallen afoul of the new constituencies opposed to the Vietnam War and Lyndon Johnson's guns-and-butter approach. The California Democratic clubs had split on the Vietnam issue and most members had sided with the students and civil rights groups who by now deeply mistrusted the Democrats.

Brown's partnership policies had always implicitly accepted the premise that California needed a steady flow of cheap, nonunion labor as well as a unionized sector of the work force. Now that premise was being tested by the uprising in Watts. In 1966, Brown was opposed in the Democratic primary by Sam Yorty, the hawkish mayor of Los Angeles who projected a harsh, antagonistic approach to rebellious minorities and antiwar dissidents. Brown, as part of his attempt to hold together his old coalition, appeared to equivocate. He promoted civil rights, while defending police actions in the ghettoes. He appointed a commission on Watts—headed by former Bechtel partner and CIA head John McCone—that was strongly biased in favor of the police.

Although Brown beat Yorty by a smaller margin than anticipated, he still felt confident that he could keep his forces together to oppose Ronald Reagan, whom he scornfully dismissed as a second-rate actor who dealt in one-liners instead of the heady issues of state. Pat Brown was mistaken about the strength of his coalition. In those days of turmoil and disintegration of the political center, he failed to recognize the importance of media symbols that would ultimately bring his opponent to the very doors of the White House.

Although an actor, Ronald Reagan in 1965 liked to think of himself as a man who understood the world of the corporate boardroom. He had been comfortable in his role as spokesman for General Electric. His involvement and identity in politics stemmed as much from his gradual absorption of the corporate ethic as the development of a conservative attitude that had moved him toward the right wing of the Republican party.

Reagan was more than happy to accept the offer of support for a gubernatorial campaign made by the "millionaires' group," an informal gathering of right-wing businessmen. The group, led by California oilmen Cy Rubel and Henry Salvatori and used-car dealer Holmes Tuttle, first became involved in politics during the Goldwater presidential candidacy. The millionaires' group also included other big names in California business, such as Justin Dart of Dart Industries, MCA's Taft Schreiber, and Los Angeles lawyer William French Smith. Many of the group, however, were not included in the circle of Republican power brokers—men like Los Angeles businessmen Asa Call and Leonard Firestone and San Francisco investment banker Leland Kaiser—who had played a dominant role in Republican party affairs through the Warren and Knight periods.

By the mid-1960s, this latter group of Republican "centrists" had faded from power and influence in party affairs. Disturbed by the divisive and ultimately unsuccessful rhetoric of the Goldwater campaign, they felt more comfortable with Ronald Reagan and his bland political pronouncements, which contrasted with his effective jibes against antiwar demonstrators. After Reagan won the Republican primary, the "centrists" were ready to join with the millionaires' group to provide a solid Republican front for the 1966 general election.

Reagan was an unusual, although effective, candidate. He had little sense of the particulars of the California political economy. *Oakland Tribune's* Bill Boyarsky recalled Reagan asking at a campaign stop in the Sacramento Valley about a hundred miles north of the delta area, "Is this what they call the Delta?" The press largely ignored the gaffes, and Reagan became one of the first California politicians adept at using the electronic media where euphemisms and vague yet catchy slogans, such as Reagan's "creative society," were effectively transmitted over the airwaves directly to the voters. Reagan's appeal as a celebrity-politician lay in his ability to go on television and speak out about the antiwar or civil rights demonstrators, who became his favorite targets. With the political center in collapse and the New Left taking to the streets rather than developing voting blocs, Reagan moved into a vacuum that seemed to touch the yearnings and angers of a disaffiliated middle class that ultimately became the constituency for a revived New Right.

When Reagan entered office in 1967, the slate in effect was clean. He had almost no program and had made few campaign commitments aside from rhetorical challenges to the protesters or generalized attacks against "bureaucracy," exemplified by such campaign statements as "Nothing is more opposed to creativeness than bureaucracy." One of his strongest programmatic thrusts involved an attack against efforts to organize farm workers. A strong advocate of cheap labor in the fields, Reagan talked about utilizing welfare recipients as farm laborers in his first months in office. "It doesn't make sense," he declared at one point, "for able-bodied people to sit by while fruit and vegetables rot."

Reagan's overall program did not challenge Pat Brown's partnership concept; if anything, Reagan strengthened several of its features. The State Water Project, the costs of which had dramatically risen in the last years of the Brown administration, continued to grow and be supported during Reagan's term in office. The California water lobby remained intact during Reagan's tenure, rallying around the sensitive negotiations for the Central Arizona Project legislation. Reagan won the 1966 election by promising a dramatic reduction in wasteful government spending. On entering office, he proceeded to raise state taxes by $900 million to deal with the burgeoning deficit accumulated through the large-scale spending policies of the partnership-oriented Brown administration.

The major difference between the Brown and Reagan periods had to do with the structure and style of decision-making rather than the substance of policy. Reagan did not contend with or oppose the bureaucracy that had grown through the Warren, Knight, and Brown eras—a public sector that worked with, but remained distinct from, the corporate world. Instead, he attempted to superimpose private-sector leadership and methodology directly over the bureaucracy. Reagan saw himself as a chairman-of-the-board governor. Many of his business advisers became heads of departments; others were members of his Businessman's Task Force, a special advisory committee that functioned as an auditor of state government.

Relying on the private sector by placing hundreds of middle-level corporate executives in positions of public power, Reagan literally handed over state government, particularly its regulatory agencies, to business. Reagan's Public Utilities Commission, for example, not only favored utilities on rate matters but gave the go-ahead to the utilities' Grand Plan for the Colorado Plateau.

The heart of Reagan's conservative, probusiness approach to state government was continued support of public-sector programs that contained subsidies for the private sector, such as the State Water Project. At the same time, he railed against New Deal social programs, particularly in the areas of education, health, and welfare. With a strong Democratic majority in the legislature during his second term, Reagan was confined largely to rhetorical outbursts rather than any substantive dismantling of the public sector. Even in the areas of development and growth, Reagan was constrained by the emergence of new and growing constituencies, which challenged a number of the premises underlying the boom.

Despite the hostility of the Reagan administration, the environmental movement achieved its greatest impact in California in the early 1970s through a number of landmark events. The Friends of Mammoth decision required environmental-impact statements on any growth-related project. The Coastal Commission created a statewide bureaucracy to implement and regulate land use in coastal areas. Further, the tensions that had begun with Watts spread to the growing Latino communities during the late 1960s and early 1970s, foreshadowing the emergence of a new era of volatile politics within one of California's key communities.

Reagan's second term became a defensive reaction to the growth of these new constituencies and issues, a defensive reaction also shared by California's corporate powers who felt increasingly restrained by the political climate of the period. The last years of the Reagan period saw the issue of the boom itself reach center stage as all eyes turned to the junior Brown, who entered office with an open-ended mandate and a reform posture which created the expectation that this time it would not be business as usual.

Jerry Brown rode to power with a well-known name and, like Ronald Reagan, an ability to manipulate symbols into media events. Unlike earlier governors, he appeared to shy away from constituency politics as embodied in the partnership notions of his father or the probusiness orientation of his predecessor. Uncomfortable with both labor leaders and corporate executives, Jerry Brown tried to avoid, beyond certain appointments, any specific commitments or obligations to his main supporters whether environmentalists, the labor movement, or the Chicano community. His notion of politics was an updated version of the idea of reconciliation of competing interests, with the governor and the state bureaucracy occupying an independent position and looking for ways to resolve apparently irreconcilable conflicts.

Brown was more than just another opportunist politician manipulating his supporters. He saw himself as a new-wave political figure, a postliberal who criticized big government as a self-serving and imperial bureaucracy that had to be weakened or at least controlled. The notion shared elements of Reagan's "creative society" critique as well as the anti–big government analysis of the New Left. Brown and his advisers, like Tom Quinn and Jacques Barzaghi, were adept at projecting the idea of a different kind of politics while maintaining an ambiguous attitude toward the politics of the past, embodied by the new governor's father. "Pat Brown," adviser Richard Maullin recalled, "became a model to achieve and to avoid."

Brown, nevertheless, maintained a liberal appeal by making a number of early appointments from outside the old-boy networks established during his father's and Reagan's tenures. Several of these appointments were drawn from the public-interest law firms, the environmental movement, women's and Chicano organizations, and even included a handful of more radical advocates. Brown also successfully maneuvered to take credit for the passage of several bills that had been bottlenecked in the legislature by Reagan's threat or use of the veto. The most important of these laws was the Agricultural Labor Relations Act, favoring unionization of farm workers.

At the same time that Brown embraced César Chavez and appealed to the growing Chicano constituency, he also cultivated the image of himself as an environmentalist interested in alternative solutions to the growth economy. Brown used the language of British socialist E. F. Schumacher's *Small Is Beautiful* to question the ethic of growth in both the public and private sectors, positing a government that slowed down or even eliminated the large public-works projects and private-sector subsidies of the Pat Brown and Reagan periods. Top Brown advisers were assigned to come up with a comprehensive urban plan that could consolidate the range of land-use proposals and planning restrictions on urban growth that were much in vogue in the mid-1970s. Brown also flirted for a time with land-reform ideas related to the enforcement of the 160-acre limit.

While Jerry Brown projected an environmentalist approach, he remained hard to pin down on certain environmental issues. When the nuclear issue came to the forefront in late 1975 and early 1976, Brown took a neutral stance during the bitter and unsuccessful initiative campaign to pass stringent nuclear safety requirements. Instead, he chose to focus on the question of disposal of nuclear waste. By 1977, Brown's early reform-minded gestures, such as his Westlands proposal and his urban land-use package, gave way to very different impulses. Brown, for example, abandoned the 160-acre fight after appointing a pro-agribusiness farmer as his top agricultural aide. And he transformed land-use reform into a regulatory reform bill that simplified the route for developer and construction permits. Brown's apparently contradictory impulses were best symbolized by his private negotiations with British Petroleum over a possible terminal in the Long Beach area on the very same day that he was attending E. F. Schumacher's funeral in London.

In response to the Watergate scandal and Brown's early reform gestures, the state's business leaders set up the California Business Roundtable. The Roundtable was modeled after the national Business Roundtable as an overt lobbying and pressure group made up of the chief executive officers of the largest companies in the state.

The Roundtable was led by David Packard, Nixon's former undersecretary of defense and chairman of Silicon Valley's Hewlett-Packard; the Southern Pacific's Ben Biaggini; and southern California's Justin Dart, former head of Dart Industries. The new organization started out on a defensive note hoping to "overcome the current trend of declining business credibility." Although California's corporate heads had made the transition through the Reagan and Pat Brown periods in terms of adjusting to Democratic majorities in the legislature, the creation of the Roundtable was the first direct statewide attempt to involve the powerful chief executive officers in lobbying the legislature and the governor. The emergence of the environmental movement with its influence over California's new-wave governor made direct Roundtable involvement in state politics seem a necessity.

When California banks and corporations expanded nationally and overseas in the 1960s and 1970s, many of the same companies also established operations throughout the state. Initially, the traditional Los Angeles–San Francisco rivalry was intensified as regional banks and companies established beachheads in each other's territory. The rate of expansion was so rapid, however, that it undercut regional rivalries and allowed these companies to become fully developed statewide institutions. The development of a statewide market laid the groundwork for a statewide organization like the California Business Roundtable.

From the start, the Roundtable's primary focus was to deliver its message through "well-established delivery systems," as one of its documents put it. "California business today is involved in a war of ideas. And for too long it's been the corporate critics who have been firing most of the shots," another declared.

During the Reagan period, access to the governor and the state bureaucracy had been direct and informal, since so many of the leading cabinet members and advisers had been pulled from the state's major companies and established law firms. That process had all but collapsed in the first years of Jerry Brown's administration. Now Roundtable leaders were particularly antagonistic to those Brown aides who appeared to have anticorporate attitudes.

The key to success for the Roundtable was Jerry Brown. Toward that end, the group set up a series of meetings with the governor and his aides in 1975 to talk about ways to deal with the economic recession that had begun to affect the California economy. It wanted Brown to recognize that the private sector, not the government, was paramount in stimulating the economy and that government's role should be oriented toward cutting back the number of regulatory restrictions on business activities. The group was willing to concede that the recession required some public-works expenditures to increase the number of jobs in the state, particularly in highway and sewer construction.

When Jerry Brown finally sat down to talk, his response confounded the organization's leaders. He criticized the public-works idea as a pork barrel and said he did not want anything to do with it. When Brown avoided any response to their overall concerns, the business leaders left the meetings angry and perplexed. "We felt," David Packard recalled, "that some people around the governor were terribly suspicious about our motivations, and they reacted to us with a combination of hostility and bemusement."

By 1976 Jerry Brown appeared to be giving off a number of mixed signals. While holding himself at arms length from the Roundtable, he was simultaneously squeezing out the more liberal members of his administration, such as James Lorenz and Robert Gnaizda. The mercurial governor seemed to be bored with the functions of state government and increasingly attracted to national politics as he prepared the first of his campaigns for the presidency.

During 1976, Brown attempted to steer a middle course on the issue of Dow Chemical's plan to build a massive petrochemical plant in Contra Costa County in the Sacramento delta. During the winter of 1976, Dow decided to bail out, in part due to an internal corporate decision to shift resources toward other, non-California-based projects. But Dow and its corporate supporters, like the Roundtable, used the opportunity to launch a major attack against the environmental movement and the corporate community's off-and-on-again antagonist Jerry Brown.

In the months following Dow's decision to scrap its plant, the California Business Roundtable went on the offensive. Its leaders attacked the governor's "small is beautiful" rhetoric and dredged out Dun and Bradstreet's Fantus Report, a business survey that ranked California extremely low (forty-seventh out of fifty states) in terms of business climate. The Fantus Report suggested that low taxes, minimum government regulation, antilabor legislation, and cooperative public officials were the key to providing a good business climate. Of these, the Roundtable focused particularly on the question of regulation and the attitude of public officials.

The Roundtable's campaign was an immediate success. News stories and editorials broadcast the Fantus charges and helped create a widespread impression that California had become a state hostile to business. Within months, the Roundtable began to modify its message, satisfied that Brown and the environmentalists had been put on the defensive. Now it worried that all the negative publicity could create "a misleading impression about California," as one Roundtable executive put it. It feared that a continued negative campaign could turn into a self-fulfilling prophecy, leading to corporate flight and a shift of capital resources outside the state. So by 1977 it announced that the boom was on again.

By late 1977 both Brown and the Roundtable leaders were ready to come to terms. Taxes, particularly the question of property-tax relief, had become a key issue in the Democratic legislature. Attempts had been made to cut taxes for apartment dwellers and small property owners while maintaining or increasing tax levels for the large property owners, including the commercial and industrial interests who paid upward of two-thirds of the state's property-tax bill. Both Brown and the organization's leaders attacked these measures as attempts to "redistribute income." Ultimately, the legislature failed to pass a tax-reform measure in 1977.

Discontent was in the air. Property owners, caught in an inflationary squeeze, were angered by their spiraling tax bills. After three years of Jerry Brown's anti–big government rhetoric, property owners linked the issues of their tax bills and the increasing growth of the public sector. Taxpayers were particularly irked by the huge state surplus that had expanded with the rise of personal income. By the spring of 1978 the attack on government was no longer simply a shibboleth of the extreme Right or the business community. Due in part to Brown, the antigovernment mood had been transformed into widespread antiestablishment sentiment waiting to be tapped by Howard Jarvis, progenitor of Proposition 13.

Proposition 13 was an anomaly from the start. The measure embodied an extreme negative redistribution of income. Its dramatic reduction of the property tax provided an enormous windfall for large property owners, primarily the largest corporations in the state. Alan Stein, a former Goldman, Sachs executive who had become Jerry Brown's business and transportation secretary, called the $4 billion windfall "the largest consolidated return to industry ever devised." With the media featuring Proposition 13 as a tax revolt, the measure enjoyed a level of support far beyond those who stood to benefit from it.

Prior to the election, both Jerry Brown and the Roundtable opposed Proposition 13. While a number of Roundtable executives supported the proposition, the organization feared that passage of the measure would create an antibusiness backlash. Once the results were in, with a 70 percent yes vote, the executives' attitudes changed quickly. The meeting at the Hyatt Regency was called to see how the governor would react to the fallout over Proposition 13 and whether he would try to trigger a new wave of antibusiness sentiment based on the measure's boon to large property owners.

Some Roundtable members were willing to accept a modest increase in commercial and industrial taxes in order to lessen the embarrassing windfall from the proposition. At the meeting, Jerry Brown once again confounded the executives. He had first encouraged rent control and then shifted position by appearing at a fund raiser for his reelection campaign organized by a large Los Angeles apartment-house owner. He also opposed any talk of new taxes. Instead, he embraced Proposition 13 as incorporating his own approach toward reducing the role of government. The meeting at the Hyatt Regency pleased the executives: here was Jerry Brown not only avoiding talk of new business taxes but echoing their belief in the primacy of the private sector. "He now recognized," a satisfied David Packard commented shortly after the meeting, "that the private sector is the largest, most important part of the economy." "His objectives are now basically our objectives," the crusty and conservative Justin Dart reluctantly admitted.

Having embraced the anti–big government cause, both Brown and the Roundtable now turned their attention to enacting the largest state-wide public-works project in history—the completion of the State Water Project. Ever since the initial proposal, water planners had attempted to find a more efficient method of transferring water southward across the Sacramento River delta. The first phase of the project had involved the transfer of Feather River water from the northern part of the state to a giant pumping plant near Tracy in the delta. The water would be sent southward through the San Joaquin Valley to another giant pumping station at the base of the Tehachapis, which in turn pumped the water over the mountains into southern California.

This system was particularly destructive to the delta area, where the pumping had dramatically increased the salt content of the water. As early as 1965 the state's Department of Water Resources had proposed a massive new canal in the delta that would create a separate man-made river to bring water through the delta on its passage southward. By 1974 the study of the Peripheral Canal proposal culminated in the Reagan administration's environmental-impact report. The report supported plans for a 43-mile long, 440-foot wide canal to divert 70 percent of the flow of the Sacramento River around the delta and into a series of aqueducts. Simultaneously portions of the river would be returned to the delta.

The report immediately drew strong opposition from environmentalists who felt the proposal would make the existing salinity and wildlife problems worse. Many northern Californians resented any further transfer of water to the southern part of the state. Others questioned the massive subsidies for large agribusiness interests in the Central Valley and Kern County.

When Jerry Brown took office, he appeared to side with environmental critics by proposing to study alternatives to the canal. As the Brown administration began to shift gears in 1977–1978, talk in the governor's office was less on alternatives and more on the reconciliation of conflicting interests. Brown, like his father twenty years earlier, attempted to construct a coalition that would include an alliance of southern California and Central Valley users together with businessmen, environmentalists, and delta residents. These apparently hostile forces could be brought together by tying the Peripheral Canal to a package of environmental safeguards and increased conservation measures. Although Brown was initially able to obtain some support from the leadership of the Sierra Club, which argued that the measure was the best that environmentalists could get, most environmental groups opposed Brown's attempts and vowed to fight the canal to the end. Brown had more success with most of the large water users, who went along with the conservation package.

Although Brown's initial efforts at compromise failed, the state's water interests geared up to push the measure through the legislature over the next two years. The Roundtable created its own water task force, run by the head of the Newhall Land Company, a southern California farm and land development corporation heavily dependent on water from the State Water Project. Officials from Newhall, southern California's Metropolitan Water District, and the Orange County–based Irvine Corporation created a powerful lobbying arm for the canal that linked up with organizations such as the California Farm Bureau in what they called the "consensus group" to promote the canal.

The procanal lobbying groups, relying on the political clout of the Metropolitan Water District, the largest single water agency in the country, and the huge financial war chest provided by the district's corporate allies, were adept at pressuring hesitant southern California legislators and influencing media coverage of the issue. District officials argued that without the canal and with a diminishing supply from the Colorado River, which would occur on completion of the Central Arizona Project, water supplies in southern California would no longer be sufficient to meet increased demand and further development in the Los Angeles basin.

Environmentalists, in turn, presented a strong front in opposition after a Sierra Club referendum overturned the leadership's support for the canal package. The environmentalists argued that talk of diminished supplies obscured the reluctance of the large agricultural users to apply conservation techniques and that the Metropolitan Water District had its own contingency planning to store existing surplus water, activities that would more than offset any diminished supplies from the Colorado.

The existence of a water surplus was critical to the longstanding alliance of the district with agribusiness interests. The creation of a surplus would allow the southern California region to continue to expand as rapidly as possible even in areas—such as northern and eastern San Diego County—which were extremely short of water. Surplus water could also be sold to large agricultural users at a subsidized rate, several of them energy companies such as Tenneco, Shell Oil, and Standard Oil of California who had purchased land development companies in anticipation of the state water project. The cost of this subsidy in turn would be absorbed by the taxpayer and the urban water user.

In the summer of 1980, Jerry Brown finally signed Senate Bill 200, enacting the second phase of the State Water Project. The environmental-safeguards provisions were severed and incorporated into separate ballot measures. It was an historic moment, the expansion of the largest public-works project ever built, a rite of passage for the son, who in this instance emulated, rather than avoided, the model of his father.

The passage of SB 200 did not lay the issue to rest. Anticanal groups succeeded in gathering more than eight hundred thousand signatures in ninety days to place the canal issue on the ballot, promising an election campaign as divisive as the vitriolic 1960 initiative battle. The Farm Bureau broke with its allies in the consensus group to oppose SB 200 after an initiative was passed in November 1980 that provided some of the environmental safeguards involved in Brown's attempted compromise. The Farm Bureau felt that Ronald Reagan's election, and a potential shift to the right, might enable them to lobby a more conservative legislature at some later date, thereby producing a bigger and better version of the canal with the north-coast rivers thrown in. Newhall and Irvine, along with the Metropolitan Water District and Kern County agribusiness interests, disagreed with the Farm Bureau analysis and maintained their support for the canal. Meanwhile environmental and reform groups like NLP and other critics of corporate power linked opposition to the canal to the long-range goals of conservation and an end to subsidies.

As the campaign got under way, sharp disagreements developed over the cost of the completion of the State Water Project. While canal backers and the media talked about $600 million just to build the canal, the state's Department of Water Resources estimated that it would cost $20 billion to complete the canal and the remaining facilities tied to the State Water Project.

One of the main issues surrounding the canal's escalating costs involved energy use. By the 1970s the State Water Project had become California's largest single consumer of electricity, utilizing nearly 4 billion kilowatt-hours of electricity each year. The Peripheral Canal would increase usage to upward of 10 billion kilowatt-hours, much of which was required to make the water run uphill to cross the mountains into the Los Angeles basin. The expansion of the State Water Project would clearly place additional strains on California and western energy systems. The Department of Water Resources had by the late 1970s contracted with an out-of-state utility, Nevada Power, to provide additional future power. The department's actions were a further indication of California's increasing involvement in securing energy supplies from the interior West, a process that dated back to the WEST concept.

By the late 1970s the growing number of environmental regulations, particularly concerning air quality, made it exceedingly difficult for California utilities to establish major new power plants inside the state's borders. Unlike the Reagan period, Jerry Brown's administration was antagonistic toward the idea that a big project was the best method of meeting future needs.

Brown moved away from the Roundtable position on energy and toward the environmentalist perspective, particularly as nuclear power took center stage in the late 1970s. Under the leadership of the state's new Energy Commission and Brown appointees on the Public Utilities Commission, the Brown administration was able to undercut the attempt by San Diego Gas and Electric to build a nuclear plant in the Mojave Desert. Brown's new-wave approach flourished as he tinkered with experimental solutions, such as wood-chip fuel, and solar and wind power, while promoting other alternatives, including cogeneration and geothermal power. Central to Brown's scenario was the projection that the boom was winding down.

The energy issue ultimately convinced the California Business Roundtable that despite the accommodation of 1977–1978, the passage of Proposition 13, and the signing of the Peripheral Canal bill, Jerry Brown would ultimately have to be opposed. Nevertheless, several of the utilities, especially Southern California Edison and Pacific Gas and Electric, tentatively dropped their plans for large coal-fired plants inside California. They moved toward a Brown-approved cogeneration pilot project, an expanded renewable-resources program, and a new regulatory approach that provided a profit incentive for conservation. In this way, the utilities were prepared to deal with Jerry Brown while making plans for the reascendancy of another Ronald Reagan, someone who still believed in and could promote big projects and a permanent boom.

For all his contradictory impulses, Jerry Brown had, in his own fashion, maintained a certain consistency in his approach to the California boom. He viewed California as a new center of power, where, as his father had once proudly proclaimed, "the full impact of a dynamic America now manifests itself."

Jerry Brown came closest to the old expansionist tradition when he spoke of California as a nation-state in the heart of the Pacific basin empire. Shortly before his meeting with the California Business Roundtable at the Hyatt Regency, Brown gave a campaign speech in which he declared, "I see California on the edge of a Pacific economy and Pacific culture. Just as Venice, Rome, and Greece and Egypt in years past have been the leaders of civilization and culture, power is shifting. It is moving toward this part of the world and the Pacific Basin is emerging as a center where the power and adventure of the remainder of this century will be."

Brown championed new trade and investment ties with Pacific basin nations, particularly Japan, China, and Mexico. California's huge internationally linked economy meant that as head of the government Brown had to have a foreign policy. He, like his presidential rival Ronald Reagan, talked of a North American Common Market. The idea of a free-trade zone binding the United States, Mexico, and Canada, the three resource giants of the region, was a new variation on the 1960s Pacific Rim trading strategies. The notion reflected the awareness that in the future more and more of America's resources would have to come from within its own borders or from its nearest neighbors. With this in mind, Brown spoke of lessening the dependence on Arab oil through the Common Market concept and a strengthened Mexican connection.

From the Chinese revolution to the Vietnamese revolution, California politicians, led by Nixon and Knowland (known as the Senator from Taiwan), championed a kind of Pacific revanchism linking militaristic anti-Communism to economic expansion into Pacific markets. Nixon finally stood this posture on its head by promoting trade and investment in an atmosphere of mutual agreement about respective spheres of political and military influence. Since the Vietnam years, the major Pacific powers—the United States, Japan, China, Mexico, and Australia—were being drawn closer and closer together as they began to develop their tremendous potential for trade, a development that benefited California more than any other state.

As a nation-state on the eastern shore of the Pacific basin, California had by the 1980s established a significant level of independence from the traditional power centers in the East. California had become so influential in national affairs that every governor since Earl Warren had been seized by presidential ambitions.

But even California, the "Pacific Republic," home of the permanent boom, had its own tendencies toward fragmentation. The state would soon have a nonwhite majority heralding new tensions within its borders as well as conflicts with Pacific basin nations that were the sources of new immigrants. California was still divided by the Tehachapis into two unique urban centers, each in its own way helping to stimulate the boom and to set the terms for developments that would ultimately influence the state, the West, and the Pacific basin.

SAN FRANCISCO: THE PORT CITY

It would enter the annals of the city as a classic "arrangement," one in a long history of deals for power and profit made in this great Pacific basin metropolis. Labor leader John Shelley had returned control of city hall to the Democrats in 1963. The big moneymen behind the party—hotelman and real estate magnate Ben Swig, clothing-store merchant Cyril Magnin, and realtor Walter Shorenstein—were never entirely happy with the mayor; they wanted their own candidate for 1967. In the wings was a more liberal segment of the party headed by Philip Burton and built around an alliance between the California Democratic clubs, some of the unions, and minority (particularly black) voters. The moneymen hoped to stop Burton's candidate, Supervisor Jack Morrison, while dumping Shelley. Their candidate was State Senator Eugene McAteer, a probusiness Democrat with strong ties to the Irish-American community, San Francisco's most powerful ethnic group. McAteer, however, died before the campaign got under way.

With McAteer gone, the moneymen turned to Joseph Alioto, an aggressive lawyer who had made his reputation in antitrust cases. Alioto, ebullient and talkative, with a crowlike voice and a balding head, was the son of a Sicilian fish merchant who had opened one of the first shops on Fisherman's Wharf. Alioto had been the president of the Redevelopment Agency.

The agency and city hall had come under attack from civil rights activists who had been conducting a fair-employment campaign against the city's hotels and auto dealers. The activists were also pushing for minority representation in the governmental agencies charged with "upgrading" the city's poorer neighborhoods. These attacks had slowed down the Redevelopment Agency's plans to transform the city into a modern corporate-headquarters city, upsetting the plans of the big real estate operators like Swig and Shorenstein.

After a meeting at Swig's Fairmont Hotel, Alioto announced his candidacy, and Shelley agreed to withdraw. Four days later, Swig hosted another meeting of financial backers at the Fairmont and raised over $200,000 for Alioto "in exactly forty-five minutes" according to Swig's biographer. Alioto, with his powerful backers, went on to defeat Morrison.

The new mayor, at his gala inaugural at the Opera House, called on the citizens of San Francisco to "join with me in a grand urban coalition." Alioto then set out to form an alliance between labor, minorities, and the downtown business community, hoping to bring to fruition the big plans for the city that had been germinating since the end of World War II.

In 1976 Alioto left city hall under a cloud, charged with pervasive conflict of interest in his dealings with the city's port. His ally, Cyril Magnin, had already resigned as head of the port commission, also because of conflict of interest.

During two terms, Alioto had built his coalition and played a major role in building the new San Francisco. In the process, the mayor had made a habit of putting relatives and friends on city commissions while staking out the port as a private satrapy for his various family enterprises. Alioto helped to transform San Francisco from a port city with a large blue-collar work force, contending constituencies, and varied neighborhoods to a major corporate center for the entire Pacific basin, a city where an increasingly homogeneous white-collar class contended with a whole new generation of minorities for control of the city's neighborhoods.

San Francisco grew up a port city along the sandy beaches and mud flats of Yerba Buena Cove. The cove provided a natural harbor adjacent to deep water and was well protected from the rough waters of the Pacific. The four-mile-wide peninsula on which the city was located and the rugged, hilly terrain to the west and south limited its ability to expand. With its physical limits clearly defined and its ready access to the sea-lanes of the world, the city fathers have spent much of their history, especially since World War II, extending their influence throughout the West and the Pacific basin, while concentrating power and control within the city's small downtown business district, bordered by Kearny Street on the west, the waterfront on the east, Broadway on the north, and Mission Street on the south.

San Francisco's port is unique. From the city, the bay extends southward to San Jose, where Silicon Valley's new suburbs have displaced the rich agricultural lands of the Santa Clara Valley and the redwood forests of the Santa Cruz Mountains. North and eastward, the bay winds through the Carquinez Straits, into the Sacramento River delta, and the very heart of the most productive farm valley in the world, the five-hundred-mile-long Central Valley.

While Los Angeles did not even start developing its port at San Pedro until the 1890s, San Francisco was from the start located at the head of a natural waterway system. At first, the Sacramento River carried miners and their gear to the diggings in the Sierra Nevada and beyond. Later, the numerous rivers that converged in the delta served as highways along which steamboats and flat-bottomed sailing vessels moved the products of the interior to the San Francisco market and from there to the markets of the world.

More than seventy years after Spanish Franciscans established Mission Dolores in 1776, the gold rush transformed the city overnight into a seaside boomtown. By the tens of thousands, people from the Atlantic Coast, Europe, South America, Australia, and Asia converged on the rough collection of adobes, frame buildings, shacks, and tents, making San Francisco their first step on the way to the goldfields. Hundreds of ships were anchored off the beach, many abandoned as crew and passengers alike set off for the interior.

Gradually, the sand dunes along the shore were leveled and used to fill the cove. Plank walkways led out over the mudflats, and the floating hulks of abandoned ships were converted into stores, saloons, warehouses, and rooming houses. The planks and roadways rose and fell unevenly, and many an errant passerby dropped from sight into the ooze. "In the finest and most frequented parts of town," wrote one newcomer, "you see old clothes, rags, crockery, boots, bottles, boxes, dead dogs and cats and enormous rats (in which the town is particularly rich) and all kinds of filth flung before the doors."

In one of its first acts, the fledgling city government authorized the incorporation of a joint stock company to build Central Wharf. As the city inched out into the bay, speculators began to trade in "water lots" sold by the city in areas to be filled. "Proceeds from the very first sale of water lots which was to provide funds to establish a city government disappeared from the treasury," wrote William Martin Camp. Thus began a tradition along the waterfront of private speculation with public property. More money, it was discovered, could be made dealing in waterfront property than from working the diggings.

Starting in 1853, the city granted ten-year franchises to new operators who built a series of piers out into Yerba Buena Cove. While easy access to public property made control of the wharves a lucrative business, there was little incentive to improve the quickly constructed piers. Who knew what would happen to the property after ten years? Every effort was put into a quick killing. Once again, most of the income from the city's leases never reached the treasury.

Finally, in 1863, the unbridled corruption that attended construction and control of the wharves led to a drastic change on the waterfront. When a series of scandals prevented the city from building a bulkhead along the waterfront, the legislature transferred control of the port to the state on the grounds that the easily suborned city government was unable to handle the most important port on the West Coast.

During these years San Francisco's first merchants, a polyglot group, established themselves along the bay. Domingo Ghirardelli, the chocolate maker, arrived from Italy via Peru. Levi Strauss, the pants manufacturer, came from Germany, as did Anthony Zellerbach, the papermaker, and Isaac Magnin, the shopkeeper. The fabulous Comstock lode brought the Bonanza Kings (Fair, Flood, O'Brien, and MacKay) to the city, where they were joined by George Hearst, another Comstock millionaire. Henry Wells and William Fargo started Wells, Fargo and Company, the banking and transportation firm. Factories, canneries, and packinghouses sprang up along the waterfront from North Beach to Potrero Point, soon the largest concentration of industry on the West Coast. Here the Union Iron Works built the first locomotive in the West and the first iron ship on the coast.

Before any other western city, San Francisco escaped from the influence of the East and established its unique identity. Isolated from the Atlantic East and flush with gold from the interior, San Francisco became a major center for the colonization of the West even before the arrival of the railroads. San Franciscans ignored the sleepy cow town of Los Angeles, but they played a role in the settlement of Hawaii, San Diego, Seattle, and Alaska, as well as the mining districts of the interior.

The railroads were a key factor in building the city into a major power in the

West. The Central Pacific (later the Southern Pacific), the most important of all the early San Francisco companies, was formed in 1863 by Leland Stanford, Mark Hopkins, Charles Crocker, and Collis Huntington, four merchants who had come to make their fortunes from the busy diggings. With the completion of the transcontinental railroad in 1869, the Big Four established themselves as a formidable political power in both California and Washington.

The Southern Pacific also played a major role in the development of wheat farming in the Central Valley. For the first time since the gold rush of 1849, California had an important export. The development of irrigated agriculture along the Kings and San Joaquin rivers added more farm products to the export list.

The Southern Pacific, having made a bid to monopolize rail traffic in and out of both San Francisco and Los Angeles, sought to dominate shipping, too. It gained control of most of the Oakland waterfront and formed the Occidental and Oriental Steamship Company with the Union Pacific to compete against the Pacific Mail Line. The new company was particularly eager to get a piece of the federal mail subsidy enjoyed exclusively by the Pacific Mail. After a hotly contested rate war, the Pacific Mail agreed to abide by the rate structure set by the railroads' shipping line. While the Southern Pacific tried to enforce its monopolistic freight structure, several new American shipping companies made a bid for the Pacific trade.

By 1900, San Francisco, thanks to the steady growth of unionism, had emerged as the first closed-shop port in the world. The early strength of the San Francisco labor movement resulted from the scarcity of labor, a product of the constant lure of the gold diggings and the general instability of western life.

As early as 1886, all the sailors in the coastal trade had been organized, and San Francisco was becoming an agitational center from which the union message was disseminated throughout the West. In response, the shippers formed the Ship Owners Protective Association, the first coastwide employers' association and the state's first anti-union organization.

After a major strike in 1886, the shippers were determined to drive the unions from the waterfront. As part of a general offensive against all unions, San Francisco businessmen joined the Board of Manufacturers and Employers of California. More than a decade of bloody confrontations followed, as the waterfront workers tried to maintain a united front and the shippers, bolstered by the economic recession of the 1890s, pursued their campaign to wipe out the unions with remarkable success.

At the turn of the century, a new burst of unionization spread throughout California. San Francisco became a closed-shop town, and in reaction, the city's employers put together a new secret organization to fight the unions. In 1901 a minor incident touched off a strike on the docks. When the waterfront workers went out, the strike took on the dimensions of a general strike. After three months and at least five deaths, the strike, which had affected the whole Bay Area, began to weaken. Gradually men returned to work, determined to gain control of city politics in part to curtail police actions that had played a major role in breaking the strike. The result was the ascendancy of the Union Labor party, which elected Eugene Schmitz mayor in 1905, ushering in a period of corruption outrageous even by San Francisco's generous standards.

Two decades of waterfront strikes led the employers to develop two approaches to unionism. First, the major steamship lines, led by the Southern Pacific and the Pacific Mail, set up an organization to promote the open shop. Then, a second organization was formed to promote bargaining with existing unions by craft rather than on an industrywide basis in order to undermine the increased strength the waterfront workers enjoyed through the alliance of all waterfront unions.

Through a series of confrontations after World War I, the employers whittled away at the unions, finally leaving them in total disarray by 1921. With the more conservative craft leaders in retreat, the Industrial Workers of the World (IWW), the hated "Wobblies," began making inroads on the waterfront through their call for industrial unionism. In 1921 a twenty-year-old Australian sailor named Harry Bridges joined the IWW after the sailors' union was all but wiped out in a strike. Two years later, Bridges went to work on the San Francisco waterfront. On the wharves, Bridges and other dockworkers experienced frequent speedups and irregular employment, which caused numerous injuries and occasional deaths. Bridges himself was injured twice. At the same time, the longshoremen had to pay off the gang bosses to get work.

As tensions along the waterfront grew during the Great Depression, Bridges worked to reorganize the East Coast–dominated International Longshoremen's Association (ILA). By the time a charter was issued in 1933 for a new ILA local, organizing had spread to all the West Coast ports. The longshoremen received important support when Franklin Roosevelt's administration recognized the right to organize through the National Recovery Act (NRA).

In 1934 the ILA drew up a list of demands, headed by the demand for a hiring hall, higher wages, shorter hours, and more employment. The shippers resisted the union's demands, calling them part of a Communist conspiracy to take over the waterfront. When efforts by the Roosevelt administration to arrange an agreement collapsed, the ILA shut down the entire West Coast. Gradually other unions, despite the opposition of some labor leaders, joined the strike. A series of violent confrontations occurred when the San Francisco police force escorted strikebreakers through the picket lines. Pitched battles between the police and strikers resulted in the deaths of two union men and the declaration of martial law. The San Francisco Labor Council called for a general strike, and public sympathy swung behind the strikers.

In the Bay Area 127,000 workers responded to the strike call. The economy of the whole area was shut down. At the height of the strike, vigilantes raided suspected Communist meeting places throughout the state. William Randolph Hearst, who led the denunciations of the strikers as Communists, even toyed with his own plans for a vigilante force called the Hollywood Hussars, with each elaborately uniformed unit led by a movie star.

After three days the general strike wound down, and the longshoremen's demands were submitted to arbitration. The general strike, occurring as it did at the height of the depression, raised the spectre of class warfare and sent shock waves throughout the country. But in San Francisco a whole new system of industrial government grew out of the strike after Bridges, who rebuffed a campaign to get him either deported or jailed for alleged Communist party membership, formed the International Longshore Workers Union (ILWU) in 1937 with his followers.

*　*　*

By the end of the war, a crucial shift in the future of the port and the city began to unfold, a shift that eventually transformed the old waterfront beyond recognition. San Francisco in 1945 was a wide-open town, a mecca of gambling and prostitution for servicemen moving to and from the Pacific battlefields. Although the preeminent western city, San Francisco was in fact more small town than booming metropolis. The city's well-entrenched elite presented its daughters at Cotillion, the men belonged to the Pacific Union and Bohemian clubs, and the women graced the St. Francis and Palace hotels. But the town was also open to outsiders with big ideas.

Roger Lapham, a Republican shipping company executive, was mayor. In the 1920s, the New York–born Lapham had moved his family's American Hawaiian Steamship Company to San Francisco. During the conflict on the waterfront, he publicly debated Bridges in the course of the 1934 strike as one of the principal spokesmen for the shipowners. Lapham moved in what former *San Francisco Chronicle* society editor Frances Moffat called the "Golden Circle," along with the Roths (who owned the Matson line), the Crockers, the Spreckels, the De Youngs (owners of the *Chronicle*), and the Floods of Comstock fame.

With their spokesman in the mayor's office, the shippers braced for another round of strikes after the war. The ninety-four-day maritime strike of 1948, which ended in a contract, turned out to be a critical turning point for the shippers and the ILWU. In time, the shippers gave up their attacks on Bridges after one last attempt to get him convicted of conspiracy failed in the early fifties. The ILWU was finally accepted as a permanent force on the docks by the shippers, and the 1948 strike turned out to be the last until 1971.

Up through the late 1940s, the shippers had been quick to blame the port's problems on Harry Bridges and the Reds. But as early as the 1930s, when the port was under virtual employer control, business leaders noted that San Francisco was losing ground to other West Coast ports. Seattle was closer to Asia by the great-circle route. San Pedro, Los Angeles' port, was located near the southern California oil fields. Even Oakland provided greater space along the waterfront for the development of maritime facilities and enjoyed readier access by rail and truck to the interior.

State control was considered the port's greatest liability, since other cities could prevent the state from spending money in San Francisco while their own ports were not subject to state control. After the war, the newly formed Bay Area Council launched a new campaign to return the port to city control.

The Bay Area Council was formed in 1945 to promote trade and investment in the Bay Area. Its board of trustees, according to Clark Beise, former chairman of both the Bank of America and the council, was "composed of the senior people of our leading business firms, presidents, and board chairmen." Among the corporations represented on the board were Standard Oil of California, Pacific Gas and Electric, Bank of America, Wells Fargo, Crocker Bank, Bechtel, Kaiser Industries, Utah Construction, and Levi Strauss.

The council soon became a major forum for the discussion of plans to modernize the city. "There was no need to promote growth," recalled council executive director Angelo Siracusa. "It took off on its own." Instead, the council focused on making San Francisco the centerpiece of the regional economy.

In a series of campaigns, the Bay Area Council promoted three key developments: the construction of the Bay Area Rapid Transit (BART) system; the redevelopment of the city's poorer neighborhoods; and the return of the port to the city.

Ben Swig, who was one of the country's biggest real estate operators and who moved to the city in the 1940s, summed up the prevalent feelings: "You've got to think big to be big. The whole San Francisco skyline is going to change. We're going to become a second New York."

The BART campaign was launched in 1951, but the final engineering recommendations, drawn up by the Bechtel Corporation, were not submitted until 1961. The key public vote on the system came in 1962 in all three counties served by the system. The campaign for a favorable vote on the tax measure was headed by two executives from the Bank of America and Kaiser, while financing for the election campaign came from another behind-the-scenes power, the Blyth-Zellerbach Committee.

The Blyth-Zellerbach Committee was formed in the 1950s by Charles Blyth, a prominent local broker, and J. D. Zellerbach, from the family that controlled the Crown-Zellerbach paper and lumber company, to strengthen local corporate control over redevelopment. The San Francisco Chamber of Commerce described the committee as "San Francisco's most powerful business leaders whose purpose is to act in concert on projects deemed good for the city." Many of the corporations represented by the Bay Area Council were also represented on the committee, including Bechtel and Standard Oil of California.

BART was a disaster. Construction carried out by Bechtel and Morrison-Knudsen, among others, was repeatedly delayed, turning Market and Mission streets, two of the city's main thoroughfares, into an extended traffic nightmare. Project costs skyrocketed. When a small part of the system was finally opened in the 1970s, it was plagued by endless breakdowns and other technical problems. In addition to lucrative construction contracts financed by public funds, BART's corporate promoters achieved a major goal: the creation of a mass-transit system, however shaky, that provided a means by which tens of thousands of commuters could daily make their way to the downtown area to work in the more than two dozen skyscrapers that had sprung up along the waterfront since the middle fifties.

While BART was being planned by the city's corporate powers, civic leaders were also working on plans for urban renewal. These redevelopment schemes focused on several of the city's working-class neighborhoods. The first was the area south of Market, a neighborhood of hotels, bars, and flophouses where many of the single men who made up the state's large itinerant work force lived all or part of the year. A second area, the Fillmore, which is adjacent to city hall and is the oldest neighborhood left standing after the 1906 fire and earthquake, had become increasingly inhabited by blacks during World War II, when the Fillmore's large Japanese population was moved into detention camps. The third area was the produce market, where A. P. Giannini got his start. The produce market, the most valuable real estate in the city, was a maze of old warehouses, hotels, and shops immediately adjacent to the waterfront where the streets had been built out over the old waterlots into Yerba Buena Cove. The Mission District and Bayview–Hunters Point were also designated redevelopment areas. The Mission District, once a white ethnic neighborhood inhabited by Irish, Italians, Germans, and Portuguese, was becoming increasingly Latino. The depressed area of Bayview–Hunters Point had become a black neighborhood since the war because of the construction of "temporary housing" for workers and their families at the local naval base.

The real estate magnate Benjamin Harrison Swig proposed one of the first of these redevelopment plans in 1954. Swig's San Francisco Prosperity Plan called for construction of a convention center, baseball and football stadium, high-rise office building, and parking facilities south of Market. Once the downtown business district began to expand beyond the immediate downtown area north of Market Street, Swig and others realized it would eventually have to spill over into this area known as South of the Slot.

Swig ran into problems when the city's planning director ruled that only 10 percent of the area was blighted, disqualifying it from the urban renewal process. Undaunted, Swig pushed on, donating his own funds to the Redevelopment Agency for preliminary planning studies. Swig received support from the new chairman of the Redevelopment Agency, Joseph Alioto, who explained that the purpose of the Swig-financed study was "to find the most expeditious way of declaring the area of Mr. Swig's interest a blighted area."

Swig also encountered opposition from Republican Mayor George Christopher. Christopher, a Greek-American dairy owner who had grown up south of Market, was generally supportive of redevelopment, but he agreed with the planning director's negative assessment of the Swig plan. Christopher, it turned out, was more interested in a redevelopment scheme of William Zeckendorf, the New York real estate operator, onetime Swig partner, and protégé of the Rockefellers. Zeckendorf wanted to build a very large complex containing an apartment house and various corporate headquarters known as the Golden Gateway in the centrally located produce market area. The planning director and local business leaders were opposed to giving control of a massive project like Golden Gateway to an outsider. The Blyth-Zellerbach Committee eventually intervened and forced Zeckendorf off the project.

The Zeckendorf affair convinced the corporate community that still another corporate-related organization was needed to guide the redevelopment effort. Chester Hartmann, in his detailed study of the South of Market–Yerba Buena Project, wrote that the Blyth-Zellerbach Committee's "somewhat covert character had limitations. Corporate interests needed a group which could more openly take definitive and active stands; this would be particularly important as drawing-board proposals came up for public approval and the search for funds began." In 1959 the committee provided funds to transform an older organization composed of elite-oriented urban designers into the San Francisco Planning and Urban Renewal Association (SPUR). For a time SPUR served as the mayor's committee for urban renewal. Despite its corporate backing, SPUR claimed to be the representative citizens' committee overseeing urban renewal.

In 1963 John Shelley, the new mayor, inherited redevelopment and a new era of political turmoil. As a congressman, Shelley, the former head of the San Francisco Labor Council and the State Federation of Labor, had helped get federal funds for BART. At his inauguration Shelley announced, "I intend to plan San Francisco's future with a heart as well as a bulldozer."

Political activism had returned to the city with the demonstrations against the House Un-American Activities Committee in 1960. In time, civil rights leaders and a growing number of community activists began to attack the various redevelopment plans, charging that "Downtown" was trying to destroy their neighborhoods.

Shelley responded by delaying redevelopment in the Fillmore and raising a number of criticisms of the Yerba Buena Project. In response to neighborhood protests, Shelley appointed the president of the National Association for the Advancement of Colored People (NAACP) to the board of the Redevelopment Agency. The Board of Supervisors then voted to halt redevelopment in the Fillmore and exclude the Mission from redevelopment plans. In 1966 resentment over the treatment of the city's black population mushroomed into a small-scale riot in Hunters Point. The business leaders' plans to build a second New York were in disarray, and the stage was set for Shelley's departure.

When Joseph Alioto replaced Shelley, he set out to build, on top of his business support, what he called "a kind of New Deal coalition of labor and minorities, plus flag-waving Italians." Alioto got important support from a number of unions, including the building trades, the laborers, and the ILWU.

"The ILWU did more to elect Alioto than anyone," declared his opponent, Supervisor Jack Morrison. "They gave him a liberal cachet and allowed him to get the black vote."

Alioto responded by appointing important union officials to key city posts, including the Redevelopment Agency and the Port Commission. Alioto soon had the redevelopment juggernaut rolling again in the Fillmore, South of Market, and Bayview–Hunters Point. A number of labor leaders had criticized redevelopment in the early 1960s, agreeing with the charge that real estate speculators were running the city and working to destroy its neighborhoods. With the offer of construction jobs and appointments to the bureaucracy, labor joined the Alioto coalition. As one building trades official put it, "We are in favor of building with no respect to where it is and how it is."

With redevelopment under way again, civic leaders turned their attention to the port, which was still languishing under state control. Port development had been part of the overall plans for the city put together by groups like the Bay Area Council, SPUR, and the Blyth-Zellerbach Committee. As they saw it, the construction of new port facilities dovetailed nicely with their plans for BART and for new office buildings on the waterfront.

Rapid changes in port technology introduced in the late 1950s and early 1960s were changing their assessment of the port's future, however. To facilitate handling, cargo was now loaded into containers—large metal boxes the size of a truck trailer—rather than by the old break bulk method. For years, the ILWU had resisted the introduction of labor-saving innovations on the piers in an attempt to keep as many longshoremen as possible employed. In 1957, Bridges started pushing for a new policy toward mechanization, which was embodied in the union's 1960 contract with the shippers. In exchange, the shippers agreed to contribute to a fund that provided incentives for early retirement and pay for a guaranteed workweek for those still working.

For fifty years, San Francisco had been losing ground to other West Coast ports. Now containerization speeded up the process. The location of the San Francisco waterfront immediately adjacent to the rapidly growing downtown district simply did not provide the space for the large marshaling yards needed to handle containers. Oakland, with its more spacious waterfront, provided the perfect setting for the new technology. Oakland also benefited from the construction of BART when dirt excavated from the BART tunnels was used as landfill along the waterfront. As more and more shipping shifted to Oakland, the old finger piers along the San Francisco waterfront were abandoned.

After Alioto was elected, SPUR leaders approached him to start a new campaign to get the port returned to the city. A luncheon was held "with all the movers and shakers," as SPUR executive director John Jacobs put it, including Bridges, Cyril Magnin, and representatives of the *Chronicle* and *Examiner.* Alioto then approached R. Gwinn Follis, former chairman of Standard Oil of California and head of the Blyth-Zellerbach Committee, to lead the campaign. Follis eventually worked out a deal with the Reagan administration, then in power in Sacramento, and the legislature to return control of the port to the city. Once the port was returned to city control, Alioto appointed Cyril Magnin to head the Port Commission and Harry Bridges to the commission itself.

Although Follis was assured by his acquaintances in the shipping business that "they did not want to move to Oakland," he found that "the city didn't pick up the ball in the very aggressive way necessary to correct the problem. They did build containerization facilities but never enough."

In fact, there were clear signs that civic leaders were more interested in extending commercial development into publicly owned waterfront property. As a Wells Fargo report explained, "The trends toward centralization now evident in the spate of high-rise buildings will be accompanied by an attendant rise in the value of real estate." While Alioto called the port property "one of the hottest pieces of real estate that anyone could get," business leaders argued that revenue from leases on the northern waterfront could be used to finance maritime development on the southern waterfront.

In 1959, Magnin had unveiled the first of a long series of elaborate proposals for the northern waterfront. His plan, called Embarcadero City, included office buildings, hotels, sports arenas, and other facilities. Once the port was returned to the city, the Board of Supervisors removed themselves from the review process for new development plans. The stage was set for the Port Commission and Alioto to run the waterfront as their own personal fiefdom.

As soon as the port was turned over to Alioto and company, the advertisements appeared: "Prime waterfront property in San Francisco now available for commercial development." A number of proposals were immediately forthcoming, the most spectacular of which was for a five-hundred-foot skyscraper. It was proposed by United States Steel and supported by Magnin and Walter Shorenstein.

To build the United States Steel Tower, the city would have had to scrap the restriction on the height of new buildings in part of the downtown area, which had been secured by increasingly active environmentalists. At first, the restriction did not seem to be a problem. The builders of the Transamerica Pyramid, through a careful publicity campaign that included the pampering of public officials and the media, had been able to circumvent the height limitation. This time, a number of groups, including the Sierra Club, Telegraph Hill Dwellers, and San Francisco Tomorrow, supported by the weekly *Bay Guardian* newspaper, drew greater attention to the project. Alioto and the downtown business community ignored the protests, but finally in 1971 a regional body with jurisdiction over developments within one hundred feet of the bay denied the necessary fill permits.

The defeat of the United States Steel project did not stop the prodevelopment forces. Cyril Magnin, for instance, came up with yet another plan, this one for Pier 45 in the Fisherman's Wharf area. Magnin wanted AMFAC, a Hawaii-based conglomerate that had bought the Joseph Magnin Company, to develop the pier. But the political climate was beginning to change. The high-rise fight had triggered a new kind of genteel politics that pitted the affluent residents of Telegraph Hill against Alioto's coalition of developers and unions. Describing the people who opposed the United State Steel project, the *Bay Guardian's* environmental editor wrote, "These people are wealthy, sophisticated and powerful." A union official, on the other hand, told the *Guardian*: "Eight hundred guys are sitting in our hiring hall waiting for work . . . and the conservationists are screaming about the US Steel project blocking the view. View? How many working people have a view?"

The widespread opposition to the developers' plans for the city's neighborhoods had led to a campaign for district elections. The advocates of district election noted that the Board of Supervisors, which was elected on a citywide basis with downtown financial support, was heavily representative of the city's wealthier neighborhoods, such as Pacific Heights, Saint Francis Woods, and the Richmond District. The activists proposed that the city be divided into districts, each to be represented by one supervisor.

In 1973 the growth of reform sentiment caught up with the developer-led coalition: the voters passed a stricter version of the city's conflict of interest law. In its aftermath Cyril Magnin became the first influential San Franciscan to resign from his post on the city's powerful commission.

Although his allies were being forced out of city government, Alioto pressed on with his own plans for the waterfront. First, he put his brother-in-law on the Port Commission. Then, when Magnin resigned, he appointed John Orsi, a close family friend, to head the Port Commission. With Alioto backers in command, the port negotiated a number of highly favorable sixty-six-year leases for Alioto's friends and relatives who owned restaurants around Fisherman's Wharf.

Having secured his family's and friends' interests on the northern waterfront, Alioto turned his attention to the southern waterfront. In 1974, Alioto's son John bought controlling interest in Pacific Far Eastern Lines, a shipping company that used facilities constructed with city funds after the city took control of the port. (Among the investors in Pacific Far Eastern Lines was Ben Swig.) The Aliotos were already in the shipping business, exporting rice from the inland port of Stockton. Just before taking office, Alioto, in fact, had arranged the largest rice deal ever between South Korea and the California rice industry. Deals later negotiated through the notorious Korean fixer Tongsun Park gave Alioto's company exclusive control of shipments of California rice to South Korea in 1976.

At first, the Alioto acquisition appeared to be a remarkable shipping coup. The company enjoyed a strong position in both Pacific basin and Middle East trade and was converting its ships to a new technology particularly adaptable to the anticipated trade with China. After a time, the Aliotos appeared to have other plans for Pacific Far Eastern Lines. When trade began to fall off, some company ships were sold at a handsome profit. The Alioto law firm launched a series of law suits on behalf of the company that netted large legal fees. By 1978, two years after Alioto left office, Pacific Far Eastern Lines, now headed by John Orsi, was bankrupt. Among its debtors were the port of San Francisco, to which it owed almost $2 million in back rent, and the National Maritime Administration, which had provided the company's passenger service with $130 million in subsidies during the Alioto years.

Even in a city of such easy virtue as San Francisco, Alioto's fantastic wheeling and dealing produced a public outcry and much scrutiny from the usually docile *Chronicle* and *Examiner*. With half the city's piers abandoned and many of them victims of mysterious fires, the Board of Supervisors launched an investigation of activities at the port. It uncovered a "series of questionable deals," "noncompetitive bids and leases," "deliberate concealing of real costs," and "a disregard for basic business standards and a bias for a favored lessee." Although the various developer combines had argued that commercial income would finance maritime development, the port was rapidly going broke. The Board of Supervisors concluded that "some lessees skimmed the cream from the port's potential nonmaritime income." Speaking of the port's transfer to city control, SPUR's John Jacobs concluded, "It was a good idea. We began it. But it turned out to be not such a good deal."

Alioto was succeeded in 1976 by State Senator George Moscone, who defeated John Barbagelata, a conservative realtor. In the same election, voters finally passed a referendum calling for district elections. Barbagelata immediately launched a campaign to prevent "a radical takeover" of city politics, by attempting to repeal district elections and recall Moscone. In the summer of 1977 the Barbagelata proposals were overwhelmingly defeated, clearing the way for district elections in November of that year.

The ferment of the 1970s produced a new but unstable political scene by the end of the decade. After a disastrous city workers' strike, labor was less able to defend itself against measures, inspired by the Chamber of Commerce, to weaken the city employees' union. In labor's place, newly formed neighborhood and homosexual organizations, such as the Tavern Guild, played an increasingly influential role. The first Board of Supervisors elected by district was decidedly liberal in its composition, although hardly representative of a radical takeover. Among the new supervisors was Harvey Milk, the first avowedly homosexual supervisor and an activist with ties to other community groups.

The change to district elections and the emergence of homosexuals as a political force was having an unsettling impact on the city's working-class neighborhoods. The new host of professional and white-collar workers who provided the work force for Wall Street West moved into low-income neighborhoods, bidding up the price of real estate. Castro Valley, for instance, was once the home of white working-class families, its bars the daytime home of many retired couples. In the midst of rampant real estate speculation, Castro changed almost overnight into a gay street scene offensive to many of its former residents.

The new turbulence created a sense of powerlessness and victimization, a sense that San Francisco was more interested in its tourists and its new arrivals than the people who had lived and worked in the city for years. In this context, conservative supervisor Dan White, a former fireman from a fairly typical blue-collar family, assassinated Milk and Moscone and got away with a light sentence in one of the most heinous crimes in the city's violent history.

Upon Moscone's death, the job of mayor passed to Dianne Feinstein, president of the Board of Supervisors. Feinstein had lost to Alioto in 1971, running well only in the city's wealthiest neighborhoods. By the time she ran for office again in 1979, she had built enough support among the new constituencies, including crucial support from the homosexual community, to beat Supervisor Quentin Kopp, a Democrat with strong support in the city's more conservative west side.

Although Feinstein appeared to represent some kind of new politics, the old alliance between the business community and the mayor's office, fashioned so carefully in the late 1950s and the 1960s, was still very much intact. The old insider ways of getting things done still prevailed. Feinstein developed her links with the business community through advisory committees, including one set up by the Blyth-Zellerbach Committee and headed by the Bank of America's Walter Hoadley to advise the mayor on streamlining city government in the wake of Proposition 13.

The mayor's financier husband, Richard Blum, played a role in the final selection of developers for the long-delayed Yerba Buena Project. The new plan for Yerba Buena, introduced during the Alioto years, was held up by a lawsuit brought on behalf of residents of the area who were demanding that the Redevelopment Agency build new housing to replace that which was destroyed to make room for the project. Under Moscone, an agreement for new housing was reached. Construction of a convention center (named the George R. Moscone Convention Center after his death) was begun. In 1980 the agency selected developers for the complex, which by then included a hotel, shops, and entertainment facilities to be built adjacent to the convention center. Blum represented the Marriott Corporation before the agency, and Marriott was one of the developers eventually selected.

Despite her image as an environmentalist and a supporter of neighborhood politics, Feinstein's policies reflected her connections to downtown. She purged two antideveloper members from the Planning Commission, vetoed a strong rent-control measure, and generally supported the idea of continuing the development of the downtown business district into the area south of Market although Feinstein, unlike her corporate allies, emphasized the need for more housing in the area. The mayor's modest push for some additional housing and other measures to cushion the impact of the high-rise boom eventually led to conflict with the Chamber of Commerce, the removal of the long-time president of the Chamber in 1981, and his replacement by John Jacobs, the executive director of SPUR. Her opposition to rent control drew most attention because she and her husband owned rental property in the downtown area. "She's not a front for downtown," commented Darryl Jackson, a supervisor's aide. "She's one of them."

Meanwhile, along the waterfront, restaurateur Warren Simmons had completed Pier 39, the first major commercial development on the piers. Simmons got his collection of shops and restaurants approved by the Port Commission and the Board of Supervisors through a judicious distribution of campaign funds and leases at his new enterprise to members of the Board and Commission. Once completed, Pier 39 was considered an atrocity by some of the same "genteel environmentalists" who opposed the United States Steel project. In order to prevent the recurrence of that kind of situation, a citizens' advisory committee was formed to guide the development of the rest of the northern waterfront.

By the late 1970s, the port had returned to solvency through new commercial leases and a minor revival of shipping. The ILWU and Jack Morrison, appointed to the Port Commission by Moscone, were still pushing for some maritime development on the northern waterfront. Others, including Mayor Feinstein, were waiting for the port to revive through trade with China. Port Commissioner Alan Rothenberg felt that hope for new maritime development was in the tradition of a former port manager who "was always leaning out the window and looking for the great white sails to come into the Bay."

ILWU official Herb Mills described the old waterfront as "a true community—spawned by work, strengthened by unionism, rooted in turf, and enriched by a spontaneous and diverse social contact." But, Mills concluded: "It has simply been plowed under by the commercialization of everything in sight."

Despite the hothouse political atmosphere in 1980, the plans drawn up by the city's largest corporations and their satellite organizations—SPUR, the Bay Area Council, and the Blyth-Zellerbach Committee—had been carried out. The downtown district was spreading southward along the waterfront and westward adjacent to city hall. Giant office buildings seemed to spring up daily, and the high-rise vacancy rate remained near zero.

The onslaught of real estate speculators notwithstanding, San Francisco became a city with a nonwhite majority during the 1970s. More minorities were coming every day from Asia, Mexico, and Central America. In the past, ethnic groups such as the Italians and the Irish had claimed their place in politics and the business world through the Democratic party and the unions. But today, according to political scientist Frederick Wirth, "the contemporary struggle of the 'arriving' minorities for recognition has not met with the same success."

In 1981, San Francisco was still in the hands of the rich and powerful. Their quirks and activities were covered daily by columnist Herb Caen and on the *Chronicle*'s society page. The major corporations still projected their plans in global terms, while the smaller, local businessmen still maneuvered for their piece of the action. Bank of America chairman A. W. Clausen became head of the World Bank. From Bechtel, Caspar Weinberger, once an attorney involved in the Yerba Buena Project, moved on to become secretary of defense, and George Schultz became a Reagan economic adviser. The next generation of civic leaders was somehow less awe-inspiring, perhaps because the great gray corporations had pushed the colorful businessmen-politicians out of the limelight. The death of Ben Swig in November 1980 signaled the passing of the visionary businessmen who had made San Francisco the headquarters from which the economies of the West and the Pacific basin were shaped.

LOS ANGELES: THE ULTIMATE BOOMTOWN

The air in the Chamber of Commerce meeting room was filled with tension, what the Latino United Neighborhood Organization (UNO) liked to call "sex." There was something strikingly significant about the meeting between the dozen or so UNO leaders and the sixteen top members of the Los Angeles corporate world from the Community Committee (formerly the Committee of Twenty-five). Both sides had their agendas, and both sides shared a fair amount of curiosity about the strangers on the other side of the table.

The UNO people, trained in the organizational methods of social activist Saul Alinsky, had been operating in the barrios of East Los Angeles for more than four years to fill the vacuum created by the weak political leadership in the community. UNO was organized primarily through church parishes, which functioned as community centers. With its ability to mobilize supporters around a range of community issues, generate visibility, and create confrontations, UNO had built a strong base within its area of operation.

East Los Angeles is a vast network of minineighborhoods, a hodgepodge of small incorporated cities, a large unincorporated section of the county, and thin slivers of the eastern outskirts of downtown Los Angeles. It has a thriving community culture: Spanish-language movie theaters, shopping bazaars on Broadway, and "low-riders" on Whittier and Hollywood boulevards. In the old, stately houses of Boyle Heights a sprinkling of eastern Europeans live side by side with Latino migrants, who have displaced the Jewish *shtetl* of the city's east side.

East Los Angeles is the second largest city of Mexicans in the world. An extraordinary mix of several generations of migrants resides in this city, long considered the model twentieth-century American metropolis.

Los Angeles has always been home to an unusual mixture of people. It was founded in 1781 by the Spanish as a mission twenty miles from the ocean, on the flood plain of the Los Angeles River—a flood plain that hardly ever flooded, since the river was almost always dry. The Spanish used the mission as a marketing and commercial center for the large ranchos and cattle operations of *los ricos*. "The rich ones" gave way to the Anglo cattle barons and the growing number of speculators who followed the gold rush and the laying of the transcontinental railroad. It was also a Chinese town then, the product of the cheap-labor system on the railroads, a town where a race riot exploded shortly after the railroad entered California. "Heathen Chinese," as the Los Angeles newspapers liked to call them, were raped, lynched, and murdered in an orgy of violence.

Los Angeles has experienced several waves of migration, giving the city its crazy-quilt character. First there was the constant influx of nonwhite labor—the Chinese, Mexicans, Japanese, and Filipinos. In the 1940s, southern blacks joined the expanding Mexican and Latino population. Most recently, Vietnamese, Koreans, Thais, Armenians, Iranians, and Israelis have settled there. These migrations supplied cheap labor for the extensive network of farms that dotted Los Angeles as late as the 1930s and 1940s as well as for the textile, electronics, and service businesses of the postwar years.

Los Angeles was also the city of the white man's booms. These were sponsored by an assortment of local entrepreneurs, get-rich-quick speculators, bankers, newspapermen, and calculating railroad barons from the Southern Pacific and Santa Fe. They vied for supremacy in landownership, rail transport, and local political and economic affairs. "Los Angeles wants no dudes, loafers, and paupers: people who have no means and trust to luck, failures, bummers, scrubs, impecunious clerks, bookkeepers, lawyers, doctors," the *Los Angeles Times* impetuously declared in 1886 on the eve of the town's first great boom.

"We need workers! Hustlers! Men of brains, brawn, and guts! Men who have a little capital and a great deal of energy—first-class men!"

The boom seized Los Angeles like no other city before or since. It was a speculator's heaven where pictures in advertisements were doctored to show oranges hanging from joshua trees, where the rugged, desertlike terrain with its mild climate was transformed into a promotional paradise attracting not just the foreign migrant laborer but the "first-class men," good midwesterners, the middle- and lower middle-class "American" emigrants from the "frozen East," a slice of Iowa in the southland of California.

Los Angeles has ever since remained divided between the two worlds created by the Anglo and non-Anglo migrations. The meeting at the Chamber of Commerce building seemed to capture a bit of that urban dichotomy. The men of the Community Committee were heirs to the hustlers and speculators who had created a system of wealth and power out of the raw materials of the boom. These committee members—executives such as Edward Carter, Southern California Edison's Howard Allen, or Security Pacific's Frederick Larkin—were more discreet and sophisticated than their brash ancestors. Los Angeles, after all, had become a major center of power almost despite itself. The city is the home of multinational corporations, banks, and insurance companies that conduct business on a national and international level; of law firms that operate in the very highest corridors of power; of merchants who wield control over vast chain stores and international marketing operations; of utilities whose energy load is among the most complex and extensive in the world.

The committee had been designed to function as something of a council of elders. It included the wise (read "powerful") old men of the corporate elite who would meet with key people like the mayor or the police chief on the substantial issues of the moment to communicate (informally and discreetly, of course) how committee members felt. The committee had been organized to centralize and focus the establishment's involvement in the public-policy area during the mid-1960s, when the very concept and character of the city's establishment was undergoing a change. Los Angeles had grown to such a point that its second- and third-generation leaders, such as Charles Ducommun of Ducommun Metals and Neil Petree of Barker Brothers, were considered relics, while the new powers of the region were big-league players with a national and international perspective.

The committee was essentially a device to keep in touch, to make sure that the expanded and more diffuse institutional arrangements of power were functioning smoothly or at all. The most powerful assortment of local business leaders still fretted about their changing city. Effective control of their city seemed to be eluding them. But business was booming, and these men were leaders not just of a region but executives with statewide and even national clout.

When the UNO leaders announced that they wanted to talk to the Community Committee, committee members once again felt that pang of disorientation. They feared that UNO might be looking for a confrontation. So the committee's executive secretary, insurance executive Stephen Gavin, was assigned to inquire quietly why UNO was requesting this meeting. The smooth and affable Gavin attempted to explore ground rules and to see if the proposed meeting would be kept out of the media spotlight.

"It was clear they were nervous about the whole thing," one of the UNO leaders recalled of the preparatory talks with Gavin. "I'm sure they saw the whole thing as a bunch of crazy Mexicans trying to barge in and harangue those stiff, proper, uptight businessmen who have always been so used to controlling everything. You couldn't imagine two more different kinds of groups, two more different styles and cultures."

It was a brisk December day, the kind of day Los Angeles' promoters love to advertise. The UNO members filed into the Chamber of Commerce meeting room to encounter the stern but curious expressions of the sixteen businessmen whom the UNO leaders had already carefully researched. Security guards ringed the building. The session was opened by a nervous Edward Carter, the chairman of the group and an important power broker on the state and local scene. Carter started talking even before the UNO members had taken their seats and quickly turned the floor over to the UNO president, Gloria Chavez, who presented the problems of East Los Angeles, which were being neglected by the political and business leadership of Los Angeles.

There were some nervous coughs and occasional whispers while Chavez spoke. UNO's famous tension prevailed throughout her talk. When she finished, committee members realized that no "crazy Mexican" was about to jump on the table to deliver a harangue. Anxiety soon gave way to puzzlement and curiosity. An air of uncertainty hung over the meeting. Just what did these Mexicans want anyway?

"I guess I never focused on East Los Angeles," Carter spoke up. "I am vaguely aware that 31 percent of the city is now Mexican. And I guess Watts would not have happened if we paid more attention."

Committee members tried hard to respond in an appropriate manner. "Your complaints are legitimate," Howard Allen piped up. Others agreed. The tension still hung over the room, a tension that increased when Union Oil's Fred Hartley began to speak. "My chauffeur is a Mexican," Hartley declared while other committee members blanched. "Do your people have jobs? Do they have money? Are you the kind of Mexicans that clean up after themselves? If you had any rich Mexicans where would they live?" Hartley continued. The oilman then sternly warned of the possibilities of an explosive "Quebec situation," with two divergent languages and cultures.

Committee members tried to express concern while the UNO participants attempted to gain recognition as the legitimate voice of East Los Angeles from the people they felt really held the power. Nothing as such was accomplished. The meeting was an unusual moment as two distinct forces encountered each other—the Anglo elite of the corporate city face to face with an aspiring leadership of a rising minority. UNO represented a part of the city—Third World neighborhoods and multiclass, multiethnic communities—that belied the old stereotype of Los Angeles as the archetypal suburb in search of a center.

Suburbs in search of city had always been the development leitmotiv of the leadership consortium that stage-managed the periodic southern California booms. The Los Angeles boom that originated with the madcap activities of the 1880s quickly became a state of mind as much as an economic and demographic development—the logic for a certain kind of development in which the growth of the city was built on the fact of growth itself.

By the turn of the century, the development patterns of the region had been set by promotion schemes and syndicate grandstanding. These syndicates were an ingenious device, a kind of division of labor between the players necessary for a successful development project. The syndicates bought mostly undeveloped or poorly irrigated lands to the north, east, southeast, and west of the city. Syndicate members included bankers, who put up the initial risk capital; railroad and streetcar executives, who laid out the transportation lines; utility shareholders, who plugged in the power; and newspaper publishers, who sometimes spearheaded the syndicate groups and created the ballyhoo to entice settlers. The syndicates ultimately transformed the undeveloped land into new urban subdivisions.

Subdivision sites were selected on the basis of their profit potential—a process that contributed to Los Angeles' lack of planned growth. Henry Huntington and the Southern Pacific were not only locked into the syndicates but actively speculated on their own, creating a direct incentive to organize their transportation routes along the lines of their real estate projects. By the 1930s, as the new subdivisions spread in every direction, Los Angeles found itself with the most extensive rail system in the world. Almost as soon as the tracks were laid, the local business leaders promoting the boom began to toy with the auto as the favorite means of maintaining the existing grid while "penetrating virgin territories," as one reporter put it. Changing from interurban advocates to automobile advocates, the syndicate members promoted the "Good Roads" movement. Next they became behind-the-scenes members of the Major Highways Committee and ultimately the leadership of the Southern California Auto Club. Each of those lobbying groups took on the characteristics of a de facto planning organization.

Water, even more than transportation, was the essential ingredient for the continuing boom. Water was located on or near the surface east of the original mission, but the local water supply quickly reached its limits in the aftermath of the boom of the 1880s. When the lack of water limited the scope and direction of development, Los Angeles' first great water project, the Los Angeles Aqueduct, which reached from the Owens Valley at the base of the Sierra Nevada in Inyo County 230 miles southwest to the northern reaches of the Los Angeles basin, did more than allow for the success of the Pacoima and San Fernando subdivisions (which did succeed because of the available water). Central to the boom hype, these water supplies allowed growth at any future point. "There it is, take it!" implored Los Angeles' engineering mastermind, William Mulholland, when Inyo water finally flowed into the basin in 1913.

The 1920s constituted a pivotal decade in the development of Los Angeles. What had earlier been uneven and explosive growth was transformed. The major industry of Los Angeles became growth itself. It was the period of the big oil discoveries on Rincon and Signal hills and the rise of Hollywood. Both industries exploited the boom mentality and contributed to the feverish mood that swept the city. Los Angeles became the quintessential western boom city with thousands of real estate schemes—"a real estate conspiracy rather than a municipality," one critic explained—countless stock promotions, and penny-ante manipulations, including the extraordinary Julian Petroleum stock swindle, which implicated half the town's power structure.

"It was population mad, annexation mad, and speculation mad," one observer wrote of Los Angeles in the early 1920s. "It had just become the largest city in California. Newspapers and billboards shrieked the announcement that the population would soon reach one million! two million! or five *million!* The fever of annexation was riding high."

Annexation had been made possible by Los Angeles' water policy. With abundant water from the Owens Valley, Los Angeles blackmailed its way into expanding the city limits by threatening to withhold water if a community was unwilling to become part of a greater Los Angeles.

"If you can't bring the water to the city," Noah Cross says in the film *Chinatown,* "you bring the city to the water." Even the inexhaustible supply from the Owens Valley was thought to be quickly reaching its limits during the mad migration of the 1920s and in the fierce annexation policy spearheading the growth. Water-empire builder Mulholland, in league with his civic boomers, appealed once again to his "Great Architect of the Universe" to help him envision yet another massive transfer of water, this one from the Colorado River. The city's involvement in the campaign for Hoover Dam gave an enormous boost to the dam advocates. Now able to argue for their project on the grounds of the greatest good for the greatest number, advocates could, at the same time, quietly lay the groundwork for the development of irrigated agriculture in the Imperial Valley in the desert east and south of Los Angeles. The Imperial Valley growers would not only feed the growing Los Angeles market but would also become part of the regional power structure. The giant irrigated farms would become a corporate extension of the metropolis.

The Hoover Dam agreements of 1931 linked the agricultural districts of the Imperial and Coachella valleys with urban southern California represented by the newly created Metropolitan Water District. The district had been formed as a coalition of Los Angeles and other basin communities to divide up the Colorado waters. The creation of the district marked the end of Los Angeles' annexation policy but did not stop the advocates of the boom, who looked to the new Colorado supply to create the conditions for another round of growth.

Between the formation of the Metropolitan Water District in 1928 and the Hoover Dam agreements of 1931, Los Angeles witnessed the collapse of its second great boom. The Great Depression hit Los Angeles particularly hard. The migration patterns shifted from the good Anglo stock, caught up in the town's speculation fantasies, to depression migrants, thrown off of Dust Bowl farms. These new arrivals came to California looking desperately for a ray of hope in the midst of the gloom of social and economic displacement. While the town's boosters and business leaders resented these new migrants and warned against any social changes in their conservative, Babbitt-like city, the new migrants maintained the optimistic and offbeat character of the city by embracing utopian solutions, inspirational radical politics, and newly devised promotional scams touted as redistribution-of-income programs.

Los Angeles' power structure in the 1930s, consisting of many of the members of the earlier real estate syndicates, bitterly resisted the radical impulse and mobilized against the growing revival of the town's working-class movement. Population growth, the boosters argued, resulted from the "open-shop principle of industrial relations." Any move toward unionism would undoubtedly cause the city's growth to "slow down, stop, or even reverse direction," according to a *Los Angeles Times* editorial.

The local leadership group remained true to the racist and nativist tendencies of the period. On the one hand, it aided the large-scale deportation of thousands of Mexicans from the southland. On the other hand, it attempted to resist the growing inmigration of the Arkies and Okies through such tactics as the famous "bums blockade" on the California border in 1935. The local business leaders also remained loyally Republican. They opposed any expansion of the public sector and identified the New Deal and its western proponents, such as Marriner Eccles, as betrayers of their class.

This stance was ironic, given the fact that the great public-works projects of the West and the frowned-upon migrations from the Dust Bowl provided the region with the capital and labor needed to meet the enormous changes brought about by World War II. For Los Angeles, as well as California and the West, these changes were monumental in scope. The role of the city was permanently altered, placing it at the heart of the greatest economic and demographic expansion the state would ever witness.

The war produced an industrial base for southern California. Major production facilities were established in aircraft- and shipbuilding and in the production of rubber goods, nonferrous metals and their by-products, machinery, and chemical and allied products. The Los Angeles region grew from the seventh largest manufacturing center in the country in 1939 to the second largest industrial center after Detroit during the war. From 1940 to 1944, a total of 780,000 new immigrants entered southern California.

War industry also produced a new type of corporate executive in the region: men like John McCone, who was allied with the Bechtel interests, and the Gross brothers from Lockheed. Although their businesses were locally based, the nature of their enterprises caused them to look to Washington and the international scene, particularly the lucrative Pacific market. These men were important new links to the older power centers in the East.

For every John McCone, with his high-powered Washington connections, there were dozens of conservative nativist boomers still locked into the style and politics of the prewar years. The new industrial leadership in the city came to include more easterners or those with stronger ties back east than with the local elite. Los Angeles had begun to resemble a "branch industry" town.

After the war, Los Angeles, continuing to develop its industrial base, gradually emerged as a more self-conscious and nationally oriented metropolis. The boom was once again in gear as the population growth induced by the war continued its upward spiral. National companies, such as American Potash, Carnation Milk and Justin Dart's Rexall Drugs moved corporate headquarters to Los Angeles.

The boom itself continued to remain the city's greatest attraction. "In the last analysis," *Fortune* argued in 1949, "the only thing that makes Los Angeles County much different from other big industrial centers is the extraordinary number of Americans who keep moving out there." *Fortune* concluded, "The supply of four or five or nine million people in one metropolitan area is a substantial industrial operation in itself."

This time around, the problems with growth and the checkerboard grid pattern of development caused even some of Los Angeles' most fervent boosters to realize that the boom was a mixed blessing. At the height of the war, Los Angeles experienced "Black Monday," the first of the region's potent smog attacks, which would become more serious with the rapid growth of the late 1940s and 1950s. A rapid transit system radiating from the downtown center had all but collapsed during the 1940s, a casualty of the efforts of the pro-automobile elite, who allied with a national consortium consisting of General Motors, Phillips Petroleum, and Firestone Tire and Rubber to convert the electric interurbans to an exhaust-spewing bus system.

The grid pattern, based on overspeculation, combined with population growth to create what one analyst called a "flexible labor market," which permitted the new wartime industries to set themselves up in outlying areas, beyond the central business district. This perimeter development and the vast auto-supportive highway program, the first and largest of any American city, allowed managerial and factory personnel to live considerable distances from both their places of work and the central city. Industries, in turn, became a magnet for other industrial, commercial, and residential developments, which transformed entire new areas into urban focal points.

By the 1950s, the Los Angeles region had become a sixty-mile metroplex radiating in each direction. The once extensive agricultural farmlands and undeveloped areas had given way to the new subdivisions in Los Angeles, Orange, Ventura, San Bernardino, and Riverside counties, to create what some of the local business leadership called "supercity." Industrial plants, small and medium-sized manufacturing outlets, housing developments on the magnitude of five thousand to twenty-five thousand units, and the new branch retail outlets leapfrogged each other. This growth filled in semideveloped pockets such as the new subdivision of Inglewood or the communities of the San Fernando Valley north of the Santa Monica Mountains. New communities, such as Manchester, sprang up overnight, creating a kind of homogeneity among these newly constructed working-class communities, with their middle-class aspirations. All this served to make the Los Angeles of the 1950s a collection of nondescript suburbs without a central core to give it shape and identity.

The great postwar boom had transformed Los Angeles into an instant metropolis. According to the 1950 census, more than 50 percent of the city's residents had not lived in Los Angeles for more than five years. Los Angeles, its mayor proclaimed in the early 1950s, is "the picture of a city expanding like an exploding star, dominating a vast area through the demands of a great population."

Local businessmen actively promoted perimeter development, but the decline of the central city created problems for those very same businessmen, who still maintained interests in the central business district. The need to create a downtown civic and cultural complex was obvious. Such a center could serve to end the small-town inferiority complex of the city's second- and third-generation leaders.

This first phase of a downtown revival—the creation of a cultural complex—became the cause célèbre of the old elite. Over the next thirty years, enormous efforts went into the attempt to develop a Music Center, with theater and performing-arts wings; a convention center on the southern edge of the new downtown; and the Bunker Hill high-rise office buildings on the northwest edge of the city's center. When they eventually went up, these developments displaced the area's Mexican and Anglo working-class tenants.

The downtown revival ultimately broke the parochialism of the local leadership, which was forced to listen to some of the newer voices in the region: the new crop of builders and savings-and-loan men, such as Howard Ahmanson and Mark Taper, who had replaced the syndicates as the major force in pursuing perimeter development; the new entrepreneurs of Hollywood, such as Lew Wasserman; and a host of middle-level manufacturing and financial businessmen who had muscled their way into Los Angeles society. On· the sidelines stood the multinationals; local corporations, such as the aerospace companies, which had become multinational in character; and the powerful outsiders who had transferred headquarters to an expanding Los Angeles.

Through the 1950s, the city continued to be thrust awkwardly toward its role as a major national center of power. The old elite appeared to be at the peak of its power during these years. Los Angeles mayor Norris Poulson seemed its perfect foil, a former accountant humble in the face of these powerful businessmen and more than happy to arrive at policy decisions directly derived from their informal deliberations.

Poulson had been selected to run in classic style. A handful of the most powerful men in the city—including insurance executive Asa Call, a critical force in state and local politics; *Los Angeles Times* publisher Norman Chandler; and O'Melveny and Myers lawyer James ("Lin") Beebe, a Mr. Big on the local scene—sat down one day at the California Club to brainstorm to find their candidate. "And then we thought of you, Norrie," they wrote Poulson, promising him a Cadillac to "strut around in" as mayor. Poulson quickly accepted.

Poulson was a passive mayor, allowing Lin Beebe and his aides to write the budget each year at a special retreat set up for the occasion. He went along with various taxpayer-related schemes and urban-renewal proposals to set the downtown revival in motion. Although content with their mayor and satisfied with the growth, the old elite felt slightly on edge during the late 1950s, a bit out of place in this new, aggressive city. Events and institutions appeared to be passing them by. This complex and diverse city, with its characterless suburbs and increasingly complex racial profile, became prey to social and economic problems that followed in the wake of the boom.

This sense of disorientation became particularly pronounced at the end of the 1961 mayoralty campaign, in which the bland Poulson was upset by an irascible, quick-on-the-draw, perennial politician named Sam Yorty. Yorty had attempted to run for mayor in 1937 as a self-proclaimed candidate of the New Deal–inspired liberal-left coalition. Rejected by this coalition, the opportunistic Yorty swung widely to the right and cofounded California's own version of the House Un-American Activities Committee in 1939. Yorty's career, seesawing back and forth in the 1940s and 1950s, combined Red-baiting tactics with occasional populist appeals against the powers-that-be, who had little use for the unpredictable politician.

In the 1961 race Yorty attacked Poulson's backers, threatening to "throw out" the downtown crowd. He appealed to the first generation of Anglo homeowners in the lower middle- and middle-class suburbs of the San Fernando Valley, who felt little connection with the old elite and its evocation of the downtown revival. Yorty also capitalized on the racial issue, which had already begun to flare in the Los Angeles basin, anticipating the events in Watts four years later.

Yorty rode to power on the basis of his antidowntown rhetoric, but once in office, moved to ingratiate himself with the very people he had so diligently attacked. Some of the business leadership, led by the new publisher of the *Times*, Otis Chandler, mistrusted Mayor Sam, his clowning antics, and his appeals to his suburban constituency. Yet, they realized that the new mayor ultimately defended and promoted the boom, which continued unabated in the first years of Yorty's tenure. When several more multinationals established headquarters in the region, new skyscrapers began to go up in the downtown area. The revival effort went into high gear with the opening of the Music Center in 1964, the Dorothy Chandler Pavilion, and the construction of several giant high-rises. The growth nevertheless continued to be dispersed throughout the supercity, with numerous skyscrapers and urban complexes going up in such areas as Anaheim–Santa Ana in Orange County and Encino–Sherman Oaks in the San Fernando Valley, and a new complex called Century City being built on the backlot of Twentieth Century–Fox by Alcoa in West Los Angeles.

By the 1960s, Los Angeles had also become a thoroughly segregated city, with its Anglo suburbs sharply divided from the long stretches of black, brown, and Asian neighborhoods. Watts and East Los Angeles became angry centers of discontent and protest, exacerbated by the foul, smog-ridden air; inadequate transportation system; and continuing decline of jobs, schools, and housing so characteristic of the slums of the East. The boom had directly contributed to the segregation because of the spread-out grid development patterns and the shift from the "new industrialism" of the war years to a diversified high-technology economy with a highly stratified work force.

Los Angeles had become a city of severe contrasts masked by the superficial glories of the boom and denied by the myth that slums could not possibly exist because this was the city of single-family homes. Forty years earlier, realtors and business leaders had seen dispersal and single-family homeownership as bulwarks against working-class radicalism. But a 1960s version of deteriorated single-family houses rented in highly segregated and isolated neighborhoods only served to exacerbate tensions. The Watts riot came as an extraordinary shock to a city that had prided itself on its California exceptionalism. "Is this really happening here in our Los Angeles?" bewildered business leaders asked themselves. For the first time, they began to wonder whether the boom had been undercut by social discontent.

The explosiveness and pervasiveness of the Watts riots prefigured the emergence of ethnic consciousness and racial confrontation as major factors in this polarized city. The confrontation deepened with Sam Yorty's slashing racial appeals, a style that ultimately reinforced doubts about the viability of his leadership even among his supporters within the business community, such as Neil Petree and Asa Call. Although many of his backers stuck by the mayor in his ugly, racially inspired defeat of black city councilman Tom Bradley in 1969, four years later this expanded and relatively diffused business leadership stood on the sidelines as Bradley successfully put together a coalition of minorities, west-side liberals, and environmentalists to defeat Yorty.

Tom Bradley played the dignified and moderate statesman to the erratic and harsh-sounding Yorty, a style appreciated by those corporate executives who, like Arco's Thornton Bradshaw, functioned on a state, national, and international level and wished to give credibility to Los Angeles' rise as a national center of power. Yet Bradley, like Yorty, lacked clearly defined objectives concerning the social and economic problems that were the by-products of the boom. Bradley ultimately learned to embrace this corporate constituency, particularly the nationally oriented executives and their counterparts in the financial, legal, and retail areas who envisioned the transformation of Los Angeles and its downtown into a corporate-headquarters city similar to San Francisco.

By the 1970s, the downtown revival had shifted from the push for the Music Center and the cause of "high culture" to plans for redevelopment. These plans called for an expansion of high-rise office and residential construction for the professional and managerial personnel employed at corporate headquarters.

When Bradley took office, he inherited a series of proposals for this new redevelopment effort. The proposals had been formulated, in part, through a publicly funded study conducted by the Central City Association, a group led by the downtown banks and department stores. The study called for a special tax method known as tax-increment financing designed to tap countywide funds to help subsidize construction of new offices and residential buildings. Further, under Bradley's leadership, a series of fixed-rail transit proposals oriented toward downtown, including a subway system and a people-mover, were initiated.

Throughout the 1970s, this second stage of the downtown revival continued to be plagued with economic problems and political opposition. The perimeter developments in places such as the San Fernando Valley and the west side continued to strengthen, despite such problems as Century City's economic decline during the 1973–1975 recession. By the late 1970s, the outlying centers, such as the commercially developed areas of Orange and Ventura counties, had thoroughly institutionalized the geographic diffusion of power. Groups like Orange County's Lincoln Club, consisting of conservative business-men from large corporate powers, became counterbalances to such downtown Los Angeles groups as the Central City Association. As a significant behind-the-scenes power, a group like the Lincoln Club could influence a range of development issues and political matters affecting Orange County far better than a centralized downtown group.

The Anglo suburbs to the north and east of the city opposed the downtown tax-increment and transportation proposals. The grid development and its subsequent segregated and dispersed "civic" consciousness came back to haunt the city's business leadership when suburban voters consistently rejected what increasingly looked like a plan to subsidize downtown.

Los Angeles became a constellation of separate political fiefdoms—the Jewish west side, the black south-central area, the conservative San Fernando Valley, and, of course, downtown, represented by a black city councilman who delighted in acting the court jester while vociferously defending his downtown clients. As the city's character and racial composition changed during the 1960s and 1970s, the political fiefdoms failed to include new constituencies, particularly the mushrooming barrios of the east side. Long represented by a right-wing prodevelopment councilman, East Los Angeles was the most disenfranchised of the new communities, a casualty of the consequences of "illegal" immigration, low voter turnouts, and a diffused community leader-ship. Even an organization such as UNO, which avoided the pitfalls of electoral politics, had to start close to point zero in attempting to mobilize the community.

The power structure and the media perceived the dispersed civic consciousness of Los Angeles less in terms of the city's disenfranchised minorities—who were quickly becoming the majority—than in terms of the difficulties of implementing the downtown revival. That sense of dispersal was exacerbated in the mid-1970s when a number of the leading downtown corporate powers, such as Southern California Edison, Pacific Mutual Life Insurance, and Title Insurance and Trust, moved their headquarters out of the downtown area. The political coup de grace for redevelopment turned out to be Proposition 13, which had, ironically, so benefited many of the same corporations. Proposition 13 undercut the tax-increment financing method, which had already been used to subsidize the construction of housing and offices on Bunker Hill.

The shifting fortunes of the downtown revival paralleled the attempt to regroup the city's dominant corporate, financial, and legal powers. In the spring of 1965, shortly after Yorty's reelection, Daniel Bryant, the tall, lean second-generation head of Bekins, the moving and transportation firm, was fretful about the increasing bureaucratization of leadership organizations into committees, commissions, and various other bodies that had emerged in the complex world of the 1960s corporate and political institutions. "What we need is some kind of behind-the-scenes group," Bryant told Bank of America chairman Louis Lundborg, "a place where a few of us can get together and figure things out like old Harry Chandler and [Southern Pacific head] Paul Shoup and some of the others used to do."

Bryant mentioned the idea to a few others. It quickly became clear that Asa Call, the grand old man of the establishment now that Lin Beebe had passed away, was the appropriate person to head up such an effort. Call liked the idea. He sent out twenty-eight invitations to some of the region's corporate leaders. The first meeting was held at Perino's, the exclusive restaurant in Hancock Park. Nearly all those invited showed up.

The Committee of Twenty-five, as the group came to be called, never did fulfill Bryant's hopes. The ability of a select group of people to influence policy events by handpicking candidates, by writing budgets, and by proceeding at will in extending the boom was no longer possible in the Los Angeles of the late 1960s and 1970s. The committees, commissions, agencies, and other bureaucratic mechanisms of power had continued to grow. In response, the big corporate powers, rather than attempting to eliminate such institutionalization, decided to influence, and possibly control, it. Companies created their own internal procedures to encourage, or even insist on, middle- and upper-management figures' participation in these new bureaucratic instruments of power. Groups like Mayor Bradley's Task Force on Finances were overwhelmingly dominated by banking officials, lawyers, and corporate executives from the top firms in the region. The Committee of Twenty-five complemented that effort by allowing the small handful of chief executive officers and second- and third-generation leaders to review the local issues; summon mayors, supervisors, police chiefs, and the like; and communicate their point of view.

Despite its apparent clout, the committee never functioned as a policy-setting organization. Its members largely reacted to the events rather than initiated long-term and even short-term goals and objectives. The committee also failed to attract some of the most powerful figures headquartered in southern California. At first glance, R. O. Anderson of Arco seemed a logical participant and leader for the committee. Anderson had moved Arco's corporate headquarters to Los Angeles from Philadelphia in 1972 after the eastern-based Atlantic Oil Company had merged with a long-standing southern California power, Charlie Jones's Richfield Oil.

Anderson's Arco actively backed several of the downtown-oriented proposals, including one transportation plan designed to send a commuter-based subway system through the downtown area with one of the stops located below the Arco Towers. During the 1970s, Anderson participated in the national Business Roundtable, and Arco's number-two figure, Thornton Bradshaw, was the company's representative on the California Business Roundtable. W. B. Rood, the company vice-president in charge of public affairs, became Arco's representative on the Committee of Twenty-five. The decision of Anderson not to participate in Committee of Twenty-five affairs reflected the lower priority regional policy matters now held for the largest corporate powers based in southern California.

The change in the chairmanship of the committee after Asa Call's death in 1978 symbolized that changing priority. Asa Call had for more than thirty years played a central behind-the-scenes role in both local and statewide events, helping sponsor the careers of such men as Earl Warren, Richard Nixon, and Norris Poulson. He exercised enormous influence through his long history of informal power-brokering. Call was considered a Mr. Big figure even as late as the 1960s, when no single individual could still exercise power in that manner. Part of the Committee of Twenty-five's early mystique had been derived from Call's presence, a kind of historical residue of power that was to last as long as Call remained active.

When Call died in 1978, his place was taken by department store magnate Edward Carter, chairman of the locally based multinational Carter-Hawley-Hale. When Carter took over the chairmanship of the Committee of Twenty-five, he simultaneously expanded his role in the California Business Roundtable, assuming chairmanship of that group in late 1979. Carter, unlike Call, immediately oriented himself toward the new shape of power in California. The emergence of an organization like the Roundtable demonstrated the statewide, national, and international orientation of the most powerful regional companies.

The downtown revival, then, had both succeeded and failed. With a new skyline—especially Bunker Hill—downtown had successfully incorporated certain features of a corporate-headquarters center. But the effort to create special subsidies for the downtown revival had largely stalled by the end of the decade. Southern California remained a complex of interacting centers scattered throughout the region. These centers, like downtown, had flourished through the life of the boom.

Along with the changing fortunes of Los Angeles, there developed substantial changes among the most important local institutions, such as O'Melveny and Myers, which had once been the dominant local law firm and whose clients had constituted the very heart of the old elite. During Lin Beebe's reign, the O'Melveny firm had written the bond measures for the city and county and had directly influenced politicians, bureaucrats, and the range of public officials involved in policy areas. Twenty years after Beebe's death, O'Melveny had become a multinational law firm, following its own clients as they grew beyond the region. As the firm extended its own domain, O'Melveny picked up new, larger clients from outside Los Angeles. O'Melveny partner Richard Sherwood explained in the summer of 1980, "What's happening to us is not unique. Firms, companies, banks, some of the key businesses in Los Angeles do business anywhere, in any market, and are involved in political matters everywhere."

Los Angeles, Sherwood argued, although still of secondary importance when compared to the major power centers in New York, Washington, and Chicago, had moved closer to parity with other national centers in the last decade. "The boundaries between those centers of power are breaking down," Sherwood declared. "We might be a junior partner to New York, but that situation is shifting. We're now a great deal larger than New York population-wise, though we still have fewer economic and financial transactions. And we're now big in electing presidents, feeding at the pork barrel, and influencing legislation. Our lawyers, even our bankers and corporate executives no longer feel second-best to anyone, any place."

Los Angeles, as it entered the 1980s, had become an international city with an extensive and varied power base. Along with its counterpart to the north, Los Angeles' corporate powers now looked to California as a center of power in its own right, a nation-state with its own integrated elite and set of policy objectives. Los Angeles had become a series of corporate headquarters, a supercity or superregion integrated into the groupings and institutions of power within this superstate.

By the 1980s Los Angeles had also become an international city of another kind, an ethnically rich and diverse region rivaling even New York in its multiplicity of nationalities, languages, and cultures. The population of Los Angeles had become largely nonwhite. Its 70 percent nonwhite school population indicated that the city would be increasingly nonwhite. The undocumented migrant from Mexico who came searching for work during the 1970s was only one of several recent additions to a region that had thrived on the economic presence of a cheap surplus-labor supply. Vietnamese, Koreans, Thais, and Filipinos could be found next door to blacks and Mexicans, who in turn shared their neighborhoods with Central American immigrants from Guatemala, El Salvador, and Nicaragua. "Minorities," the *Los Angeles Times* declared, were "changing the face of Los Angeles."

The boom and its ethnic underside described not just Los Angeles but the entire state. Los Angeles and California had become the new crossroads, with the rise of the corporate headquarters matched by the rise of a western version of the "new wave" melting pot, as the *Wall Street Journal* described it. This time, instead of experiencing acculturation and integration, Los Angeles had become a fragmented center where those who held power remained far removed from those other non-Anglo Californians who maintained their own claim to the region.

5 Denver: Hub of the Interior

Around the table at a dinner meeting of the Western Regional Council sat some oilmen, an executive from a high-tech firm, some bankers, and the hip up-and-coming executive from Amoco. This energy giant, a subsidiary of Standard Oil of Indiana, was making a major move into Denver and the intermountain West. Amoco planned another skyscraper to grace the new Denver downtown to accommodate its expanding oil business in the nearby Overthrust Belt and its coal, shale, and uranium interests.

The young executive and his wife, transplanted Texans, chatted about the new styles, the theater in New York, California boutiques, Jerry Brown, things that were happening in Houston. "I love Denver," the young executive told the others seated around the table. "You know, it's the last place left where you have people like R. O. [Anderson of Arco]—adventuresome types, not some robot doing the routine work of a faceless management. Denver is like a last frontier where the great plays can still be made."

Seated next to him was the president of one of the big local banks. This Denver banker and his colleagues were happy to share in the divvying up of the interior West among the big energy companies, more than happy to take the crumbs of the big development bucks dropped by the New York and California banks. The banker, a Denver native, felt a little out of place dealing with these high-flying energy boys, a cowhand among wheeler-dealers. Dressed casually in his red sports jacket and striped pants, he was out of place in conversations about last frontiers and the newest cultural events to hit the intermountain West.

Not the trendy oilman, however. "Say," he asked the banker, ready to make an elaborate point, "did you hear about this new film? All about Jack Kerouac, Neal Cassady, and the Beats."

"What's that you say?" the banker interjected. "Sugar beets?"

Awkwardly, the subject was dropped, and the two men continued their dinner, feeling comfortable only with the subject of how, where, and when the big boom would strike next.

*   *   *

The youngish newspaperman was as wired as you could get. Coffee and cigarette stains were on the desk, on his clothes, on the floor. He liked to characterize himself as someone who had been a "drug-crazed, brain-addled, coke-sniffing" hot dog, an example of "too much, too soon." Now he saw himself as a big-league newspaper editor, the scion of the Scripps-Howard dynasty, the publisher of the wealthy Denver morning daily, the *Rocky Mountain News.*

Mike Howard, with his cost-cutting techniques and mercurial moods, was not well loved in his newsroom. Turnover was constant and high. The paper was a nondescript product that had little feel for the rapidly moving events that were transforming this queen city of the intermountain West.

A few blocks away sat Howard's counterpart at the rival afternoon *Denver Post.* In the publisher's suite, Donald Seawell tried to give every indication that he was the cultured man in town, gently running his fingers through his silver hair, slowly articulating his words. He became more animated when talk shifted to his latest plans for the Denver Center for the Performing Arts rather than the plans of the big energy giants to reshape the city and bulldoze their way through the state. He had little feel for such things as water projects or oil-shale deals. This sixty-five-year-old self-defined connoisseur of the arts was in reality a corporate lawyer rather than a newspaperman. He had gradually moved into a position of power by untangling the stock wars of the two Bonfils sisters, the daughters of the scalawag Frederick Bonfils, who had scandalized Denver and the world of journalism with his fiery, outlandish sensationalism, muckraking, and self-dealing that passed for news.

Seawell's real passion was the Denver Center for the Performing Arts. The *Post* publisher used the funds from the Bonfils Foundation and the editorial resources of the paper to finance and promote this central-city cultural complex to the detriment, some said, of the paper's own development. The center was not only Seawell's personal passion, but it was his way of seeking a class identity for his city, a Denver-Seawell version of the Chandler–Los Angeles Music Center or New York's Rockefeller-Ochs-Sulzberger–Lincoln Center.

"Can I show you around?" he gestured, his voice rising in passion. "You *must* see our center. You cannot *see* Denver unless you come to a perform-ance," he tells reporters writing about his city.

He and Mike Howard had even buried the hatchet to crusade together to reroute some downtown traffic lanes that passed by the new theater building and concert hall, to the polluted and congested arteries that touched the classroom buildings shared by the University of Colorado, Metropolitan State College, and the Community College of Denver.

The Seawell-Howard approach to journalism meant that the publishers preferred to dabble in their favorite pastimes rather than covering the changing face of power. Now their journalism had reached a critical impasse. Abruptly in the fall of 1980, Mike Howard was sent to pasture after yet another round of personal scandal. With the center's increasing financial needs and the necessity for refurbishing funds for the *Denver Post,* Donald Seawell also prepared to abandon ship, seeking out other buyers after Marvin Davis, a wealthy Denver oilman, came up with a bundle of cash to try to purchase Denver's onetime establishment voice. A buyer was finally found when the big Times-Mirror

Company, the Los Angeles media conglomerate, came up with an offer that Seawell would not refuse. Denver's paper, like so much else in the city, had gone "downstream" to the big outsiders who happily looked at Denver as one of their own.

Gerald H. Phipps of the Denver Phippses, who trace their wealth to the Carnegie Steel fortune, sat in his modest office in the warehouse district. The Phippses, although one of Denver's first families, were always somewhat of a strange breed. Gerald's grandfather Lawrence joined Carnegie at the age of sixteen and soon rose to the position of treasurer and vice-president, thanks to the fact that the Phippses had a piece of the growing Carnegie fortune and Uncle Harry was Carnegie's chief partner.

When J. P. Morgan created the United States Steel trust, thirty-eight-year-old Lawrence Phipps exchanged his Carnegie shares for United States Steel stock and then went off to Denver to "retire." His wealth increased dramatically when United States Steel stock went through the roof during World War I. So Phipps decided to do what many rich westerners had done—buy his way into the United States Senate.

Once in that rich man's club, Phipps plugged for pork barrel expenditures for his state, but railed against those on the dole. For a time, he flirted with the Ku Klux Klan when it dominated Colorado politics in the 1920s. The good senator feared that the rabble might immigrate to Denver and give his adopted home a foreign cast. Denver, Phipps felt, should be a proper town, comfortable, secure, an enclave for displaced millionaires and assorted entrepreneurs who agreed that "westward the course of empire takes its way."

Senator Phipps's grandson had not done particularly well for himself nor his family, despite his modest construction business, his directorships on the banks and railroads, and his stocks and bonds from the family fortune. His big passion, his contribution with his brother Allen to the new Denver, was the Broncos, the football team that gave Denver its brief moment in the sun.

In Gerald Phipps' office, there were dozens of Denver Broncos memorabilia, all hung next to the family photos and other Phipps regalia. The thin, almost gaunt Phipps sat there awkwardly, without much to say about the issues facing the new Denver. Then the phone rang, and his face lit up. "That goddamn fool! There is no way we can stop him," he said into the phone. Phipps was talking about the big tackle Lyle Alzado. Alzado's decision to try a boxing career was in fact the big news in town. And it was not just Phipps who was impassioned over the affair, a controversy that only faded when Phipps traded the star to the Cleveland Browns. The Broncos gave Phipps a tie-in to his city, a way to link the team's mementos with its hoped-for trophies of the future until the day in 1981 when he sold the club to an outsider, none other than Edgar Kaiser, Jr., the heir to the Kaiser family fortune.

About a mile west of the Phipps office in the heart of the downtown district stands the Anaconda Tower, the recently constructed ultramodern thirty-six-story office building. The Anaconda of mining fame controlled Montana but faltered in later years and was taken over and restructured by Arco. The tower is a symbol of the new Anaconda, the sleek corporate subsidiary of the sleekest of the new players among the energy giants investing in Denver. While the tower is the town's tallest skyscraper today, it too will be surpassed when Arco, with the Marriott Hotel people, completes its forty-three-story tower, which will in turn be surpassed by some other tower as the skyscrapers go up faster than anyone in Denver ever thought possible.

Downtown Denver—the Oil Patch, as local residents call it—is where the action is in this wide-open town. If you want to find the people who are making it happen, enter the tower and take the express elevator all the way to the very top. The decor of the top floors is future-oriented: white walls, ore samples in display windows, soft black chairs, and a spectacular view of the Rockies.

When you are buzzed through the closed glass doors leading to the offices on the thirty-third floor, you enter the Denver where the real power lies and where the crucial decisions get made, to be okayed at similar offices in Los Angeles or New York or Chicago. These decisions will shape this region. The old-line heirs, such as the Phipps family and the inheritors of the local banks and newspapers, all watch in awe, happy to feed off the boom, while attempting to provide Denver with an identity that is really no identity at all.

THE INSTANT CITY

Denver, like most of the cities of the interior West, has little sense of its own history. It has been characterized as a series of boomtowns, a process that began with the discovery of gold by a group of Georgia prospectors and Indian Territory half-breeds on the South Platte River in 1858. From the gold-rush days, Denver, as the *Wall Street Journal* put it, "reeled and caroused through a silver boom, a lead boom, a zinc boom, and, in the 1950s, a uranium boom." There was also a government-spending boom in the 1940s, a military-hardware and -software boom from the 1940s to the 1960s, and a big real estate boom in the 1950s. Today, the town is being rapidly transformed by the onslaught of the multinational energy and mining companies in what promises to be the most extensive and far-reaching boom to date.

The early growth of Denver was phenomenal, so much so that Gunther Barth has likened it to the creation of an "instant city." Population jumped from 4,759 in 1870 to 106,713 in 1890, a growth rate faster than that of any other city in the country for that period.

Denver, like Los Angeles and Phoenix, was not a "natural" city. It did not lie on the original east-west thoroughfare of the Union Pacific. Nevertheless, this new town on the western edge of the High Plains, the base of the Rockies, did become a crossroads for the interior West. It became a transportation center because of the rail lines to Cheyenne, Omaha, and Chicago. Denver also became a commercial center for the Rocky Mountain region, helping to sustain early mining activities. In its rapid rise, Denver replaced the boom-and-bust towns, such as Leadville, as the dominant metropolis of the Rocky Mountain region.

Although a native Denver elite emerged within two or three decades after the city's founding in 1858, the key decisions affecting the region were made in the East. Major financing of the great mining fortunes came from New York and Boston. Powerful families such as the Rockefellers and the Guggenheims took over the main mining operations by the turn of the century. Early loans to budding Denver entrepreneurs were screened through the New York house of

R. G. Dun and Company (forerunner of Dun and Bradstreet), which sent confidential investigators, mostly young lawyers in the firm, to evaluate those prospective members of the Denver power structure who depended on New York financing for their activities.

By the 1920s the leading families of Denver, such as the Boettchers (the Great Western Sugar fortune), the Hugheses (Denver's First National Bank), the Evanses, and the Phippses, had already developed the distinctive western version of the old free-market ideology. They attacked regulation of the private sector and what they considered excessive government spending on social matters. At the same time, they pushed for massive federal subsidies for oil-shale development and highway construction to promote tourism. The Denver elite also joined their counterparts farther west in strongly urging government aid for crucial water projects.

The old elite also supported a strategy of modest growth based on development of natural—particularly extractive—resources as well as agriculture and tourism, while they opposed any kind of large-scale industrialization. The opposition to industrialization came out of a basic nativist ideology that grew out of sharply divisive class and racial antagonisms built up during nearly half a century of bitter struggles in the mines. According to historian Lyle Dorsett, a leading Denver establishment figure attacked industrialization because it would bring "low-brows, foreigners, and dirt into a respectable city." This attitude lasted well into the World War II period when Denver's longtime mayor, Benjamin Stapleton, said of the increasing immigration, "If these people just go back where they came from, we wouldn't have any problems here."

The anti-immigration, anti-industrialization perspective of the elite helped spawn the local Ku Klux Klan, which became extremely strong in Colorado during the Klan's brief national rise to prominence in the 1920s. In the 1924 elections, Klan support was responsible for the election of the governor, Senator Lawrence Phipps, and the mayor and police chief of Denver. When Colorado Klan leader Dr. John Galen Locke was jailed in 1925 for contempt of court and the Klan-backed officials performed poorly in office, the group's popularity quickly faded. By the end of the decade, the Klan had vanished from the scene, although the nativist undercurrent remained.

In 1936, Colorado's populist-inclined Governor Edwin Johnson invoked that same tradition by imposing a border blockade against Mexican immigrants, who worked in Colorado's sugar-beet fields and as sheep-shearers and track laborers. Johnson, after declaring martial law on Colorado's southern border, ordered National Guardsmen to "prevent and repel further invasion of . . . aliens, indigent persons, or invaders," on the grounds that "jobs in this state are for our citizens."

The advent of World War II was a turning point in the development of Denver as an "instant city." To establish a major military presence throughout the West, decentralize war production, and focus on the Pacific, the federal government established a number of defense plants in Denver, many of them operated by out-of-state companies. The first large plant, operated by Remington Arms, became a major factor in Denver's growth during this period. At its height the plant employed twenty thousand workers, about 40 percent of Denver's factory personnel.

After the war, the government converted the plant into a massive government complex. This complex combined with Denver's historical role as a crossroads city to make an attractive location for the massive federal regional center that was needed to handle the postwar growth of the interior West. By 1980 Denver had more than thirty-three thousand employees on the federal government payroll, more than in any other city except Washington, D.C.

Simultaneously, Denver became a major center for the defense industry. The Rocky Flats Nuclear Weapons Center, west of the city; the Air Force Academy in Colorado Springs, south of Denver; and the headquarters of the North American Air Defense Command (NORAD) helped launched the Front Range urban growth of the postwar years. The impressive NORAD facility, built inside hollowed-out Cheyenne Mountain, controlled the nuclear-oriented air defense of the entire country and employed a substantial number of military personnel.

With the development of major government military-hardware and -software centers, a number of high-technology aerospace and electronics firms opened their own regional headquarters or major branch plant operations in the area. These included the Baltimore-based Martin Company (later Martin-Marietta), Hewlett-Packard (in Colorado Springs), Dow Chemical (which, with the army, operated the controversial Rocky Flats Arsenal, a facility for storing nerve gas), IBM, Honeywell, and Johns-Manville.

A number of early cold-war military strategists encouraged further development of the area as the major military site in the post-Hiroshima age. As the military focus began to shift from the Atlantic to the Pacific, Denver quickly became the key military and high-tech location in the interior West.

Despite such massive changes, the old Denver elite was slow to accept the changes in their city. It remained wary of the government-induced growth of the war years. These grand old men fostered conservative lending policies that bucked the developing trend in their city and throughout the interior West. Charles Graham and Robert Perkin, in their bitter essay on the town's elite, characterized the policy as "abhorrent of risk-taking, chary of progress. Its contentment is a colonial complacency, and its uninspired, rock-sound motto is 'Don't diminish the principal.'"

The reluctance of the Denver elite contributed to the inordinate role of outside (mostly New York) capital. Eastern financiers still dominated the resource industries and even played a role in local construction and manufacturing. For example, Gates Rubber, the largest industry in Denver after World War II, needed to float a multimillion-dollar expansion bond in the late 1940s to underwrite further development. Gates approached some local bankers to see if they would back the deal with their own capital. The arrangement never got off the ground. Gates turned instead to New York's First National Bank, which not only provided the underwriting but also sent a vice-president to Denver to oversee the transaction.

Denver was ready to expand despite the absence of adequate venture capital from the local bankers and the big New York financial houses. It was a situation ripe for new investors. Instead of an increase in local capital, investors like New York's William Zeckendorf and the Murchison brothers from Dallas filled the vacuum, keeping Denver's fate linked to the movement of outside capital.

"The biggest change in Denver was when Zeckendorf came to town," declared former Governor John Love. Zeckendorf was a free-wheeling real estate man who had orchestrated the United Nations and Rockefeller Center deals for the Rockefellers and who once tried to buy the Howard Hughes holdings for his patrons. In the late 1940s and early 1950s, Zeckendorf began to acquire Denver real estate in anticipation of the postwar boom. He acquired the municipally owned area known as Courthouse Square and came up with a construction program that included the twenty-three-story Mile High Center, a five-story department store sheathed in gold-colored aluminum, and a hotel complex with one thousand rooms. Not to be outdone, the Murchisons, awash in oil dollars, also began to invest in downtown Denver.

As Denver expanded, the town's most enthusiastic booster, *Denver Post* editor Palmer Hoyt saw by the mid-1950s the possibility of realizing his dream of Denver's becoming the capital of a Rocky Mountain empire. The empire notion was in part a marketing strategy designed by Hoyt when he first came to the *Post* in 1946 to establish the paper as the major regional voice for the interior West, from New Mexico to Utah and Wyoming.

During the 1950s the town's boosters considered the regional economy recession-proof because of the continuing increase in government and military expenditures. Like many of the western metropolitan economies of the postwar years, Denver's was susceptible to shifting fortunes among its military-related companies. The dependence of the regional economy on decisions made in Washington paralleled its dependence on eastern-based financial institutions, whose decisions continued to affect the pace and pattern of regional expansion. According to Love, "From the beginning of the development of this community, capital came into Denver from the East, and we and the whole West were a province or possession of the money centers." The establishment of branch plants and even the occasional shift of corporate headquarters to Denver did not necessarily signal a shift in the balance of power, since decision-making authority continued to remain outside the state.

The relocation of the Johns-Manville Company to Denver in the early 1970s symbolized that dependence. Johns-Manville had long been considered a conservative, even stodgy, New York company, controlled since the late 1920s by the Morgan banking interests and headquartered in an old brick building on Madison Avenue. The company, in an attempt to revamp its image and performance, hired W. Richard Goodwin, a consultant who had previously worked in California for the Rand Corporation.

Goodwin, who soon became president, was a modishly dressed, high-flying executive, who had originally received a doctorate in experimental psychology. His first big move was to transfer headquarters to Denver, to break with the company's "dreary, almost dingy" style, as one business analyst put it. He forced many of the middle- and upper-management people to retire.

In Denver, Goodwin immediately acquired the 10,000-acre Ken Caryl ranch sixteen miles southwest of downtown and prepared to spend $43 million to build what *Forbes* magazine called "a corporate palace in the foothills of the Rocky Mountains." This new headquarters was an essential component of Goodwin's plans to refashion the company. "A company's headquarters is its signature," Goodwin told *Fortune* magazine. "I wanted a new signature for Johns-Manville that frankly would attract attention, that would tell everybody, including ourselves, that things were changing."

The Ken Caryl ranch became an attention-getting device all its own. Visitors were picked up at the Denver airport by helicopter, driven around the huge estate in four-wheel-drive vehicles, and then lunched at the turn-of-the-century manor house. The ranch also became a marketing tool, especially for foreign customers who had never seen a western ranch before. "It's the greatest place in the world to close a deal," Goodwin declared.

Goodwin's efforts appeared at first to pay off. His plans became so talked about that, according to *Fortune*, Johns-Manville became "about the liveliest, most prominent corporation in the Rocky Mountain region." Goodwin's motivation was not simply to attract attention but to actually transfer power westward. He made plans to expand the board of directors from twelve to twenty, to offset the power of the nine outside directors controlled by Morgan. Goodwin also insisted that Morgan Stanley, the investment banking house that had been Johns-Manville's traditional manager of stock offerings, share a major offering of stock. When Morgan Stanley balked, Goodwin dropped the investment house and turned instead to two of its rivals.

Goodwin, to Morgan and its allies on the board, was clearly making a bid for power and using the shift to Denver to accomplish his goal. Just two weeks before the completion of the Ken Caryl facilities the Morgan directors made their move: they peremptorily dumped Goodwin and named new executives to head the company. Johns-Manville remained in Denver, stayed in the profitable land business, and even increased its percentage of Denver- and western-based investors, but the company gradually downplayed its new western image. Now the *Wall Street Journal* characterized the new "dull silver and glass headquarters" as a lonely site, "hidden in the stark foothills," with a "fortresslike look."

About the time of Johns-Manville's relocation, Denver experienced its most extensive expansion, caused by the energy crisis of the 1970s. Denver once again attracted outside capital as numerous energy giants opened regional headquarters in the city. They did so not because of Denver's proximity to energy resources—Cheyenne, Casper, or Salt Lake City might have been better locations—but because of Denver's existing infrastructure of financial services, transportation, trade, and government facilities.

By 1980, Denver had become what Continental Oil Company executive A. B. ("Pete") Slaybaugh called "a wide-open town," still influenced by outside investors and decision-makers, or what one local magazine called "a city under the influence." Zeckendorf's and Murchison's accomplishments in the 1950s were dwarfed by the immense building and construction work in downtown Denver—the "energy capital," as the local press began to call their city. Oil-company money, California money, New York money, Canadian money, and European money all poured in. Every six months the downtown skyline was revamped, and the local residents watched in amazement as their city became a transformed metropolis in the space of a few short years.

Denver in the 1980s had become an instant city grafted on to a progression of earlier instant cities. This transformation had been made possible by all the ingredients of the western urban mix: government expenditures and subsidies; a work force consisting of skilled technicians, managers, and professionals at the top and low-paid non-Anglos at the bottom; an assortment of antigovernment right-wing and elusive "liberal" politicians; and a water supply system dependent on big intermountain transfers. The starting point for Denver's development, like that of all the cities of the interior West, was the search for water.

WATER UNDER THE MOUNTAINS

Driving through the warehouse district on the western edge of downtown Denver, by the Union Pacific tracks, you come upon the sprawling modernistic headquarters of the Denver Water Board, the most powerful public agency in the state. Despite the fact that it is raining, the sprinklers are turned on, watering the already lush grassy areas surrounding the building. "We're supposed to have them on only once every three days," the Water Board manager explains. "It's a conservation program. And this was the third day."

The new headquarters for the Denver Water Board are even more striking on the inside than on the outside. The long, flat three-story building has an open circular corridor on each floor, facing the center where a massive waterfall sends a cascade of water into a large pool that dominates the view. No matter where you stand, the strong sense of a lush, plentiful water supply permeates the building. You feel the water, it fixates you, it defines the surroundings in this back-city lot where the Water Board holds court—autonomous, obscure, discreet, and powerful.

The control and utilization of available water supplies has played the central role in the development of western regional economies, including the structure of urban growth. Denver was founded at the confluence of Cherry Creek and the South Platte River. In its early years, the waters of the South Platte were used to accommodate the rapidly growing city.

After the city bought the privately owned water system, the Denver Water Board was formed, like the Los Angeles Water Department, to coordinate and centralize the expansion of the city's water supplies. As far back as the turn of the century, water planners and engineers had warned local businessmen and politicians that the South Platte system was insufficient for continued expansion of the city. The key to future supplies was the Colorado River, situated on the western slope of the Rockies. The western slope's weather system provided 70 percent to 80 percent more moisture than the drier eastern slope. As early as 1921, the Denver Water Board began to file for claims on the western slope and after the signing of the Colorado Compact purchased land for potential diversions of water under the mountains.

As the Moffat Tunnel, the first major water-diversion project in the state, neared completion in the 1930s, Denver Water Board engineers, along with their counterparts from other Front Range communities, began to discuss other water-diversion projects. In 1934 two engineers, backed by Secretary of Interior Harold Ickes, called for the transfer of up to 300,000 acre-feet of water from the Colorado River to the eastern slope. This Reclamation Service project brought into the open the long-standing hostility between western-slope and eastern-slope interests. Western-slope farmers had already begun to depend on irrigation and feared that any intermountain diversions would impinge on irrigated farming.

Colorado's Governor Edwin Johnson helped to work out a compromise between the two groups. The compromise called for the construction of a thirteen-mile tunnel under the continental divide and two large storage reservoirs on the western side of the divide. The reservoirs would collect water for diversion to the eastern slope as well as store water for western-slope farmers. The project was heralded as the largest intermountain diversion for purposes of storage, power, and irrigation, ever attempted.

The major opposition to the plan, known as the Colorado–Big Thompson Project, came from the National Park Service, which considered the storage projects to be potentially harmful to Rocky Mountain National Park. Despite Park Service opposition, construction got under way in 1938 and immediately ran into severe cost overruns and criticism that the project was a federal subsidy of agricultural interests and urban developers. When costs skyrocketed during the early years of the war, the project was halted. Agricultural lobbyists were able to pressure the government to renew construction on the grounds that the increased food production resulting from the additional irrigation was necessary for the war effort. In 1947 water flowed through the completed tunnel for the first time. The overall project was completed in 1956. Final cost for the thirteen dams, ten reservoirs, and seven hydroelectric plants came to nearly four times the original estimate.

The Colorado–Big Thompson Project had been dominated by the irrigated agricultural interests, while urban interests had played a secondary role. As resistance to Denver's growth began to break down after World War II, the activities of the Denver Water Board took on increasing importance. During the 1950s and early 1960s, the board undertook a series of massive construction projects, including the 23.3-mile Roberts Tunnel, running under the continental divide. By the early 1970s it had become a large bureaucracy that ruled over a system of thirty-one pumping stations, thirty-two storage reservoirs, several treatment plants, and a billion-dollar capital expenditure program.

In 1973 a bond issue was passed to finance the Foothills Project southwest of Denver, which included a huge treatment plant, a storage dam, a reservoir, a tunnel system, and several access roads and conduits. In the course of the election, major opposition to the plant began to coalesce, coming from the environmental movement as well as western-slope interests. The environmental groups criticized the extensive acquisition of private land for the project and pointed to possible conflicts of interest involving Denver Water Board members tied into construction companies and law firms whose clients had a stake in the development.

By the early 1970s the rate and capital expenditure structure made it clear that the Denver Water Board encouraged growth and development. Since its inception, the board had favored the concept of "cheap water," the idea that the greater the use of the water, the cheaper the cost. That rate structure not only favored heavy users, such as agriculture and industry, but also encouraged the board to invest greater and greater amounts of capital into future water supplies. These policies, which led to the Foothills Project, necessitated a huge capital investment in the board's various storage dams and treatment plants, which in turn forced the board to sell the existing and future supplies as rapidly as possible.

By the time the Foothills Project began construction in the mid-1970s, the Denver Water Board, according to state water official Felix Sparks, had more water at its disposal than it could possibly sell. Such a situation encouraged profligate use and put greater demand on an already overbooked Colorado River. Sparks predicted a crisis for Denver by 1990 unless major changes take place in reversing the rate structure and instituting large-scale conservation and selective pricing.

Environmental critics insisted that larger users pay more for greater use, a reversal of the board's long-standing policy. To change the rate structure and to offset a decline in use would severely affect the board's existing amortization process. With so much capital invested, the board needed to increase use in order to obtain the revenues necessary to amortize its costs. This situation ultimately pitted the board against not just the environmentalists but anyone who questioned Denver's growth patterns established since World War II.

Although largely on the defensive, the Denver Water Board quietly continued to plan for growth. The board developed financial arrangements with Front Range communities to provide them with an expanded water supply, which in turn encouraged future growth. While downplaying its relationship to future growth, the board used the most optimistic projections for population increases as a basis for the expansion of its major capital projects. Taking a lunge forward toward expansion and a step back for conservation, the board entered the 1980s as a force under siege, its new, isolated headquarters offering a haven from the realities building up on the outside.

CLUB 20 AND THE WESTERN SLOPE

Former governor John Vanderhoof and former representative Wayne As-pinall had their work cut out for them. Both men had been defeated for public office and both were concerned with the "new politics" associated with environmentalists and limited-growth advocates who had swept to power in the 1974 elections.

John Vanderhoof, who liked his constituents to call him Johnny Van, was a folksy politician; the *New York Times* called him "a shrewd rube." Vanderhoof had lost a difficult election for governor to a new-breed politician, Richard Lamm, and was now looking for both a job and a new political base. Vanderhoof had been an effective politician, serving twenty years in the Colorado house of representatives, six years as speaker, three as lieutenant governor, and then, after Governor John Love left office to serve as a top energy official in the Nixon administration, as governor of Colorado until the disastrous 1974 election. Johnny Van had campaigned that year as a reasonable advocate of measured growth, not as a wild-eyed booster but as someone who felt that growth was inevitable. Denver, he said during the campaign, was going to become the "energy capital of the world"; and the rest of Colorado, he warned his constituents, "had doggone well get ready." Now Johnny Van was himself getting ready for the big energy play.

Wayne Aspinall was also ready. The longtime representative for the western slope was not exactly an outgoing, backslapping, just-plain-folks politician like Johnny Van. Born in Ohio, Aspinall arrived in Denver as a youngster and was graduated from the University of Denver in 1919 after obtaining a law degree. He went into the peach-growing business and soon after into politics, winning election to the state assembly for a western-slope district near Grand Junction. He served in the Colorado legislature for nearly twenty years before entering the United States Congress. Aspinall, a good behind-the-scenes operator, became a troubleshooter not just for western Colorado agriculture but for the energy companies, mining companies, and others who wanted a piece of the western-slope pie. He became a premier lobbyist for the big water projects, trying to juggle the narrower interests of his own constituents, who wanted the upper Colorado basin projects, with the overall plans of the Bureau of Reclamation, energy companies, and lower-basin interests. As chairman of the House Interior and Insular Activities Committee, which oversaw the big water projects and the management of public lands, Aspinall was in a key place to influence decisions.

Through the 1960s and early 1970s, Aspinall was a strong opponent of environmental legislation and a fixer who used his chairmanship to make big deals happen. By 1970, environmentalists tagged Aspinall one of the "dirty dozen" members of Congress targeted for defeat. Their effort paid off two years later when a young lawyer named Alan Merson, funded by out-of-state environmental money, upset the cagey deal-maker in the Democratic primary. Since that election, Aspinall had turned his attention toward western-slope projects and an organization that both he and Johnny Van had decided would provide the right vehicle for overseeing the coming boom on the western slope.

The vehicle was called Club 20, a booster organization that had been organized in 1953 by the editor of the *Grand Junction Sentinel.* Club 20 initially consisted of representatives of the twenty counties west of the continental divide. A tourism program was an essential part of the Club 20 effort.

By the early 1970s, the club had become a chamber-of-commerce type of organization. Much of its leadership was provided by western-slope development interests and power brokers like Aspinall, who chaired the club's natural-resources committee. Aspinall had also helped select Johnny Van to head up the club after Van's 1974 defeat. With Van and Aspinall in the leadership, Club 20 became a new and potent force, financed primarily by the energy companies who had replaced the counties as the major contributors to the club. These donors had helped shift the club from a tourism-promotion group to a powerful lobby for energy development on the slope. Opposition to the club's change came from such nouveau chic areas as Aspen and Crested Butte while San Juan County actually dropped out of the coalition.

The other major effort of the new Club 20 focused on water development. Western-slope water-project advocates had become very wary of the increased power of the Denver Water Board, which coveted western-slope water sources. Conflicts between the two users, compounded by the new factor of the energy companies, threatened to unravel their fragile truce. When the energy companies quietly began to buy water rights throughout the western slope, some officials predicted that the competition among users would ultimately lead to cutbacks in farming on the western slope.

The passage of the Foothills Project bond in 1973 had been engineered by a pro–eastern-slope water lobby group without western-slope backing. Relations between the two areas continued to deteriorate between 1973 and 1977. The rise of the environmental movement complicated the situation by raising the possibility that the construction of some of the large projects, including the five involved in the Central Arizona Project legislation and the massive Foothills treatment plant, might actually be halted.

Hostilities between the two slopes had reached their high point when Jimmy Carter came to power. With the public disclosure of the hit list an abrupt change took place. Within a month after the hit-list announcement, secret off-the-record meetings took place between a Denver Water Board-led coalition and Club 20 members led by Johnny Van and Wayne Aspinall.

The secret negotiations eventually led to a trade-off: western-slope support for Foothills, which continued to face federal hurdles, for eastern-slope backing of the western-slope projects threatened by the hit list. A combined effort would be launched to influence the Colorado congressional delegation to back both sets of projects. The key to the new coalition was the groups' shared hostility to the environmental movement, now perceived as "larger than life," as eastern-slope lobbyist Bob Tonsing put it. "The hit list," Tonsing declared, "bridged the continental divide more than anything else."

Over the next two years this alliance solidified. When the General Accounting Office (GAO) issued in May 1979 a report suggesting that the five Colorado projects be scrapped in order to reduce future salinity levels in the Colorado River, the new coalition used the report as an opportunity to launch a more systematic attack against its opponents through a statewide coalition. This coalition would be able to lash out at common enemies, such as environmentalists, the budget-conscious GAO, and, if necessary, that old bugaboo, California water interests. The new coalition also attempted to bring in energy interests on the grounds that the hit-list projects could be used for energy development as well as urban growth and irrigated agriculture.

By the late 1970s, the water for energy and growth equations had become a prominent component of the water development perspective. Implicit in the new strategy was the notion that agricultural lands and water rights would eventually give way to other uses, particularly energy development. A number of Colorado farmers, like their counterparts in Arizona and Utah, had begun to realize that the sale of land and water rights could be extremely profitable. "Development is their only opportunity to bail out," environmentalist Bob Weaver said of the farmers. "They want to sell out either to the subdividers or energy companies, both of whom are willing to pay a significantly higher price for water rights."

By 1980, Colorado water politics were in a state of flux. A new coalition of the two slopes had emerged. Despite the revival of the water lobby, fears continued to surface about diminished supplies, a renewed attempt by California to restrict upper-basin development, budget cuts, Indians, and environmentalists. With the advent of the energy boom in the 1970s and a bigger development cycle on the horizon, the old equation that more water projects equal greater development had somehow gone awry. "Eventually," Felix Sparks promised, "nobody's going to have enough water." At that point, new choices, unusual choices for the booming Denver metropolis, will have to be made.

*   *   *

THE RISE AND FALL OF THE ENVIRONMENTALISTS

A change was in the air in 1972. The voters of Denver had rejected a bond issue for the construction of downtown facilities. The voters had also said no to a new plan by the Denver Water Board to bring more water to the growing metropolitan region through another tunnel system. A relatively unknown moderate Democrat named Floyd Haskell had upset Gordon Allott for the United States Senate by raising environmental issues and by picking up the new eighteen- to twenty-one-year-old voters, a factor that also aided Patricia Schroeder in her upset victory for Denver's congressional seat. By far the biggest and most significant vote had been the Winter Olympics referendum, a vote that had not only been a major defeat for the old elite but signaled the emergence of a new force in Colorado politics, a force that in two years would make an even greater bid for power.

The Olympics referendum vote resulted from a sequence of events that traced back to the spring of 1970 when Governor John Love, Denver's Mayor William McNichols, former astronaut Walter Schirra, and fourteen businessmen and public officials arrived in Amsterdam to make a successful presentation to the International Olympics Committee proposing Denver as the site of the 1976 Winter Olympics.

At first, it seemed a simple matter to mobilize support for hosting the games and assuming all the attendant expenses and problems that went with it. Pro-Olympics committees were formed, headed by the leaders of the business community, including such old-line figures as Eugene Adams of the First National Bank and Chris Dobbins, representing the Boettcher interests, along with such new, high-flying corporate players as Richard Goodwin of Johns-Manville (before his unceremonious fall). Political backers included not only Love and McNichols, but Lieutenant Governor Vanderhoof and William Armstrong, then leader of the Colorado state senate and later a United States senator. There was strong backing from the two major newspapers as well.

As soon as the site selection was announced, difficulties surfaced. Speculators with such names as Olympic Properties, Olympic Realty, and Olympic Land Sales moved in. Accusations of conflict of interest plagued the backers of the Olympics. For example, the airline and hotel interests stood to gain from the increased traffic, as did the real estate developers, who controlled landholdings in the areas where the games were to take place or housing was to be built.

The business and political backers of the Olympics made a long series of miscalculations. They failed to take their opposition seriously, underestimated the costs of the games, and peremptorily dismissed fears about possible environmental problems. While big corporate and celebrity names were trotted out as Olympic backers—people such as Arco's R. O. Anderson, Hewlett-Packard's David Packard, Bob Hope, and Billy Graham—the ostentatious display behind the effort, such as the expenditure of $100,000 for the book in which the backers presented their original bid, only served to alienate voters.

The opposition to the games, which built up during 1971 and 1972, was led by environmental groups such as the Colorado Open Space Council and the weekly newspaper *Straight Creek Journal*. The growing opposition and the mistakes of the Olympic sponsors pushed some established politicians—Colorado house minority leader Richard Lamm, among them—and several of the state's new political activists such as Vietnam War opponent Sam Brown, into the opposition camp. A referendum initiative on whether to finance the games with statewide funds was placed on the November 1972 ballot. By November, a ground swell of opposition had emerged despite proponents being outspent more than twenty-five to one by the games' backers. When the votes were counted, the initiative had passed by a three-to-two margin.

The vote indicated that a powerful new force had emerged in Colorado politics. The opposition had drawn not just on the new environmentalists but also on a number of rural and more conservative voters who were outraged at the sponsors' tactics and the costs involved in the games. Games opponent John Parr characterized this coalition as one of fiscal conservatives, environmental liberals, exploited minorities, threatened homeowners, and antiestablishment radicals. "This was an issue that had something for everybody," Parr told the *Straight Creek Journal* shortly after the election. "If you didn't like the Governor or the Mayor or Big Business, you could vote against the Olympics."

The Olympics also signaled problems for the Colorado political establishment. That group, like Denver's old families and long-standing business leaders, had not been known for its overpowering personalities and innovative policies. Since World War II, the state government had been controlled by "centrists" who believed in water development, energy activities, and urban growth, combined with modest government support for social and human services. Democratic Governor Stephen McNichols, older brother of Denver's mayor, talked about a public- and private-sector partnership—a concept Pat Brown had also used to promote western development. "If something is big, it isn't necessarily bad," McNichols (who was governor from 1958 to 1962) said of his progrowth policies. "You have to think big. We did it in Vietnam. The key thing is balance. You have to have the incentives for the private sector, but give the feeling of equality through the activities of the public sector."

McNichols was defeated in 1962 by John Love, a Colorado Springs lawyer who had been president of the local Rotary Club. Love, handpicked by the inner circle of the Republican party, was a noncontroversial politician who liked to attend ceremonial affairs and had no political history and no scars but a recognized name. Love was a progrowth politician when such a position seemed natural and was puzzled by the new antidevelopment constituency that emerged in the late 1960s and early 1970s. Love organized the establishment-dominated Committee of Seventy-six to finance the campaign for the Olympics and was thoroughly mystified when his committee's efforts only seemed to backfire. By 1973, Love felt out of touch with a Colorado where the slogan "Don't Californicate Colorado" was seen more frequently than the long-standing promotional appeal to "Keep Colorado Growing."

While the political center shifted in the early and middle 1970s, one figure, Denver's Mayor William McNichols, still managed to hold on to his power. McNichols, who became mayor in 1969, systematically built his political base through patronage and a carefully nurtured depoliticized image. By creating the elements of a political machine and managing to stay in office for more than a decade, McNichols earned a reputation as the Mayor Daley of the Rockies— "Mayor Daley with the edges smoothed off," as one local lobbyist characterized him.

Entering McNichols' office was like a flashback to an earlier period: a

Spencer Tracy–type political boss, with his cigar, white shoes, and aides who looked more like "the boys" than political specialists or bureaucrats. McNichols ultimately became a nuts-and-bolts man who identified with "sewer politics" rather than the explosive and more ideological issues then permeating the Colorado political scene. "The things that go on at this level," McNichols said of his job, "are not really political things. They are streets, sewers, chuckholes, weeds, garbage."

This nuts-and-bolts politician managed to get elected time and again despite the growing problems that had begun to surface in Denver, the metropolitan area surrounding the city, and the long urban corridor running along the base of the Rockies. The city of Denver, whose boundaries coincided with Denver County, had grown rapidly through the 1960s, but its half-million population stabilized and even shrank slightly in the 1970s. The zero-growth figures for Denver were largely due to a 1974 constitutional amendment passed by Colorado voters as part of a suburban antibusing move. The amendment forbids the city to annex land to make room for new residents, thereby shifting growth to the suburbs in Arapahoe County to the south and Jefferson County to the west. New housing in the suburbs went up at the same time as the new office buildings downtown.

While Greater Denver grew rapidly in the 1970s, the Front Range, stretching from Fort Collins on the north through Boulder and Denver to the military complex at Colorado Springs on the south, experienced such extraordinary growth that it threatened to turn the entire corridor into one long urban center. Connecting all the cities was Interstate 25, which seemed to hold these growing population centers together like "beads on a string," as the Conservation Foundation described it.

As Denver and the Front Range grew, so did such urban problems as transportation, air quality, and a limited water supply. The availability of water was an obvious problem, since annual rainfall along the Front Range averaged only eight to sixteen inches. To gather sufficient water supplies Front Range and Denver engineers relied not only on interbasin transfers but the acquisition of agricultural water rights. The resulting loss of agricultural production and open space furthered the transformation of the area into one integrated urban corridor.

Growing urbanization also brought about increasing air pollution. Denver, which had long publicized its clean, crisp air, began to witness a bad case of urban smog, with thick brown skies hiding the scenic panorama and dirtying the once-pure mountain air. Smog quickly became the Front Range's most embarrassing problem. By 1978 the Environmental Protection Agency labeled Denver's air the second worst in the country, trailing only Los Angeles. Smog alerts—a term once used only in reference to southern California—had become a common occurrence in the Mile High City.

The failure of Denver to develop a substantial rapid transit system compounded its smog difficulties, because much of the problem stemmed from automobile emissions trapped by temperature inversions. Rocky Mountain High, some residents complained bitterly, had become a metaphor for lung cancer.

As the Front Range and Greater Denver expanded rapidly, different pressures began to build inside Denver's inner city. While the suburbs attracted skilled, professional, and managerial employees, Latinos and blacks flocked to the inner city. The city's minority residents, constituting upward of 40 percent of the Denver population, had become both victims and minor beneficiaries of the most recent energy boom in the region. Energy activities had produced a larger secondary labor market in the metropolitan area, and the increase in unskilled, largely service-related work acted as a magnet for minorities.

The rapid move of the energy companies into the area had also stimulated the process of gentrification. Entire neighborhoods bordering the downtown area were reshaped by the influx of managerial, professional, and other white-collar personnel who took over the old brownstones and single-family dwellings in the inner city. "A concentric white ring around the city core now exists in Denver. We're feeling it. The blacks are feeling it. It's become an issue of displacement," Chicano city council member Sal Carpio remarked in 1979. The gentrified inner core, thanks to urban renewal, condominium conversions, and upgrading, led to the development of suburban ghettoes.

While blacks and Latinos complained about displacement and felt squeezed by the energy boom and while environmentalists feared the impact of future growth in the urban corridor, Colorado's "centrist" establishment, including Mayor McNichols, welcomed the growth and discounted its problems. "Smog?" McNichols said of his city's brown skies. "Why, it might have blown in here from Seattle for all any of us know."

By the early 1970s the progrowth policies began to catch up with their most prominent advocates, including Wayne Aspinall. Aspinall's opponent in the September 1972 Democratic primary, a few months before the Olympics debacle, was Alan Merson, a young lawyer from New York who later became Carter's regional EPA administrator. Because of the redistricting dictated by the 1970 census, Aspinall's district was changed to include Adams County, where an increasing number of Latinos had settled. Merson hit hard at Aspinall's wheeling-dealing maneuvers and sent out reprints of articles critical of Aspinall's methods from *Field and Stream* and *Reader's Digest*. Aspinall lost a bitter primary fight. Although Merson lost the general election to Republican James Johnson, the Aspinall defeat, along with the Olympics vote, set the stage for the rise of the new wave of environmentalist-backed politicians who swept to power in 1974.

The key 1974 election was the gubernatorial race between Johnny Van, the shrewdest candidate of the establishment centrists, and Richard Lamm, a major figure behind the Olympics opposition. Lamm, the son of a Wisconsin-based coal operator, went to Denver in 1961 to work as an accountant and then a lawyer. During the 1960s, Lamm, who became minority leader after his election to the Colorado house of representatives, established a maverick reputation. He authored the state's first abortion law and was a major backer of liberal legislation relating to land use, marijuana possession, homosexual activity, and the availability of contraceptive devices for unmarried teenage girls. In the 1974 election, Lamm played down his social liberalism, emphasizing instead environmental issues because they seemed capable of attracting a majority of the voters.

Lamm's victory in November, along with the election of Gary Hart to the United States Senate and Sam Brown as treasurer (he won with the slogan "Me Against the Banks"), and a dramatic increase in the number of Democrats in the legislature, seemed to herald a new era in Colorado. "There's a new breed of Democrats here," the *New Republic* commented after the election, "issue-minded, young, aggressive, adept at organization. They are going to be heard from."

Throughout the state, the new environmentalists were now perceived as giant killers. Before the election, Lamm commented that if he lost, it would certainly not be because of any weakness in the environmental movement. "That movement is growing stronger," Lamm declared, "and it is spreading. It will prevail—if not in my election, in other elections; if not this year, other years. It has to, because the stake is survival."

Such rhetoric gave the new activists a sense of security in the aftermath of the victories of Lamm, Hart, and others. Colorado Open Space Council leader Carolyn Johnson recalled, "After the election things became diffused. We saw their victories as a 'quick fix' and so we kind of laid back and expected things to now fall into place. We never put on any pressure, we remained passive, we never put his [Lamm's] feet to the fire. And, as it turned out, that's exactly what we should have done."

No sooner had Lamm taken office than he found himself having to retreat on issues while trying to turn these retreats into face-saving victories. The plan for a new interstate highway ringing Denver was a case in point. Interstate 470 was already in the planning stages when Lamm was elected. Lamm and his advisers had campaigned against the highway because it would provide easier access to the rapidly expanding suburban areas southwest of the city. Once in office, Lamm wanted the environmentalists to speak out on the issue and to lead the campaign against the highway forces in order to position himself in the center of the dispute between the two antagonists. The environmentalists refused. Since they had campaigned so heavily for his election, they now expected the governor to take the lead in stopping the highway.

Within a few months, the besieged governor began to retreat under attack by the highway interests. To take the heat off, he appointed a commission that represented various interests. The commission, with Lamm's blessing, worked out a compromise that substituted a parkway with a more controlled access plan. "We were really defeated badly on that one," Lamm adviser John Parr recalled. "We and the press called it a kind of victory for Lamm because it was no longer an interstate. . . . But from a planning point of view it was just no good. It was a defeat. The growth was still going to continue, period."

For the next four years, Lamm and several other new-breed politicians began to soften their arguments and to look for ways to accommodate diverse interests rather than function in an adversarial capacity. Senator Gary Hart, in particular, was adept at neutralizing, and even winning over, his former corporate detractors as he gradually shifted toward support of water development projects and tax breaks for the oil-shale industry. Even Sam Brown, who had built a strong populist-inclined political base, faded from the scene when he accepted an appointment as Carter's head of the Peace Corps and Vista in 1977.

The 1978 election saw the resurgence of the right wing in Colorado politics and a renewed push for such long-standing conservative causes as the antiunion open shop, along with opposition to environmental regulation, plant safety and industrial health restrictions, affirmative action, abortion, and other programs affecting minorities and women. The political right in Colorado had a long tradition dating back to the Klan and the strong antiunion practices of the mining companies. Figures such as Joseph Coors of the Coors Brewing Company have long funded various right-wing causes. Coors and the Monfort cattle interests promoted an effective antiunion strategy. Coors, Aspinall, and conservative Arizona media baron Karl Eller organized the Denver-based Mountain States Legal Foundation. The organization, headed by James Watt, adopted a "public-interest" approach to oppose environmentalists and Indians on a range of resource-development questions. While advocating federal subsidies for such traditional regional objectives as water and energy development, the Right decried federal actions in regulating that development.

The right had only mixed success in the state. Conservative William Armstrong successfully unseated the moderate Floyd Haskell in their 1978 Senate race. Ted Strickland "snatched defeat from victory," as local newspapers characterized his loss, by allowing his own right-wing politics to become the issue in his campaign against Richard Lamm's reelection. Gary Hart won reelection during the Reagan landslide after shedding much of his earlier liberalism.

While the aggressive right and the retreating environmentalists failed to sustain initial victories, the new, self-defined centrists, like Lamm and Hart, moved to fill the political vacuum that had emerged. Hart and Lamm hoped to situate themselves between the environmentalists on their left and the urban growth and resource development forces on their right. Through such efforts as the Lamm-initiated Front Range Project, the centrists hoped to redefine the state political scene.

The Front Range Project was an attempt to create a coalition of environmentalists, Lamm supporters, and those corporate executives open to a "problem-solving" approach to growth. The project focused on ways to control, rather than curtail, growth along the Front Range. Through the project, Lamm hoped to educate new constituencies about such problems as water supply and the costs of urban sprawl so that "reasonable," planned development might emerge. Lamm would no longer have to be out front on the issues, vulnerable to the decline of his onetime environmental allies. His new politics would be neither liberal nor conservative; neither environmentalist nor prodevelopment. He would be able to activate constituent support but without having to fulfill constituent obligations, practicing a politics of adjustment rather than confrontation.

After Lamm's 1978 election, several of his advisers began to circulate between the state and federal bureaucracies and Denver's major corporate-oriented law firms. Aide Harris Sherman, for example, went from the Environmental Defense Fund to Lamm's cabinet as head of the Natural Resources Department and then on to the Denver office of Arnold and Porter, the Washington, D.C., firm whose clients included many of the top energy companies in the West. Although the big energy companies welcomed these changes and kept up a "dialogue" with politicians like Lamm and Hart, they also kept open their "fast-track" option, supporting candidates ready to raise the banner of free enterprise, rugged individualism, and the celebration of the corporate ethos. By the 1980s, Colorado's politics had shifted once again from a debate over whether there should be development to a debate over the best way to handle the anticipated boom caused by the unstoppable energy juggernaut.

BOOM AND BOOM AGAIN

By far the biggest source of change in Denver was the energy companies. Historically, Denver had been headquarters for independent oil and gas companies whose activities in the 1940s and 1950s were centered east of Denver, in the Julesberg basin, where oil had been discovered in the postwar period. By the late 1960s and early 1970s, energy-related exploration and production focused on three key resources: coal (with vast reserves in the intermountain area from New Mexico to Montana); oil and gas (in the Overthrust Belt near the Wyoming-Utah border); and uranium (in Colorado, New Mexico, and Wyoming). In the 1970s and especially after passage of the 1980 legislation creating the Energy Security Corporation, oil shale and synfuels also became factors in Denver's growth. In addition, the activity around solar energy increased because of the Denver-based Solar Research Institute. Thus, Denver became second only to Houston among energy capitals of the country.

Thanks to its role as a hub city, Denver became regional headquarters for such companies as Amoco, Arco, Conoco, Amax, and Union Pacific. Denver became a major air terminal for the interior West, a center for the federal bureaucracy, the home of a large university system, and—perhaps most important—the home of a ski-oriented "mountain chic" life-style attractive to the highly paid managerial and technical personnel of the energy and high-technology industries of the area.

The impact of the energy companies on the economy of the region was substantial. Most of the estimated twenty-eight thousand people employed directly by the more than two thousand energy companies based in Denver earned significantly higher salaries than the rest of the Denver work force. Although those twenty-eight thousand employees represented only about 4 percent of the total Denver work force, energy activities were considered "prime movers," generating income that in turn created other economic activities. The Colorado Energy Research Institute calculated that energy activities accounted for between 11 percent and 19 percent of Denver's 1979 total economic base, an increase of 30 percent over 1970 figures.

Despite the boom, the large Colorado banks felt excluded from major participation in investment opportunities because of the particular history of the region as a capital-short area. The lack of deposits and capital funds has meant that the large local banks have been unable to underwrite some of the nonenergy expansion as well as the activities of the capital-intensive energy companies.

Still searching for a way to participate in the boom, the large Colorado banks also concentrated on overturning the state's unit-banking laws to allow these larger banks to practice branch banking. Through the 1970s, the big banks, organized as the Convenience Banking Association, failed to get legislation through the state legislature, because of a coalition of urban liberals and rural conservatives who maintained a healthy mistrust of the downtown banks. The big local banks unsuccessfully resorted to the initiative process in 1980 in a last-ditch effort to expand into branch banking.

Meanwhile, many of the financial giants from New York and California have begun to look toward Colorado. According to Colorado banker Bruce Rockwell, the New York and California financial powers plunged into Colorado as the big push in energy in the late 1970s began to transform the state. The out-of-state banks established loan production offices, correspondent banks, and provided for direct financing of the major multinationals doing business in the state. New York's Citicorp; California's First Interstate Bank, Bank of America, and Wells Fargo; Texas' Republic National Bank; and Chicago's Continental Illinois Bank, all became involved either through loan production offices or the mortgage market.

Booming Denver also became the capital of the penny stocks (so called because of their small initial value and speculative origin) through companies, like Jade Petroleum or Oil Tech, that turned to the stock market to generate capital. These companies came to Denver not only because it was an energy city but because Colorado required minimal corporate disclosures, which allowed the most "wild-assed scheme," as one banker put it, to be promoted. In the late 1970s, the penny stocks dominated the Denver market.

The penny stocks were a speculator's dream come true. Companies created incredible promotional schemes. One company, for example, claimed to have invented the process for extracting gold, silver, and platinum from burnt coal. The promoter hid his three previous fraud convictions. Penny stocks attracted investors from New York, California, and Europe, all looking for tax breaks and possible get-rich-quick opportunities. "The Denver market," the Security and Exchange Commission regional administrator said of penny stocks, "operates on the 'greater fool' theory. Irrespective of a company's merits, people will buy its stock because they reckon a bigger fool will come along later to buy it at a higher price."

Despite the speculators, the uncertainties involved in activities like shale production, and the boom-and-bust quality of some businesses, the energy companies had permanently altered the structure of power in the region and the nature of its economy. The power vacuum originally created by a fading old guard that had lost control of its region over several decades made Denver ripe for the energy boys to come in and take over.

It did not take long for the new energy players to dominate local affairs, although they did so almost as an afterthought and not because it was central to any corporate game plan. Many of the energy companies were multinationals with regional headquarters in Denver. These regional headquarters oversaw activities throughout the West and reported back to corporate headquarters in New York, Los Angeles, or Chicago.

Yet Denver leadership positions were theirs for the taking. Pete Slaybaugh of Conoco, for example, became head of the Denver Chamber of Commerce less than five years after he arrived in town. After a bruising experience in Houston he was astounded at how quickly he was accepted. "I guess you don't find any group that functions as the town city fathers," Slaybaugh remarked, adding, "It's hard to find a native Denverite."

Anaconda's Ralph Cox, to whom top executives point as the man to watch in the 1980s, continued to spend far more of his time on national and intermountain issues than those having to do with Denver. Cox could be transferred out of Denver at any time to another, perhaps more powerful position inside Arco, which owns Anaconda. The fact that Anaconda shifted headquarters to Denver after Arco's acquisition of the company could well stimulate other large companies to relocate in Denver. Relocation of corporate headquarters to Denver would improve the city's standing as a center of power by providing a stable leadership pool and a source of nationally and internationally oriented activities. The situation parallels what happened to southern California in the 1950s and 1960s.

The creation of an independent, autonomous center of power still seemed far removed. Despite the population growth, despite the energy boom, and despite the emerging "professionalism" of its business elite, Denver remains, as it enters the 1980s, a city "under the influence."

Today Denver looks eastward to New York and westward to California for leadership and direction from those companies and money centers that continue to dominate the crossroads of the interior West. Ultimately, Denver remains a secondary center of power whose major role consists of dominating other, more exploited regions of the interior.

6 Salt Lake City: Zion at the Crossroads

It was 1969 and this was to be the last meeting of this self-appointed group of three, a most unusual and perhaps fitting finale to nearly two decades of information-swapping, problem-solving, and decision-making in an effort to keep their city in hand. A meeting in an oxygen tent! What a sad but apt way to describe the end of an era.

First and foremost there was David O. McKay. The silver-haired president of the Church of Jesus Christ of Latter-day Saints was the "prophet, seer, and revelator," the spiritual and temporal leader of the church for which Salt Lake City was the capital, the centerpiece of the Mormon economic, political, and religious empire of Zion. McKay was a key figure in the growth and development of Salt Lake City from World War II through the 1960s. Intensely interested in political and economic affairs, he had set up regular breakfast meetings at Lamb's Cafe, across the street from the Mormon-owned Hotel Utah, where McKay lived, to keep abreast of city affairs and to direct them in appropriate ways. McKay was also something of a folk legend in his declining years, a man who liked big, fast cars, although he could not always control them, a man about whom everybody in the city had some kind of story to tell.

Now the ninety-six-year-old David O. McKay was in an oxygen tent, plagued with the illnesses that would define his remaining days. A new church leadership had emerged to take over the practical affairs of the church. This new leadership was best represented by Nathan Eldon Tanner, the dour and efficient Canadian oilman who reorganized the church's vast economic holdings along more modern corporate lines, and Spencer W. Kimball, who assumed the office of "first president" in 1973.

Next to McKay in the oxygen tent stood Gus Backman, the head of the Salt Lake City Chamber of Commerce, the non-Mormon businessman who linked the gentile and Mormon business worlds. Backman was a business fixer who derived his power from his connections and the pivotal role he occupied between Salt Lake City's two elites. He had led the fight for Utah's share of the Colorado River and had been instrumental in making non-Mormon business-men feel more comfortable with these "peculiar people," as the Mormons

140

called themselves. But Gus Backman was also getting on in years. He could see the passing of an era and the arrival of new businessmen from the outside, many of them from California, eyeing the rich coal deposits on the Colorado Plateau. These businessmen had already begun to bypass Backman and go directly to the new fixers in the state—politicians like Governor Calvin Rampton and his successor Scott Matheson.

The third man in the oxygen tent was John Gallivan, the publisher of the gentile *Salt Lake Tribune,* a comparative youngster although already in his late fifties. The *Tribune* was the establishment paper and spoke for the business community as a whole. In 1950 the *Tribune* made peace with its Mormon-owned rival, the *Deseret News,* through a joint operating agreement that pooled the advertising, distribution, and production of the papers into a single corporate entity. Now, nearly twenty years later, with both papers running in the black, the *Salt Lake Tribune* helped direct the business affairs of the city with its Mormon counterpart. It was a far cry from the origins of the *Tribune* in 1870, when it led the attack on Mormon control of the territory.

Gallivan had replaced his father-in-law, John F. Fitzpatrick, the *Tribune's* longtime publisher, at the breakfast meetings when Fitzpatrick died in 1960. Gallivan came into his own by successfully establishing and promoting, like the Chandlers in Los Angeles and Donald Seawell at the *Denver Post,* a downtown cultural center. The idea for the Salt Palace had originally been advanced at the Hotel Utah breakfast meetings. The group of three quickly realized the benefits of such a project for the downtown district and the business community as a whole. "It was our finest moment," Gallivan recalled. Indeed, the idea capped a long history of Mormon-gentile cooperation that began tentatively when both Mormons and gentiles signed the articles of incorporation for the new Salt Lake City Chamber of Commerce in 1887.

Every Wednesday the three men met at the Hotel Utah. The gentiles drank their coffee and McKay his Postum while they exchanged bits of information and gossip, discussed who was buying and who was selling, and decided, when a big issue came along, what needed to be done. Although their time was now passing, Salt Lake was still their kind of city. The planned capital of Brigham Young's State of Deseret, Salt Lake was more of a village than the other sprawling, amorphous metropolises of the West, a city where close personal ties were still important—what Mayor Ted Wilson would later call a city of brothers-in-law. On the horizon loomed new, powerful forces eager to turn Utah inside out to satisfy their thirst for energy.

THE DEPENDENT COMMONWEALTH

Born of the martyred prophet Joseph Smith's socialistic frontier evangelism, reared and given identity during their dramatic exodus to the Promised Land on the shores of the Great Salt Lake, and consolidated and expanded into the communitarian and centralized State of Deseret by the organizational genius Brigham Young, the Mormons created their own commonwealth in the West in the days of the first Anglo migrations. "The Mormons had, in effect," wrote Leonard J. Arrington and Davis Bitton, "leaped beyond the line of American frontier settlement, moving to a region that others would not approach in significant numbers for three decades."

Utah's history derives from the efforts of the Saints to build an autonomous society in a largely hostile world of gentiles. From their arrival in 1847 through the coming of the transcontinental railroad in 1869, the Saints, with Brigham Youg's leadership, attempted to establish a self-sufficient theocratic society based primarily on irrigated agriculture and village industry. Defying the federal invasion of 1857 and a series of natural disasters, the Saints created their state as a grand experiment in centralized planning and cooperative organization. At first, Deseret was bypassed by the chaotic and antagonistic mining frontier and the schemes of Manifest Destiny emanating from Washington.

With the driving of the golden spike at Promontory Point north of Ogden, signaling the completion of the transcontinental railroad, the Saints could no longer avoid a confrontation with the gentile world. The coming of the railroad coincided with the opening of the Utah mining frontier and the arrival of eastern capital to finance the new mines. When the railroads marched across northern Utah and the local silver kings and eastern mining companies opened Utah's ore veins, boomtowns sprang up with values diametrically opposed to the Mormon's tightly controlled theocracy.

With his community threatened to its roots by the corruption and departure of its young people, Young preached against mining. After the arrival of the railroads, Young reemphasized the need for the church to build and direct its own economy according to its own principles. At the same time, he tried to accommodate some of the new outside forces. Beginning with the Union Pacific, Young organized work crews to subcontract grade work for the new railroads, gave church land for stations and warehouses, and later sold the church-developed intrastate roads to the Union Pacific. In the process, the church developed a close relationship with the Union Pacific that has continued to the present. As *Fortune* magazine once commented, "You can't do business with the [Union Pacific] unless you work through Utah." Young's relationship with the emerging world of corporate capital was facilitated by Mormon businessmen, like David Eccles, who were strong links between the church community and eastern-based power.

Despite eastern fears of theocracy, which were aroused to a new pitch by the early feminists' campaign against polygamy, the church continued to maintain its control over the territory's politics and economy. Local gentile merchants feared that church economic schemes, such as Zion's Cooperative Mercantile Institute, were an attempt to monopolize all economic activity. Led by the *Tribune*, the local merchants argued for the development of mining and the freeing of politics from "ecclesiastical directive and control." The fight raged until the church, weakened by the attacks of the federal government, began the inevitable process of accommodation by officially opposing polygamy in exchange for statehood.

By the turn of the century the conflict between the Mormon and gentile elites within Utah had diminished. Mining had become the dominant economic activity. The early mining which attracted thousands of speculators and individual mining entrepreneurs soon gave way to forms of mining dependent on large capital expenditures. The shift to this kind of mining paralleled the rise of such eastern-based companies as Kennecott, which became, along with the Union Pacific, the major corporate power in the state.

By 1914, Utah had become the most industrialized state in the interior West through the processing of ore. Since a high percentage of the profits and products of the mines were taken out of the state, mining did not provide a sufficient foundation for broader economic development. The mining profits that remained went to build the great mansions east of the Temple or were siphoned off into political contributions to keep the state legislature in tow. When Thomas Kearns, whose family operated one of the Park City mines, bought the *Tribune* in 1901, he also became a major political power in the state.

With the rise of mining and a new business class, a local financier named Heber Grant led the church to rebuild its own economic base, much of which had been confiscated by the federal government or quietly sold to high-ranking church members. In the 1890s Grant, a member of the church's Council of Twelve (the highest ranking body in the hierarchy below the president), went hat in hand to Wall Street to attract outside capital to Utah. He was told to come back when economic conditions were more propitious. Grant then turned to a number of wealthy Mormons, including David Eccles, and persuaded them to purchase $1 million worth of church bonds. Looking for profitable business ventures, the church decided to make a second attempt at sugar-beet production—its first effort having failed in Young's day. The Saints first guaranteed a $400,000 bond issue, which was sold to an eastern financier. Then Grant consolidated several processing plants into a $13 million agribusiness giant called Utah and Idaho Sugar Company (U and I). With the help of Utah Senator Reed Smoot, a member of the Twelve and a prominent Republican, U and I successfully sought the imposition of high tariffs to protect its output from the cheap imports from American-owned plantations in Cuba and Hawaii.

Grant was also instrumental in the formation, with church funds, of Utah Power and Light, Utah's principal utility. The church later sold Utah Power to E. H. Harriman, whose ownership of both the Union Pacific and Southern Pacific made him the foremost eastern capitalist seeking to control western resources. Utah Power was eventually reacquired by Mormons, and the church became the largest single stockholder.

After Heber Grant became church president in 1918, the Utah economy began a long slide that hit bottom in the Great Depression. Output had been artificially expanded during World War I, but soon after, the mining economy collapsed, and farmers faced a severe downturn from which they would not recover until World War II. Discriminatory freight rates further hurt local industry, which also suffered from growing competition with California. The decline in basic industries through the 1920s and 1930s became so severe that the state's industrial capacity, despite the recovery during World War II, was smaller in 1950 than it had been in 1920.

With the economy in a state of collapse, people began to leave the state in large numbers. Nearly thirty thousand people emigrated from Utah in the 1920s. Radical insurgencies erupted after World War I, culminating in a Workers, Soldiers, and Sailors Council in Salt Lake City in 1918 and a bitter miners' strike in 1922. Under the influence of radicals, the Utah Federation of Labor endorsed the Russian Revolution. Soon a concerted counterattack led by the church and local bankers, Marriner Eccles among them, virtually destroyed the labor movement.

During the Great Depression, United Orders—local communal organizations that had been promoted by Brigham Young—were revived, and many poor Mormons established cooperatives throughout the state. The growing popularity of the United Orders and the defeat of Reed Smoot by Elbert Thomas, a pro–New Deal professor of political science at the University of Utah, frightened the church hierarchy. J. Reuben Clark, Grant's top adviser, attacked the revival, saying that "Communism and the United Order are the same thing, Communism being merely a forerunner, so to speak, of a reestablishment of the United Order. . . . I am informed that ex-bishops, and indeed bishops, who belong to Communistic organizations are preaching this doctrine."

In reaction to the revival of the United Orders, the church established the Church Security Program under Clark's leadership. This self-help program, the hierarchy's version of the correct connection with its socialistic past, was presented as an alternative to New Deal relief programs. Encouraged by articles in such conservative publications as the *Saturday Evening Post, Cosmopolitan,* and *American Banker,* the Republican-oriented church leadership touted the church program as the answer to Roosevelt's "big government." It claimed to have taken more than eighty-five thousand Mormons off the dole, but in fact, Utah's proportion of indigents on relief remained high throughout the decade. At the height of the depression, more federal funds poured into Utah than most other states. The Mormon welfare program ultimately failed to stem the "revolt of the Mormon congregations" as Carey McWilliams characterized it. Utah residents through the 1930s and 1940s remained attracted to New Deal programs and candidates. Church members frequently preferred government relief checks to bishops' storehouse supplies.

The Great Depression also hit the church hard economically despite Heber Grant's attempts to rebuild its economic base. Church investments in the late 1920s and early 1930s were largely unproductive. One of its major banks was sold for a song to the Eccles interests in order to forestall a collapse of the entire Salt Lake banking system. Utah and Idaho Sugar was also forced to sell its Canadian factory to meet long-overdue payments for sugar beets and to gain capital to keep the company going.

While the church floundered, the Eccles interests prospered. Led by George Eccles after Marriner went to Washington, the family was more in tune with the shifts in the regional economy and the new forces emerging from the New Deal. The Eccles brothers in the late 1920s had created the first bank holding company in the interior West, which allowed their First Security Corporation not only to weather the depression but to swallow up at bargain prices weaker banks in Utah and Idaho. The central organizing force in the region, First Security maintained influence throughout Utah, southern Idaho, and Wyoming and established a presence in Nevada and northern Arizona. First Security became heavily involved in the home-mortgage market by tapping loans from the new Federal Housing Administration, in the design of which Marriner had played a central role.

The Eccles brothers were not the only Utah businessmen to establish a Wachington link. By the late 1930s, a number of key people, some of them Mormons who had gotten their start as Reed Smoot's bright young men, became a force in the Washington bureaucracy. These Washington connections paid off for Utah with the advent of World War II. George Eccles promoted Ogden as a desirable site for military installations because of its role as a railroad nexus. In the late 1930s, Hill Air Force Base was established on land donated by Eccles and other members of the Ogden Chamber of Commerce. During the war, ten major military bases were opened in Utah. New capital investment from 1941 to 1945, almost all of it from federal sources, equaled the total capital investment in the state in 1939.

Wartime expenditures soon led to the diversification of Utah's mining-dominated economy. Hill Air Force Base became a magnet for further defense installations and for defense-related industries. By 1960, Hill was the major missile center in the West, and Utah was the third most defense-oriented state in the nation. At the same time, Utah's military installations attracted such corporations as Thiokol Chemical Corporation, Sperry Rand, and Hewlett-Packard.

Utah farming was also undergoing major changes. The size of farms grew as they came to resemble large outdoor factories. First Security worked closely with the Idaho-based Jack Simplot agribusiness interests and U and I Sugar to foster the integration of farming with processing and packing. Simplot is best known for its development of mass marketing of potatoes for the McDonald's fast-food chain.

The war was also responsible for the interior West's first steel plant at Geneva, Utah, south of Salt Lake City. Built with federal funds by Utah Construction, the plant was leased during the war to United States Steel. When United States Steel proposed purchasing the plant outright in 1948, the church opposed the move because it feared the plant would disorganize nearby communities and undermine the church's influence in an area not far from Brigham Young University at Provo. Negotiations between J. Reuben Clark and United States Steel's Dr. Walter Mathesius eventually led to an agreement over hiring policies and the role of the corporation in the community. With United States Steel firmly established in Utah, the Geneva plant played a major role in generating related economic activity in the area. Utah resources, in the spirit of the self-industrializing West, were being fully processed within the state and used to build its own economy.

The momentum from the war-inspired boom had carried Utah forward, eventually establishing it as an important growth center of the interior. The strong presence of corporations from outside the state was complemented by the rise of such regional powers as First Security, U and I, Simplot Industries, Idaho-based Morrison-Knudsen, the Browning armament interests, and regional marketing operations such as Albertson's and Food King. "If one word had to be chosen to summarize the economic history of Utah for the past thirty years," wrote James Clayton in *Utah's History*, "a good choice would be *dependency*." According to J. L. Shoemaker, a Utah Power and Light executive who had worked for Dun and Bradstreet, the New York brokerage houses were still identifying Utah as federally dominated in the 1960s.

By the late 1960s the boom began to shift toward resource development. The issues underlying this boom traced back to the very roots of Deseret, when control over resources, particularly control of water, the most precious western resource, was considered the key not just to growth but to survival. Despite its dependency, Salt Lake City grew apace, fueled by Mormon population policies. As he city spread along the Wasatch Front, the city's leaders mounted a campaign to get Utah's share of the Colorado.

GRABBING UTAH'S SHARE: THE CENTRAL UTAH PROJECT

Immediately upon arriving in the Salt Lake Valley in 1847, the Mormon settlers realized that the proper development of water was the key to food production and economic self-sufficiency. By the following spring, over 5,000 acres had been brought under cultivation by diverting the streams that flowed from the Wasatch Mountains. Settlements were established near the mouth of every canyon with at least one irrigation system for each settlement. The effort was entirely on a cooperative basis defined by a system of "beneficial use." Brigham Young told the settlers, "No man has the right to waste one drop of water that another man can turn into bread." Consistent with the practice of "prior appropriations," which would later develop in Colorado and other western states to serve mining, the Mormons linked water use to their overall concept of the cooperative community, in which no individual rights for use of the water were recognized. Prior appropriation, with its principle of "first in time, first in right," was a mechanical application of a western-invented system for an arid environment, which required control with some degree of cooperation. The Mormon model of cooperative action impressed the first great appraiser of western water, John Wesley Powell, who believed further land development in the West could only be achieved through cooperative action rather than individual, government, or corporate action.

Throughout the late nineteenth century, the Mormon settlements experimented with dam and reservoir construction, encountering the usual difficulties with financing. By the turn of the century, irrigation efforts began to dwindle in number because of the growing costs of projects. One of the key projects explored but postponed was a diversion of the Strawberry River into the area of Spanish Forks in the Utah Valley southeast of Salt Lake City, one of the major agricultural valleys in central Utah. The local farmers realized that they would need to find outside financing and resources to pay the high costs of diverting the water through the mountains north and east of the valley. With the creation of the Reclamation Service, the farmers quickly turned to the federal government for irrigation subsidies. The Strawberry Creek Project, one of the Reclamation Service's first, was initiated in 1906 and completed in 1922.

When Utah agriculture was in collapse during the 1920s and 1930s, the Reclamation Service became the central planning body for future Utah water development. The bureau conducted nearly all the field investigations and planning for a series of projects for the storage and diversion of water.

By the mid-1940s local Utah business and agricultural interests formed the Utah Water Users Association and later the Water and Power Board to build the state's own water lobby rather than relying solely on the Bureau of Reclamation. The plans of Arizona and California to take more water from the Colorado generated the first systematic push for water development among the upper-basin states. Utah water interests began to talk of massive development of the upper Colorado basin, including a series of long-term projects known collectively as the Central Utah Project.

The Colorado had been a major concern of the Mormons ever since they had built early settlements adjacent to the river. Brigham Young had explored the possibility of using the Colorado as the main transportation route from Salt Lake

City to the sea. In the late 1920s Senator Reed Smoot, in response to California's plans for the Colorado, raised the possibility of a dam at Flaming Gorge on the Utah-Wyoming border.

By the late 1940s Utah's growing water lobby was committed to large-scale utilization of the Colorado for agricultural and urban needs as well as a source of cheap hydroelectric power. The upper-basin agreement of 1948 made water allotments by state, with Utah entitled to 23 percent of the upper-basin total. The upper-basin states, working with the Bureau of Reclamation, planned a series of major multipurpose dams called the Colorado River Storage Project, which was introduced in Congress in the early 1950s. The major Utah components of the plan, the Central Utah Project, were budgeted at more than a billion dollars.

In a curious episode in 1950, the head of southern California's Metropolitan Water District, Joseph Jensen, used his Utah Mormon background to try to persuade church officials to back California instead of Arizona in the fight over the Central Arizona Project. In a letter to J. Reuben Clark, Jensen argued that the Mormon church in southern California was growing rapidly. The increase in Mormons meant in turn a greater church investment in the area, thanks to tithing and other income-generating activities. Such growth and economic investment, Jensen argued, was "dependent upon the security of the water supply in southern California." Jensen then set up a meeting with Clark in Salt Lake City through Gus Backman while simultaneously attempting to influence his cousin, senatorial candidate Wallace Bennett, and Governor J. Bracken Lee. Jensen argued with the conservative Lee that the Arizona project ought to be opposed because it was "federally dominated."

Jensen's efforts were to no avail. The church stood by its support for Arizona and its substantial Mormon population, located in the area where development by the project might occur. Church counselor Clark also felt that California represented the major obstacle to the plans of Utah and the upper-basin states. "We have large areas in Utah that might be irrigated from the Colorado River," Clark wrote back to Jensen, arguing that "Arizona has elaborate ambitions along the same direction of providing water for their lands and they have great quantities of land." Clark concluded, "In all of these, we have and must have a direct interest."

Jensen discovered that the growing consensus in the state around the Central Utah and Colorado River Storage projects was overwhelming. Even Lee, although strongly opposed to federal government intervention, backed them. The breakfast trio of McKay, Backman, and Fitzpatrick, along with other Salt Lake business leaders, had a hand in mobilizing support through the Aqualantes, the promotional organization of the upper-basin states. The *Deseret News*, treating the Colorado River Storage Project as a crusade, called on upper-basin groups to subscribe to a publicity fund to fight the conservationists who opposed the project.

Republican Senator Arthur Watkins became the state's chief spokesman on water issues through the 1950s. Watkins, with senators from Wyoming, Colorado, and New Mexico, became a field general for the storage-project legislation and maintained an almost evangelical fervor in promoting the reclamation project. When the bitter fight between Senator Joseph McCarthy and the Eisenhower administration broke out in 1954–1955, Watkins played a pivotal role. He eventually introduced the successful censure motion against the Wisconsin senator. Watkins' emergence as a key figure in the McCarthy situation was a trade-off for Eisenhower's reluctant support for the storage project. Watkins denied any explicit deal but explained in his autobiography that when Eisenhower called him in to congratulate him after the censure motion, the Utah senator "quite coincidentally—because a State of the Union message was in preparation—asked him [Eisenhower] to include a statement in support of the Colorado River project, and he did."

After Congress passed the storage-project act in 1956, the Central Utah Water Conservancy District was established to act as local government sponsor for the Central Utah Project. The Water Conservancy Board, appointed by state judges, became a self-perpetuating pro–water-development lobbying group that functioned as tax collector, administrator, and lobbyist.

As it was originally designed in the 1950s, the Central Utah Project was structured to divert water from the south slopes of the Uinta Mountains and the Colorado River to the Great Basin in Central Utah. The water from the Bonneville unit of the project would be diverted via extensive reservoirs, tmnnels, and canals over the Wasatch Mountains, a substantial distance to marinal farmland in central Utah as well as the more densely populated and industrialized Wasatch Front. The project's six separate units, Bonneville, Vernal, Jensen, Uintah, Upalco, and the Ute Indian unit, were designed for different urban and agricultural purposes.

From the outset, the Central Utah Project was never a clearly defined project. When it was authorized, it was presented primarily as a plan to bring irrigation water to previously unirrigated lands. After 1956 the overall project, particularly the key Bonneville unit, was modified several times to offset criticisms of excessive costs and unwarranted subsidies. Ultimately, a substantial amount of the water was redefined as supplemental municipal water so that the quantity of water for urban and industrial use could be increased. "In analyzing the CUP, the economist does not know exactly what to analyze," wrote University of Montana economist Tom Powers. "The CUP is a shifting project," he concluded.

The shifting rationale for the project paralleled similar shifts involving other Colorado basin projects. The underlying motivation for completing the revised projects revolved around the fears associated with the "use it or lose it" mentality. "The goal to 'fully utilize the whole supply' has had all the force of revealed truth from pioneer days to the present," wrote Utah water analyst Jay Bagley. "Every generation sees some unrealized water development opportunities and is driven toward development from an implicit faith in the economic and social transformation that could be triggered by it. This faith has been reinforced by a constant fear that if water-development potentials are not soon realized, someone else will find a way to put the water to use so that identified opportunities are lost forever." In Utah's case, that "someone else" was primarily California, with its apparently insatiable thirst for the Colorado.

"For those of us who live in the arid West," Utah Water Conservancy District attorney Ed Clyde declared in defense of the project, "it is unthinkable that we should permit our water resources to waste, either by nondevelopment or wasteful use." Such thinking became the rationale underlying support for the project as well as the basis for environmental opposition to the Central Utah

Project and other massive western water projects. Through the 1970s, public criticism mounted over project costs and subsidies. As the attacks increased, advocates of the Utah project restructured the project to allow for greater urban use. Under the new plan up to 99,000 acre-feet were to be delivered to the urban corridor stretching from Salt Lake in the north to Provo and Orem in the south. The new urban-oriented system meant additional costs from plans to deliver the water to satisfy summer peak loads, particularly during a drought. One Salt Lake County water study estimated that upward of 40 percent of residential and municipal water use during the year was earmarked for such nonconsumptive purposes as watering lawns, trees, and flower gardens. "Thus the Bureau of Reclamation is using federal subsidies intended for support of family farms," Powers wrote, "to construct mammoth facilities so that suburban lawns in prosperous communities can be watered whenever their owners desire."

The Central Utah Project also generated criticism concerning the project's diversion and storage components, which would, according to one critic, "hack up the mountains and screw up the stream flows." Another key area of concern was the problems related to the Ute tribe, which was entitled to a substantial portion of the project. Many of these criticisms were incorporated into the arguments justifying Jimmy Carter's hit list, which jeopardized the project's future when the list was first announced. Unlike the situation in Colorado, Utah water lobbyists were already united and prepared to act to save their project. Farming and urban interests, along with the Mormon church, had long maintained a common front for the project. Time and again Utah's governor, congressional delegation, and legislature would invoke their support of the project. One exception to this powerful support was Paul Van Dam, Salt Lake County Attorney from 1975 to 1979. Van Dam and his assistant Gerald Kinghorn risked career and political backing by issuing two reports questioning CUP economics and its ostensible advantages for the Salt Lake area.

The strong support for the Central Utah Project proved crucial in the months following the hit-list announcement. The Utah water lobby continued to pressure Congress for new authorizations on the Bonneville unit. The lobby used considerable muscle to fend off the Carter administration's attempts to scale down the project. In 1979 the EPA, working closely with local critics, proposed an independent review process for the project that would have substantially delayed the project and quite possibly killed it. But the Utah water lobby immediately moved to keep the project on line using its biggest weapon, Congressman Gunn McKay, the nephew of David O. McKay. Gunn McKay was a strong project advocate and a power in the House as chairman of the House Military Appropriations Subcommittee. When the EPA began to move on its independent-review proposal, the Carter administration sought support for the MX missile system to be built in Utah and Nevada. McKay would clearly play a central role in the MX debates.

By late 1979, an obvious quid pro quo had been arranged. If Carter would agree to support McKay and the project, McKay would support basing the MX missile in Utah and Nevada. As the EPA started to make its move for an independent review, the agency was called off. "EPA got a call from [the president's] Domestic Council saying do not defer this project," the Environmental Policy Center's Peter Carlson told *High Country News*. "For various political reasons, Interior Secretary Cecil Andrus has committed his agency to constructing the CUP, and EPA's involvement was just not acceptable," said Carlson. As a consequence, CUP not only remained on line, but in January 1980 an additional $20 million was added to the appropriation request for the project. "Utah has found itself marvelously favored by Mr. Carter," the *Deseret News* noted in March 1980, in light of the situation. "The number of federal policy reversals in the past three months has been amazing," the *Deseret News* concluded. MX support eventually helped deny McKay his reelection in 1980.

Despite lobbying successes, the project continued to face a range of criticisms, particularly as the project shifted to a more urban orientation. EPA administrator Alan Merson pointed out in 1979 that construction of the Utah project would "defer the need for water conservation measures for several decades, and this in a metropolitan area with one of the highest per capita water use rates in the nation."

Using conservation and cost comparisons as their yardstick, critics were able to develop full-blown alternatives. Gerald Kinghorn, director of Salt Lake County's Division of Water Quality and Water Pollution Control, proposed an urban-oriented "dual water system." Such a system would provide low-quality water for such uses as watering lawns, while high-quality water would be earmarked for personal consumption. In this way enough high-quality water would be conserved to eliminate the need for Bonneville-unit supplies to urban areas. This alternative plan would cost only about one-fourth as much as the Central Utah Project.

The idea of an alternative to the project, particularly one of limited size and purpose, was anathema to the development-oriented business and political leadership in Utah. By the late 1970s, a small but significant opposition to that development ethic had emerged. The opposition called attention to the "physical limitations of the region," as Powers put it. Utah's water lobby, committed for so long to the completion of the project, still dominated the politics of water in the state. But Utah, which never had as powerful an agribusiness lobby as California or Arizona, found it increasingly difficult to justify the project. With the question of resource development in flux, the problems with the CUP refocused that other central resource issue of the Interior: energy, by whom and for whom.

ENERGY BROKER

While the focus of efforts to divert the Colorado River shifted toward the urban corridor, the attention of the major energy players was fixed on the rich deposits of coal, uranium, oil shale, and a variety of other mineral ores in eastern, central, and southern Utah. Increasingly Salt Lake City's future was tied to its new role as an energy broker.

Utah coal deposits had been coveted by energy producers since the development of deep mines in the Emery County coal fields in central Utah in the late nineteenth and early twentieth century. By the 1960s, with the emergence of the Grand Plan and WEST Associates' regional energy strategy, attention shifted from central Utah to strip mines on the Colorado Plateau. The region's rich deposits of low-sulfur coal offered a major opportunity for energy producers, particularly the California utilities attracted by its proximity to California.

The first big play for these coal deposits on the Utah side of the Utah-Arizona border was the epic Kaiparowits fight in the early 1970s. The Kaiparowits project fit the state's development ethos. Local residents accepted the argument that construction of the plant would aid the local community. Unlike the urban corridor to the north, southeastern Utah, according to sociologist Ronald Little, had been "undergoing dedevelopment since 1940, and its residents faced a reality of high unemployment, low wages, and the expected outmigration of its youth." The utilities argued that the Kaiparowits plant would revitalize the area economically, providing more than six thousand new jobs as well as indirect economic benefits. Most important, the utilities appeared to offer the solution for halting outmigration. Widespread concern over the exodus of the young was particularly intense in Mormon communities, in which people desperately wanted to keep their families and communities intact.

As the Kaiparowits fight heated up, local residents felt torn between the different parties to the dispute. The major participants—the utilities, the environmentalists, the federal government (which owned the land on which the coal was located), and the railroads (which debated whether to build a new transportation route for the coal)—were all outsiders. No one seemed to have much concern for the impact on the residents, whatever the outcome. Even the church, which strongly backed the Kaiparowits project, appeared more interested in the overall dynamic of energy development in the state than the actual impact on the local Mormon communities.

The effects, many argued, would be severe. In an area that was basically agricultural, the Kaiparowits project would consume 41,400 acre-feet of Utah's annual allotment from the Colorado River. The project would also create boomtown conditions then prevalent in other energy development areas such as Page, Arizona, across the border. A number of boomtown studies pointed out that jobs for local residents generated by projects like Kaiparowits were few and far between, primarily because of the skill requirements of the jobs. A transient work force would be brought in that would likely undermine local institutions and sharply conflict with community values. Ultimately, the studies concluded, the economic impact—including increased property-tax, welfare, sewer, police, and education assessments and skyrocketing inflation in such areas as housing—would be extremely negative.

One Mormon academic who had studied the potential impact of Kaiparowits concluded that the plant would indeed hurt the area, contrary to what the utilities were saying. The academic met with a member of the church hierarchy who followed the Kaiparowits situation, to communicate his views. "We are now an international church," the church leader told the professor. "Do you realize how many members we now have in Latin America, in Europe? How many new stakes, how many new temples we're building? We can't be oriented just toward a few small communities in southern Utah."

When the Kaiparowits project was suspended after Southern California Edison dropped out, the decision highlighted the crucial role of the California utilities and the California market on the Utah energy situation. While the Kaiparowits fight was being waged, another proposed coal-fired plant in southern Utah, the Intermountain Power Project (known as Son of Kaiparowits), began to wend its way through the federal bureaucracy. The Interior Department approved the project after its relocation to Lynndyl, north of Interstate 70. After Kaiparowits, the Intermountain project became the focus of efforts to develop Utah's energy resources. Once again California utilities, led by the Los Angeles Department of Water and Power, provided a major share of the project's front end financing and planned to take 58 percent of the power supply. Their presence on the project was, like Edison at Kaiparowits, essential to its survival. Further, the proposed coal-fired Warner Valley plant, also in southern Utah and advocated by southern Utah development interests, was equally dependent on California participation.

The dependence on California, particularly after the Kaiparowits fight, became more and more unpopular in the state. The opposition was joined by some southern Utah residents formerly wedded to energy development. The state's major electrical utility, Utah Power and Light, took note of the increased antagonism toward California and used the opportunity to shift away from an integrated regional energy strategy with California in the driver's seat toward a new role for Utah as an energy broker.

The Mormon church had for a number of years owned and controlled Utah Power and Light, but in the dispersal of church investments at the turn of the century, it divested itself of most of its interest in the company. Through the 1970s, there was a strong Mormon presence within the company's management and on its board, although many of the utility's stockholders were eastern investors. During the 1960s and early 1970s, Utah Power and Light had been a participant in WEST Associates, sharing the assumptions of the Grand Plan. But shortly after Kaiparowits collapsed, the company's leadership decided to pull out of the WEST group and reorient its approach. It decided to extricate itself from the southern Utah situation by seeking to trade long-term leases held on the Kaiparowits Plateau for coal leases in Emery County that were held by the Bureau of Reclamation. The company continued to consider coal development central to its continuing strategy as a self-sufficient energy broker. But even the wily utility realized it could never maintain a fully independent role, given the great energy play developing within the state and throughout the interior West. Utah Power's primary source of capital now came from California rather than the East, as in the past. Utah, like Colorado and Arizona, was a capital-deficit state and showed no signs in the foreseeable future of generating its own funds. Despite significant church investment, Utah Power and Light had to look outside the state for funding for new projects.

Utah Power and Light pursued a regional energy strategy even after pulling out of WEST. As part of an overall campaign to promote the Utah boom, the utility ran a series of ads in the *Wall Street Journal.* "We sit atop some of the world's great coal deposits," the utility proclaimed to these national business readers, encouraging them to tap into Utah's boom. Utah Power and Light, despite its fling as an independent energy broker, still expressed the same "Come and Get 'Em" attitude that dominated the mood of the state.

The emergence of the energy issue in the 1960s and 1970s witnessed the rise of a new type of power broker in the state—the energy-connected lawyer and politician. Two of the most influential figures were Calvin Rampton and Scott Matheson, who occupied the governor's post through most of the period. Rampton, elected in 1964 as a moderate Democrat over weak Republican opposition, was a consummate politician. The son of a Mormon salesman from Bountiful, Utah, Rampton became a powerful local lawyer with a wide range of political and corporate ties. As governor, he worked closely with Pro-Utah, a Republican-oriented business group, to establish the Utah Industrial Promotion Council and the Utah Travel Council.

As governor when the boom took off in Utah, Rampton established himself as a champion of corporate relocation and a probusiness environment. His prodevelopment stance made him equally attractive to Republicans and Democrats, allowing him to become the consensus candidate of the business and political establishment. Rampton also became the champion of energy development in Utah, declaring that he was "perfectly willing to produce energy for sale outside the state." The foremost champion of the Kaiparowits project, he scoffed at the anti-California perspective and worked closely with corporate lobbyists to promote the big energy developments.

Although Rampton won reelection easily in 1968 and again in 1972, he decided to leave office in 1976 to devote his time to his law practice, in which he functioned as a high-powered broker on the statewide, western, and national levels. Rampton's handpicked successor, Scott Matheson, narrowly defeated Vernon Romney in the 1976 election. Matheson, the son of a Mormon judge, had worked for eighteen years in the legal department of the Union Pacific and as legal counsel for the Anaconda Copper Company.

Although Matheson was a less crafty politician than Rampton, he was nevertheless a crucial link between the big energy companies and the new Democratic politicians of the 1970s: Lamm of Colorado, Judge of Montana, Herschler of Wyoming, and Babbitt of Arizona. When Matheson became chairman of the Western Governors' Policy Office (WESTPO) in 1979, his election was welcomed by the Western Regional Council. The council's chairman during that period was James Wilson, the head of the Union Pacific's energy subsidiary, Rocky Mountain Energy Company. Wilson characterized Matheson's ascendancy in WESTPO as providing "a basis of trust already established."

Matheson in turn looked to the council as a key component of what the Utah governor characterized as "the new coalition of the 1980s." Speaking at the council's annual meeting in Phoenix in December 1979, Matheson described "the fast-blooming romance" between WESTPO and the council, comparing their relationship to the "romance period" that precedes the marriage. Looking to the big energy play in the West and in his own state, Matheson also spoke of "a new western consciousness" underlying his proposed coalition of governors, the congressional delegation, the various federal bureaucrats overseeing development in the western states, and the corporate community. WESTPO and the council would provide the leadership for this coalition, Matheson declared. The Utah governor projected a new kind of regionalism—not the conservative and potentially unproductive concept of the Sagebrush Rebellion, which neither he nor his corporate hosts backed, but a regionalism based on a developing energy economy.

Matheson knew that Utah was well situated to cash in on the development of its resources. He actively backed the mammoth Intermountain Power and Warner Valley plants, hoping they might launch a new coal boom in southern Utah. Anticipating such tentative projects as a proposed coal-gasification plant in the California desert or the Harry Allen coal-fired plant in Nevada might use Utah coal, Matheson and his allies explored the possibility of constructing a coal-slurry pipeline, using Utah water to transport coal to the California coast, where it could be shipped to Japan.

Shale was another resource being touted. Every participant in the proposed Matheson coalition saw rich possibilities for Utah Shale, particularly after the "money supermarket" became available in 1980. The possibility of shale development turned cautious Utah bankers and businessmen into wild-eyed optimists. "We're incredibly optimistic about future growth in the area and energy is the key to it all," Kelly Matthews, chief economist of the First Security Corporation, said of the Utah economy. "Right now, however, we're the weak sister to Denver in the battle for the big money coming in around that development, especially oil and gas exploration. But most of the synthetics are on our side of the mountain," Matthews happily went on, "and all that money for development should rub off on us here in Salt Lake."

Matthews and other Utah businessmen realized that shale could be a tremendous boon, but even the massive subsidies from the Energy Security Corporation would be dwarfed by what could be the largest and most expensive public-works project and boom stimulator in history—the MX missile project. "The MX," Matthews declared in 1980, "is an absolutely imponderable situation. They're talking about $60 billion or more, much of which will undoubtedly be oriented toward Salt Lake City. Even if the people here in Utah don't like it, I'm not sure they can block it in any case. The MX could be our blockbuster."

The MX idea was initially proposed by the Carter administration in June 1979, shortly after the president signed the SALT II treaty. The system consisted of a looped track winding twenty-five square miles through the desert along the Nevada-Utah border. Two hundred missile transporters or launchers would move up and down the track through twenty-three horizontal shelters on each loop, creating all together forty-six hundred different shelters. This MX was a monstrosity, a multibillion-dollar project that some estimates projected would cost as much as $100 billion or more. It would have employed more than twenty-three hundred construction workers, creating boomtown conditions far greater than any previous project. The Carter administration and the Air Force dismissed the boomtown problems by emphasizing, as with the Kaiparowits project, the economic advantages for the area.

Unlike Kaiparowits, local residents, particularly in the south-central part of the state and Nevada, where the MX was to be built, quickly opposed the project. Opposition building through 1979 and 1980 focused not only on boomtown fears but also the availability of water. Politicians such as Matheson soon began to retreat on the issue, shifting from their earlier advocacy to a more studied neutrality or opposition. The MX opposition signaled a shift in attitude that raised the question of large-scale development throughout the state.

Mistrust of the federal government, always present, grew in the late 1970s because of the effects of the 1950s atom bomb tests that were conducted in Nevada upwind from southern Utah. With neighbors and family members dying of cancer and the federal government's Nuclear Regulatory Commission continuing to downplay the consequences of the tests, the Utah media quickly moved in on the story, transforming the tests into a major issue in the state. Even the Mormon church maintained a neutral position on the MX in part because of the anger of a number of church members over the nuclear-test issue. By 1981, opposition to the MX had spread to a substantial number of the state's residents. The Mormon church, after major internal debate, issued a strong statement attacking not only the MX, but the proliferation of nuclear weapons as well.

For the first time, Utahans began to question the impact of the massive projects—whether the MX, the Intermountain Power Project, or the huge nuclear park proposed for the Green River area—on local communities. Residents were more amenable to the arguments of environmentalists, although a great deal of mistrust still remained. The actor Robert Redford, who had been involved in the fight against Kaiparowits, had symbolized unwelcome outsider meddling in Utah's affairs. At the height of the controversy, Redford had been burned in effigy in Kanab. But in the period after Kaiparowits, the actor tried to mend fences in the state while continuing his opposition to big energy projects. Now established as a Utah resident, he criticized, in retrospect, the way he and fellow environmentalists had disregarded the fears and needs of the local residents. Redford now supported the idea of economic development but proposed instead "nonpolluting" industry, such as film production, as an alternative to the energy game plans.

The film *The Electric Horseman*, shot both in Las Vegas and southern Utah in 1978 and released in 1979, was conceived in part as an element of Redford's "southern Utah strategy." It provided some employment for local residents. Redford also attempted to establish an interesting counterpoint through the story line of the film. The cowboy played by Redford is linked to the good people of southern Utah and its celebrated landscape but is pitted against a rapacious development-minded corporation that operates out of the iniquitous Las Vegas.

Despite the success of the film, the local residents ultimately remained interested in Redford the celebrity—the quintessential outsider—more than Redford the advocate. But by 1980 the hostility toward environmentalists had begun to dissipate. The idea of resource development no longer produced an easy consensus. Utah, indeed, was a changing state, susceptible to all the characteristics of the western boom. The speed and direction of that change could no longer just be a simple matter of what someone in New York, Los Angeles, Denver, or even downtown Salt Lake City, decided to do.

CHURCH POWER

When Heber Grant made his pilgrimage to Wall Street in the 1890s, he embraced Brigham Young's realpolitik of seeking accommodation with the larger economic and political forces shaping Utah. Before he reached the top of the church hierarchy, the uneasy relationship between leaders of the Mormon and gentile communities had developed into a more permanent detente. The Grant presidency (1918–1945) became a pivotal era for the church.

The church had begun as one of the great nineteenth-century millenarian movements emphasizing that the creation of Deseret through cooperative action meant the realization of the commonwealth of heaven on earth. With the growing ties between church and gentile leaders, church attitudes shifted profoundly. The attack on the church led by feminists and a number of exposés written during the early muckraking period had identified the church in the popular mind with socialistic practices and polygamy. In response to this popular view of the church and the changes in the Utah economy that weakened church-controlled enterprise, church leaders began to preach the virtues of Americanism, hard work, and free enterprise. Politically, the church became identified with the most orthodox wing of the Republican party. According to Robert Mullen, Heber Grant's time "was taken up in forwarding the economic interests of the church."

The first two decades of the Grant presidency embraced a period of difficulties and decline for the church. Restrictive immigration laws cut off the church from its main source of new recruits—its missionary efforts in northern and western Europe. The collapse of the Utah economy forced more and more saints to emigrate, many to California. The Saints had weathered infinitely more difficult periods, and they survived the Great Depression, divided politically but still intact.

With the rapid spread of American influence overseas after World War II, the church renewed its missionary effort in countries from which it had previously been excluded. Consistent with the Mormon definition of success as success in the business world, the church developed a missionary approach modeled after sales techniques used in the commercial world. In the postwar era the church identified itself not only as the one Christian church native to America but also as the fastest-growing church in the country. By the 1960s the top levels of the church hierarchy—the First Presidency, the Council of Twelve, the presiding bishopric, and the Quorum of the Seventy—were overwhelmingly composed of small businessmen or corporate executives.

In addition to being the principal center of influence in what Arrington called the Great Basin Kingdom, the church was heard in Washington. The role of Marriner Eccles and other Mormons in the Roosevelt administration highlighted Roosevelt's alliance of regional power centers. The New Deal Mormons represented a liberal tendency within the church, but they did not speak for the hierarchy, which was decidedly anti-Roosevelt. During the Eisenhower years, Ezra Taft Benson served as secretary of agriculture, symbolizing the emergence of Great Basin agribusiness and representing an important tie to western conservatives. Eisenhower characterized Benson's church connections as "a distinct asset." In every election year, presidential candidates regarded an appearance at the Tabernacle as a must. Despite its power, the church remained passive in many crucial areas, following rather than initiating key economic and political decisions. From the Great Depression through the 1950s, the federal government played the major role in reviving a moribund Utah economy. In this period New York investment houses defined Utah as "a sphere of influence" of the federal government and tended to discount the nature and importance of the influence of the Mormon church and its extensive holdings.

Throughout David O. McKay's presidency, the church's holdings grew steadily in value, beginning with the assets left intact or reacquired after the divestitures forced by the Edmunds-Tucker Act of 1887. These assets included several insurance companies, a local bank, a woolen mill, the ZCMI department store chain, Utah and Idaho Sugar, and large amounts of land around the Temple in downtown Salt Lake City, plus the growing holdings of local stakes (parishes). Other major economic powers such as Kennecott Copper, the Union Pacific, and the Eccles interests continued to be linked to the church. During the McKay presidency, George Eccles was a regular visitor to McKay's suite at the Hotel Utah, while Marriner maintained a suite upstairs. Although George in particular became an informal adviser to the church and church leaders sat on the First Security Board, both George and Marriner remained distinct from the church.

After Marriner returned to Salt Lake City, he decided to run for the United States Senate as a Republican against Arthur Watkins. Out of tune with the state's conservative politics, he was accused of aiding and abetting Communists because he advocated recognition of China and was soundly defeated. Soon after the defeat, Marriner began dividing his time between Salt Lake City and San Francisco. As Utah Mining and Construction expanded in the Pacific basin, Marriner decided that San Francisco was a much more appropriate city for the headquarters of a major multinational corporation.

The church, having weathered a liberal challenge from within its own ranks during the New Deal, felt much more at home with the conservative politics of the cold-war era. In 1948 and 1950 the church played a role in the defeat of pro–New Deal candidates for governor and United States senator. Then with the advent of the Eisenhower years, McKay became the new prophet, seer, and revelator. He and church leader Henry D. Moyle began to orient the church away from its earlier passive and reactive role to a more aggressive policy of growth and recruitment. McKay and Moyle put particular emphasis on the international missionary effort. To send thousands of missionaries around the world and build new stakes and temples required a great deal of money.

Under Moyle, the church upgraded its portfolio, even selling its own Zion's First Security Bank to Mormon businessmen, who kept the bank within the church's sphere of influence. By 1962, Moyle would boast to Salt Lake City's Mayor J. Bracken Lee that church investments and internal sources of income such as tithing were generating an annual income of $1 million a day. But the church was also spending its money as fast as it was coming in. The drive for new members overwhelmed all other aspects of church policy. As a regional economic power, the church continued to remain relatively passive, removed from, although supportive of, the gradual growth that preceded the takeoff of the economy in the 1960s.

When Moyle died in 1963, his place as counselor and chief economic policy maker was assumed by Nathan Eldon Tanner, who became the pivotal figure in church economic affairs for most of the next two decades. Tanner, who comes from an old Mormon family, settled in western Canada in the early part of the twentieth century and became active in politics. Elected to the Alberta legislature, he eventually became speaker of its house. With a background in mining, oil, and gas, Tanner later became minister of lands and mines in the provincial government. He developed extensive interests in the energy area, becoming the head of the Trans-Canada Pipeline Company and the Canadian Gas Association. Called to Zion in 1960, he was soon appointed to the Council of Twelve and then became second counselor in the First Presidency on Moyle's death.

As counselor, Tanner reorganized the economic side of the church, attempting to create a more professional, corporate-oriented approach that treated church investments more as a business opportunity than simply as a source of expansion funds. He was able to consolidate his power and overcome remaining resistance in the wake of a scandal in the late 1960s. Two church accountants had been able to embezzle at least $600,000 before getting caught because of the antiquated nature of the church bookkeeping system. The embezzlement so shocked church authorities that Tanner was able to computerize the accounts and to bring in a number of "money managers." These professional aides were in charge of day-to-day decisions under Tanner, as well as the preparation of annual budgets and long-term investment strategies.

In 1968, Tanner created the Deseret Management Corporation as an overall holding company for church-owned businesses. Zion's Securities Corporation was established as the holding company for the church's real estate interests, stock portfolio, and other investments. Further reorganization took place in 1972 as the corporatist approach became entrenched within the church organization and Tannerism became synonymous with church economics.

In economic affairs the church also turned to several national corporate figures, who were given no formal leadership position but served as informal financial advisers and decision-makers. Such behind-the-scenes figures included David Kennedy, Richard Nixon's Secretary of Treasury, and J. Willard Marriott, founder of the Marriott hotel and entertainment empire. Kennedy, prior to his Treasury appointment, had been Nixon's roving ambassador, a kind of international economic troubleshooter, a natural outgrowth of his work as head of the internationally minded Chicago-based Continental Illinois Bank. In his memoirs, Nixon said of Kennedy, "He also met my requirement that my Secretary of the Treasury not be part of the New York-Boston banking establishment that had dominated the department for too long." During the 1970s Kennedy, relying on earlier contacts, also functioned as the church's international ambassador.

The expansion of the church's media holdings showed best how the church used its economic power to further its spiritual quest. Prior to Tanner's emergence, the church's media holdings were limited to Salt Lake's afternoon newspaper, the *Deseret News;* a couple of radio stations in southern Idaho; and KSL, the CBS television and radio outlet in Salt Lake City. Under Tanner, the church reorganized its media holdings into what would ultimately become a major international media conglomerate. In 1964 the church leadership called on Arch Madsen, the sharp-tongued conservative head of the church's Salt Lake broadcast operations, to head up this new church-media operation. Madsen had lived in New York, operated an advertising agency, and had some contact with the world of media financing. With Madsen in charge, the church created the Bonneville International Corporation and immediately acquired radio and television properties in Seattle and New York City to expand it holdings. Through the late 1960s and 1970s Bonneville systematically picked up broadcast properties in Los Angeles, Kansas City, San Francisco, Chicago, and Washington, D.C., and created a broadcast consulting arm to advise Bonneville's stations and other like-minded media groups. Bonneville also created a film-production arm, a computer operation, and a number of audio production facilities.

Under Madsen's leadership, Bonneville functioned as a professional, "profit-oriented" operation within which church policies and goals would still be implemented. Madsen and other church leaders became wedded to the idea that mass communications were, as Madsen put it, "the ultimate power on the face of the earth today. . . . The proper use of the mass media is going to mean the difference between chaos and the solid values of civilization." Madsen referred in part to Bonneville's decision to buy a couple of Dallas radio stations in 1978 in order to "clean them up."

As Bonneville attempted to project itself as a modern media conglomerate subject to Federal Communications Commission (FCC) programming standards, the appearance of overt church influence on programming, news, and public affairs, particularly in its Salt Lake outlets, had to be diminished. Nevertheless, when conflict developed because church interests were at stake, invariably the church hierarchy would step in, stories would be killed, and programming would be affected.

By 1980 the church had greatly expanded its area of economic influence. Since Eldon Tanner's appointment to the first-presidency seventeen years earlier, the church had moved from a passive supporter of downtown redevelopment to an active participant in reshaping the area. New high-rises were built, notably the church's own twenty-six-story office building adjacent to the Temple. The church also leased land to Salt Lake County for the Salt Palace Convention Center. It ultimately attempted to influence the direction of development in both the downtown and outlying areas of Salt Lake City through its own real estate activities as well as links with individual real estate developers. In the process, redevelopment obliterated some of the most spectacular examples of Utah's architectural heritage, including a number of beautiful church and commercial buildings and stately downtown mansions associated with the heyday of the mining frontier. The church was obsessed with recording its own history, but history could not stand in the way of making Salt Lake City a modern, more characterless metropolis.

Tanner's effort to reorganize the church economic holdings was part of a larger effort to consolidate church functions and programs to bring them under centralized control from Salt Lake City. Through its missionary effort, the church had become a worldwide organization with more and more of its membership located overseas in Asia, Europe, Latin America (particularly Mexico), the Pacific basin and Africa. This new situation required a more streamlined administrative structure and greater control over the content of church programs.

The general consolidation of church authority paralleled changes in the use and disposition of its political power in its historical area of influence. The church was especially concerned about its influence in the Utah state legislature, where direct church interests were at stake. "Clear it with the church" was an unwritten rule for politicians in areas in which church policy was directly involved. The church, for example, was active in the right-to-work issue, a long-standing church concern, and it played a prominent role in passage of the provision in Utah as well as in Nevada, Idaho, and Arizona. By 1980 the Utah legislature was overwhelmingly Mormon and conservative, by some estimates as high as 80 percent Mormon.

The increasing political turmoil of the 1960s had a profound effect on the church. The most publicized issue was the church's policy on black members. Although the church was actively recruiting in Third World countries, black members were banned from the priesthood, a position attained by white Mormon men at the age of thirteen. In Joseph Smith's day, ironically, the church was considered abolitionist. Civil rights activists began to attack the church, and Brigham Young University sports teams were often picketed when they appeared out of the state.

Divisions within the church over the civil rights issue were exacerbated by a growing right wing within the church. Divisions became increasingly pronounced between an Ezra Taft Benson wing and a more moderate faction led by First Counselor Hugh B. Brown. By the early 1960s Benson had become a confirmed "conspiracy" advocate who praised the John Birch Society and called its founder, Robert Welsh, "a great American patriot." When Benson's son Reed became Utah chairman of the John Birch Society, father and son were constantly inveighing against liberal-cum-socialist perfidy. "Today the devil as a wolf in a supposedly new suit of sheep's clothing is enticing some men to parrot his line by advocating planned government-guaranteed security programs at the expense of liberty," the elder Benson wrote in 1962 about John Kennedy's New Frontier.

By the mid-1960s the Benson followers found themselves increasingly isolated within the church. Brown was able to stave off the Benson thrust within the church by sending Reed Benson to London on a church mission and by attempting to tone down some of the more virulent anti-Communism and liberal-baiting that had characterized the church over the previous decade. With the collapse of the civil rights movement and the end of the war in Vietnam in the early seventies, the moral issues that most concerned the church leadership became increasingly important political issues throughout the country.

In 1973 Spencer W. Kimball became the new prophet. Kimball came from an old and worthy Mormon family. His grandfather was Heber Kimball, Brigham Young's closest adviser. Spencer was related through complex and extensive family ties to many past and present church leaders. He grew up in Thatcher, Arizona, in the Gila Valley east of Phoenix, where he counted Stewart and Morris Udall's father among his high school classmates. Before becoming president of the church, Kimball was best known for his missionary work among the Indians, whom the Saints identified as their brothers, the Lamanites. In 1978 he announced that he had a revelation that called for the admission of blacks into the priesthood. Kimball's revelation ended a bitter fight within the church and appeared to represent a new move toward the mainstream.

In Utah this was the period of the consensus candidacy of Calvin Rampton. The common understanding among Utah politicians by the mid-1970s was that the church, although not necessarily endorsing particular candidates, would still actively oppose those who attacked or threatened church interests or opposed a prodevelopment approach. Thus a politician like Salt Lake Mayor Ted Wilson, with his youthful liberal image, could get elected mayor of Salt Lake City twice in the 1970s precisely because of the absence of any active church opposition. Wilson brought a new image to the city, the publicity-conscious church hierarchy decided. Such prestige was considered crucial in changing the image of Salt Lake from its "once provincial, religiously oriented" aura to a "cosmopolitan city," as a Hotel Utah promotional brochure put it. Wilson was inevitably influenced by the church, however. He consulted with church leaders on a number of issues and his reelection campaign was run by J. Allen Blodgett, the church's comptroller.

The turmoil of the civil rights and Vietnam eras led the church to create a new institutional mechanism to look after its interests in the political sphere. The new Special Affairs Committee included Gordon Hinckley from the Council of Twelve; James Faust, also a member of the Twelve and a former member of the Utah legislature; David Haight, former mayor of Palo Alto, California; and Neal Maxwell, the former director of the church's educational institutions. The committee was staffed by a number of individuals who played an active role in Utah and western politics. Special Affairs member Maxwell, for one, symbolized the new breed of church leadership involved in political affairs. Formerly a member of the CIA and vice-president for public affairs at the University of Utah during the turbulent 1960s, the smooth-talking Maxwell blended in well with the more modern-sounding corporate-oriented leadership emerging within the church.

The Special Affairs Committee became the leading edge of the church's new role in politics. Its members looked into issues the church considered crucial, such as the MX, how changes in the 160-acre law would affect the church agricultural holdings, how the Indian Child Welfare Act of 1976 related to the church's Indian programs, and the fate of the Central Utah Project. Mormons in Congress—and the entire Utah delegation was Mormon—also looked after the church's interests, getting the church's Indian programs exempted from the Indian Child Welfare Act and promoting the version of the reclamation reform bill that exempted church holdings from the 160-acre limit.

The relatively bland probusiness political outlook of the Special Affairs Committee did not lay to rest the long-simmering right-wing traditions within the church. In 1974 the church took a dramatic stand against the Equal Rights Amendment (ERA) and subsequently helped defeat passage of the measure in at least five states, including Virginia, Florida, and Nevada. This new line on the ERA grew out of the response to the liberal and permissive trends of the 1960s and put a renewed emphasis on what the church considered the moral issues confronting and threatening the family—issues such as the role of women, abortion, and homosexuality. This increasing concern over family issues led to a conservative revival in the church. While some members attacked this conservative revival and questioned the patriarchal and authoritarian outlook associated with it, a new and more powerful right wing began to gather momentum within the church.

Meanwhile, the church, more than ever, actively encouraged its members to get involved in politics. Such activities were extraordinarily effective, since the church remained a highly disciplined, centralized structure with a strong authoritarian cast in all its internal procedures. When the church decided to get involved, it was capable of mobilizing large numbers of people at short notice, as it proved during the International Women's Year meetings in 1977.

In many minds, the question boiled down to whether the eighty-two-year-old Ezra Taft Benson would outlast the ailing eighty-six-year-old Kimball and assume the role of prophet. Once that question is settled, then the conflict within the church between the more modernist element and the Benson conservatives will be resumed within the newly arranged hierarchy.

*   *   *

A NEW SALT LAKE CITY

In the early 1970s, the Eastman Kodak Company decided to open a regional headquarters in the interior West. Company officials narrowed the choice of location to Denver or Salt Lake City. An internal study was commissioned to weigh the pros and cons of each city. When the firm issued a report, Kodak's choice was Denver. Calvin Rampton, recalling the report, commented that what made it so unusual was that it openly referred to Mormon influence in Salt Lake as a crucial factor. "Those fears about the church are seldom articulated and thus seldom addressed," Rampton commented. "When you're trying to persuade a company to bring their headquarters here, you have to raise the problem, since they're undoubtedly thinking about it." Rampton concluded a little wistfully, "But the problem is hopefully diminishing."

Discussing the problem, one non-Mormon Utah Power and Light executive compared his feelings about working in a state surrounded by the pervasive Mormon cultural, political, and economic influence to the feelings of a young man he read about in *National Geographic*. The magazine profiled a man who was walking across the country. When he crossed the Utah state line, the walker commented that entering Utah felt like entering a foreign country.

Northwest Energy, a major pipeline company and the largest single corporation headquartered in Salt Lake City, decided that church influence had its advantages. "The church people are businessmen and that's what's important," Vice-President William Owens said of the situation. "They will support growth and development," he declared, referring to the state's business and tax climate.

Despite this favorable assessment, Owens, like other non-Mormon executives, complained of feeling that he and his wife were "strangers in a strange land." The company was also concerned for its younger, non-Mormon employees with children who had to deal with the thoroughly Mormon-influenced school system. It was fearful that its employees' social life was inevitably constricted by the community's prohibitions on drinking and the general stern moral tone projected by the church and its active believers. "You know, you can't just invite people over for drinks or maybe some bridge, or a cup of coffee," an executive's wife complained.

Despite its rapid growth, Utah remains a relatively small state, with a population under 2 million. While the recent rise in population was in part related to the development of new plants and new jobs, Utah also maintained the highest birthrate in the country, a phenomenon directly related to the church's emphasis on large families. "If we can't beat 'em, we can outpopulate 'em" is a common quip among the Mormons. Utah's growth has not fully weakened Mormon influence, with the exception, perhaps, of Salt Lake City. The Mormon population in the state hovered around 72 percent, while it dipped to slightly over 50 percent in the Salt Lake metropolitan area and under 50 percent in Salt Lake City proper.

As the Mormon factor prevents a greater shift of regional headquarters to Salt Lake, the city will fall short of achieving the status of a new energy capital like Denver. The large corporations, which have moved so easily into Denver and assumed power, remain wary of Salt Lake and the church, although they are tempted by such favorable variables as the probusiness environment, the large energy deposits, the high level of education, and the focus on maintaining a nonunion labor force.

New industries recently attracted to Utah include energy-related companies and a range of labor-intensive operations such as electronics, light industry, and the garment industry. New companies opening plants in the state include multinationals such as Litton, General Telephone and Electric, and Union Carbide and big energy combines such as Standard of Indiana, Exxon, Texaco, and Union Oil.

Energy-related growth was clearly the key to Utah's economic development. Mining operations were a big source of employment, and copper was to a great extent still king, with the value of its output still surpassing the value of coal output, although not for long. Kennecott, with its regional headquarters in Salt Lake City, was still a major influence in the state. In fact, the company was crucial in the initial organization of the Western Regional Council. In the mid-1970s, Kennecott faced increasing difficulties over the extensive pollution generated from its massive smelter west of Salt Lake City, pollution that was contributing heavily to the rapid decline of Salt Lake's air quality. The EPA attempted to force Kennecott to put in new antipollution equipment or face a possible plant closure. Kennecott, at that point, turned to several of its business and political allies, including the head of the Mountain Fuel Supply Company, the local gas company, and Calvin Rampton, who had recently stepped down as governor. The newly formed Western Regional Council took on the Kennecott air-quality issue as its first major project, and Kennecott regional vice-president Robert Pratt was the council's first chairman.

After the council began operations in 1977, staff work was contracted to a newly formed consulting firm called Bonneville Associates, based in Salt Lake. Bonneville was part of a new breed of ambitious, young Salt Lake professionals and entrepreneurs attracted to the potential power and profits of the intermountain region. The Bonneville staff was more attracted to the sleek corporate world of Denver than the stuffy "Neanderthal" world of Salt Lake. Although Bonneville helped smooth the council's transition from a Salt Lake–oriented to a multinational-oriented and Denver-influenced organization, Bonneville remained in Salt Lake City because many of the staff liked what they perceived as a new Salt Lake emerging from the confines of an earlier Mormon-shaped city.

Around the time that Bonneville began operations in the late 1970s, Salt Lake City began to witness a growing influx of like-minded young professionals and middle-management figures. The arrival of new corporate types who liked to drink in turn led to the proliferation of private clubs, the only places in which the state's liquor laws permit the sale by the drink of alcohol. These private clubs, resembling a cross between a singles' bar and a businessman's club, were the main center of afterwork socializing. A rapidly growing ski culture, similar to the fast-growing areas that had so influenced the political climate of Colorado, began to take off in the late 1970s with Park City, about thirty miles from Salt Lake City, providing the proper old mining-town setting. The notion of a new outdoor life-style, complete with booze, drugs, and wife-swapping, became the new Salt Lake's answer to that pervasive "other" culture.

A counterpoint of change and reaction set in. Salt Lake, unlike any other western city, resembled something of a battleground between contrasting cultures and life-styles. As the new corporate life-style invaded Salt Lake, Mormon fundamentalism, linked in part to the revived Mormon right wing, also began to grow. Inspired by the church's own strong emphasis on the social issues surrounding the family, a number of Mormons reacted strongly to what they perceived as new antifamily values. This reaction was intensified by the contemporary corporate ideology, which emphasized loyalty to the company above loyalty to the family. As several business publications pointed out, the preferred 1980s executive, as opposed to the 1950s executive, was someone engaged in the more open-ended, less attached life-style of a single or divorced person.

With growing mistrust of the modern life-style, Mormon fundamentalists became more aggressive in seeking out new political solutions to combat these contemporary trends. There were even widespread signs that polygamy has never fully disappeared. Some estimates put the number of polygamists as high as 35,000. Polygamous households, including one behind a high wall in Salt Lake City, existed throughout the state. Polygamists could be spotted on the street because of their distinctive old-fashioned dress and were treated by some with a measure of respect due to society's committed traditionalists.

Groups like the Salt Lake–based Freemen Institute, headed by former Salt Lake police chief and FBI man W. Cleon Skousen combined a profamily position with a new conspiracy theory focused on such corporate pillars as the Trilateral Commission. Skousen's group, which claimed that more than twenty members in the state legislature had gone through the group's intensive seminar program, represented one possible direction for a Salt Lake caught between countervailing cultural and political currents.

Ezra Taft Benson's sons, Reed and Mark, who continue to work with right-wing groups, contrast sharply with the more moderate go-getters such as J. Allen Blodgett and Mayor Ted Wilson. Blodgett, one of the rising men in the church financial bureaucracy, is a technocrat whose moderate conservatism was shaped more by business issues than an ideological anti-Communism. Blodgett, in turn, contrasts with the young Bonneville Associates staff. The Bonneville people are more representative of the new corporate-influenced generation on the rise in Salt Lake. Deeply attracted to the values of money and corporate power, wedded to the outdoor life-style of the new Utah, these corporate go-fers simply ignore that "other" culture, which intersects and severely contrasts with their own.

Behind this unique cultural confrontation lie the region's two contending, but essentially linked, powers. On the inside sits the church, looking once again to become a power in the West and beyond. And on the outside, looking in, are the big energy companies and their corporate counterparts. They are ready to make their move, potentially capable of overwhelming the region in their search for new sources of energy and other investments.

7 Phoenix: On the Edge

It is a potent vision, the empire on the desert. A strong sense of violation permeates the urban landscape. The city looks something like a war zone. Unfinished roads pass through agricultural fields or barren land and then run adjacent to half-completed new subdivisions. Saguaro cacti sit on the lawns of gaudy split-level ranch-style homes. Orange trees run along the downtown thoroughfares leading to the half-empty, forty-story Valley National Bank Center. A civilization, they say, is in its formative stage as America moves west and its newest power center emerges, superimposed on the desert terrain.

Phoenix is a developer's city, a pivot in the Southwest's growth machine, an expansive capitalism's dream come true. It is the prototypical Sun Belt city, with aggressive taxation policies that favor corporate relocation and new plant development, probooster media and political machinery, new planned communities and subdivision schemes used to attract a continuous wave of American immigration.

Phoenix has become a major center of power in the interior West in the space of just a few decades. The city has become a meeting place for all kinds of power brokers and influence-peddlers trading off the boom. Just down the street from the shiny curves of the Valley National Bank Building, the squat and bulky Adams Hotel carries on the old traditions of the town, blending them with the new ways. After the hotel became a trading center for cattle interests, old J. C. Adams decided to boost the hotel's image as a political headquarters. It became in time "the meeting place of Arizona," as a hotel plaque boasts, the real capital "where more legislation was passed than at the capitol building." In the tradition of the hotel, Phoenix became a town where the deals got made: big developments, small ripoffs, backroom maneuvers, stock manipulations, real estate swindles. The city became a magnet that drew developers, agribusiness lobbyists, big mining executives, wheeling and dealing lawyers, good-old-boy bankers, fast-talking financial promoters and speculators of every size and shape.

Like much else in the West, Phoenix' history has been distorted by myth-makers. According to establishment folklore, the city emerged from an ancient civilization to dominate the Southwest and to share power with Los Angeles to the west and Salt Lake and Denver to the north. The city was founded in 1867 as a hay camp for the cavalry at Fort McDowell on the floodplains of the Salt River adjacent to the canal system of the Hohokam Indians. It was named after the phoenix, the mythic bird that burned itself up and emerged renewed from its own ashes. The city, similarly, rose on the ashes of the lost Hohokam Indian civilization, which, the popular interpretation goes, somehow vanished in the fourteenth or fifteenth century, a casualty of the fierce demands of the desert. Yet the modern city bears little resemblance to the peaceful, environmentally adaptive Hohokam. The myth has been skewed to fit its new meaning: this aggressive, money-seeking city can and will grow, defying the desert in its quest for power and immortality.

THE OLD BOY NETWORK

The early development of the Salt River valley by Anglos originated in the 1870s and 1880s with the farming settlements that used the irrigation canals of the Hohokam. The Phoenix farmers marketed their products to the military posts northeast of the town and the mining camps in the mountains. The joining of the local Maricopa and Phoenix Railway with the Southern Pacific's main east-west line in 1889 strengthened the role of this growing agricultural center. Two years later, when the town was named the capital of the Arizona Territory, the local farmers and merchants talked of eventually turning their township of thirty-two hundred residents into the "Denver of the Southwest."

These were the days when Arizona was dominated by copper interests led by William Andrews Clark and the Phelps-Dodge interests from New York. Clark, who had substantial interests in the Rocky Mountain states, bought and developed the United Verde mine near the Arizona-Mexico border. Having created his own company town called Clarkdale, he eventually made off with about $72 million in profits, which he never reinvested in Arizona. It was the era of the Three Cs: copper, cattle, and cotton. The men who dominated the business and political affairs of the state were locked in battle with a powerful labor movement. A strong Mormon influence existed through extensive migration and settlement by the Saints in the northern part of the state and the founding of the Mormon town of Mesa, just east of Phoenix in 1878.

The federal government remained the critical force that helped to underwrite much of the early twentieth-century development. Irrigated water projects subsidized local agriculture, and a massive road and highway system situated Phoenix as a central market and distribution center, linking the farms to their urban markets. During the Great Depression, the government provided a bail-out service for the local economy, created jobs and stimulated production through construction contracts, enlargement of the airport, further road and highway programs, and the expansion of the government bureaucracy. A Phoenix builder named Del Webb characterized local construction during the 1930s as "no longer a private enterprise but rather a subsidiary of the federal government."

World War I also provided a stimulus for growth. In 1916, Goodyear made a deal with the federal government to produce cotton for tire and airplane fabric. A major cotton factory and the new settlement of Litchfield Park to the east of

Phoenix were created to provide housing for the Goodyear workers and managers.

The Goodyear executives liked the potential for development in Phoenix. As war clouds gathered in the late 1930s, Goodyear chairman Edward Littlefield convinced Arizona Senator Carl Hayden that the state could successfully procure military installations (with potential economic gain for Goodyear) if the powerful senator lobbied exclusively for Air Force bases. The construction in 1941 of Luke Air Force Base, complete with a training facility for pilots, was one of the early results of the Hayden-Goodyear lobbying effort.

No sooner had the base opened than Luke's commanding officer, Colonel Ellis Whitehead, started complaining about the situation in Phoenix, which was rife with corruption. Whitehead was particularly outraged by the activities of the chief of police, the city manager, and the chief magistrate. The police, rumor had it, would make periodic sweeps of the houses of prostitution when publicity got especially bad. Instead of locking up the women they would send them to a doctor for a checkup and then let them back out on the streets. Whitehead decided he needed to do something dramatic about the continuing spread of gambling and prostitution. He called the chairman of the Phoenix United Service Organizations [USO], a powerful young lawyer named Frank Snell, and warned Snell that he would declare Phoenix off limits if conditions did not change. Snell and the other local merchants were alarmed at the possibility of an off-limits order, given the town's widespread dependency on business with the military bases.

Snell contacted his friend Walter Bimson, the head of the major bank, some of the department-store owners, and other businessmen in town. An evening meeting was called to take place at the cardroom of the Adams Hotel. City council members were also invited although they were reluctant to have this outside body review and possibly alter their own patronage-linked system of appointments and rewards. This time the businessmen put the squeeze on the council members. More than seventy-five business leaders showed up at the Adams, where the arguments lasted through the night. By the early hours of the morning, the council had reluctantly agreed to remove the three key officials and replace them with candidates selected by the business leaders. The off-limits order was never implemented and the income from the base kept flowing into town. "It was," recalled participant Frank Snell, "kind of like a coup, and we called it 'The Cardroom Putsch.'"

The Cardroom Putsch in fact became a pivotal event in the creation of a more unified, growth-oriented power structure in the Phoenix area. There emerged an informal network of key power brokers who shaped the politics of the region and called on their less powerful counterparts in the financial, legal, manufacturing, and agricultural sectors to implement their short- and long-term objectives. That power structure was dominated by three individuals: Walter Bimson of the Valley National Bank, Frank Snell of the law firm of Snell and Wilmer, and Eugene Pulliam, publisher of the *Arizona Republic* and the *Phoenix Gazette*, the state's dominant papers.

By the late 1940s, the business community began to explore the notion of Phoenix as an emerging center of power in an expanding Southwest, although the city was still relatively undeveloped. Phoenix's dry, warm climate would attract not only tourists but new industry, particularly the fast-growing electronics industry whose specialized and well-paid work force would fit in well with the suburban life-style that had already been grafted onto the region's development.

Within a few years, the combination of government-expanded air travel and the mass marketing of air-conditioning necessary for the 115° summers, generated the city's initial rapid expansion. When Motorola's Edward Noble decided to relocate his company to Phoenix in 1949, he set a precedent that helped set in motion the extraordinary boom of the post–World War II period.

The Valley National Bank was a key institution in the emergence of Phoenix, and Walter Bimson was the man who helped put it all together. "Walter Bimson did more for the Valley than anybody else," Robert Goldwater said of his longtime friend. The bank became the dominant financial institution in the state, through which a number of interests met: agriculture (both cotton and cattle), tourism, real estate, construction, water, and industry (then settling in the valley.)

The Valley National Bank was formed in 1922 through a merger of the huge Gila Valley Bank and Trust Company, which dominated the copper-mining district, and the smaller Valley Bank of Phoenix. When Bimson took charge in 1933, the bank was able to survive and expand during the Great Depression by actively utilizing government programs, including the RFC. The bank borrowed money under RFC's liberal terms and then proceeded to loan that money to many of the bank's key clients in the valley.

Bimson, a Colorado boy who established his reputation as a vice-president of the Harris Trust and Savings Bank in Chicago, brought to the Phoenix business elite the enthusiasm of a new booster, with a feel for advertising his bank, his city, and the economic interests with which he was associated. Like Los Angeles' top boosters, Bimson sent Valley National Bank emissaries all over the country to attract new businesses, Air Force flying schools and new bases, branch factories, government housing, and aircraft firms. Although the bank remained primarily agriculture-oriented, it also moved into the tourism area. At one point in the early 1940s, the bank printed envelopes with a sticker reading "The Sun Is Shining Today in Arizona."

With Bimson at the helm, Valley National financed the creation of the Del Webb empire in its early years, smoothed the way for Motorola's relocation to the Valley of the Sun, helped to finance the Las Vegas Flamingo casino, and lent several million dollars to San Diego financier C. Arnholt Smith shortly before he was indicted and convicted for fraud and embezzlement. Through the 1950s and the 1960s, the bank made major loans to the key agribusiness operations throughout the state, eventually becoming the country's fifth largest agricultural lender. Developing an international presence, the bank made major loans in Mexico and Asia (primarily Japan), with more than 20 percent of its commercial loan portfolio going abroad by 1980. Loans also went to national companies that did business in Arizona and throughout the Rocky Mountain states. As the bank grew along with Phoenix, it projected itself as the dominant financial institution in the Southwest.

Bimson used the bank to intersect with other corporate interests, but much of his influence in Phoenix came through his informal working alliance with Snell (whose law firm represented the bank) and Pulliam. The three were constantly putting together coalitions "to get things done," as Snell put it.

Snell, cofounder of Phoenix's most powerful law firm, Snell and Wilmer, played a role in literally every aspect of the Phoenix political economy. Besides representing the bank, Snell and Wilmer were counsel for most of the large financial, industrial, agricultural, and media interests in the city. The firm represented Arizona in its major water battles and played a central role in Indian land and water claims. Snell himself sat on the board of directors of several key corporations and banks. He organized the group that eventually became the board of Arizona Public Service, the leading utility in the state, for which he served as first chairman of the board.

The third member of the informal network, Eugene Pulliam, inherited his position through the purchase of the *Arizona Republic* and *Phoenix Gazette* in 1946. Pulliam, the son of a Methodist frontier missionary, had acquired several midwestern papers before purchasing the Phoenix morning and afternoon papers. He quickly made Phoenix his home. Thanks to a forceful style and a newspaper that grew with the boom, Pulliam readily established himself as one of the men to reckon with in the Phoenix power structure. He made the *Republic* and *Gazette* his mouthpiece and, as one friendly power broker put it, "could build issues and men up, or tear them down."

The "old man," as he came to be known around the newsroom, had his quirks and was prone to arbitrary decisions that occasionally ruffled his colleagues in the business community.

Although the paper was overtly conservative and booster-oriented, occasionally some investigative work got through. It was just such an investigation into organized crime and the greyhound racing industry that led *Republic* reporter Don Bolles to his fateful appointment in the summer of 1976. Bolles's death (one year after Pulliam's) signified not only an end to the Pulliam era but a key moment in the changing nature of the Phoenix power structure.

THE TWO-TIER POWER STRUCTURE

Off a main street in downtown Phoenix, between the new Valley National Bank building and the seedier bars, restaurants, and shops that eventually lead to the barrios of the south side, sits a jewelry store with its marquee proclaiming that Rosenzweig Jewelers has been in existence for more than seventy-five years. Although no longer owned by the Rosenzweig family, the dapper septuagenarian Harry Rosenzweig still maintains his office on the second-floor balcony overlooking the store.

Rosenzweig is a short, swarthy man, with neatly trimmed gray hair slicked back and a big diamond pinky ring. On the wall there are pictures of Rosenzweig, his intimate friend Barry Goldwater, and a shot of the 1950 members of the Phoenix City Council, which included Goldwater and Rosenzweig.

In the midst of an interview, Rosenzweig receives a call from a friend who has been sick. Harry consoles him and suggests, "Hey, you want me to send you one of those pretty twenty-year old nurses?" He cracks a smile, guffaws, and hangs up the phone. Could this be the same man who has been characterized as one of the two or three most powerful men in the state, the alter ego of the senator from Arizona who made a bid for the United States presidency?

*   *   *

When the bomb went off in Don Bolles's car in the fall of 1976, it also appeared that it might blow the lid off the underside of Phoenix and reveal the power that a figure like Harry Rosenzweig had accumulated. A twenty-member journalistic task force led by *Newsday*'s Bob Greene was created by the newly formed Investigative Reporters and Editors (IRE) to expose the forces responsible for Bolles's killing. Although this task force threatened to expose the power structure and some of its seamier activities, IRE focused on a narrower, although substantial, subject: the penetration of organized crime into the state and its relation to some key corporate and political figures. The central figures in the IRE stories were the Goldwater brothers—Barry, the family politician and Robert, the family businessman—and their intimate friend, political ally, and business partner, Harry Rosenzweig.

The Goldwater brothers came from a wealthy Phoenix family that owned the largest local department store and held the second largest block of stock in the Valley National Bank. When Barry and Bob's father died, Walter Bimson approached their mother and asked the family to select a representative for the Valley National Bank board. Bob was chosen for the bank, while Barry was given work at the department store. Bob eventually returned to Goldwater's to replace his brother, who did not seem cut out to run his family's store. Instead, Barry went into politics to run as a candidate for the city council.

So reads the story of how the Goldwater brothers embarked on successful careers in the world of business and politics. But IRE was able to document another side to the Goldwater careers. Along with their close friend Harry Rosenzweig, the Goldwaters befriended, received favors from, and, in some cases, went into business with some of the best-known figures of organized crime. These mobster types had begun by the late 1940s to make investments throughout the Southwest.

Bob Goldwater was an early investor and founder of La Costa Country Club near San Clemente, California, along with former Cleveland mobster Moe Dalitz and convicted embezzler C. Arnholt Smith. The Goldwaters also got the exclusive franchise for their department store in Dalitz' Las Vegas hotel and casino, the Desert Inn. Bob Goldwater also helped form a restaurant chain called Hobo Joe's, which was granted a $3 million expansion loan from the Valley National Bank. One of the partners in the restaurant enterprise, Herbert Applegate, who also functioned as president and manager of the operation, was a longtime associate of Peter Licavoli, a Detroit mobster who had settled in Arizona. In the course of his reign as manager, Applegate diverted more than $15 million from the operation to finance fancy Las Vegas parties, to buy equipment and supplies that then vanished, and to subsidize his own extravagant life-style.

IRE also described Bob Goldwater's agricultural holdings (in conjunction with Joseph Martori, his partner in the Hobo Joe affair), which included an immense citrus ranch northeast of Phoenix. IRE reporters witnessed first-hand the ranch's large-scale use of undocumented Mexican workers, who were forced to live "amid their own excrement and garbage in orange-crate shelters, and fly-infested camps shielded from curious eyes by black plastic sheets hung on trees." The undocumented workers were paid as little as $5 a day, which was then further reduced by phony Social Security deductions.

Paralleling the Goldwater ties to mobsters and seamy labor practices were the activities of Harry Rosenzweig. Rosenzweig, who had been heavily involved in numerous Phoenix business-oriented "civic" activities, had engineered the revitalization of the statewide Republican party, a feat made possible by Barry Goldwater's ascendancy. IRE wrote of Rosenzweig's "power brokering in prostitution, gambling, and the police agencies responsible for enforcement of laws against them," as well as his ties with "mob-connected bookmakers and syndicate hoodlums who midwifed the birth of Las Vegas as the gambling capital of the nation."

The Goldwaters, Rosenzweig, and their friend Del Webb, the Phoenix builder who was also heavily involved in Las Vegas activities, were key members of the Phoenix elite, although they did not have the clout of Bimson or Snell. Webb was a loner and had little to do with the informal network that ran the city, but he still played an enormous role through his Vegas operations, his building and development schemes, and his presence on the Valley National Bank board. Complementing this underside to the Phoenix business world were the myriad of individuals and companies involved in outrageous, often illegal activities, especially land fraud. Many people such as Ned Warren, Kemper Marley, and Robert McCulloch functioned as individual entrepreneurs, who got involved in multimillion-dollar operations through political bribes, bulldozing tactics, and a business climate that encouraged rapid growth and development.

Arizona Governor Bruce Babbitt recalls the period in the late 1960s when development schemes and fraudulent operations were de rigueur in Arizona. Half the state legislators and county supervisors were on the take. The other half wanted in, ready at a moment's notice to give up some land or zoning restriction for a development package complete with a politician's "finder's fee." "Has the lid been on in Arizona? The answer is yes," Babbitt told "60 Minutes" shortly after Bolles's murder. "Anything that purports to be business is not to be critically examined. State government exists for the purpose of facilitating business deals."

Ned Warren, who was introduced to the Phoenix community by Harry Rosenzweig, became known as the Godfather of Arizona land fraud. He was a small-time con man who cleaned up in Arizona through an elaborate web of corporations that bought and sold land—and politicians. The common bond between many of these Warren-linked corporations was "bad paper," fraudulent contracts and mortgages used to swindle land buyers and investors of millions of dollars. Warren was put behind bars partly as a result of the outcry caused by Bolles's death and the murder of a onetime Warren lieutenant who was prepared to turn state's evidence against his former boss. Yet the conditions that generated the possibilities for land fraud still remained.

What had emerged was a two-tier power structure: the visible, dominant layer of banks, law firms, and corporations that laid the groundwork for growth and development and a favorable business climate; and a second, less visible layer linked to the enormous risk capital of organized crime and assorted petty-fraud operators involved in a variety of Arizona "leisure-time" investments.

The Bolles murder proved to be such an enormous embarrassment to the business and political elite that they immediately closed ranks after IRE departed and claimed that the "crime problem" was being solved.

Even the Bolles murder continued to remain largely a mystery, despite early arrests and convictions (later overturned). The early efforts of the *Republic* to look into the Bolles murder and its aftermath had been disbanded by 1979, as the paper went into a crisis beset by the suicide of a key editor, the resignation or squeezing out of some top investigative reporters, and a unionization effort by reporters.

In 1980 a report from the state attorney general's office only confirmed what the two-tier power structure had continually tried to downplay: namely; that "organized crime" in the state, whatever the form, remained powerful and continued to expand. The underbelly of the Arizona boom had become the flip side of this brassy, expanding Sun Belt success story.

LOOKING FOR AN ESTABLISHMENT

The Bolles murder and the increasing publicity surrounding the seamier side of Phoenix development took place precisely at a time when the Phoenix business community was witnessing the decline of the Charter Government Committee, its consensus-generating political organization. Despite the changes generated by the Cardroom Putsch, Phoenix city government during and shortly after World War II continued to be volatile, corrupt, and patronage-linked. Phoenix had continued to maintain its share of gambling, prostitution, and illegal bookmaking, and its system of contract awards left much to be desired in terms of competitive bidding.

In 1947 the Phoenix mayor, partly in an attempt to undercut this patronage system, created the Charter Review Committee, which was to propose changes in the election of council members and the appointment of the city manager. The local business community, much in the manner of the Cardroom Putsch leaders, rallied behind the charter-reform proposal in an effort to pass an initiative in the 1948 election to restructure the city government.

The following year the Charter Government Committee, led by the cream of the local business elite, was organized to select candidates for the city-council election, a slate that included Barry Goldwater and Harry Rosenzweig. The Charter Government candidates, with vigorous backing from Pulliam's *Republic* and *Gazette* and a considerable financial war chest, swept to victory. A new, non-Phoenix-based city manager was immediately installed, the former civic secretary of the Kansas City Chamber of Commerce.

Shortly after the 1949 election the Charter Government Committee formally disbanded, fearful of the charges it was attempting to "run things." Several of the business leaders felt the need to consolidate their victory and to create what would be a nonpartisan organization of the local elite that would sanction candidates. Through this process, they could maintain complete hegemony in the screening, as well as ultimate election, of candidates.

These were the furious growth years of the city. The actions of what became a city government run by the committee, such as land annexation, zoning policies, public-works expenditures, and an active Phoenix promotional program, strongly complemented the region's economic and population boom. The Charter Government Committee, which formed and disbanded before and after each municipal election, held a monopoly on political power from its formation in 1949 to the mid-1970s, during which time only two council candidates were able to win election without the committee's backing. The committee was particularly successful in recruiting middle- and upper-level business executives to run for office. In this way they provided a direct link between the informal business leadership, expressed through the old-boy network (and its darker underside), and city government.

By the mid-1970s, Charter Committee-run government was fast becoming an obsolete institution. The valley had grown by leaps and bounds, and groups like the committee had begun to lose their cohesiveness. By 1975, a probusiness city-council member, Margaret Hance, defied the committee's decision not to back her because, as she put it, she was a "woman, and therefore couldn't win." When Hance decided to run without charter's endorsement, her successful candidacy caused a significant split within the Charter Government Committee coalition.

Yet, significantly, the broad objectives of the financial and corporate powers still remained intact in the Hance administration. Hance, whose father was a vice-president of the Valley National Bank, also sat on the bank board while mayor, despite a potential conflict of interest. She was a strong growth advocate, constantly seeking out new industries and people to settle in the Phoenix area through favorable tax breaks, right-to-work laws, and development notions whereby the public sector acted as purchasing agent and risk-taker for private-sector investments.

Hance was, in many respects, a perfect complement to the city's business interests, yet her move to power came at a time when the informal and formal mechanisms of the old-boy network were in decline. By the mid-1970s, some of the network's participants had died or retired, and its power base—the banks, law firms, and local merchants—had grown and become more complex than during the heyday of the Charter Government Committee. It had become harder to recruit local businessmen to run for political office, since many of the top leadership of the growing corporations were obligated to spend so much time on their own corporate affairs.

Changes were also stimulated by the shift toward corporate and branch relocation in the Southwest. That trend, already set in motion in 1949 when Motorola arrived in Phoenix, had become a significant factor in altering the political economy of the region. Several large national corporations such as Greyhound or major subsidiaries such as Garrett Corporation's AiResearch moved corporate headquarters to Phoenix, aided by a new Arizona law tailored for Greyhound that gave a tax break to companies moving headquarters into the state. Their move paralleled the growth of a number of local companies, including Webb, Ramada Inn, and Southwestern Forest Products, which had become major national conglomerates in their own right.

The corporate shift to Phoenix had an effect on the power structure and the way things "got done" in Arizona. The local merchants, for example, played a lesser role in the power structure as national companies moved to acquire every major Phoenix department store, including Goldwater's. The new managers who ran these stores were not as involved as power brokers in the day-to-day life of the city. Similarly, the expansion of an organization like the Valley National Bank resulted in group management rather than a single man at the top. "I just can't do what a Bimson was able to do," the Valley National chairman Gil Bradley complained. "The bank has gotten too big, and I'm too tied up with it to spend the same kind of time that Walter did on Phoenix matters."

By the mid-1970s, many of the old and new Phoenix elite understood that a power vacuum had developed. In 1974, Frank Snell and Eugene Pulliam decided that with the demise of the old informal network, a new, slightly enlarged power grouping was needed. Using models like the Los Angeles Committee of Twenty-five, Snell and Pulliam organized a group they called the Phoenix Forty. The organization was not intended to be a decision-making body as such but a group of the top men in the region who would review major policy questions and intervene informally as individuals to make things happen. The group's key leaders were Snell and an up-and-coming young lawyer from Snell's firm, Richard Mallery; the new chairman of the Valley National Bank; and the president of Arizona Public Service.

The Phoenix Forty immediately plunged into the question of organized crime and the resulting bad publicity for Phoenix, which depended on its image to attract newcomers and to stimulate growth. When IRE arrived on the scene, the Forty successfully convinced the journalists' group that a distinction had to be made between the "good" anticrime power structure and "bad" organized-crime types and land-fraud operators such as Warren. Once IRE completed its work and departed, the Forty declared that the IRE stories were simply a case of sensational journalism.

As the repercussions from the Bolles killing began to fade, the Forty expanded their area of interest to include the key issues of water and transportation at once-a-month meetings. Despite the enormous power represented in the group, the Phoenix Forty, as Bradley put it, was not an "action" group as such and simply could not function the way the old informal network did in influencing overall regional policies. Not only had the city grown and corporations become larger and more diversified, but the functions of government, with its varieties of agencies, commissions, and public and quasi-public policy-making bodies, had vastly increased. Through the 1960s, governmental decision-making was crude and influenced by such direct pressures as a telephone call from one of the big three or a Ned Warren. By the late 1970s, that decision-making process had become more institutionalized, multiplying the number of people necessary to make the decisions.

Many of the middle-management figures drafted for policy involvement were not able to pull the kind of weight on a particular commission or board that a Walter Bimson or Frank Snell or some chief executive officer might have in the same situation. Consequently, a certain dispersal of power had resulted, and the power vacuum, despite even the presence of a Phoenix Forty, persisted.

By the late 1970s, some broader, intercorporate organizations were formed to try to change the situation. In the political sphere, several key corporate figures created the United for Arizona Committee, based on a similar organization in California. Its goal was to utilize, and to teach other companies throughout the state how to use, the new and potent Political Action Committee concept to finance candidates and educate employees on political matters. On the ideological level, many of the same executives behind United for Arizona hired Herman Kahn's Hudson Institute in 1976 to study Arizona's future. Called *Arizona Tomorrow*, the study, commissioned shortly before the expected arrival of the IRE team, would become, its sponsors hoped, a promotional and policy-generating document to provide a rationale for continuing growth and future economic development for the region.

Arizona Tomorrow celebrated Arizona's future, while discounting problems such as water supply. It proclaimed that Arizona's growth model "may indeed be a development prototype for post-industrial society," and that its life-style had become largely responsible "for redefining the very term *desert*," with the term now signifying an "appealing landscape, an attractive place to live, and a new kind of adult playground. . . . Desert living with air conditioning, water fountains, swimming pools—getting back to nature with a motorized houseboat on Lake Powell (itself a man-made lake), and going for an ocean swim in a man-made ocean are all contemporary examples of the marriage between life-style and technology."

The ideas put forth in *Arizona Tomorrow* inspired one of the report's sponsors, Richard Mallery, who saw himself as Frank Snell's heir apparent, to propose, along with one of Kahn's associates, Paul Bracken (the co-author of *Arizona Tomorrow*), a Phoenix-based Pacific basin institute. The institute would eventually contribute to turning Phoenix and Arizona into "a little Switzerland of the Americas," in Mallery's words. The immediate impetus for the creation of such an institute was the desire of Valley National Bank to expand its contacts, influence, and economic projects with Mexico. A Pacific basin institute with Mexican businessmen as central participants could facilitate such contacts. The idea that Phoenix could actually establish itself as a major Pacific basin center, somehow outpositioning California and Texas, seemed at best a long-term hope and probably just a pipe dream.

Yet Mallery symbolized the new hope of the Phoenix establishment—"the big thinker," as State Senator Alfredo Gutierrez characterized the ambitious lawyer. His dreams of a Pacific basin institute indicated a desire on the part of business and political leaders to see themselves and Phoenix as part of a national and international elite. Mallery also projected a sense of insecurity, a feeling that despite the dream, he was not really in touch with the big power centers of New York, California, or Texas. He fretted that he and his Phoenix were disregarded or misunderstood at best.

Mallery's feeling of insecurity reflected Phoenix's continuing dependence on corporate forces and decisions outside its control, such as the dependence of Arizona utilities on decisions by their California counterparts. Even the major national corporate powers such as Greyhound remained largely aloof from the Phoenix power structure, far more absorbed by their corporate, rather than regional, policy concerns. Mallery and his associates maintained their big hopes, transforming the projected rapid expansion of the region into dreams of empire. And, they told themselves, even the desert environment, with its limited rainfall, could not prevent the development steamroller from reaching its next—and greater—economic plateau.

WATERING THE DESERT

The emergency meeting was called to order. In perhaps its most important discussion to date, the Phoenix Forty gathered round to hear about President Carter's threat to veto funding for the Arizona business community's long-cherished Central Arizona Project. Interior Secretary Andrus was also making allocations of water contingent on a statewide groundwater reform. The problem was far too important to leave to the main water-lobbying organization, the Central Arizona Project Association (CAPA), or traditional arm-twisting methods. CAPA had become a bit rusty, a bit out of touch. The bankers, lawyers, utility executives, and others of the Phoenix Forty were needed, even those men who had done little previous lobbying on the issue. The project, after all, had historically been the great issue of the establishment, and these corporate leaders had no intention of abandoning the project, despite major changes in its focus and purpose.

Water, they knew, had always been the key resource in the Southwest. More than two thousand years ago, the Hohokam learned through a sophisticated system of irrigation ditches and canals that tapped the turbulent waters of the Salt River how to practice agriculture in the valley. Many of the early Anglo settlers in the Salt River Valley used the old canal systems of the Hohokam, but they soon were replaced by large farms that pumped groundwater. The new dominant farmer class was "true to the aggressive values [of] Anglo-American society," as one study on Arizona water practices put it, a society that "struggled against the dictates of the environment and increasingly sought to adapt the environment to the purposes of the society."

By the turn of the century those central Arizona farmers who had relied on groundwater pumps discovered that the existing technology was inefficient and the water supply uneconomic. The situation was compounded by a severe drought in the late 1890s that affected the entire Southwest. The Phoenix farmers realized they needed a water-storage facility, a project that required far more capital than the local farmers could generate on their own. Thus, the 1902 Reclamation Act was a godsend.

In 1903, Congress authorized the Salt River Project, the government's first large multipurpose project, which allowed valley farmers to regulate the flow of the Salt and Verde rivers and create storage basins to allow for an inexpensive and plentiful supply. The project also foreshadowed further settlement and subdivision in the valley, a prospect favored by the railroads, which were contributors to the National Irrigation Movement.

Valley landowners, organized into the Water Users Association, created a structure in which each acre pledged as collateral for Salt River Project loans entitled its owner to one vote in project elections. That "one acre, one vote" formula, favoring large landowners, lasted more than sixty years and was only struck down by the United States Court of Appeals in 1979 after public-interest lawyers successfully argued that the project had become increasingly an urban-related project that required a "one man, one vote" method of representation. That decision, however, was reversed by the Supreme Court two years later.

By the 1940s, the agriculture-dominated Salt River Project had become linked to a number of other interests, including mining, utilities, and urban real estate. Unlike the Bureau of Reclamation, the project maintained friendly relations with its private-sector competitors. During the 1960s, the project, expanding its role in power generation, became linked to the western utilities' Grand Plan projects such as Four Corners, Mojave, and the Navajo generating station near Page. The power generation aspect of the Salt River Project not only financed the water-storage and delivery components favoring valley farmers but also paved the way for the conversion of irrigated cropland into urban subdivision.

The developing relationship between agribusiness and urban-development forces was the key to the changing fortunes of the state's most celebrated water project, the Central Arizona Project. That project's origins dated back to the late 1930s and early 1940s, when the state's agricultural interests faced a crisis due to a massive drought that had caused Arizona's farmers to rely heavily on groundwater withdrawals to maintain adequate water supplies for their irrigated crop production. Fearful of declining groundwater levels, the state's key economic interests, led by the farmers, mining interests, and bankers, decided to bury their long-standing dispute with the other Colorado basin states, ratify the 1922 compact, and draft legislation to acquire Arizona's share of the Colorado.

Support for the Central Arizona Project among Arizona's business and political elite was dogma. Every major political or business figure in the state joined the fight at one point or another. A generation of leaders, particularly in the Phoenix area, were weaned on the notion that project water was crucial to Arizona development. Arizona business interests were particularly sensitive to the notion that the state's postwar boom would be short-lived because of a lack of water. When *Life* magazine published a pictorial essay on Arizona in August 1951 that depicted desert lands cracked by drought and lined with the skulls of dead cattle, one eastern investment company canceled a $3 million acquisition of mortgage notes on a Phoenix subdivision. Bimson then immediately mailed a five-page letter to eastern insurance companies, banks, and bond houses, declaring, "There need be no fear that the shortage of water, either now or in the future, would adversely affect the growth of our cities."

By the late 1950s, it was becoming clear that the original rationale behind the Central Arizona Project was no longer compelling. The process of urban conversion of agricultural lands had begun to wind its way through central Arizona. Farmers sold parts or all of their land and water rights to land developers who then sought to convert the cropland into real estate developments.

The shift of agricultural land to urban development undercut the project lobby's arguments for the need to transfer Colorado water to the central part of the state for irrigated agriculture. In June 1959 the CAPA created a special committee to "take a fresh look at the CAP plan in light of the changing circumstances," as director Rich Johnson wrote. The committee, headed by First National Bank chairman Sherman Hazeltine, concluded that urban development and greater industrial activity in the cities increased rather than lessened the need for the water. "It is apparent that although the project was originally conceived almost entirely as an agricultural irrigation development," one CAPA leader told the press, "a substantial portion of Arizona's share of the river may find its ultimate usage in direct support of expanding urban and industrial segments."

Under the leadership of H.S. Raymond, the new president of CAPA and the head of the Boswell land interests in Arizona, project supporters now emphasized the twin benefits of urban and agricultural development, with more and more emphasis on "m & i" (municipal and industrial) aspects of the plan. "Wherever a cow pasture or citrus grove is converted into a residential subdivision," a vice-president of Valley National wrote in 1962 on the conversion theme, "there is both a saving in water and a tremendous property increase."

By the early 1960s, urban developers and financiers had become wedded to the notion of an unlimited water supply making possible future investments. Since Phoenix existed in a desert environment, it was crucial for the developers to promote the idea that new residents could luxuriate in water-lush, rather than water-scarce, surroundings. So much of the "Arizona life-style," a crucial part of the Sun Belt appeal, was focused on water—and its availability. Everywhere in Phoenix were reminders that water was plentiful: fountains; sprinklers; rich, dark-green bermuda grass; and, of course, lakes. Artificial lakes created by the vast array of dams and irrigation projects were located throughout central Arizona and developers liked to boast that Arizona had more registered boats than any other state in the country.

For the growing need of m & i water, CAPA called in the Bureau of Reclamation to justify the project. The bureau issued a report, financed by an Arizona water agency, that found that without Colorado water, urban use in Arizona would retire agricultural lands at far too rapid a pace. Such a shift would ultimately be reflected in reduced urban growth, because of a lack of an agricultural base to support it. Consequently, according to the logic of the report, water would be needed for both uses.

In 1963 a team of University of Arizona economists decided to look into the water issue as a new round of project hearings and congressional maneuvers began. According to William Martin, a member of the team, it started from the conventional assumption that it was necessary to pump more water into the state. During the next few years, the team interviewed one-quarter of all the farmers of the state, did a cost analysis of the new project plan in relation to other sources of water (such as groundwater pumping), and looked at the overall nature of Arizona agriculture and the conversion process to urban lands. In 1967 it published its initial findings in a magazine article questioning the cost effectiveness of the project and some of the assumptions underlying the plan.

The reaction was extraordinary. "The politicians just didn't want to hear it," Martin recalled. "It seemed so far out. After you've spent thirty years trying to get a project authorized you don't want some upstart economist telling you it's not right. There were front page editorials suggesting that me and my colleagues were double agents from California."

Six years later, the University of Arizona group published their complete findings. Arizona's farmers, the team wrote, tended to use the existing water supply as quickly and inefficiently as possible. The farmers feared either the possibility of future shortages or that someone else—perhaps the copper companies, Indians, or urban interests—would successfully lay claim to the water unless the farmers claimed the water first through the "first in right, first in time" system. Since agriculture utilized about 90 percent of the supply, their practices had created a cycle wherein rapid and inefficient use created a fear of shortage, which in turn led to the push for new supplies.

By the late 1960s and early 1970s, the water-use cycle had gotten out of hand. The need for a new supply source, encompassed by the latest project proposal, raised the amount of subsidization to new and incredibly high levels. The University of Arizona study suggested that some kind of public or governmental intervention would be necessary either to shift agriculture to less water-intensive crops or to retire some agricultural lands in an orderly manner.

The water issue, it concluded, was a management or institutional problem, not simply a question of "supply."

The 1973 University of Arizona report found a far more receptive audience than did the initial critique six years earlier. Despite the passage of Central Arizona Project legislation in 1968, organized opposition had surfaced in Arizona, bolstered in part by the growing national environmental movement. Critics focused on the project's cost, which had escalated from the original estimate of $823 million in 1968 to a 1980 Bureau of Reclamation estimate of $1.9 billion. The bureau figures, economist Tom Powers wrote, were themselves far too low, since they failed to account for numerous hidden subsidies based on the low or nonexistent interest rates for repayment of the capital costs of the project. Powers calculated hidden subsidies at an additional $5.5 billion.

By the late 1970s, the most troublesome opponents of the project were not the environmentalists, academics, or angry taxpayers but the Yavapai Indian tribe located at the Fort McDowell reservation, twenty-five miles northeast of Phoenix. This reservation, four miles wide and ten miles long, had been established in 1903 for the Yavapai tribe. The Yavapai, like several of their southwestern counterparts, had been frequently relocated in the late nineteenth century. Their own forced "March of Tears" led to their imprisonment at San Carlos for about twenty-five years. Over the years a number of Yavapai had returned to their ancestral lands and settled on the hills overlooking McDowell. When the reservation was set up by executive order, the order basically recognized the existing remigration.

From the establishment of the Fort McDowell reservation, the Yavapai had to fight to retain their lands. After completion of the Roosevelt Dam in 1911, continuous attempts were made by valley farmers to transfer the Yavapai and to gain access to Fort McDowell land and water rights. Thanks to the leadership of Dr. Carlos Montezuma, a Yavapai Indian and surgeon who had settled in Chicago but returned to the reservation in the last years of his life, the tribe was able to resist efforts to acquire the Indian lands.

The Central Arizona Project plans raised once again the issue of access to the lands of the Yavapai reservation. They included the Orme Dam, a multipurpose flood-control dam that would inundate twenty-five miles of this stretch of Sonoran desert, create a large lake available for boating and other recreational purposes, and flood the Yavapai reservation.

The Orme Dam had been one of the features added to the plans in order to meet urban as well as agricultural interests. Phoenix had a history of flooding problems, which had been compounded by the city's helter-skelter development (including the construction of new subdivisions on floodplains and the building of bridges in precarious locations). The flood situation was exacerbated by the Salt River Project's storage basins, which were kept as full as possible in normal periods to offset potential drought problems for the farmers. The prodevelopment bias of public officials during the mid-1960s was such that the Holly Acres development to the west of the city was approved despite a warning from the county flood-control engineer that the proposed subdivision was located within the floodplain of the Gila River. When Holly Acres flooded in February 1980,

Arizona's water lobbyists blamed the problem on the Yavapai resistance to the Orme Dam.

During those same 1980 floods, the *Arizona Republic*'s chief editorial writer, Pat Murphy, launched a campaign to try to force the federal government to act on Orme Dam despite the Indian opposition. The *Republic* and the water lobby vowed to break the resistance of the Indians and "reeducate them," as one task-force group described its effort. The Yavapai held firm, "uneducated" and unsympathetic to the lure of big bucks that the water lobbyists waved in their face. The water lobbyists contended that such funds would allow the Indians to "build a marina, a restaurant, perhaps even a motel for the use of recreation seekers," as a Murphy editorial declared. But the unreconstructed Indians held out. One elder of the tribe answered the frustrated water lobbyists: "If Phoenix wants so much water, why don't they move to the ocean!"

PUMPING DOWN

The Central Arizona Project's shifting fortunes brought into perspective another critical feature of the Arizona water situation—the declining groundwater supply. Since the turn of the century, Arizona farmers had been pumping from ever greater depths as the technology improved and the amount of water withdrawn exceeded the amount replenished by rainfall. By the 1930s, these overdrafts had become a serious problem. Part of the rationale for the Central Arizona Project was to substitute Colorado River water for water pumped out of the ground. By the late 1970s, the overdraft had become so severe that the groundwater issue supplanted even Orme Dam as the main concern of the state's business and political community.

The implications of the groundwater overdraft were both immediate and long-term. By the mid-1970s, big gaps or fissures caused by the declining groundwater tables had appeared in the land. The continuing practices of the farmers, combined with the growing needs of the cities and mines, could seriously affect the groundwater supply to the point where more severe and even permanent water shortages might result. The additional supply from the Arizona project would only reduce the current overdraft in central Arizona by two-thirds, thereby postponing rather than eliminating the problem.

The use and disposition of groundwater had been monopolized by agricultural interests through outdated practices and legislative codes. Groundwater bills passed in 1948 and the early 1950s codified this monopoly while only producing stopgap measures designed to slow the overdraft. The courts sustained agriculture's position by ruling that groundwater was not a public resource and not subject to the doctrine of prior appropriation, which applied to surface water. The court defined groundwater as a private property right, a situation complicated by the fact that groundwater did not limit itself to property ownership boundaries. Therefore, an owner who pumped the groundwater first might take groundwater from beneath adjacent property as well.

The coalition of agribusiness, the mine owners, the financial community, and various urban interests that had for years held together to support the Central Arizona Project began to show signs of strain over the groundwater issue. Those strains turned into active warfare after the Farmers Investment Company (FICO) case in 1976. FICO owned several hundred acres of irrigated land in an area where several large copper mining companies and the city of Tucson pumped groundwater transported to the mines and the city. FICO went to court and won. The court ruled that since FICO, the property owner, was able to show that the pumping was taking place in a "critical groundwater area" without a reasonably safe supply for agriculture, the pumping and transporting of the groundwater by the mines and Tucson for use outside the critical groundwater area was illegal.

After the FICO ruling, the mining interests teamed up with municipal officials to create a coalition against the farmers. The lawyer for the Anaconda and Amax interests in Arizona told the press, "The farmer leases the land from the state at a cheap rate, plus he gets power breaks, a cheap tax rate, government subsidies. He's pumping me dry; he's pumping the state dry; and when he's got that done, he's going to move to La Jolla and raise martinis."

The farmers resisted yielding their monopoly rights. They knew they could continue their irrigated farming with subsidized water until the markets for their products declined. Certain Arizona crops were already being undercut by a stronger and equally well subsidized California agribusiness. In the event of declining markets, the farmers could sell their land and precious water rights to developers as the urban sprawl expanded throughout central Arizona. Water rights could also be sold to the revived mining industry.

With the pressure from Carter's Interior Department to come up with a groundwater reform plan before receiving any project allocations and the beginning of open warfare between old allies, the Arizona legislature created the Groundwater Management Study Commission in 1977. The commission, led by a young former Utahan, Kathy Ferris, was composed of members appointed by the legislature from the ranks of agribusiness and mining, a labor official, an Indian, and several municipal representatives. Ferris had while she was attending the University of Utah law school worked with Utah Governor Calvin Rampton. Ferris' technical experience gave her credibility among Arizona's politicians and lobbyists that landed her the job as executive director of the groundwater commission. To the politicians, Ferris was an unknown quantity. Unlike Rampton or most others involved in the water industry, Ferris represented a new kind of public official, influenced by the mood for reform, conservation, and a rational use of existing resources rather than the big water project.

Ferris and commission members immediately became embroiled in the growing conflict between the urban interests, the mines, Indians, and the farmers. Under the leadership of the municipal forces and the mines, the commission majority came up with an unusual package of reforms for the anticonservation, farmer-dominated state. The reforms called for "grandfathered rights" and "quantified rights" that would allow a new groundwatermanagement body to force the big agricultural users of groundwater and all other users to "quantify" the amount of water they used. That amount would then either remain stable (the grandfathered rights) or be reduced through conservation or "pro-rata reductions" (that is, an across-the-board reduction of users). The package also included provisions that would make it difficult for developers to acquire and convert agricultural land into urban subdivisions.

This mining-municipal coalition sprung these reforms at a commission retreat at Castle Hot Springs in the summer of 1979. "We were not ready for their move at Castle Hot Springs," recalled Bob Moore, the director of the Agribusiness Council, a coalition of the big farmers, equipment suppliers, processors, ranchers, and financial interests that had been set up to deal with the groundwater issue. "We didn't anticipate that they would have developed a scheme. We got kicked in the teeth and everywhere else you can get kicked."

But the agribusiness forces were not ready to give up. They approached the mining interests as compatible, "profit-oriented" businesses and, after a series of meetings at the Adams Hotel, tried to come up with a new, modified package. After some further maneuvering, with the cities and some of the mining interests holding fast on several areas of the reform package, a new proposal was worked out. The resulting compromise did provide management limits on the withdrawal of groundwater and used various conservation requirements to reduce the overall groundwater withdrawal. The compromise included what turned out to be the sleeper of the entire package: the prohibition of any urban development in areas where there was no assured water supply for at least a hundred years.

The new proposals eliminated the controversial quantified rights and pro-rata reduction components—a major plus for agribusiness. The farmers had complained that those measures were a form of "confiscation without compensation," but the cities argued in turn that those reforms were critical to bringing about conservation and breaking agriculture's monopoly over the pace of crop reductions and the price of the sale of land with its water rights. "The cities had been saying, 'By God, we're not going to buy one more farm [for the water under it],' but with these new proposals they're going to have to eat their words," proclaimed Bob Moore.

Nevertheless, the groundwater reform advocates had been able to salvage what for Arizona and the rest of the West was the seed of a revolutionary new approach to western water practices. With the threat of the Carter Interior Department holding back project allocations, the compromise proposal went through the state legislature with breakneck speed in June 1980 and was quickly signed into law by Bruce Babbitt. The core to the reforms was the existence of mandatory conservation procedures aimed at cutting back the profligate use of groundwater. A centralized groundwater management body was created to oversee the conservation measures to the year 2006, when the state would be allowed, if necessary, to purchase and retire specific amounts of lands for the use of groundwater. "In some ways it seems incredible that we got what we did," one water reformer remarked. "But we're still holding our breath."

No sooner had the reform measures passed, than some of the dominant water users started having second thoughts. The process accelerated in December 1980 when Secretary Andrus increased project allotments to several Indian tribes, thereby reducing the allotments for other users. By the winter of 1980 a number of developers had begun to gear up to eliminate the provision in the new law requiring the hundred-year water supply for new developments. The controversy over the "assured water supply" raised the issue that most fully characterized the new Phoenix: rapid, chaotic urban development; a development that had made Phoenix synonymous with explosive urban expansion in the Sun Belt.

THE SPREADING GROWTH

If you drive northeast past the Phoenix city limits, past Scottsdale, just south of the McDowell Mountains near the Yavapai reservation, you enter the central Arizona desert, with its saguaro cactus, piñon, and sagebrush dotting the red and brown terrain. About twelve miles down the road you come across a most incongruous spectacle: a giant white spout of water rising three hundred feet in the air, visible from miles away. This "snow white column of water," as the promo reads, is the centerpiece of the Fountain Hills subdivision, with its projected population of 40,000.

McCulloch Properties, the real estate subsidiary of the McCulloch Corporation, which has interests in oil, chain saws, and land, acquired this desert property in 1971. McCulloch was one of Arizona's unsavory land developers. He successfully developed the Lake Havasu project by purchasing at extraordinary bargain prices—greased by hefty campaign contributions and "gifts" to state legislators—state lands bordering on the artificial lake created behind the Powell Dam, near the California-Arizona border. With the Fountain Hills development, McCulloch acquired the necessary permits and licenses to uproot the terrain, to put in an artificial lake and to rip out the desert growth for the "green" look of a new subdivision. McCulloch's bulldozers leveled the land, causing one planning commissioner to complain that McCulloch did not need a zoning permit but a permit to open a mine. "You people," the commissioner said of the McCulloch group, "have committed the biggest rape of the earth I've ever seen."

The heart of the development was the Fountain. Situated in the middle of a thirty-acre artificial lake, the fountain shoots off a spray powered by the three giant turbine pumps located in the power station next to the lake, belching out seven thousand gallons of water per minute, every fifteen minutes on the hour. Monstrous symbol that it is, the Fountain, like McCulloch's reconstruction of London Bridge for his Lake Havasu project, served as a "unique landmark" for the developer.

Yet the Fountain's ultimate meaning lies in the incongruity of the situation. Like much of the Phoenix development package, the McCulloch subdivision offered new settlers the luxuries of the Arizona life-style while attempting to convince them that they were located somewhere else than where they actually were—in the midst of the great southwestern Sonoran desert.

Fountain Hills was the rule rather than the exception to Phoenix development. The signs of that development in 1980 were everywhere as the city oozed with new planned communities and subdivisions. Leisure World–Golden Hills, Sun City, McCormick Ranch, Carefree, Dreamland Village—the names of the projects match their promo. "Your Place in the Sun for a Carefree Life-style"; "Why Wait? Move into the Best Years of Your Life"; "The Excitement is Here and the Dust Hasn't Even Settled"; "Some Call It a Holiday. You Can Call It Home"; "Do It Now Before the Rest of the World Finds Out."

The growth of these new subdivisions parallels Phoenix's extraordinary population growth in the 1960s and 1970s. By 1980 there were forty-three different development projects either approved or under construction that would occupy 125,000 acres of land with a projected population of eight hundred thousand. The people who settle in the new subdivisions are largely from out of state. By 1980 more than one hundred thousand people were moving to Phoenix each year; that is, nearly 10 percent of the entire regional population settled in Phoenix annually.

The granddaddy of the new subdivisions, Del Webb's Sun City, was in many ways a model for a number of the planned communities now sprinkled throughout the Salt River Valley. According to Owen Childress, a Webb vice-president, Sun City grew out of company interest in Youngtown, a planned retirement community outside Phoenix that had been featured on the television show "Omnibus." The Webb company had already established a housing and development division but had never previously explored the possibility of a planned community. After the "Omnibus" show, the company undertook some market surveys, explored different location possibilities in Florida and southern California as well as Phoenix, and then decided to go ahead in 1959.

Webb acquired thousands of acres of land in an area near Youngtown from the cotton-growing J. G. Boswell Company which led to the partnership that established the Sun City development. Webb created a new subsidiary, the Del Webb Development Company (DEVCO), 49 percent owned by Boswell. DEVCO proceeded to transform the cotton fields into new housing subdivisions with grassy medians between paved roads, artificial lakes, golf course, recreation centers, banks, shopping centers, restaurants, and other features that constituted an urbanized enclave amid agricultural lands.

During the first several years of the Sun City operation, Webb attempted to attract a fairly broad population—from lower middle-income retirees who might swing a deal through federal government financing, to wealthier seniors who financed their purchase out of pocket. When sales began to decline by 1965, a major shakeup occurred within the company, and a new strategy and executive group emerged as a consequence.

Webb turned away from its broad-based income-group "concept" to exclusive upper-middle income retirees who would settle in what was now characterized as "comfortable surroundings with amenities," as one Webb executive put it. Promotional campaigns were revised and geared toward golfing, hunting, and fishing periodicals with high demographics. Several new golf courses and recreation facilities were established and an exclusive "country club" was formed. A hospital well endowed by the J. G. Boswell Foundation and designed primarily to serve the needs of Sun Citians was also established. New roads were built, and a wall was constructed on the two sides of the main street that intersected the development and led to the freeway about six miles to the east. Sun City had an exclusive Anglo, largely midwestern, over-fifty population. The Project had become by the 1980s its own self-contained, walled-in city.

Sun City was a major success for Webb. Within twenty years Webb had built on all the land originally acquired in 1959 and had convinced forty-eight thousand people to migrate and settle in the development. By the late 1970s the project's success inspired the giant developer to purchase more cotton lands from Boswell for yet another project, adjoining the original development. Sun City West opened its doors in 1978. More than three thousand houses were purchased within the first several months of operation. Eventually, the Webb-Boswell interests hoped Sun City West would attract seventy thousand new immigrants to the area within a period of fifteen years. Profit margins for Sun City could well double and even triple earlier Sun City figures.

The consequences of creating this minicity on the politics and life-style of the region have been extraordinary. Sun Citians have become an important economic and political force in the Phoenix area. Banks proudly declare that the well-to-do migrants of Sun City have more money (1 billion in 1978) on deposit than any single group in the valley.

Since Sun Citians also vote, the legislature and county supervisors have become sprinkled with conservative to extremely right-wing Sun City representatives who stand firm against the forces of fiscal irresponsibility and godless Communism. Sun Citians form a strong voting bloc, affecting statewide elections and particular local issues. The area surrounding Sun City consists of large-scale citrus and cotton ranches worked largely by the undocumented migrants from Mexico who live in cardboard shacks—a severe contrast with the affluent Sun City environment. When local elections are held concerning school bonds or other services desperately needed by the farm labor residents, Sun City voters consistently reject such measures, invoking the conservative credo, "I won't pay a dime for those illegal aliens." The Boswell Memorial Hospital refused to accept those who could not pay for their services—that is, undocumented workers. A law suit was filed in 1977 against the hospital when an undocumented worker lost his arm after being refused service. The result was a $200,000 judgment against Boswell Hospital.

The Webb–Sun City bloc has not consistently held together. Early Sun City residents disapproved of Webb's expansion policies, feeling, as several longtime residents put it, that the growing development undermined the feeling of community that had existed initially. Residents also complained of the cheaper construction of the prefab houses and the general decline in housing stock despite the substantial increase in sale prices.

Ironically, the one problem area consistently raised by Sun City residents is future growth in the area. The continuing push for development and population growth, so strongly advocated by developers and other members of the Phoenix power structure, is not necessarily endorsed by residents of the new developments. New inmigrants, once settled, frequently share with a number of other Phoenix constituents a strong dislike for the unending growth spiral. Polls conducted during the 1970s that appeared in the progrowth *Republic* pointed to an overwhelmingly antidevelopment majority that cut across class lines from the barrios on the south side to the working-class communities on the west, and the middle-class communities and planned subdivisions sprinkled throughout the valley.

In many ways, the growth explosion of the 1970s has turned Phoenix into a scarred battlefield. The Phoenix city limits continued to stretch in all directions, reaching 325 square miles by 1980. Annexation, as one official from the Arizona Public Service declared, inevitably stimulates growth. Since services have to be provided, the land becomes *ipso facto* more appealing to developer interests. With the leapfrogging of one site to the next by developers, the population spreads in every direction and without any planning logic behind the geography of annexation and development.

Sprawl might well be a misnomer for such a pattern. The urban expansion process has no center, no ecological boundary. The urban cancer notion works better: Phoenix can be seen, as one critic put it, as a "slurb infestation." "I guess what we call sprawl, they call Arizona life-style," *Arizona Republic* publisher "Duke" Tulley, a newcomer to the Phoenix power structure, declared.

Although a large constituency did exist for stopping the growth machine, no organized political force has allied itself with such subversive notions. Mayor Hance spoke of the "constitutional right to relocate," and much of the Phoenix power structure believes strongly in the Sun Belt, particularly in relation to the promotional, tourist, immigrant-attracting angle of climate. When it rains in Phoenix, corporate and financial executives constantly fret that such unnatural acts spoil the region's most attractive selling point. Nevertheless, optimism reigns even with changing weather patterns. "After all," one savings-and-loan executive smugly declared to an out-of-state reporter, "our rain becomes their blizzards."

HOPE WITHOUT HOPE: POLITICS IN THE FACE OF THE "OVERWHELMING MARKET"

By the late 1970s, nothing seemed able to stop the growth machine—"our economic engine," as the chairman of the Valley National Bank affectionately called it. The framework for political debate in the state had been defined by various conservative and progrowth positions staked out by the two parties.

From the period prior to statehood, up through World War II, Arizona had been dominated by the Democratic party. The party was deeply divided between a labor-progressive wing, which drew its basic support from the mining towns, and a conservative faction, dominated by the Three Cs of copper, cattle, and cotton. Although the prolabor forces maintained a strong influence in the statehouse, particularly during the popular reign of Governor Sidney Osborn (1941–1948), the conservative faction held power in the state legislature, drawing strength from gerrymandered rural districts and key committee posts in the state senate and house. Arizona's most powerful politician, its longtime senator Carl Hayden, directly articulated the interests of the Three Cs, although he also maintained an aura of popularity and "untouchability" through his accumulated senatorial seniority (he was chairman of the Senate Appropriations Committee for fourteen years) and his effective use of geographically based pork-barrel politics that allowed the senator to obtain dams, roads, air bases, and power facilities for Arizona.

After World War II the state began to change economically and politically. Through the 1950s and 1960s, mining declined in importance, as did the mining work force and the tightly knit constituency that provided the glue for the labor-progressive political wing of the Democratic party. The new immigrants to the state, many of whom worked in the new electronics and high-technology industries of Phoenix and Tucson, considered themselves middle class in economic terms and consumerist, rather than class-conscious, in orientation. They favored the growth policies of the new business-dominated urban coalitions such as the Charter Government Committee and tended to mistrust trade unions after the highly charged right-to-work campaigns of the late 1940s. They became the new suburban-based constituency of a rapidly growing Republican party, which began in the 1950s to undercut the long-entrenched one-party system in the state.

In 1952 Charter Government–backed city-council member Barry Goldwater decided to run for the United States Senate against incumbent Ernest McFarland, a New Dealer who was then Senate majority leader. Goldwater was a novice in politics. Prior to his city-council election, according to Nicholas Udall, he was considered a "young merchant prince who liked to get his picture taken and fly airplanes." Goldwater's own Republican party registration had been decided by a flip of the coin between himself and his brother Bob. The brothers had decided after their father died that they would register with different parties in order to serve their store's interests most effectively.

By 1952 the Democratic party appeared vulnerable. Goldwater was able to raise more than $30,000 for his campaign—including $5,000 from the national Republican party, another $5,000 from a convicted labor racketeer who would later be murdered gangland style for his running afoul of Las Vegas interests, another $3,000 from H. L. Hunt, and $2,500 from a wealthy Texas oilman. With his ample funds and an effective campaign that mixed conservative positions on social legislation with appeals to Mexican and Indian support, Goldwater squeaked through in the same year in which Arizona voted for a Republican for president for the first time.

The 1952 Goldwater election became a turning point in state politics, leading to the emergence of a powerful Republican establishment headed by Goldwater, state party chairman Harry Rosenzweig, and their political allies Richard Kleindienst and Robert Mardian, both of whom were convicted for Watergate-related activities. The shift to the Republicans coincided with the continuing economic and demographic changes in the state related to the growth of Phoenix, the new planned subdivisions, and an increasing number of retirement communities.

The 1974 election, influenced as it was by Watergate, Nixon's resignation, and the disgrace of Kleindienst and Mardian, appeared to loosen the strong grip of the Republican party on statewide politics. One of the bright new faces for the Democrats was a young, reform-minded lawyer who entered politics by running for state attorney general. Bruce Babbitt came from old and powerful Arizona stock. His family had been influential in the economic and political affairs of Flagstaff in northern Arizona for three generations by providing commercial links with northern Arizona Indian tribes through the Babbitt Brothers' Navajo Trading Posts.

Although heir to a prosperous family business, young Babbitt saw himself as something of an outsider, shifting from a passion for geology to a strong liberal, if not radical, advocate at law school. "I remember how Bruce joined our rap sessions, and talked about subverting the system and using environmentally inspired law suits," one fellow law student recalled.

After graduation, Babbitt joined the law firm of Brown, Vlassis and Bain, which had strong ties to the Democratic party. Babbitt campaigned and won election for attorney general as a reformer concerned with land fraud and syndicate crimes, appealing to a white-collar constituency of recent inmigrants who, unlike the previous generation of inmigrants, worried about the underside of the growth machine. They liked Babbitt's Mr. Clean image, an image strengthened by the new attorney general's investigation and prosecution in the Ned Warren case and the aftermath of the Don Bolles murder (although two of Babbitt's convictions in the Bolles case were later thrown out by the Arizona Supreme Court).

By 1977 the attorney general appeared to have a bright political future. Talk began of a Babbitt run for the Senate in 1980 or 1982, but through a series of unexpected events, the Flagstaff heir found himself in the governor's chair. Shortly after Governor Raul Castro had been appointed ambassador to Argentina, his replacement, Lieutenant Governor Wesley Bolin, an older conservative Democrat who was well liked and well connected to the state's leading business interests, had a heart attack and died. By state law Bruce Babbitt was next in line.

To remain in office Babbitt, who faced election the following year, had his political work cut out for him. As the new Governor, Babbitt cultivated the popular western political image of the youthful social liberal but fiscal conservative. He was a media-wise environment-conscious but prodevelopment (with constraints) politician who defied political labels. He emphasized his "Arizonian" qualities: he was a lover of the outdoors, especially the desert; author of a book on the Grand Canyon; a hiker; a jogger; and a member of a "pioneer" family. Running against a right-wing car salesman whom even conservative business leaders had trouble supporting, Babbitt won election as a full-fledged governor.

Babbitt continued to try to avoid the "liberal" tag, despite his early reform-minded appeal to certain constituencies. Like Jerry Brown and other Democratic western governors of the 1970s, Babbitt liked to see himself as an anticonstituency politician—someone who managed to obtain the support of diverse constituencies without committing himself to their particular needs or interests. Babbitt saw state government as a neutral force, reconciling diverse, possibly antagonistic, interests and projecting a measure of control over the growth forces. To development-oriented business interests, the new governor looked suspiciously like a public-sector activist, a possible no-growther. "Many of these people," Babbitt said of such critics, "saw Arizona as the last stronghold of rugged individualism, with government as a socialist bureaucracy out to destroy free enterprise." Their notion of free enterprise, according to Babbitt, meant a developer taking an elected official out to lunch and obtaining his zoning variance.

The apparent contradiction between an antigovernment "rugged individualism" political ideology and Arizona's long-standing reliance on federal expenditures and subsidies, epitomized by the multibillion-dollar Central Arizona Project, never phased conservative Arizona politicians. Elected officials such as Barry Goldwater loved to invoke the name of Arizona's pioneers, who had apparently defied nature and the federal government in carving out their empire. This myth was cherished and nurtured by the *Arizona Republic* and much of the Phoenix establishment.

Babbitt, as an anticonstituent politician, also evoked pioneer mythology but hinted that the state needed to play a modest yet significant role in directing Arizona development. Arizona, in Babbitt's view, had to adjust its ideological blinders to accommodate some form of private- and public-sector partnership—

perhaps a modest version of Pat Brown's old coalition—in order to control the enormous expansion of the state and its major metropolis. During the campaign, for example, Babbitt talked of the need for protecting state lands from speculators. After his election, Babbitt appointed a committee to develop a program to reconcile apparently contradictory interests. The committee had strong developer and progrowth representation, led by its chairman Gary Driggs, head of Western Savings and Loan, a major Phoenix developer. Driggs, like Richard Mallery, symbolized the new corporate leadership of Phoenix, aware of Phoenix's emerging national reputation as a fast-growing Sun Belt center and comfortable with Bruce Babbitt's modern-sounding partnership approach. Driggs's committee issued a report criticizing earlier sales of state lands for their low price tags. The problem, the commission declared, was the rip-off of public land, not development per se. Underlying that critique was an attempt to set the stage for lifting the existing limits on sale and lease of state lands. The leases had been limited to rural commerce, such as grazing or running country stores. Driggs and his committee argued that urban-development leases would bring in a lot more money.

What Driggs, Babbitt, Mallery, and others had in mind were new "planned" developments—perhaps what one developer called a "planned hometown of the future" to be built on twenty thousand acres of the state-owned land north of Phoenix. Mallery, as business' "big thinker", projected a partnership between the state and private industry regarding these planned communities, with leasing funds going toward a stronger university system. This arrangement, in turn, could produce the high-level managers, technicians, and skilled personnel to make Phoenix and Arizona competitive with other major centers of power. Gary Driggs supported the idea of the state mediating and underwriting future development. The developer-financier, from an influential Mormon family in Mesa, also saw the market as the ultimate determinant, the real linchpin of Arizona's and Phoenix's future expansion. And it was Driggs's rather than Mallery's vision that spoke to corporate Phoenix's understanding of its region's place in the Sun Belt.

The market, stated Driggs, would dominate Phoenix's future and lead it inevitably to more development and expansion. "The market is overwhelming and will overwhelm all in its path," Driggs declared, pointing to maps of state lands and future developer plans. "It's just what the people want. Popular enterprise is just following the popular will," he continued.

He moved his pointer around the maps, to the north, to the east, demonstrating an even larger and expansive Greater Phoenix. "Who will be the next Del Webb?" he asked rhetorically. "You don't need state planning. The market does its own planning. Free enterprise prevails! That's what's really happening."

Phoenix: free enterprise in the saddle, the market as king. Even the most fervent free-enterprise advocate and Sun Belt enthusiast worried about the boom collapsing, the bottom falling out. Developments have peaked in Phoenix, as elsewhere in the southwest, and then dramatically declined, only to peak again. The fear of collapse has become the hidden side of Sun Belt optimism. "This has always been boom-and-bust country and it always will be," declared former Arizona State Lands commissioner Andrew Bettwy. "We found silver and built mining towns with opera houses, the works; when the silver went, so did they. Maybe the next bust will come when the water's gone. In the meantime, we'll eat the chicken today, and have the feathers tomorrow."

But the developers, corporate and financial leaders, partnership advocates, free-enterprise believers, water lobbyists, and urban-growth promoters all continue to look for more of the same, as if they believe it can never end, that their empire in the desert will grow as wide as the desert itself. Phoenix is becoming southwestern capitalism's quest for immortality, creating something profitable out of nothing, something that appears vast and limitless, defying the sun, the land, and all the elements of an apparently redeemable nature.

If you watch the Fountain at Fountain Hills, you can see some of the spray evaporate into the desert heat before it falls into the artificial lake. When fifteen minutes have passed, the turbines are turned off, and you hear a sound like "woosh." Instantly, the column of water collapses, and with a thump disappears into the lake. And then, nothing. Just the quiet of the land and the silence of the desert.

8 Las Vegas: End of the Desert Road

Through the desert they drove, on the road from Los Angeles into Nevada leading nowhere. The sun was unbearable, and the car kept on overheating. Gas and water cans were loaded in the back. Their moods were a bit raw. Meyer Lansky, the "Little Man," kept on trying to calm his volatile longtime friend and partner, Benjamin ("Bugsy") Siegel. Meyer said that it would not be long before they hit the Nevada border and entered the Las Vegas valley, for which he had big dreams. Bugsy thought Meyer was a lunatic to try to create something out here in the desert, and he kept on grumbling as they drove on. But Meyer told his boyhood friend from the Lower East Side of New York that the two of them were going to be "pioneers." They would transform a "dinky, horrible, little oasis town," as Meyer called it, into a spectacular haven. They would build "the greatest, most luxurious hotel casino in the world and invite people from all over America—maybe the high-rollers from all over the world—to come and spend their money there," as Meyer described his dream forty years later to an Israeli journalist.

"The choice of the desert was deliberate," Lansky told the Israeli. "Once you got the tourists there, after they had eaten and drunk all they could, there was only one thing left—to go gambling."

To Bugsy, it was still only a dream, and the bleak desert they were driving through was an overwhelming reality. Past Death Valley and into the mountains they drove, on the same road the dam builders from the Six Companies had taken a dozen years earlier, playing poker on the floor of their big touring car as they crossed the mountains and entered a new desert valley on the Nevada side of the border. The area, surrounded by a majestic range called the Spring Mountains, was named by the Spanish Las Vegas ("the meadows") because of grass patches in the vicinity of springs on this otherwise barren and godforsaken valley floor.

For more than a thousand years, the Paiutes and their ancestors had roamed the desert valley unseen by white men until the Spaniards visited the area in the late 1700s. In 1855 a Mormon settlement was established along the Mormon

191

Corridor from Salt Lake to the sea. The first Mormon mission lasted only until 1857, when the settlers were recalled during the United States Army's invasion of Utah. For the next forty-five years, development in the desert valley was limited to a few cattle ranches and some occasional alfalfa production.

While southern Nevada remained sparsely developed and populated, the northern part of the state witnessed a series of boom-and-bust cycles. The boom began with the notorious Comstock lode in the northeast, which enriched San Francisco entrepreneurs such as George Hearst while depleting the area of its mineral resources. In the latter half of the nineteenth and early part of the twentieth century Nevada was a mining colony, divvied up among the Guggenheims, Bernard Baruch, Charles Schwab, and other eastern capitalists; the big railroads, such as the Union Pacific and Southern Pacific; and San Francisco businessmen involved in financing the mining towns.

Southern Nevada was largely ignored, even after the Union Pacific established a way stop at Las Vegas in 1905 on the line between Salt Lake City and Los Angeles. Las Vegas became a division point, providing an interesting contrast between its raucous, rough-and-tumble character as a railroad town and the more industrious mood of the Mormons.

The town grew rapidly twenty-five years later when Frank Crowe and the Six Companies came to the desert to build Hoover Dam thirty miles south of Vegas. The same year that Crowe's work crews got started, the state of Nevada legalized gambling. The town found itself uniquely situated to provide entertainment as well as basic services and supplies to the influx of construction workers. A wild real estate and gambling boom soon began. While most of the workers lived in the federally constructed Boulder City situated between the dam and Las Vegas, they still went up to Vegas to do their gambling, boozing, and whoring, all of which had been outlawed at Boulder City. For nearly four years Las Vegas was alive and booming. When Franklin Roosevelt cut the tape in 1935, the ceremony signified the end of another Nevada boom-and-bust cycle.

Nevada achieved its first real stable commercial success with the opening of Harold's Club in Reno in 1937, owned by a promoter-showman who had once been in street carnival work and run a bingo parlor in San Francisco. Harold's Club revolutionized the gambling trade, which had up to then been associated with speakeasies, illegal liquor, and backroom games that took the money of miners, cowboys, and roustabouts who passed through Nevada's towns. Harold's, with gimmicks such as "mouse roulette" (in which the winning number was selected by a live mouse) and its emphasis on high volume, attracted large numbers of people and gave Nevada gambling a more businesslike appearance. Lee Hunt, a Californian who had played a role in the development of Palm Springs, came to Las Vegas with the idea of creating a similar desert resort area. The resort idea was encouraged by the Union Pacific, which donated some land as well as obtained local backing for the project. A year after Harold's opened in Reno, a Los Angeles hotel magnate named Thomas Hull took the resort idea one step further. He built El Rancho Vegas, complete with gambling casinos, swimming pools, and guest cottages, on land filled with sand and sagebrush alongside Highway 91, the road to Los Angeles.

The El Rancho became a rendezvous for members of the Hollywood movie colony, for whom the gambling hall and the characters who frequented it held an allure. To the Hollywood crowd, Bugsy Siegel and his cohort were exciting personalities whose mysterious activities made them very appealing. Siegel was frequently seen with his friends from the movie industry—George Raft, Jack Warner, Cary Grant, Jean Harlow, Clark Gable, and Gary Cooper. The movie colony was particularly intrigued and fascinated by this freewheeling, good-looking playboy who used his Hollywood connections to establish a certain legitimacy for his activities.

The Siegel-Hollywood connection was just one element in an overall web of relationships between the Hollywood studios, its films, and organized crime. Several studios, studio executives, talent agencies, and actors and actresses maintained intimate ties to the world of organized crime, whose members provided the financing for numerous film operations, invested in joint ventures with studio executives such as Mexico's Agua Caliente gambling complex, and controlled the trade unions, which held a monopoly of production jobs. The links between Hollywood celebrities and gangsters dominated the gossip columns and blurred the line between the real world and the cinematic world, where the gangster as popular hero and/or tragic figure frequented the screen.

Meyer Lansky and his associates from the East were not particularly happy with Siegel's hobnobbing with Hollywood celebrities and flair for publicity. Siegel had worked effectively on the West Coast since his arrival in Los Angeles in the 1930s, when he became head of a number of illegal operations ranging from bookmaking to gambling along the Los Angeles waterfront.

Siegel's and Lansky's ties to the Sicilian-dominated organization based in New York headed by Lucky Luciano and other organized crime outfits, such as Morris ("Moe") Dalitz' Mayfield Road Gang in Cleveland, have been well documented through congressional and law-enforcement investigations. Siegel, when he came out to Los Angeles, served as a representative of those eastern-based organizations while carving out an empire of his own. Los Angeles and the western region were so wide open, Meyer Lansky would later remark, that there seemed enough for everyone.

Now Lansky and Siegel were on the verge of something new, something Lansky felt might be bigger than anything they had ever touched before. What the Little Man had in mind was a lavish hotel-casino complex outside Las Vegas on the road to Los Angeles. Siegel, who had first become involved in Las Vegas in 1941 when his aide Moe Sedway established a wire service for bookmakers, would coordinate the construction and management of this gambling palace, while the Luciano-Lansky group would provide the financial backing and maintain hidden interests, or "points."

Meyer Lansky was a persuasive man, and even the reluctant Siegel finally went along with the idea. Siegel decided to name the place the Flamingo, after the birds that nested at Florida's Hialeah Park race track, in which both Siegel and Lansky held an interest. Although the Flamingo name was meant to signify good luck, the hotel-casino at first became nothing but trouble for both Siegel and his financial backers. Siegel was able to obtain extremely scarce materials and labor from Los Angeles thanks to the influence of his organization and union connections to groups such as the Teamsters, but the shortage of supplies also caused costs to skyrocket. Siegel hired Phoenix contractor Del Webb to oversee the building of the Flamingo, which was scheduled for completion in 1946. The high cost worried Siegel's East Coast backers. Even Lansky was concerned about the mercurial Siegel and the rumors that his friend had begun to take kickbacks.

At a meeting in Havana, Cuba, of top organized-crime members, including the exiled Luciano, a deadline was set for completion of the Flamingo and for the hotel-casino to move into the black. Siegel and Webb aimed for an opening date of December 26 but were only able to complete the casino, and not the hotel, by opening night. Nevertheless, Siegel decided to open the Flamingo with a lavish ceremony and an expensive show, featuring George Jessel as master of ceremonies and entertainers Jimmy Durante, Xavier Cugat, Spike Jones, and Danny Thomas, with many of Siegel's Hollywood friends attending. Ticket admission was a hefty $15. Despite the grand opening, the Flamingo lost money because the casino drew disappointing crowds during its first couple of weeks. Christmas–New Year's week, it turned out, was a disastrous time to launch such an operation. Losses for the first weeks were estimated at $100,000. With the overall price tag estimated at somewhere between $5 million and $7 million, the losses placed severe strains on Siegel's ties with his East Coast friends.

Despite the warnings, Siegel remained optimistic. He closed down the casino until the hotel was completed. When the Flamingo reopened several months later, it began to turn a profit, much to the delight of the Los Angeles gangster. In early June 1947 Siegel told an interviewer about Las Vegas, "What you see here is nothing. More and more people are moving to California every day, and they love to gamble. In ten years, this'll be the biggest gambling center in the world."

Unfortunately for Siegel, his eastern backers refused to wait. On the night of June 23, 1947, Bugsy Siegel was gunned down at the home of his girlfriend, Virginia Hill, in Beverly Hills. That same evening Maurice Rosen and Gus Greenbaum, associates of Lansky, walked into the Flamingo, where Moe Sedway was in charge, and told him that a change in ownership had occurred and that they now represented the interests of the new management. They told Sedway that he and his staff were to remain and that the casino would continue to operate as if nothing had happened.

The "change in ownership," with all the publicity about Siegel's death, had an immediate impact on the fortunes of the Flamingo. Hundreds of new tourists hoping to rub shoulders with the gangsters flocked to Las Vegas to see "the house that Bugsy Siegel built," as *Las Vegas Sun* editor Hank Greenspun later called it. In his death Bugsy Siegel brought his vision of the biggest gambling center in the world and Meyer Lansky's dream of high-rollers in the desert that much closer to becoming a reality.

TAKE THE MONEY AND RUN

By the late 1940s Las Vegas had taken on the appearance of a glittering boomtown. Local lawyer Paul Ralli wrote in 1949, "The people in the streets were jingling coins in their hands and pockets; they talked money, thought money, and did everything but eat it. A 'hoopla atmosphere' prevailed." The people who built the casinos, like the people who came to Las Vegas to gamble, were looking to get rich quick and do it before the boom collapsed. There were those, like Wilbur Ivern Clark, a small-time gambler who had first come to

Nevada in 1941, who were terribly ambitious and dreamed of building giant casinos similar to the Flamingo but who lacked the capital. Clark wanted to build a massive hotel-casino to be called Wilbur Clark's Desert Inn. He was unable to obtain capital from traditional sources and even, at one point, unsuccessfully attempted to negotiate a loan with the RFC.

Word traveled fast in Las Vegas that Clark was looking for some front-end money. The early success of the Flamingo, and other hotel-casinos, such as the Thunderbird, Golden Nugget, and Fremont, made his proposal appealing. As Clark's predicament became known, one group from Cleveland, the former associates of the Mayfield Road Gang who were led by Moe Dalitz, took an interest in the situation. The Mayfield Road Gang, as the Kefauver congressional hearings later detailed, had a particularly ruthless reputation among federal and local law-enforcement personnel as a rum-running and bootlegging operation. Dalitz and his allies were also particularly adept at commingling their investments with "legitimate" businesses such as the Reliance Steel Corporation. When they learned of the Wilbur Clark situation, they immediately offered up to $1.3 million to finish construction of the Desert Inn, in exchange for 74 percent interest in the new hotel-casino.

The opening of the Desert Inn in April 1950 was even more lavish than the Flamingo event three years earlier. The heavily publicized affair was called by local residents "the most brilliant social event in the entire history of the Strip." Painted Bermuda pink with green trim, the new hotel casino had three hundred rooms, a ninety foot bar, a ceiling dotted with twinkling electric stars, and a "Doll Ranch" nursery for children, with registered nurses in attendance. Once again Hollywood celebrities attended en masse, with Edgar Bergen and Charlie McCarthy headlining the floor show. The event was even granted "semiofficial" status with the appearance of a number of high state officials, including Governor Vail Pittman.

The relationship between the casino owners and the politicians had indeed become close. Vail Pittman's lieutenant governor, Clifford Jones, for example, owned 11 percent of the Thunderbird Hotel and was a partner in the law firm of Jones, Weiner, and Jones, which played a critical role in statewide politics and the early regulation of the gambling industry. Gamblers favored politicians through hefty campaign contributions; "perks" such as complimentary hotel and casino accommodations; and, at times, outright bribes, all in order to maintain direct control of statewide and local political affairs. "We don't have to say to ourselves, like we used to say in the old days back east, 'Is this guy going to be a crusader?'" Moe Dalitz told a reporter from the *Saturday Evening Post*. The gamblers, argued the former Cleveland bootlegger, had a monopoly on a politician's source of funds. "They can't get it anywhere else," Dalitz gloated.

By far the gambler's most important political friend in the days of the Flamingo and Desert Inn was Nevada's Senator Pat McCarran. During Estes Kefauver's hearings on organized crime in 1950 and 1951, McCarran tried to block contempt citations against a number of top organized-crime figures, including Joe Adonis and Jack Dragna. (Dragna, who had inherited the number-one mob position in Los Angeles after Siegel's death, was Siegel's suspected killer.) McCarran, as later court depositions revealed, was a frequent guest at expensive Strip hotels. But the senator never paid a bill and on several occasions used the hotels as campaign headquarters at no cost. In 1950

McCarran interceded with the Internal Revenue Service in a case involving the Flamingo's Gus Greenbaum and Moe Sedway.

The only real independent force separate from the gamblers and their political allies was an ambitious, pugnacious Brooklyn kid turned gunrunner for the Israeli underground. Herman ("Hank") Greenspun came to Las Vegas just before Meyer Lansky and Bugsy Siegel had begun to build their desert mecca. Greenspun, who had a way with words, quickly understood the value of a certain kind of media hype. He began publishing *Las Vegas Life*, a promotional sheet that covered, as he put it, "the more stimulating aspects of Las Vegas Nightlife." The magazine's financial problems were helped by a generous advertising contract from Bugsy Siegel's Flamingo, which also hired Greenspun to do some public-relations work. Soon after, Greenspun acquired the *Las Vegas Sun*, a onetime union newspaper, and quickly turned it into an instrument of personal power.

While Greenspun liked the wide-open mood of Las Vegas, he was involved in a long-standing vendetta with the gambler's favorite politician, Pat McCarran. During a congressional hearing on McCarran's restrictive immigration bill, McCarran, Greenspun told reporter J. Anthony Lukas, attacked New York's Senator Herbert Lehman as representative of a "handful of cloak and suiters on Seventh Avenue." Greenspun, a fierce Jewish nationalist, vowed to Lehman that although he was "just a small newspaper publisher from Nevada, for what that man said to you just now, I'm going to hound him into his grave."

Soon after the incident, Greenspun began to attack McCarran in the pages of the *Sun*, using a prose style that made him famous as a gunslinging frontier editor. Word quickly went out among the casino owners that something had to be done to protect their friend. As court documents later revealed, a boycott, initiated by a telephone call from Thunderbird owner Marion Hicks, was launched against the *Sun*. Within a half hour of Hicks's call, 30 percent of the *Sun*'s advertising had been withdrawn, including the lucrative ads from Moe Dalitz' Desert Inn. Greenspun immediately brought suit against McCarran and fifty-six hotel and casino operators for conspiracy to drive him out of business. After a particularly damaging deposition by the Nevada senator in which some of McCarran's ties with the gamblers were revealed, the casino operators settled out of court, paying Greenspun $80,000 and pledging to continue advertising in the *Sun*.

The opening of the Desert Inn, according to longtime gambling executive L. C. Jacobsen, "opened the gates" for a flood of "black-market money" that transformed the desert town. "There was tons of it back then," said Jacobsen recalling the rapid entry of new capital and the host of unsavory characters who assumed the management of several new hotel-casinos that opened in the 1950s. The takeover of Las Vegas by organized crime did not detract from the volume of business that continued to occur at the casinos. "Everybody just loved to hobnob with these guys," an old-time casino executive recalled, pointing out that the national publicity generated by Moe Dalitz' and Wilbur Clark's testimony at the Kefauver hearings only served to heighten the allure of the Desert Inn and the other casinos. The successful opening of the Desert Inn, and of the Sands, Sahara, Riviera, Dunes, and Royal Nevada soon after, also eliminated the fear that more casinos would cut profit margins. Las Vegas itself became the attraction rather than particular casinos.

By the late 1950s, two distinct gambling entities had emerged, each with its own power structure and its own method of operation, although some overlap did exist. The Strip hotel-casinos, such as the Flamingo and Desert Inn, were located outside the Las Vegas city limits along the main highway to Los Angeles. The Strip served a wealthier patron, who was encouraged to bet higher stakes on the more glamorous games such as craps and twenty-one. Strip operations had a high overhead, which included high entertainment costs for the lavish productions offered nightly and the extensive use of "comps," or complimentary services, ranging from free food and drinks to free travel expenses. Up to 25 percent of Strip hotel-casino's expenses went for comps, which were also used to solicit or pay back favors from politicians, union leaders, or anyone who might have some say or influence over casino operations. Pat McCarran was neither the first nor last high-ranking politician to obtain comps, the most recent publicized example occurring in 1978 with Nevada Governor Robert List.

In contrast to the Strip hotel-casinos, which tended to dominate news coverage because of their organized-crime connections, were the downtown hotel-casinos, whose owners maintained a lower profile than their Strip counterparts. The downtown casinos were mostly situated along Fremont Street, which received the name Glitter Gulch for its honky-tonk fluorescent-lit atmosphere. The downtown casinos throve on volume, attracting more traffic than places on the Strip. Some of the downtown casinos had smaller hotels but none of the lavish entertainment offered on the Strip. Bunched together, the downtown casinos catered to the walk-in traffic of tourists who stayed in the cheap motels and then made the rounds of Glitter Gulch by foot.

As the character of the Strip and downtown operations began to emerge and tourism in Las Vegas increased, the casino owners became proficient at taking their profits both over and under the table. Throughout the 1950s, while the gamblers and politicians tried to downplay their mob associations, working control of the casinos by organized crime began to function in a variety of ways. The system of hidden ownership through "points" was widespread and maintained through a variety of guises, such as underpriced or overpriced real estate transactions or payments by courier. One of the more famous incidents of hidden ownership involved Lucky Luciano associate Frank Costello, who was shot in a New York hotel in 1957. After being rushed to a hospital, New York police discovered a small piece of paper in his jacket pocket with a set of numbers totaling $651,284. After an extensive search law-enforcement officials were able to identify the figure as the exact amount of the new Tropicana Hotel's revenues for its first twenty-four days in operation. The handwriting on the note was traced to another well-known mobster, "Dandy" Phil Kastel, who at the time was an employee of the Tropicana and had worked for the Costello organization at several Louisiana gambling houses.

Other methods for obtaining "nontaxable," under-the-table winnings utilized during this period included making phony-money transactions, "skimming" profits before they were officially entered as taxable income, laundering money obtained from other illegal means, self-dealing, and bloating expenses that could be turned into available cash. Bribery, secret fund-raising and campaign contributions, influence peddling, loan sharking, prostitution, and murder all took place.

The gamblers, like almost everyone else, believed there were limits to the growth of Las Vegas and the continuing profitability of the casinos. "It felt like a short-term risk, since we were sure it was inevitably going to bust," a top casino executive recalled. "It was like a gambler's crap shoot. In a way, the mood of the people who built Las Vegas resembled the mood of the people who came to gamble. If you can get the money, you take it and get out."

Like the western speculator, gambling, to the early casino operators, was essentially a short-term investment. The casino owners feared strong-armed competitors or even the possibility that all the bad publicity surrounding their activities might eventually cause Nevada residents to outlaw gambling. If any of this happened, Wallace Turner wrote, "the money is gone. But if the money is scooped out and shoved into the pocket or in some other safer investment, then the gambler can rest his head more easily."

By the late 1950s, business was booming, not declining. A growing tourist clientele called for greater investments to keep up with the growth. Money had to be poured in, not out. The question then was who would take the risk.

FINANCING THE DEALS

The gamblers were worried by their success. New casino plans were on the drawing boards, and several of the established operations wanted to expand, increase the number of hotel rooms available, and generally upgrade their facilities. None of the traditional banking institutions would touch the casino business, so several of the most powerful individuals in Las Vegas, including real estate promoter Nate Mack, members of the Jones, Weiner, and Jones law firm, and Beverly Hills lawyer Sam Kurland, began to explore the possibility in 1954 of opening their own bank, a bank for gamblers.

A young Utah banker named E. Parry Thomas was also attracted to the idea. Thomas had dabbled in Las Vegas real estate for several years and grew to know several of the big shots who ran the town. He convinced his boss, Walter Cosgriff, who ran the Continental Bank in Salt Lake City, to help capitalize this new bank for gamblers to be called the Bank of Las Vegas.

While Cosgriff, Thomas, and their Las Vegas friends began to work out the terms for the new bank, another Las Vegas–Utah link was being forged. The leaders of the Las Vegas Mormon community, including influential politician James Gibson, were having their periodic meeting with the top leaders of the Mormon church in Salt Lake City. Despite its stated opposition to gambling, the Las Vegas Mormon church still functioned at the heart of civic, political, and economic affairs of the community. Mormon stake President Reed Whipple was mayor pro tem of Las Vegas, and Jim Gibson would soon become the key figure in reworking Nevada's gambling regulatory laws. The membership of the local church had kept up with the growth of Las Vegas to such an extent that in order to continue to keep pace, the local church needed funds from Salt Lake City for such projects as the acquisition of land for a welfare farm and the construction of new chapels and a big meeting hall. The local church leadership wanted the Salt Lake general authorities to provide church funds as "a substantial investment in the future of Las Vegas and the church's role in the community," as Gibson recalled their request.

The Salt Lake officials were at first "cautious and conservative," according to

Whipple. "They argued that what had been created here in Las Vegas was a false economy, an economy that would boom and then bust," Gibson remembered. Gibson, Whipple, and others of the local Las Vegas church leadership felt otherwise. They knew of the plans for the new bank and that local Mormon entrepreneurs were about to launch a huge shopping center, the largest of its kind, to be called Vegas Village. Other Mormons in real estate, construction, and finance, as well as those who were top local politicians felt that the gambling business was not only in Las Vegas to stay but would ultimately cause the entire community to prosper. "The Mormon community grew up with Las Vegas. Our leaders had lots of optimism and they looked wisely on the future of this valley," local church leader Jim Seastrand recalled. "They would say, 'It's coming; get your land. The time will come when people will come to Las Vegas.' They went forth with real faith in the future."

The Salt Lake general authorities decided to go along with the Las Vegas leadership. Not long after making their decision, Salt Lake leaders concluded that they had been wise in their investment. "Things moved so fast that soon after, the general authorities were encouraging us to buy more land and keep up with the growth, which we did," recalled Whipple.

Things were also moving fast with the new Bank of Las Vegas. By 1955, when Parry Thomas arrived in Las Vegas, along with Continental executive Kenneth Sullivan, to run the new bank, he quickly established himself in both the world of the Mormons and the gamblers. Thomas was a "jack Mormon"— that is, a Mormon by name but not in practice or one who takes "an occasional highball," as the banker put it to a *Business Week* reporter. Thomas' family, including his wife and several of his children, were, unlike him, active members of the church. According to people close to the banker, including high officials of the local church, Thomas used his Mormonism as a means to establish himself in the community. His being Mormon helped the Mormon businessmen to feel comfortable with him, "since they know that he knows them and who they are, and that they can talk the same language to do business together," as Mormon casino executive Shannon Bybee put it. This functional Mormonism was expressed in Thomas' widely known remark that he worked for "the Mormons until noon, and from noon on for my Jewish friends."

The term "Jewish friends" referred to the gamblers who ran the casinos when Thomas and his Bank of Las Vegas set up shop in 1955. The new bank immediately became involved in casino financing, the first and only bank to do so for more than twenty years. It financed the remodeling of the Sahara hotel-casino at a time when the Sahara, according to law-enforcement files, was considered to be a front for Meyer Lansky and his brother Jake. In rapid-fire order, the bank then financed the development or expansion of the Fremont, the Sands, the Desert Inn, the Dunes, the Hacienda, the Stardust, the Riviera, and the Thunderbird.

By the late 1950s and early 1960s, as the casinos continued to thrive and expand, new sources of capital became even more crucial. Through Thomas and a group of close associates, a new financial network was built. Thomas became closely linked with Morris Shenker, a St. Louis attorney and powerful political figure who was Teamster president Jimmy Hoffa's personal attorney as well as the lawyer for a number of top organized-crime figures. Shenker was also the attorney for a small Texas-based insurance company, American National

Insurance Company. American National began to funnel major loans through the Bank of Las Vegas, including $13.3 million to Shenker, who became involved in the ownership of several Las Vegas hotel-casinos. American National also lent $5 million to the Thomas group, which used the money to purchase a fleet of oil tankers. At the same time, American National invested more than $1.5 million in the stock of Parvin-Dohrmann, a publicly owned company involved in the ownership of several casinos. Thomas became a director of Parvin-Dohrmann around the time of the loan. Eventually Parvin-Dohrmann collapsed after a scandal over stock manipulations and links to organized crime.

The Thomas group's biggest move was its acquisition of the Continental Connector Corporation, a small publicly held specialty electronics company based in Woodside, New York, which held a coveted listing on the American Stock Exchange. From assets of $5 million, Continental, under the Thomas-Shenker leadership, went on a whirlwind of acquisitions and investments dozens of times the value of the original company. Within the space of a year, the company bought a Chicago trucking firm, the Dunes hotel-casino, and the Mormon controlled and Parry Thomas-linked Vegas Village shopping center. They eventually sold Vegas Village back to a group of Mormon investors. Continental attempted to acquire the Golden Nugget hotel-casino but failed because of intervention by the Securities and Exchange Commission which charged that the company's proxy statement contained false and misleading information and violated accepted accounting practices. Though Continental signed a consent decree with the SEC and abandoned the takeover attempt, Thomas continued to maintain close ties with Golden Nugget management. According to Nugget vice president Shannon Bybee, Nugget chairman Steve Wynn was like an "adopted son to Parry" and the Las Vegas banker also served as Wynn's "financial guide." Wynn and Nugget, through Thomas' connections, developed a relationship with George Eccles and his Utah-based First Security Corporation. Eccles and First Security, according to Bybee, used Thomas' bank as a conduit (thereby avoiding any publicity about the investment) for financing a major addition to the downtown hotel-casino. In fact, according to Parry's son Peter, the Eccles' bank participated in all of the Thomas bank's loans to the casinos.

Aside from this web of relationships, the use of publicly held companies to raise and manipulate funds, and the use of various financial institutions to serve as conduits for hidden investments, the major role of Thomas and his bank were the ties they established with the Teamsters Union and its vast store of pension fund money. In March 1955 the Central States Southeast-Southwest Areas Pension Fund was established to serve more than 175,000 Teamster members in the midwest. Unlike the other Teamster Funds, the Central States pension money was run directly by a group responsible to Jimmy Hoffa who used the fund in part to consolidate power in his drive toward national leadership in the union. Soon after Hoffa became president, the pension fund became heavily involved in financing Las Vegas projects, frequently using Parry Thomas' bank as a conduit. The first loans went to Moe Dalitz to build his Sunrise Hospital. Teamster money then was dispersed to places like the Stardust, the Desert Inn, the Fremont, the Dunes, the Landmark, the Four Queens, the Aladdin, Circus Circus, and Caesar's Palace.

Throughout this period the Teamsters' funds went to some of the most unsavory characters and operations in Las Vegas. By far the most spectacular of the loans went to Allen Glick, a young San Diego lawyer and real estate salesman. Glick, who mysteriously burst on the scene in Las Vegas in the early 1970s, was the apparent owner of the privately held Argent Corporation, which in the short space of a few years received $160 million from the Teamsters. Of this, $62 million went for the acquisition of the Stardust and Fremont hotel-casinos in 1974. Glick was quickly surrounded by figures, such as Frank ("Lefty") Rosenthal, who were linked to the Chicago crime network headed by Anthony ("Tough Tony") Spilotro. Glick's meteoric rise and fall has been the subject of numerous investigations, almost all of which point to the apparently inescapable conclusion that Glick, as writer Steve Brill put it, "was a front for hidden organized-crime ownership of his Las Vegas Properties." Glick's fall came about after intense investigation from various law-enforcement bodies, which, among other things, were able to link the former real estate salesman to a major skim of the slot-machine revenues at the Stardust. After the skim became public, Glick lost his license and bailed out, selling the Stardust and Fremont to an old Moe Dalitz ally.

The Glick episode was just another example of union money ending up in the hands of organized-crime figures or Teamster loans turned bad. The use of the pension fund eventually led to congressional action. In 1974 the Employment Retirement Income Security Act (ERISA) was passed, allowing the Department of Labor to regulate the activities of pension-fund trustees. With the Department of Labor, Internal Revenue Service, and the Securities and Exchange Commission all involved in investigations, a number of Las Vegas–related or organized-crime–linked Teamster loans, including a huge one to Morris Shenker, were canceled. Ultimately, the fund was restructured and outside managers brought in. But the search for outside capital continued, as the gambling business, despite all the bad publicity and ongoing investigations, managed to keep its profit levels high. By hook or crook, the deals got made and the money was obtained somewhere, somehow.

THE HUGHES INTERLUDE

All through the 1950s and early 1960s, a cycle of bad publicity followed by pledges of politicians and regulators to "clean up" the industry, followed by yet another scandal, continued to plague the business. One of those cycles was initiated by a series of stories by Sandy Smith in the *Chicago Sun Times* about the skimming of millions of untaxed dollars from casino earnings. "The skimming charges," wrote *Philadelphia Inquirer* reporters Donald Barlett and James Steele of Smith's stories, "had undermined a carefully nurtured Nevada myth—that through rigid licensing standards and zealous enforcement, the state had freed its gaming industry of any criminal element."

In November 1966, Paul Laxalt was elected governor of Nevada, with the support of some "unofficial" fund-raising on the Strip by a Moe Dalitz partner who had been convicted in an extortion-murder plot in Denver the year before. After his election, Laxalt immediately sought ways to reinvigorate the state's economy and its tourist trade, which had been hurt by the continuing bad publicity. One possible solution, Laxalt thought, was to work with Howard

Hughes, the eccentric billionaire who had suddenly relocated to Las Vegas in 1966. Laxalt and the gambling industry considered the arrival of Hughes a godsend, for he brought a level of business credibility and political influence that might conceivably discourage further government investigations. After Hughes had settled in his new headquarters at the Desert Inn, the industry newsletter *Nevada Report* happily declared that "by getting into the gambling business, he [Hughes] convinced millions that gambling can't be dirty or Hughes—genius of helicopters, space vehicles, electronics—wouldn't get into it. It was a public-relations breakthrough for Nevada that could not have been delivered by Madison Avenue for $50 million."

Since the days of Bugsy Siegel, Hughes had expressed an interest in Las Vegas because of his Hollywood activities; his control of Trans World Airlines (TWA), which began to fly into Las Vegas; and his ownership of some real estate adjoining the airport. Hughes was induced to settle in Las Vegas by the Washington lawyer Edward P. Morgan, a close friend of Hank Greenspun, and former FBI agent Robert Maheu, who quickly established himself as Hughes's top representative on Las Vegas matters. When Hughes made his dramatic entry into the city—wheeled in on a stretcher in the dead of night from a private railroad car that had brought him from Boston—Greenspun, who had been alerted beforehand but had not breathed a word about the move, ran a front-page editorial the next day urging the press to "give this man the privacy he wants."

Soon after his arrival, Hughes decided to buy the Desert Inn to eliminate the bother of tourists trying to make their way up to the top floor, where the Hughes entourage had been renting space. Hughes paid the Dalitz group $13.2 million for the right to operate the hotel and casino for the next fifty years. The Dalitz group also received $1 million a year until the lease ran out. Title to the land and buildings remained in the Dalitz group's hands. Several interested parties were involved in the deal to make sure the quixotic Hughes followed through. This network included Maheu, Dalitz, Thomas (who had been hired by Hughes via Maheu to ascertain the worth of the Desert Inn despite Thomas' own financial ties to Dalitz), Greenspun, Morgan, and Johnny Roselli. (Roselli was the acknowledged representative of the national crime syndicate in Las Vegas and had been involved with Maheu in discussions with the CIA about poisoning Fidel Castro.) When the Desert Inn sale was concluded, Dalitz paid a $150,000 finder's fee to Edward Morgan, who shared it with Greenspun and Roselli. Hughes then asked Dalitz to advise him on operating the Desert Inn, to which Dalitz gladly agreed. Hughes explained in a memo to Maheu that "other deals would materialize and that if I had an opportunity I would like to have him [Dalitz] involve himself as my legal advisor in some other deals that I'd been contemplating."

And deals there were. "Over the next three years Dalitz, Morgan, Greenspun, Maheu, Parry Thomas, and many others would profit handsomely by Hughes's presence in Las Vegas," Barlett and Steele wrote in their exhaustive account of Hughes. "The only loser in the lot would be Hughes himself, and he would count his losses in the millions of dollars." In that short period of time Hughes became the largest hotel-casino operator in Las Vegas, the owner of substantial real estate and television station KLAS, the CBS outlet, which he bought from Greenspun at a handsome profit for the newspaper publisher. In a one-year stretch, Hughes spent $65 million for several Strip casinos, giving him 20 percent of all hotel accommodations in the area. Hughes's buying spree was to come to an end only after the Justice Department objected on antitrust grounds to his attempt to acquire the Stardust and Silver Slipper. Hughes did manage to go through with the Silver Slipper deal only after agreeing to forgo his purchase of the Stardust.

Throughout this period the Greenspun-Dalitz-Maheu network continued to encourage the billionaire's buying activities, as did Nevada politicians such as Laxalt. In early 1968, after a meeting with Hughes in which the entrepreneur expressed fears about germs in the Las Vegas water supply, Laxalt told the press that Hughes was a boon to Nevada because he "added a degree of credibility to the state that it might have taken years of advertising to secure." The Hughes game—fleecing the billionaire while trying to cash in on the public-relations value of a "legitimate" investor in the gambling business—ended only after an internal power struggle broke out between Maheu and Hughes's Mormon advisers. Maheu lost. Thereupon, Maheu, with Greenspun's backing, struck back at Hughes and his new Summa Corporation with a multimillion-dollar law suit and constant attacks from the once-friendly *Las Vegas Sun*. Hughes fled town. Ultimately, the whole Hughes episode served as an example, not of the "new" Las Vegas, but of the old con game extended to some new players.

THE REGULATION MERRY-GO-ROUND

In January 1977 a young investigator for the State Gaming Control Board, Dennis Gomes, filed a long memo to board chairman Phil Hannifin on investigations being carried out by the board's auditing division. The Gomes report, which was later printed in an industry newsletter, described forty-three different investigations, most of them substantial, and all but seven completed inquiries. The memo outlined how casino managers from some of the biggest operations in town, such as the Aladdin, the Stardust, Caesar's Palace, the MGM Grand, and the Tropicana, engaged in embezzlement of gaming revenues, credit frauds, payments to unlicensed interests (or hidden ownership), collaboration with organized-crime elements, evasion of gaming taxes, and violations of gaming regulations. Gomes, a Nevada high school graduate, grew up believing that the old ways of Las Vegas—skimming, hidden ownership, mob control—might become a thing of the past if he and others on the board, like Hannifin and the burly Mormon accountant (and, later, casino executive) Shannon Bybee had investigative clout and backing from the politicians.

The industry was at a crisis point in the 1970s. The Teamsters' money was in jeopardy. Many of the companies were going public and therefore subject to the regulations of a feisty SEC, which had its own ideas on how to clean up the Vegas situation. Gomes and the others approached their job with some spirit, often running into confrontations with key people in the industry.

The origins of gaming regulations date back to the period following the Bugsy Siegel killing, when key Las Vegas politicians and casino operators decided that some kind of regulation was necessary to offset the sensational headlines stemming from the murder. Under the initiative of Las Vegas District Attorney Robert Jones, a senior partner in the Jones, Weiner, and Jones firm, in 1948 the Nevada legislature passed a series of reforms designed to give licensing power to the Nevada Tax Commission, although a grandfather clause also provided exemptions for existing casinos such as the Flamingo.

About the time Parry Thomas and his Bank of Las Vegas made their appearance in 1955, the Nevada legislature passed a bill that established the Gaming Control Board as an adjunct of the Tax Commission "to inaugurate a policy to eliminate the undesirables in Nevada's gaming and to provide regulations for the licensing and the operation of gaming." Four years later, after more adverse publicity about the mob in Las Vegas, the legislature, under the leadership of Mormon politician James Gibson, created the Nevada Gaming Commission, consisting of five members appointed by the governor. The commission, for which the Gaming Board became an investigative and enforcement arm, had the power to grant or deny any license application for anyone wanting to own or to manage a casino.

Time and again, the regulatory agencies appeared ready to take decisive action—particularly when the threat of action by an outside agency, such as the Justice Department's organized-crime task force or the SEC, appeared imminent—only to reverse itself afterward and deny that major problems existed at all. The board received most of its publicity from the use of a black book of organized-crime figures. Licensees were told not to associate with black-book figures nor allow them admittance into the casinos. This practice led to the board's most widely publicized action in the 1960s when Frank Sinatra was threatened with loss of license because of his association with Chicago mobster Sam Giancana.

By the 1970s new pressures on the regulators and the industry had developed. Federal investigators were deeply involved in the Teamster situation, and the SEC was actively pursuing security violations by a number of publicly held gambling corporations. With securities fraud rampant throughout the early 1970s, the SEC was constantly investigating companies such as Continental Connector. Continental engaged in such unusual practices as advancing several hundred thousand dollars in markers to customers "whose identities are not known," as one Continental filing with the SEC described it, or paying more than $100,000 in construction money that went "to an individual who cannot now be located."

When the Hannifin board was appointed, the new group immediately set out to push the industry to eliminate its dependency on Teamster and Valley Bank of Nevada (formerly Bank of Las Vegas) money. The Hughes interlude had raised the possibility that new, more respectable corporate interests might become involved in the gambling business and thereby attract more traditional sources of investment capital either from the New York, Chicago, and California banks and insurance companies or from the stock market. As part of an attempt to act in what it perceived to be the industry's best interest, the Hannifin board decided to set up meetings with the SEC to demonstrate, as Shannon Bybee put it, that Nevada types "didn't all wear pin stripes and panamas and smoke cigars. . . . We wanted to develop a comfort level not only with them but with the money-center people, but we had very little success at first."

While the Hannifin board attempted to convince people in the East and in California that a new era had arrived in gaming, it simultaneously began to move more forcefully against the industry's more blatant activities involving fraud and organized crime. In doing so, it frequently antagonized industry figures, who resented the board's initiative even though the group thought it was acting in the industry's interest. A few companies, such as Hilton Hotels and Harrah's in Reno and Lake Tahoe, gave modest support, but most of the casino operators disliked what they perceived as negative attention focused on the industry. Despite these first modest moves against organized-crime influence, the Hannifin board never did seriously challenge the pervasive influence of Las Vegas' more notorious powers. Of forty-three different investigations by audit-division agents, several never got off the ground, including the key inquiries into transactions at the Alladin, Caesar's Palace, and the Tropicana. "There are no heroes in Las Vegas," longtime investigative reporter Al Delugach commented about the role of the regulators and their continuing ties to the industry.

Those ties became even more pronounced when a new governor, Republican Robert List, appointed new chairmen of the Gaming Control Board and the Gaming Commission in 1979. These appointees brought a strong proindustry bias to their jobs, causing several of the Hannifin group to depart. Some, like Hannifin, Bybee, and Gomes, eventually took high-level jobs with the casinos. This was a common occurrence in the industry. Nevada gaming officials and other law-enforcement personnel from the FBI and Justice Department frequently moved through the revolving door into the casinos' executive suites. A few, like Dennis Gomes, left their jobs with bitterness. "Everything that functions in this state," Gomes told *Fortune* magazine, "functions for the protection and furthering of the gaming industry. A lot of form and no real substance. . . . I used to feel that society wanted real law enforcement." The disillusioned investigator concluded, "Now I'm convinced they don't care. All they want is to walk away from a casino without being mugged."

The new regulators—Mormons Harry Reid, chairman of the Gaming Commission, and Richard Bunker, chairman of the Gaming Control Board—continued the quest for acceptance of the gambling industry by the financial community. They downplayed the organized-crime element and focused on "professionalizing" the board with better-paid accountants, lawyers, and other staff personnel. Bunker emphasized new accounting procedures that he wanted the industry to adopt, not because of skimming problems, but in order to foster a better image with the banks and insurance companies. Bunker's and Reid's work with the casino managers was a "cooperative venture," as Bunker put it, based on a "productive dialogue. . . . Now when we go to the legislature, we will go as cooperative partners rather than adversaries, since we all want the industry to have the best possible image."

Reid was even more explicit in his rejection of what he characterized as the previous board's "cops and robbers" stance. "I'm not supposed to be a cop," Reid said of his job. "What's most important to me is to be fair," he said, citing the situation facing Frank Sinatra in the summer of 1980. Sinatra had applied for a gaming license to operate out of Caesar's Palace, using Ronald Reagan as one of his character references. The popular singer's reputation, according to Reid, was creating an unfair situation. "We used to say that the poor and downtrodden didn't get a fair shake, but that's also true now of the Frank Sinatras with all their notoriety. And that's what stands out most in my mind about this situation," Reid declared. Sinatra received his license in February 1981 with support from both Bunker and Reid.

As practicing Mormons, the two regulators were closely linked to powerful networks of Mormon officials and businessmen. Mormon connections were helpful to individual Mormons, particularly when difficulties arose. For example, casino executive Frank Mooney, who worked for Allen Glick's Argent Corporation, was heavily implicated in the Stardust skimming scandal. Although Mooney lost his license and left the casino business, the Mormon district attorney, George Holt, never criminally prosecuted him for his actions. Throughout the period of investigation Mooney was helped by the Mormon network of businessmen and politicians. "Frank Mooney's Mormonism was one of the big things he had going for him," Harry Reid recalled. "Mormons would stick up for him. I would get letters and phone calls and visits from Mormon leaders asking me 'What have you heard about Brother Mooney?'"

The increasing focus of the gambling industry on the money markets and "corporate gaming" highlighted the presence of Mormons inside, and on the edges of, the industry. A generation of managers, many of them schooled in the ways of the illegal gambling business of the 1930s and 1940s, were slowly passing from the scene, to be replaced by professional managers acquainted with the world of bond offerings and debt equity financing. Mormons such as Richard Bunker were at the center of that shift, encouraging it, and hoping that with the advent of the more professionalized approach, a new kind of gaming executive would come to dominate the industry. The description of the new gambling man could easily be that of the representative Mormon business executive—proficient in the ways of banking, accounting, and the world of the highly stratified corporation. "There are certainly an awful lot of them employed by these establishments, and a number of them are in influential positions. They believe in giving a good day's work for a good day's pay, and they're hardworking, excellent people to have," declared Caesar's Palace executive Cornelius Smythe of the Mormons in casino management.

Since the early part of the century, the church had formally stated its opposition to gambling. In that light church leaders devised an elaborate policy to deal with the apparent contradiction of Mormons being a crucial part of the gambling industry. With the concurrence of the Salt Lake authorities, local church leaders evolved a three-point policy: members should not gamble; members should not hold certain kinds of gambling jobs, particularly those (such as card dealers or pit bosses) that put them on the casino floor and made them visible to others; and most important, casino management or ownership positions are not forbidden and can be held by any good Mormon. "Our counsel to people who work in management positions is that it is not wrong to work there as long as you're earning money as legitimate work. It's no different than someone who would be working for a company like the Union Pacific," church leader Reed Whipple declared. Some church leaders, such as Jim Gibson, have encouraged other church members, such as Bunker, to get involved, particularly in the area of regulation, where church members have had a long-standing influence. The convergence of Mormon businessmen and politicians with the gambling industry, a convergence that dates back to the days of Parry Thomas and the investment of the Salt Lake general authorities in this gambling town, is reinforced as corporate gaming replaces the old-style godfathers or Mr. Las Vegases, as both Thomas and Moe Dalitz have been called. Everybody in Las Vegas, as Shannon Bybee put it, ultimately makes their money off the gambling industry, and that fact, more than anything else, shapes the character of the area. Money, as the town folklore has it, is the root of all activity in Las Vegas, and it is where the community's different cultures eventually meet.

THE ADVENT OF CORPORATE GAMING

By 1980 the gambling industry had thoroughly penetrated the social, political, and economic fabric of Las Vegas and, to a slightly lesser extent, the entire state of Nevada. The industry itself employed about 30 percent of the Las Vegas work force, with another 30 percent in jobs indirectly linked to the industry. The huge revenues involved also meant, as Dean Witter specialist Alan Duncan told the *Valley Times* newspaper, that "the days of the guy opening a small casino are gone forever," given construction costs, overhead, and all the new methods of accounting controls. That leaves the winnings for either the people who get in on the ground floor, like Moe Dalitz and Morris Shenker, or some of the big publicly held companies, like MGM, Hilton, or Del Webb.

The publicity involving organized crime, pension-fund abuse, and the skimming scandals of the 1970s, all put a damper on potential investment by the traditional money center institutions. Skeptical but curious, the banks and insurance companies by and large kept their distance in the early and middle 1970s. Even after a number of large publicly held companies, such as MGM and Hilton Hotels, either built new hotel-casinos, as in the case of the MGM Grand, or acquired existing operations, as when Hilton purchased the Flamingo, establishment financiers kept their distance. That is, until Atlantic City.

"Atlantic City," declared Shannon Bybee, "changed everything." Shortly after Resorts International opened the first New Jersey casino in the spring of 1977 and began to earn an extraordinary return on its initial investment, the big eastern and California financial institutions began to stir. A top executive at Del Webb corporation recalled the difference. "When bankers heard requests for loans," the executive said of the pre–Atlantic City attitude, "they went through the motions, but they would give you the idiot treatment." The Webb company's experience was an interesting case in point. Since the days when Webb did construction work for Bugsy Siegel and became the nominal owner of the Flamingo when Siegel's inheritors failed to pay off construction debts, the company and Del Webb himself straddled the line between the worlds of legitimate business and the underside of gambling and construction. Webb was a recognized "civic leader," in part because of his 50 percent ownership interest in the New York Yankees. He was a major political campaign contributor and used his connections to develop ties with presidents, other elected officials, and J. Edgar Hoover. In the early 1960s, the Webb company went public to establish new sources of capital and to extend lines of credit with major financial institutions that had already invested in Webb's construction business and his Sun City housing project.

The other side of Webb was related to the company's ownership interests in various Las Vegas hotel-casinos. Webb shared ownership of the Flamingo with Meyer Lansky and fellow Phoenix businessman Gus Greenbaum. Webb eventually took over ownership of the Sahara and Mint hotels after being paid in points for his construction work. In the case of the Thunderbird, which had been linked to the Lansky brothers in the 1950s, Webb purchased the hotel-casino in 1964 and then immediately sold it to a ten-member investment group headed by Meyer Lansky's neighbor in Florida. Webb was also tied into E. Parry Thomas' group. Thomas sat on the Webb board of directors. The American National Insurance Company, closely linked to the Thomas bank, loaned Webb money in the 1960s for his hotel-casino operations.

After Webb's death on July 4, 1974, his successor, Robert Johnson, made a major effort to strengthen Webb's corporate image by turning to the traditional money markets to finance the expansion of its business. Johnson and Webb executives talked to several New York banks, including Morgan Guaranty, about financing the expansion of the Sahara as well as a possible Webb move into Atlantic City and Miami, if that city legalized gambling. The banks were interested but still reluctant, particularly since Webb wanted as much as a $125 million loan, an unheard of investment at the time. But the good news from Atlantic City had begun to turn heads.

When the meeting with the bankers took place, the Webb executives held their breath. "I remember the meeting well," one executive who participated recalled. "The meeting was at the Sahara. We were seated around a large table with the bankers on one side and us on the other end. We started by laying out our plans for the expansion of the Sahara and tentatively raised the $125 million figure. But instead of hearing the amount whittled down, which was the best we expected, all of a sudden these bankers started insisting on raising their own stake in the loan, asking for a bigger piece of the action. We went away with $10 million more than we had come in asking for."

Shortly before the $135 million loan went through, Caesar's World, whose chairman had some problems with the SEC and other agencies about financial transactions with a Lansky associate, was able to convince the Aetna Insurance Company to lend the casino operator $60 million for expansion purposes. The Atlantic City lesson appeared to be undermining the resistance of the traditional lenders. *Banking* magazine, the journal of the American Banker's Association, signaled the changing attitude in an October 1977 article profiling Parry Thomas' Valley Bank of Nevada. "Gambling is a subject that is bound to make bankers uncomfortable," the magazine commented. "By definition it's the opposite of prudent management of money. But the fact is, legalized gambling is now spreading. . . . This is a $50 billion a year industry, at the very least." The article concluded, "The point is, these are businesses—unconventional to be sure—but nevertheless businesses."

Corporate gaming had arrived. The venerable MGM, now controlled by the high-flying Kirk Kerkorian, spent upward of $125 million for the Grand Hotel, across the street from the Flamingo and Caesar's Palace, and spent almost double the amount for its Grand Hotel in Reno. The Hilton Hotels acquired two Las Vegas hotel-casinos, including the Flamingo, and discovered by 1977 that its two gambling properties accounted for about 40 percent of revenues and 30 percent of pretax income of its 185 hotels in the United States. By 1980 the five dominant gambling operations in Nevada were all large publicly held corporations: MGM, Webb, Hilton, Caesar's World, and northern Nevada's Harrah's.

In the months after the casinos opened in Atlantic City, *Forbes, Fortune, Business Week,* and the *Wall Street Journal* all did feature stories on corporate gaming, quoting various financial lenders and gambling executives on the potential strength of the industry. "Gambling is more acceptable," a Summa executive told the *Wall Street Journal.* "There's a great deal of money to be made in this industry. Witness the fervor and heat generated by Atlantic City. The puritanical ethic is eroding and will continue to erode."

Despite *Fortune's* 1979 comment that "the patina of disrepute that shrouded casino gambling has so eroded that the most prestigious financial institutions stand ready to help underwrite the construction of new pleasure domes costing in excess of $100 million," corporate gaming could not completely shake its old association. "When you get right down to it, that's a big part of our reluctance," a Citicorp spokesman told the *Wall Street Journal,* referring to the industry's continuing unsavory reputation. "It's a high-cash, fast-turnover business with an attraction for undesirable elements," an insurance lender commented to the *Journal.* A Webb director pointed to the "reputation" issue and the influence of organized crime as continuing problems raised by the money people, even after the Morgan-led bank loan.

The early enthusiasm for the casino business in 1977 and 1978, on the heels of the Atlantic City opening, began to taper off by 1979. The inflationary rise in labor and construction costs, the lack of experienced casino managers for "professionalized" corporate gaming, the fires at the MGM Grand and Hilton, and the problems associated with raising capital through a fluctuating stock market, all helped to take the shine off the boom. Financing, even for the confirmed "legitimate" corporations such as MGM and Hilton, was becoming difficult—and expensive—to obtain. Most new capital came from stock and equity offerings rather than king-sized loans. Consequently, the casinos became more sensitive to the effects of shifts in the economy. The gas crisis in the spring of 1979 worried the gambling men, although they proudly proclaimed in their press releases that the tourists kept on coming and that the industry had become both recession and energy-crisis-proof, a theory disputed by declining revenues during the 1980 recession. Ultimately, the evolution toward corporate gaming, despite the continuing participation of the "boys," upgraded Bugsy Siegel's debate with Meyer Lansky as to whether an empire of gambling palaces could really be created in the middle of nowhere.

STUMBLING ONTO THE LIMITS OF GROWTH

Although gambling thoroughly dominated the politics and economics of southern Nevada, the region had developed a secondary economic infrastructure which evolved from World War II military and industrial operations. In 1941, the Las Vegas Aerial Gunnery School was established eight miles northeast of Las Vegas to train flyers in the use of military aircraft weaponry. The following year, the school was enlarged into Nellis Air Force Base, complementing the range of Air Force installations established throughout the interior West during the war years.

On the opposite end of Las Vegas, midway between the town and Hoover Dam, the government made plans in 1941 to build a massive magnesium plant. The plant was to be called Basic Magnesium, after the large Cleveland industrial firm that was hired to build and operate the plant for the government. The creation of the Basic Magnesium complex created the boomtown of Henderson, settled by the more than twelve-thousand workers brought in to build and run the factories. The Basic Magnesium operation fit into the federal government's plans to generate a western industrial capacity to decentralize the nation's military and industrial operations for the war in the Pacific. The site was selected because of the area's access to raw materials, the water supply and power generation from the Hoover Dam, and the easy transportation routes to the coast.

In the early 1950s, a consortium of several national companies, including Kerr-McGee and Stauffer Chemical, incorporated as a joint venture under the name Basic Magnesium, Inc. (BMI) and took over the plant and facilities. As part of the arrangement, the corporation received the low-cost hydroelectric power and a large water supply from Hoover Dam. The advantage of the cheap power and water was essential for the companies to offset transportation costs for shipment to eastern markets as well as to California and some of the growing southwestern metropolises.

A few other industries settled in Henderson through the 1960s, including Pacific Engineering and Production Company (PEPCO), a producer of ammonium perchlorate, the solid fuel for intercontinental ballistic missiles. PEPCO, headed by Mormon leader James Gibson and his brother Fred, and Kerr-McGee (which also made ammonium perchlorate) were particularly interested in the construction of the gigantic MX system. The military's presence in southern Nevada consisted of Air Force facilities and the Nevada Test Site for nuclear weapons. The MX program would have a far greater effect than the earlier military operations.

To construct the system, scheduled to begin in the fall of 1982, the government estimated the need for twenty-three thousand workers. A population of one hundred thousand would eventually settle in the immediate construction area as well as places like Ely and Las Vegas. Each MX shelter also required 5 to 10 kilowatts of power and upward of 30,000 acre-feet of water per year during the construction period and 12,000 acre-feet thereafter.

The MX plans generated a great deal of controversy in Nevada and Utah. Although the Air Force considered alternative technologies for energy and water requirements, it prepared to contract with local utilities for most power needs, which affected the overall power supply in the area. The water issue raised the hackles of local residents in these two water-conscious states. In private, many politicians had initially applauded the MX as a great boon to their economies. After opposition began to grow, they shifted gears and started questioning different aspects of the system. Some politicians, such as Nevada's Representative James Santini, suggested utilizing the moribund NAWAPA plan to bring water from Canada and the Pacific Northwest.

The MX situation also raised the long-standing western issue of boomtown impact. In this instance a number of small Mormon towns and farming communities on both sides of the Nevada-Utah border were involved. Prominent Mormon politicians tried to balance their conservative promilitary and progrowth point of view with the belief that the MX would devastate those communities. James Gibson, the most powerful Mormon politician in Nevada as state senate majority leader and a regional representative in the church hierarchy, faced the additional factor that his PEPCO business stood to receive an extraordinary windfall if the system went through. As head of the legislative committee dealing with the MX-water issue, Gibson and his allies gingerly tried to avoid taking a definite position, but in private the Mormon leader spoke of the "inevitability" of the MX coming to Nevada. Even after the church First Presidency issued its anti-MX statement, several Nevada Mormons privately expressed support for the effort.

The MX question served to highlight the question of growth, which had reached astronomical proportions by 1980. Las Vegas had become the fastest-growing city in the country for cities with a population under 500,000, having grown from about 20,000 in Bugsy Siegel's days to more than 475,000 at the end of the 1970s. Estimates by the Regional Planning Committee of Clark County put the future population figures at 900,000 by the year 2000, estimates that did not include the possible impact of the MX.

Population growth has created enormous strains on existing resources, including the air quality, in the Las Vegas Valley. Smog had arrived in the Las Vegas region by the 1970s. In the Henderson area, residents suffered from a highly visible, dense, low-lying white cloud, known as the Henderson cloud, which formed weekday mornings from the combination of BMI gases and automobile pollution from Las Vegas.

The Las Vegas Valley, according to the Bureau of Reclamation, "is one of the driest and warmest areas of the country." The normal annual rainfall is between two and four inches a year, with much of that occurring during July and August from localized thunderstorms and cloudbursts that cause flash flooding with severe erosion, rapid runoff, and minimum penetration of moisture into the soil. Las Vegas is severely water-deficient, with problems potentially even greater than the water-short areas of central and southern Arizona.

Without much agriculture in the area, most of the water supply in the region has been used for municipal and industrial purposes. Although much of the early water supply came from groundwater pumping, a pipeline from Lake Mead to Clark County was constructed by the federal government in 1942 primarily to serve Henderson and the Basic Magnesium plant. That system was expanded in 1954 to include Las Vegas.

As Las Vegas grew, it quickly became apparent that the groundwater supplies, which provided the bulk of the early use, were being rapidly depleted. In 1955 a Bureau of Reclamation report regarding water resources declared that diversion of Lake Mead water could wait another twenty years. The extraordinary growth of the city quickly caused a revision of those estimates. By 1963, after pressure from local and state authorities, a bureau feasibility study recommended that the federal government spend about $50 million more to build the Southern Nevada Water Project in two successive stages. The second stage was to be built only after the need for additional water was determined. Most projections estimated that the first-stage supply of 132,000 acre-feet from Lake Mead would last until 1990.

The first stage, which consists of intake facilities from Lake Mead, pumping plants, aqueducts, tunnels, and underground pipelines, was completed in 1971. Las Vegas' astronomical growth put major strains on the region's water supply. Per capita Las Vegas consumption had jumped to a rate of 436 gallons a day—

the highest in the country, more than double the use by Tucson, with its equivalent population and environment. Las Vegas' high rate was due in part to the massive influx of tourists. The second stage of the project, the completion date now advanced to the early 1980s, would add another 166,800 acre-feet to Las Vegas' overall supply, which would exhaust Nevada's allocation of 300,000 acre-feet of Colorado River water. The Bureau of Reclamation optimistically estimated that this new water supply could serve a population of 750,000 and would last until the year 2000.

During the discussion over the first stage of the plan, only Howard Hughes, who was afraid of the germs filtering into the water supply, voiced major objections. The second stage plan received several criticisms centering on the growth factor. Little effort had been made to implement an urban water-conservation plan on the grounds, as the bureau's environmental-impact statement coyly put it, that to do so would interfere with the "quality of life" appeal of the gambling industry. A conservation plan with such features as zoning laws to prohibit new residential or commercial developments; more waste water for the parks, golf courses, and other public facilities; and a return to more natural desert vegetation would impose population and construction limits on the area. Neither the bureau, the local power structure, nor the gamblers were prepared to entertain the idea of planning controls. Instead, the local leaders continued to rely on the second stage of the Southern Nevada Water Project, which avoided imposing any structural limits on the population growth rate. Without limits, the growth spiral threatened to use up the water supply almost as soon as the second stage was completed.

The energy issue had become a problem as serious as the limited water supply. Ever since the construction of Hoover Dam, the issues of water and energy have been intertwined for southern Nevada. The Nevada Power Company, which serves the southern part of the state, was incorporated in 1929 just as plans to construct the dam got under way. The early leaders of the community and the power company fought the dam project, opposing federal control of the power generation and the impact on their community. After the dam was completed, Nevada Power was allocated more than 90 percent of Nevada's share of the 100,000 kilowatts available to the state.

Through the early 1950s the privately owned utility was "very conservative," according to the company's current chief executive officer, Conrad Ryan. The company closed the books on the twenty-fifth of each month and made no new purchases of power from Hoover Dam until inventory was taken during that week. "They adopted the use of a load regulator," Ryan explained of the old management groups. "Almost everything then was heated with electricity, and the usage was over double the national average. They put a regulator on each home. When the load reached a certain point the regulator cut the voltage, restricting the use of electricity." That mandatory conservation device, Ryan declared, might not sound like such a bad device today, but he quickly added, "I'm not for it."

At a time when the gambling industry and its profligate use of electricity were rapidly expanding, the old management soon lost favor with the casino operators. With pressure building for a change in the utility's management, the First National Bank of Chicago, the company's main financial agent, brought in a new staff led by Reid Gardner, a Mormon utility executive from Arizona.

Under Gardner's leadership, the company sought new sources of supply and joined others in exploring the possible use of Utah coal. Interested in WEST Associates' grid plan for the Southwest, the company decided to participate in the Mohave and Navajo power plant projects, with a 14 percent and 11.3 percent interest in the two operations, respectively. As part of the Mohave deal the WEST utilities promised to hire only Nevada residents for the plant, in exchange for Nevada's provision of the site and the water for cooling purposes.

By the late 1960s, Nevada Power experienced an extraordinary growth rate, which caused its leadership to look for the "big solution." Like its southwestern counterparts, the company was far too small to come up with the front-end financing for a plant as large as 500,000 to 1 million kilowatts, then considered the necessary volume for a profitable project. To meet the problem, company management devised the Allen–Warner Valley plan to build two massive operations: a 500,000-kilowatt coal-fired plant near Saint George, Utah, in the Warner Valley, and a second 2-million-kilowatt coal-fired Harry Allen plant (named after a Nevada Power officer), near Las Vegas.

The key to the Allen–Warner Valley plan was the distribution of costs and power generation. Although Nevada Power was to remain project manager, initial front-end costs and power distribution were to be divided 20 percent for Nevada Power and 80 percent for larger utilities in California. Nevada Power also reserved the right to increase its share of the output from the Allen plant thirteen years after the first unit entered commercial operation. The Nevada utility reduced its front-end capital and interest costs, while keeping a long-term reserve available. The California utilities, in exchange for some initial costs, received a stable medium-term supply of power without having to face the problem of burning coal in California. For Nevada Power it seemed the ideal solution to future growth problems, without requiring the kind of massive investment that could bankrupt the company.

Despite the initial enthusiasm of the utilities, the plant repeatedly ran into problems. The Los Angeles Department of Water and Power dropped out of the project because of a tax ruling. Southern California Edison and Pacific Gas and Electric withdrew because of a shrinking growth rate and overestimated demand in California. The enormous environmental problems related to the Allen–Warner Valley effort involved southern Utah strip mines and the Warner plant, which threatened air quality in Bryce and Zion national parks in Utah. With negative assessments in 1980 and early 1981 from the Office of Surface Mining, the California Public Utilities Commission, and the Bureau of Land Management, Allen–Warner Valley seemed problematic.

The Nevada-California energy link raised old fears in Nevada about its dependency on its Pacific neighbor. "Though California has some nuclear plants, they haven't authorized any new coal or nuclear plants since 1974," former Governor O'Callaghan complained of the situation. "Then they dump their waste in Beatty. . . . Well, that doesn't set too well here. We used to get up in the morning to watch the bombs go off," O'Callaghan continued, referring to the atomic tests at the Nevada Test Site in the early 1950s. "Now, people are dying. We used to feel wanted and now we feel used."

Nevada Power and Las Vegas' approach to water and power questions highlighted most dramatically the common western practice of clamoring about scarce resources but then overutilizing them. Las Vegas was built on an industry that never closed its doors. Scarce resources concerned casino executives, who had no intention of "dimming their lights," as Shannon Bybee put it. Instead, Las Vegas sought bigger solutions.

In the summer of 1979, as problems continued to mount, Nevada Power executives called a meeting of top Las Vegas figures, including the leaders from the hotel-casino industry. Nevada Power made a presentation of its difficulties with the Allen–Warner Valley Project, urging that everyone understand that resource issues had to be handled by the entire community elite, not just the utility executives and a handful of public officials. Nevada Power's exhortations made little impact on the gamblers who hardly ever thought about water and energy and tended to dismiss the fears concerning possible limits on growth. For an industry that grew up on the notion that long-term planning meant transferring cash out the next day, resource issues were as foreign as the concept of conservation. The idea of conservation was equally foreign to the utility executives and water planners. Nevada Power, like its customers in the casinos, was a power junkie. For the lights to dim, however briefly, seemed cataclysmic.

The business of Las Vegas is cash flow, and as so many have written, that is the sound of the city. "It's the money," an executive at the Sands told Ed Reid and Ovid Demaris in the early 1960s, "the presence of it, the obviousness of it, that distorts all other values. It's the only thing that matters in this town." Fifteen years later, in 1978, Jerome Skolnick, in his sociological study *House of Cards*, commented on the irony of a society that had made legalized gambling so successful while simultaneously refusing to legalize other victimless crimes. "Apparently," Skolnick wrote, "the only heritage strong enough to challenge puritanism is capitalism." Capitalism in the gambling town is at its most overt— "a city that has constructed the architecture of money," as one critic put it.

In Las Vegas, streets are named after casinos rather than the city's founders. "But what does gambling produce?" former Governor O'Callaghan rhetorically asks. "A carpenter sees a building. A farmer sees his produce. But what does the gambler see? What is all this built on?"

People who run the industry like to boast that they never gamble, but they still act like crap-shoot artists who pray that their luck will not run out. Efforts to woo the traditional money markets of New York and California proceed unevenly, complicated by the fact that Las Vegas ultimately remains a mob town—or, to put it politely, a town that continues to use untraditional sources of high-risk capital, unusual management practices, and "creative" accounting methods. "There's a saying in this town," one high-level government law-enforcement official said of Las Vegas. 'It used to be great when the hoods ran this town.' The fact is, they still do, only now they have button-down shirts." A local gambling columnist said simply, "This city is a den of thieves."

Las Vegas, as Meyer Lansky and Bugsy Siegel knew in their desolate drive across the desert, is the end of the road in the middle of nowhere. It is the West's most contrived, most artificial city, whose needs for survival and growth compound existing western problems. As the problems deepen, whether in terms of water supplies, energy resources, or the nature and speed of urbanization, they precipitate the crises facing the entire region. The air gets dirtier, and the water saltier and scarcer. Dredging up the coal, uranium, and shale threatens to mar some of the oldest untouched landscapes of the West.

Las Vegas becomes the most tangible example of the contradictions involved in the western conflict. The city's leaders optimistically move forward "with faith in the future," as Mormon politician Jim Seastrand remarked, and with that peculiar western boom mentality. One has to wonder whether this superimposition on the desert will grow, be transformed, or, like the ancient civilization of the Hohokam, fade out in history, having self-destructed from the demands of an impossible future.

PART THREE
POINTS OF CONFLICT

The rise of the Southwest's new regional power has been fraught with conflict. The settling of the region through the Anglo migrations of the latter half of the nineteenth century was achieved by the military conquest and resettlement of the Indian tribes and Mexican pueblos. Genocide and annexation preceded a conscious labor policy based on the importation of cheap foreign labor from the Pacific and from below the American-imposed Mexican border.

The conflict over control of land can be redefined in contemporary terms with the realization that the new resource push in the Southwest must now contend with Indian tribes whose water rights and land base—once deemed worthless desert but now discovered to hold vast resources—conflicts with the designs of emerging southwestern capitalism. The issue of the Mexican border also brings into play the hundred-year quest to ease the way for a flow of capital south into Mexico and a continuing flow of labor north. Oil and undocumented workers are the new Mexican factors, and both issues have become crucial to the future of the region's power.

Conflicts in this region have a class dimension, a political dimension, and an environmental dimension, all of which go to the heart of the issues of urban development and the energy boom. The dependency on cheap labor has led to the passage of antiunion right-to-work laws setting the stage for a new attack on labor in the western energy belt. As an urban civilization in the desert, the region has bred the politically potent environmental movement and popular movements of the Left and the Right—potential citizens' armies—whose own struggle for influence sharpens the differences between contending policies and visions of the future of the region.

9   The Indian Wars

George Vlassis, the tribal attorney for the Navajo Nation, was eating a delicatessen sandwich between calls to keep him posted about the arrival of Peter MacDonald, Navajo tribal chairman. Vlassis' office, done in modern western style with Indian crafts and artifacts, is located in Phoenix, one of the urban centers from which white America has attempted to direct the destiny of Indian America.

Vlassis was in an expansive mood reminiscing about the business propositions that a tribal attorney has to deal with. After leaving Wall Street for Phoenix, he did his first work for the Navajo in 1967. He learned then that the tribe had invested $1 million in the Navajo Bancorporation in 1962, but after five years, their investment had dwindled to $275,000. The Navajo Bancorporation was chaired by Bing Crosby, with a board that included a number of Phoenix businessmen with ties to organized-crime figures. The Navajo Bancorporation had opened a branch in Window Rock, the Navajo capital, where it handled tribal funds. Despite the $1 million investment, the Navajo never did get a seat on the board of directors. Instead of ending Navajo participation in this questionable operation, Vlassis got the tribe further involved. "I went on the board," Vlassis explained, "and got the investment up to $3 million after three years."

Vlassis became tribal attorney in 1970 after Peter MacDonald was elected tribal chairman. The Department of the Interior's Bureau of Indian Affairs (BIA) had wanted to impose on the tribe Ernest Wilkinson, president of Brigham Young University and founding partner of the influential Washington-based Republican law firm of Wilkinson, Cragun, and Barker. Narrowing the field to three candidates, MacDonald chose Vlassis over Wilkinson and Nixon protégé Herbert Kleindienst. With annual receipts of $25 million from its mineral resources and another $405 million from the federal government, Navajo economic affairs are big business, the biggest of any Indian tribe. The Navajo, according to MacDonald, needed high-powered legal talent. After Vlassis was hired, MacDonald then hired a Washington-based Democratic

219

firm, Freed, Frank, Harris, Shriver, and Kampelman, to help deal with the increasing pressures on Navajo resources from the energy companies and utilities.

Vlassis' first job as tribal attorney was to check on another investment scheme. A company calling itself Westward Coach had persuaded the tribe to invest $1 million in an operation to make storage discs for computers at an abandoned uranium mill in Mexican Hat, Utah. Westward Coach suddenly decided it would rather make recreational vehicles out of used police vans, so it invited Vlassis to take a look at their assembly line in El Segundo, California. When he got there, he found only one vehicle surrounded with the kind of tools weekend handymen buy at the local hardware store. The Westward Coach people did put on an impressive slide show about their plans, however. Vlassis said that after a while, "they conceded that the pitch wasn't going well because I wanted to turn off the slide show and look at their balance sheet." When they could not persuade Vlassis to go to Las Vegas for some "entertainment," they brought out their new Navajo president, who attacked Vlassis as a typical white. In the end, the tribe sued Westward Coach for stock fraud, settling for 12 cents on the dollar.

In 1980 Vlassis was working on the tribe's biggest deal—negotiating a royalty adjustment on the tribe's first coal lease, signed in 1957 with Utah International to provide coal from one of the West's biggest strip mines for the Four Corners power plant. Vlassis had gone to his first meeting with Utah in 1971—just before radical changes in Indian politics brought on by the revelations about the nature of Indian leases approved by the BIA, the subsequent attack on the BIA offices in Washington, and the seizure of Wounded Knee Village by American Indian Movement militants. "In a polite way," Vlassis described the 1971 meeting, "they let me in the front door and threw me out the back door. I was like a poor boy from the country." When Vlassis explained the tribe's demands, "They simply said, 'Are you kidding?'"

If the Navajo were besieged by deals, rip-offs, and energy company maneuvers, part of the responsibility lay with the tribe's ostensible guardian, the BIA. In a spacious office tucked away in an obscure corridor in the Department of the Interior in Washington, BIA official David Harrison discussed the "Indian business," as it is often called by the tens of thousands of tribal employees, bureaucrats, businessmen, social scientists, lawyers, missionaries, and assorted hustlers who make their living off dealing with the country's Indian tribes. The BIA, the energy companies and the Navajo were aware that negotiations in 1980 were substantially different from George Vlassis' encounter with Utah International in 1971. "It is beginning to look," said Harrison, "like the Indians have most of what is running short in the rest of the country—water, oil, gas, uranium, and tremendous amounts of western coal." Today Edmund Wattis Littlefield, Utah's chairman, personally flies to Window Rock to negotiate with tribal leaders. "Now they are much more organized and conscious of their political position," Littlefield conceded.

After all, Harrison explained, those Indian resources are extensive: 52 million acres located mostly in the western United States; 30 percent of the country's strippable coal; 15 percent to 40 percent of the nation's uranium; an annual timber harvest of 1 billion board feet; 6 million to 8 million acres of grazing land, used by 1 million cattle, 800,000 sheep and goats, and 100,000 horses. As director of trust responsibility, Harrison, an Osage from Oklahoma, was a key government official responsible for administering and managing this huge estate as part of the trust relationship between the government, represented by the Department of the Interior, and the Indian people. His role in the trust relationship requires that Harrison, for instance, approve all leases between the tribes and private businesses.

"Today the philosophy is self-determination," asserted Harrison. "The ultimate decisions will be made by those Indian owners about the control, pace, and mitigations of the effects of resource development." The BIA's concept of self-determination is a special sort that grew out of the long and sordid history of the country's first experience with the role of colonial master. Today, after the New Deal encouraged Indians to form Anglo-style tribal governments and after the uprisings of the 1960s and 1970s gave the concept of self-determination a new meaning, Indian affairs are still ultimately under the control of the Secretary of the Interior. "There is no power for the tribes to make unilateral decisions without the approval of the secretary or for the secretary to make decisions without the approval of the tribe," Harrison explained.

In reality, there are numerous definitions of self-determination. To some Indian leaders, often identified as "traditionals," self-determination means recognition by the United States that the Indian people are members of sovereign nations within the United States, with their own forms of religiopolitical government, protected by scores of treaties, most of which have been broken. To others, like MacDonald, self-determination means a more equitable partnership with the energy companies in the development of Indian resources. Still others, tied to the bureaucracy, are divided between the emerging ideas of self-determination and the tribal governments imposed on them by the BIA. Regardless of earlier forms of Indian government, almost all tribes practice a peculiarly flawed kind of self-governance designed for them by an earlier generation of Anglo-Indian reformers.

THE INDIAN NEW DEAL

Foremost among Indian reformers was John Collier, Franklin Roosevelt's Indian commissioner and the person who had the greatest impact on Indian affairs of perhaps any man in the twentieth century. Collier was born and raised in Atlanta, Georgia, where his father served as mayor. Orphaned as a teenager, Collier was free to indulge his naturalism and romanticism in the wilds of Appalachia, where he was impressed by the lives of the backwoods people, including the local Cherokee. On numerous camping and hiking trips, he witnessed the steady erosion of this civilization as the forests were cleared and the hill people were forced into the cotton mills. Collier was also inspired by utopian socialism and the Russian anarchists with their beliefs that preindustrial communities could form the basis of the new cooperative commonwealth.

Collier's intellectual curiosity and interest in public affairs took him to New York, where he immersed himself in the life of an activist social worker. In pre–World War I New York, Collier visited the Greenwich Village salon of Mabel Dodge, an acquaintance of a wide range of artists and political figures, including D.H. Lawrence and "Big Bill" Haywood, the founder of the International Workers of the World (IWW). After the war, Dodge got Collier to visit Taos, New Mexico, where she had married a Pueblo Indian named Tony Luhan. Inspired in part by Lawrence, the Taos artistic community was infused with a romantic view of the nearby Pueblo Indians, who were seen as the key to a new communal life. Writing years later about a meeting with some Seminole, Collier revealed a highly idealized view of Indian life. "What dark hands—electric hands, vibrant with a heatless fire, hands of men and women deeply involved as living spirits and yet faithfully animal—and possessed of the long-lost unrecoverable wilderness heritage that we white men have given up."

In the early 1920s, the remnants of the nation's Indian communities were barely surviving. The Indian population had been falling steadily even though active warfare against it had all but ended with the massacre at Wounded Knee in 1890. The level of poverty and disease in Indian communities was beyond comprehension. In the era of the Teapot Dome scandal, the best of the remaining Indian lands were being removed from their control. As the period of overt genocide came to an end, Indian affairs were epitomized by the Dawes Severalty Act of 1887. The act, which provided for allotment of Indian lands to individual Indians and the sale of whatever else remained, was designed to break up tribal structures and remake the Indian in the mold of the white farmer. Although the government curtailed the allotments in the early 1920s, Secretary of the Interior Albert Fall threw open the remaining Indian lands to mineral leasing, assigning most of the income from the leases to the Reclamation Fund, where it would pay for irrigation for white ranchers.

During these years, recalcitrant Indian leaders were imprisoned; a number of Indian religious ceremonies, obnoxious to whites, were banned; and Indian children were transported to Indian schools far from their homes, where they were systematically brutalized and forbidden to speak their native language. "Until the third decade of the present century," wrote D'Arcy McNickle, "Indian policy was rooted in the assumption that the Indians would disappear."

White reform groups, including one founded by Collier, publicized the Indian situation through a successful campaign to protect the lands of one of the New Mexico pueblos. Collier's effort took him to Washington, where he worked with other reformers, including Harold Ickes, to bring about a number of investigations of conditions in Indian country. These investigations led to the beginnings of Indian reform under President Herbert Hoover.

When Roosevelt appointed Ickes Secretary of the Interior, Ickes made Collier Commissioner of Indian Affairs. Collier immediately set out to bring about a new era in Indian-white relations. Inspired by the Cherokee he knew as a youth and by what he learned from the Pueblo Indians, he urged an end to paternalism and the development of what he called "indirect administration" of tribal affairs, an idea he took from the British decolonization process.

In 1934 Congress passed the Indian Reorganization Act (the Wheeler-Howard Act), which brought about three important changes: economic rehabilitation through the end of the allotment system, the return of surplus lands to the tribes, and a commitment to extend and consolidate tribal lands; the organization through elections of tribal governments; and civil and cultural freedom and opportunity. The act called for the tribes to vote on the law and then draw up a constitution and elect a tribal government. Within a short time, 181 tribes voted for the law, but Collier's reforms triggered controversy and bitter opposition on numerous reservations.

The Navajo were at the center of this controversy. They had a tribal council, which had been set up while Albert Fall was still Secretary of the Interior. Eager to open Navajo lands for leasing to oil companies, Fall appointed as superintendent of the Navajo Agency a former territorial governor of New Mexico who had made his fortune in land speculation, railroads, and mining. When Fall's leasing plans were opposed by a council of leaders from the San Juan area of the reservation, the superintendent formed a new tribal council, which finally approved the leases.

With this recent experience in Washington's version of self-government, the Navajo were confronted in 1934 with Collier's plan for the reservation. Part of Collier's plan was to apply the new principles of the Soil Conservation Act to Indian reservations as a model of how the country's heavily eroded and depleted grazing lands could be protected. The Navajo, unlike other Indians, had grown steadily in numbers since their release from Bosque Redondo, where they had been imprisoned in 1863. (At that time, an army contingent led by Kit Carson rounded up thousands of Navajo, destroyed their crops, and forced them to make the infamous "Long Walk" hundreds of miles to the Rio Grande Valley.) The Navajo rise in population had been accompanied by a huge growth in livestock on the reservation, since sheep, goats, and horses were a principal means of exchange, a food source, and a measure of material well-being.

Although Collier went repeatedly to the Navajo reservation to campaign for his plan to reduce the tribe's livestock population by four hundred thousand head, the Navajo registered their opposition by voting down the Indian Reorganization Act. A year later, Collier, determined not to be thwarted in his attempt to convey the benefits of the New Deal, intervened by introducing a resolution that called for the reorganization of the existing tribal council. When the tribal superintendent warned that the political climate was not right for elections, Collier approved designation of seventy tribal leaders as the new tribal council and charged it to act as a constitutional assembly. With final right to approve the constitution, Collier recommended that the writers of the new constitution "should consider the inchoate, amorphous condition of the Navajo and that, in view of this inchoate condition, it should be short, concise, simple, limited to a few objectives and conferring initially a limited number of powers." When the new constitution was finally approved by Washington, the Navajo elected a tribal chairman who was a leader of the opposition to stock reduction.

One student of Navajo affairs has concluded that "in effect, the tribal government was a superimposition from the top rather than a grass-roots movement beginning with the people." Soon the stock reduction became an ugly test of strength between the Navajo and the Indian Service employees, who, in some instances, rounded up and burned stock in an attempt to enforce the reduction. In the end, the stock reduction, like the Long Walk, entered Navajo memory as another attack on their way of life perpetrated by a hostile world.

Despite numerous instances of tribes opposing reforms imposed on them by Washington, the Indian New Deal was a crucial reversal of the gradual trend toward extinction of all Indians. The tribes were given the wherewithal, meager as it was, to allow births to exceed deaths for the first time since the Indian wars of the previous century. In another reversal, government action added 6 million acres to Indian lands. Collier's efforts to impose self-determination on the

Indians were often self-defeating. Tribal society would never again be the same.

"The tribal governments," wrote Joseph Jorgensen, "were little states administered by an arm of the federal bureaucracy, and both the BIA and the tribes, in turn, were controlled by the Secretary of the Interior . . . and by the House Committee on Interior and Insular Affairs," which approved expenditures of many tribes. According to a former Sioux chairman, "This was a radical change from the traditional tribal government which had total democracy in council, advised by a smaller council of wise elders who had to agree unanimously on every decision and even then could not force their decisions on any adult male."

Collier led a successful attack on the old missionary-inspired idea that the ultimate goal of Indian-white relations was to save the Indian from his Indianness by turning him into a white man. Instead, Collier wanted to make the Indian Service into "a laboratory of ethnic relations" where mutual respect for each other's culture was the most important goal. In his reforming zeal, Collier, aided by anthropologists (a new force on the Indian scene), played the role of head scientist. He designed experiments in education, government, and other areas and then carried them out, often without consulting those who had to live with the results of his idealism. In the end, Indian life did not become the model for a new communitarian democracy as Collier had hoped. In fact, Collier brought the white world to the reservation by introducing wage labor through public-works programs and creating tribal bureaucracies. But the Indian New Deal did provide Indian people with what Vine Deloria, Jr., has called "the basis for communal survival in the postwar world."

COLLIER UNDER ATTACK: TERMINATION

Collier came under attack from Indians and whites alike from the very beginning of his term as Indian commissioner: poor Indians accused him of stealing their livestock, and wealthy Indians charged him with threatening their meager property rights by ending allotments. At the end of World War II, the BIA and Collier, in particular, were attacked as "Communistic" and "anti-religionistic" in a series of congressional hearings as Congress gradually assumed a larger and larger role in the formulation of Indian policy. After Collier was replaced as commissioner in 1945, his successor purged numerous New Deal figures from the agency. Congress began to call for the elimination of services provided by the BIA. The Hoover Commission on Government Reorganization recommended in 1948 "the complete integration" of all Indians into American society. During this period, more than a hundred anti-Indian bills made it into the congressional hopper.

When Dillon Myer became Indian commissioner in 1950, the campaign to force the Indian into the American mainstream gained momentum. Myer had been director of the agency that ran the internment camps for Japanese-Americans during World War II. Collier later wrote that "Dillon Myer's image of concentration camps as places of unmitigated misery . . . remained at the center of his mind, and when he became Commissioner of Indian Affairs in 1950, he transposed the idea to the Indian reservations. They were concentration camps, and his business was to relocate the Indians out of them." Thus began the attempt to dismantle, or "terminate," numerous Indian tribes.

Myer's policies and the whole mood of the period evoked the era of Indian reform that culminated in the disastrous Dawes Act. As with other commissioners, Myer decided to make the Hopi and Navajo the centerpiece of his ideas through programs which allocated funds to move Indians to the city while providing other funds for reservation rehabilitation for those who could not be forced to migrate. Myer also believed that the Indians should take up farming, but this time without the help of government funds. He called for the gradual reduction in the credit fund set up during the New Deal to help Indians establish cooperatives.

Finally, in 1953, more than a decade of attacks on Indian policy culminated in the passage of a resolution calling for "freeing" Indians from government supervision and control and for a review of existing laws and treaties to see how they could be nullified. Another law called for the states to assume legal jurisdiction on the reservations. In the ensuing years, numerous laws were passed that chipped away at the power of the BIA. In all, about twenty tribes, bands, and remnants of tribes were slated for termination. Best known of the terminated tribes were the Southern Paiute of Utah, whose land was transferred to the control of a Salt Lake City bank; the Menominee of Wisconsin; and the Klamath of Oregon. In some instances, the termination was carried out by simply going to a reservation and posting a notice on a building.

The Navajo-Hopi rehabilitation program, relocation, and termination, according to Jorgensen, "were right and left hand." One urged the Indians to leave the reservation for the big city; the other assured that there would be no tribal government or tribal lands for them to cling to or return to. In the 1950s, Indians were not in vogue with the mass media or white reformers, and so the fight against termination was a bitter and lonely one.

After visiting the Klamath in 1969, a senate committee concluded, "The termination of the Klamath reservation in Oregon has led to extreme social disorganization of the tribal group. Many of them can be found in state mental and penal institutions." Salt Lake attorney Parker Nielson, who had defended the rights of terminated Indians, insisted that termination "caused the urban Indian problem," by forcing the Indians off the reservation and into the cities. The Paiute, he went on, were "actually going out and committing suicide by walking under motor vehicles."

President Eisenhower denounced termination as "unchristian" but signed the necessary legislation anyway. After he appointed Fred Seaton Secretary of the Interior, Seaton repudiated termination. Slowly the pendulum began to swing in the direction of reform. Eventually the Menominee and the Southern Paiute were restored to tribal status, but the attack on the nation's Indian communities left another legacy of permanent damage and lingering hostility.

THE LAND-CLAIMS RACKET

The attack on Collier's reform policies began with the passage of the Indian Claims Commission Act in 1946. This law, hailed at first as another major reform beneficial to Indians, allowed Indians to bring cases against the federal government before the United States Court of Claims for failure to spend funds appropriated for Indian tribes and for lands taken from the Indians. Individual claims against the federal government had soared after Indians were granted citizenship in the 1920s. Almost all of these claims ultimately worked against the Indians who filed them. Once a settlement was reached, the government charged "offsets" against the claim for services rendered through government programs, and the claimant usually ended without a reward. During the 1930s Collier and others pushed for a more just and efficient claims process without success.

The claims law introduced by Senators Arthur Watkins of Utah and McCarran of Nevada, was finally passed. The law was the brainchild of Mormon attorney Ernest Wilkinson, who had already won two important land-claim cases for the Ute tribe. He wrote about the new claims act to a Ute leader, "As your attorney I spent considerable time assisting in the writing of that particular bill." He attached a letter from a North Dakota congressman describing how Wilkinson rewrote the law with a solicitor from the Department of the Interior and helped move it through Congress.

The new law called for the creation of the Indian Claims Commission, which first would rule on the legitimacy of a tribe's claim, then set a date at which the land was taken from the tribe, and finally determine the amount owed the Indians for their lost lands based on the value of the land *at the time it was taken from the Indians.* Although on the surface the law looked like another advance for the Indian people, it was designed to end Indian claims to their traditional homelands once and for all, legitimizing the entire history of Indian land seizures.

The law was quickly interpreted by the courts to mean that all settlements would be in the form of *monetary payments rather than restoration of land.* The courts also stated that once the claim was settled, the Indians no longer retained any claim to the land. In effect, the law meant a massive and final buy-out of disputed Indian land claims at nineteenth-century prices. The law—dubbed the Indian Lawyers Welfare Act by its critics—also provided fees for tribal lawyers, which were usually set at 7 percent to 10 percent of the settlement. In other words, Wilkinson, the successful claims lawyer, wrote a piece of legislation with a built-in incentive for lawyers to encourage the tribal governments, created by BIA bureaucrats during the New Deal, to file land claims that would result in monetary payments representing a fraction of present value. "The more you lost, the more money you got," noted Parker Nielson.

Having pioneered in the land-claims business, Wilkinson and his firm signed up a number of tribes including the Ute, the Shoshone, the Goshiute, the Paiute, the Klamath, and the Hopi. Wilkinson was soon joined by John Boyden, another Mormon attorney from Salt Lake City. Although Boyden had wanted to replace John Collier as Indian commissioner, he instead went to work with Wilkinson on the Ute claim case, which resulted in a $50 million settlement.

The claims process dovetailed nicely with the congressional attack on Indian government. When Senator Watkins, another Mormon, began to work for termination, he argued that the cash settlements awarded by the claims court provided the necessary funds for numerous Indians to get a start in the white world. The claims process did place significant amounts of cash in the hands of Indians. To a limited extent, this helped them survive in a hostile world. In cases like the Klamath claim, white entrepreneurs very quickly relieved the Indians of their funds. The ultimate insult was that the awards were paid to the

United States Treasury, from which they could only be dispensed by congressional appropriation. "When tribal officials appeared in Washington," wrote D'Arcy McNickle, "they found Senator Watkins of Utah standing in the way." When Watkins was finally defeated in his bid to remain in the Senate, Eisenhower made him head of the Indian Claims Commission.

Cash payments were at the heart of the controversy over the new law. Indian leaders have repeatedly stated that they never understood this provision of the law and that their lawyers had led them to believe that filing a claim meant an attempt to get their lands back, when this was precluded by the court's interpretation of the law.

In a typical case in 1973, Mary and Carrie Dann, two sisters who were Nevada ranchers and members of the Temoak band of the Western Shoshone, received a trespass notice from the Bureau of Land Management. The notice threatened to seize the Danns' livestock if they did not get off bureau land. The Danns' response was that they and their ancestors had always lived on this land, which had been part of the 24 million acres set aside for the Western Shoshone by an 1863 treaty.

When the Bureau of Land Management threatened to run the Dann sisters off their ancestral land, the Indians challenged the trespass charge in court, arguing that they were raising cattle and horses on what had always been Shoshone land. Inspired by the Danns' challenges to the federal government, a group of tribal members formed the Western Shoshone Legal Defense and Education Association (later, the Western Shoshone Sacred Land Association) and went to court. Their attorney argued that the government had never taken the land from the Shoshone.

Although the Shoshone lost their challenge before the Claims Commission in 1976, the effort inspired new interest in the claims case among new tribal leaders, who were elected in part through the efforts of the association. As a result the tribal council petitioned President Carter and the Department of the Interior to rule that the Shoshone still owned their traditional homeland. Ultimately, the Claims Commission ruled against the new tribal attorneys. In February 1979 the courts turned down the Shoshone appeal of the decision. Despite Shoshone opposition, the government awarded the tribe $26 million, or $1.07 an acre for land currently worth about $200 an acre. The Shoshone, however, refused to accept the money, knowing that would end their claim to their land. Robert Barker, who had been fired by the Shoshones, received his multimillion-dollar fee, however.

Meanwhile, Shoshone leaders were working quietly with sympathetic figures in the Interior Department to set aside as a reservation 3 million acres of the 24 million claimed by the tribe. By early 1979 the Shoshone thought they were making some headway with Interior despite their legal setbacks. The tribe had scaled down its demands for the amount of land to be restored, and both sides were talking about setting up a task force to recommend a solution. In May 1979, Secretary Cecil Andrus suddenly ruled out the establishment of a task force. The two-pronged Shoshone attack on the Claims Commission ground to a halt. Soon after, the Carter administration announced plans for building the MX missile within the boundaries of the traditional Shoshone homeland in Nevada.

The struggle to regain control of their traditional homelands was a central issue in the 1960s renewal of Indian resistance to the encroachment of the white world. At the heart of the struggle was an attack on the claims process as one of the most notorious and disputed pieces of Indian legislation ever passed. The Sioux, in a celebrated case that led in part to the Wounded Knee uprising of 1973, attempted to regain control of the Black Hills promised them in the Treaty of 1868. After fifty-eight years of litigation, the Supreme Court finally awarded the Sioux $17.5 million for the Black Hills. The Sioux decided to refuse the settlement and pursue the fight for the return of their lands.

By 1980, at least twenty-three tribes and groups of traditionals decided to fight for the return of their land, many of them through the assistance of the Indian Law Resource Center in Washington, D.C. Having exhausted most of the legal avenues in the courts, Resource Center lawyers Tim Coulter and Steve Tulberg decided to take their cases before the United Nations, where they are charging the United States with violations of the Indians' human rights.

In 1978, the Indian Claims Commission went out of business, and further claims were turned over to the Court of Claims. During the commission's existence, tribes filed claims for $2 billion. The commission awarded about $800 million, with about $60 million going to the lawyers who handled the cases. The claims process is responsible for the tribal land base remaining the same since Collier's attempts to add to Indian lands in the 1930s. There have been three significant restorations of Indian lands. The restorations include the return in 1970 of the sacred Blue Lake, and 44,000 acres, to the Taos Pueblo, which, ironically, was represented by Wilkinson, Cragun, and Barker. Between 1934 and 1977, the tribes acquired 1.5 million acres (excluding Alaska), but the government managed to relieve the Indians of 1.8 million acres. Much of that land was taken by the Bureau of Reclamation for water projects.

Ernest Wilkinson, the prominent Mormon who went on to become president of Brigham Young University, played the central role in getting a claims law passed. In fact, the file where the record of cash awards and legal fees is kept is known as the Wilkinson file. Wilkinson's effort to put cold cash in the hands of Indians to prepare them for assimilation into the white world coincided with the missionary offensive of the Mormon church launched after World War II to effect the final reconciliation between white Mormons and their lost brothers, the dark-skinned Lamanites.

THE LAST OF THE MISSIONARIES

Among Mormons, it is one of the most popular modern parables. In 1947 a ranch family in Sevier County, Utah, brought a young Navajo girl to visit Golden Buchanan, the stake president in the area. The girl was a member of a large group of migrant workers who were harvesting sugar beets for Mormon ranchers. At the end of the harvest, she asked her employers if she could spend the winter in a tent on their property so that she could attend the local school. Buchanan wrote to Spencer W. Kimball for advice. Kimball, who had been called in 1943 to work in the church's first modern Indian mission among the Navajo and the Zuni, was then an apostle. Kimball suggested that the Buchanans board the young girl. At first, the family resisted for fear of what their neighbors might say, but they eventually relented. Their decision to board the young Indian girl is considered by the church to be the beginning of its most successful Indian program, the Indian Placement Service.

The Mormons' obsession with the American Indian went back to Joseph Smith's first visions. Smith was fascinated by the Indian mounds scattered around the New York countryside. According to his account, the golden plates revealed to him by the Angel Moroni told the story of the relations between these mounds and the Mormons' spiritual ancestors. According to the Book of Mormon, the Mormons were originally a band of Israelites who fled Jerusalem and then embarked on a voyage that took them across the Pacific to the western hemisphere. Here the descendants of the Israelites built the great pre-Columbian civilizations of Central America. Once in the New World, the Israelites divided into two warrings groups, one "white and delightsome" (the Nephites), the other "dark and loathsome" (the Lamanites). Fighting repeatedly with the Lamanites and among themselves, the Nephites finally wandered north, where they fought one last great battle with the Lamanites near the Hill of Cummorah, where Joseph found the plates. In this way, Joseph Smith took the folklore of the Bible and the tales of ancient battles and ancient civilizations to create a native Christian church that linked the white immigrants to the aboriginal people of the continent.

As soon as the Saints platted their new Jerusalem on the shores of the Great Salt Lake, Brigham Young urged his followers to push out into the surrounding country in all directions. Since the lands around the lake were within the sphere of the Ute and the Shoshone, the first Mormon colonizing efforts brought the Mormons face to face with Indian resistance. According to some historians, the Indians recognized a difference between the "Mormonee" settlers and the more murderous "Americats." Mormon policy, by these accounts, was guided by Young's counsel that it was "less expensive to feed and clothe them than to fight them." In reality, the Mormon approach to the "Indian problem" was very much like the approach of other white settlers—racist and genocidal.

Spencer Kimball's grandfather, Heber C. Kimball, for example, "discouraged the idea of paying the Indians for the lands, for if the Shoshonis [sic] should be considered, the Utes and the other tribes would claim pay also." When Mormon settlers clashed with the Ute over control of the Utah Valley south of Great Salt Lake, Young, according to Brigham Young University Press editor Howard Christy, "ordered that all men were to be killed—women and children to be saved if they 'behave themselves.'"

In time the Indians—defeated militarily, cut off from their food sources, and wracked by the white man's diseases—were forced to sign treaties that confined them to reservation lands. Although they drove the Indians from the best lands, the Saints also experimented with more benevolent approaches such as confining some Ute to an experimental farm.

The Utah Ute were assigned to about 2 million acres in the majestic but arid Uintah basin in the mountains of eastern Utah by order of President Abraham Lincoln. They were soon joined there by their old enemies, the Mormon settlers, who were following plans for new settlements that Young had drawn up even before the basin became an Indian reservation, and by a large number of Ute who were driven out of Colorado after an abortive uprising known to white historians as the Meeker Massacre.

In one generation, the Ute, once the most feared raiders of the Rocky

Mountain West, had been reduced to a few pathetic bands of stragglers. In less than twenty years, according to one estimate, the number of Utah Ute had fallen from forty-five hundred to about eight hundred. The residue of bitterness is still felt among the Indians of the Great Basin. "A lot of things are not reported in history," said one Ute tribal employee. She heard from her grandmother, whose people came from central Utah, that the Mormons would hold big feeds, inviting the Indians to join them. The Ute would then be slipped poison in their food. Others tell how Goshiute Indians, baptized in an irrigation ditch, contracted a fever and died soon after.

Gradually Mormon settlers took up land within almost every major Indian community in Utah, Nevada, southern Idaho, and northern and central Arizona, while compressing the remaining tribesmen into smaller and smaller areas. Despite the Indians' special status in Mormon folklore, when Spencer Kimball was called to the Navajo-Zuni mission, Mormon-Indian relations were very much like white-Indian relations throughout the West. The two societies coexisted, but aside from the use of Indians as farm labor, both had as little to do with one another as possible.

During the great postwar missionary revival, the Mormon church turned its attention once again to its Lamanite brothers. The idea of providing foster homes for Indian children turned into an official church program known as the Indian Placement Service. By the 1960s, thousands of Indian children between the ages of eight and eighteen were bussed from reservations to live for nine months with Mormon families and attend local schools.

George Lee, a Navajo and the highest-ranking Indian in the church hierarchy, described his experiences with the Placement Service to Jon Stewart of Pacific News Service. Lee, the son of a medicine man, was raised in a large family on the Navajo reservation. His parents were both illiterate, "very traditional and very exposed to the world. We lived off the land, had a herd of sheep. I was raised on prairie dogs and rattlesnakes for breakfast, lunch, and dinner. The first six years of my life I ran around naked. Dad taught the traditional ways, to get up early, pray facing the rising sun, and his prayers were long. We slept on a dirt floor on a sheepskin, no toilets, no electricity.

"And then one day an Anglo couple, traders who lived near us, came over and started talking to us about the Mormon church. Mom and Dad said we should not listen to these people because they were trying to convert us to their ways. So whenever they came around we'd head for the hills.

"So they tried another approach. Next time they came they brought sacks of canned goods, potatoes and so on from the trading post. Mom and Dad liked that. And finally it came around to religion again."

After George joined the church, the trader persuaded George's parents to place him in a Mormon home near Salt Lake City. "On the bus everyone was crying, all the kids, saying, 'I want to go home, I want to go home.' I cried till I fell asleep." At his new home Lee did not speak a word to his foster parents for two long months despite a shower of gifts, which included a cowboy suit. "I had to make a complete transition from one way of life to another. I got sick a lot because I wasn't used to their food. Back home I never got sick; we were immune to disease. I had hives all over my body."

Lee, however, finally went on to Brigham Young, became a college president, and entered the church hierarchy. Today he has one more ambition: to be Navajo tribal chairman.

Opponents of the Indian Placement Service have often charged the Mormons with "kidnapping" Indian children to indoctrinate them into the white world. Church leaders dismiss these criticisms as the work of militant groups like the American Indian Movement, but critics of the program come from a variety of backgrounds—from Indian social workers to the Indian representative at a major southern California aerospace corporation. Claudine Arthur, a Navajo lawyer, called the program "dangerous," saying, "They want children who are emotionally stable, who come from decent, good homes. Those are the children they want to take off to their homes in Utah and brainwash for their own purposes. If they really believe that home and family is good, then they must believe that it's best for children like these to be in their own homes with their own people."

Dr. Martin Topper, who works at the Mental Health Branch of the Indian Health Service near the Navajo and Hopi reservations in Tuba City, Arizona, followed twenty-five Indian students in the placement program for a number of years. Of the students that Topper followed, twenty-three dropped out of the program and almost all of them eventually rejected their new Mormon families. "This dramatic change in cultural orientation," he said, "was not without emotional consequences. Strong psychological pressures were generated by the temporary loss of their Mormon foster families, the resumption of a poverty-level standard of living, the need to reintegrate socially and emotionally with their Navajo households and the local Navajo community, and the realization that they must grow up to be adult Navajos." For young women, this meant primarily hysterical seizures and conversion reactions. For men, it meant binges of adolescent drinking.

Criticism of all programs, church and private, aimed at off-reservation placement of Indian children led to the passage of the Indian Child Welfare Act in 1978. The Mormon church's program was specifically excluded from the careful supervision called for by the new law at the request of the church after Congress was lobbied by the Wilkinson firm. By church accounts, thousands of Hopi and Navajo have converted to Mormonism. Some tribal employees estimate that there are more than a dozen Mormons on the Navajo tribal council, while some Hopi claim that 70 percent of the reservation has been converted. In an interview just before he died in 1980, the late Wayne Sekakquaptewa, brother of the Hopi tribal chairman and president of the Mormon stake in Hopi country, laughed off the estimate, saying that "maybe 10 percent of the 70 percent are real Mormons."

Spencer Kimball rose to the top of the Mormon hierarchy in part on the strength of his reputation as a missionary among the Indians of North and South America. Kimball was a strong critic of racism among his own brethren, saying once, "The first part of the Church Indian program is education of the Latter-day Saints at home, some of whom need their hearts opened, cleansed, and purged. . . . Racial prejudice is of the devil and ignorance." Kimball, the critic of Mormon racism, clung to his own peculiar racial views, telling a Mormon conference in 1960 that "the children in the home placement program are often lighter than their brothers and sisters in the hogans on the reservation." The reason for this, he later told a reporter, was that the whitening process resulted from the care, feeding, education, and music lessons that are given to the children in the program. When George Lee, the highest-ranking Mormon Indian, was asked about Kimball's views, he responded, "The [Mormon] scriptures say . . . that the Lamanites will become white and delightsome if they live the Gospel and keep the commandments. Yes . . . I agree with the prophet President Kimball."

A RESOURCE STRATEGY FOR INDIAN COUNTRY

Although the Indian Placement Service gained the church a certain notoriety among Indians, the activity of Mormon attorneys such as John Boyden became even more controversial, particularly when the big energy and mining companies turned their attention to Indian resources in the 1950s and 1960s. The Hopi, who live in a group of villages on three narrow mesas in northern Arizona, occupy the oldest continuously inhabited village site in North America, dating to about A.D. 1150. Isolated in the high desert, the Hopis' problems with Americans did not begin until the middle of the last century. By some accounts, Hopi resistance to the arrival of the white man began with a dispute with Mormons over lands near Tuba City and the villages of Upper and Lower Moenkopi, once claimed by Jacob Hamblin, a Mormon missionary who was generally respected by the Hopi.

Resistance grew when clan leaders realized that the United States government was not going to assist them in their efforts to stop the encroachment of the more aggressive and numerous Navajo, who were pressing in on lands designated by the United States government as part of the Hopi reservation. The resistance blossomed into a tragic standoff when the local Indian agent, with the help of the United States Army, rounded up Hopi children and shipped them to the Indian boarding school at Keams Canyon. "A feud developed over the years," wrote Helen Sekakquaptewa, "as the people divided into sides for and against those who came from the outside. These two factions were known as the 'Friendlies' (to the government) and the 'Hostiles' (to the government)." Later these groups became known as the progressives and traditionals.

Until the Collier period, a succession of Indian agents presided over a deeply factionalized, impoverished, and demoralized Hopi population. When New Deal reformers tried to set up a tribal government, they could only find a small number of Hopi to vote for their scheme. When the BIA unilaterally reduced the Hopi reservation in 1937 to one-third its original size to accommodate the Navajo living on what had previously been designated Hopi land, the BIA-created tribal council lapsed into a comatose state from which it would only emerge after a prolonged campaign by the BIA and Boyden to revive it.

While the Hopi villages reverted to traditional rule in the 1940s, BIA officials considered plans to revive the tribal council. Among their concerns were the oil companies which were continually hounding the Department of the Interior to open the remaining Hopi lands for prospecting and leasing. As one Interior official put it, "It does not appear that leases acceptable to oil companies may be made under existing law unless the Hopi Indians will organize a tribal council as provided in the Hopi constitution."

In 1951, Boyden, using the numerous contacts he made while handling

Indian cases as a United States attorney, became the Hopi attorney in a land-claims case. Boyden canvassed the villages, discussing the claim and the possibility of restoring some of the "lost" Hopi land, a possibility ruled out by the claims act. He also made vague references to oil on the reservation, suggesting that oil could provide funds to purchase more land. Five villages identified as centers of traditionalism opposed Boyden's plan. After the BIA superintendent, who accompanied Boyden, conducted votes at the progressive villages, he concluded that they represented the majority of the Hopi people.

With a contract in hand that would eventually pay him at least $2 million in legal fees, Boyden filed a brief before the Claims Commission. At the same time, he set out to revive the tribal government. A confidential BIA memo reported, "When he has obtained the trust of a solid majority, he believes that he can then develop a representative tribal council with whom the BIA and outside interests may deal." Boyden, in fact, saw an important link between resource development and his own future as tribal attorney. "Remuneration for his services," wrote a BIA official, "will depend largely on working out a solution to many of the Hopi problems to such a point that oil leases will provide funds."

By the end of 1955, Boyden had succeeded in gaining official recognition for his version of the tribal government. Within four years, the tribal council had passed the necessary ordinances to open the reservation for mineral prospecting. In 1961 the tribal council signed its first lease—for mineral exploration. Interior Secretary Udall had ruled that it was legal for mining companies to enter into leases with the Hopi tribal council, even though a group of Hopi leaders contested the council's legitimacy and therefore its right to sign leases. When the first major oil lease was worked out in 1964, with a handful of oil companies, including Aztec Oil and Gas Company, Boyden was also working for Aztec. As Boyden had predicted, the oil leases brought a steady flow of funds into tribal coffers—a reported $3 million for oil leases alone, of which $1 million went to Boyden.

With all legal barriers to mineral development on the reservation removed, Boyden moved quickly to arrange further leases. In 1966 the tribal council signed the best known of the Hopi leases: the lease turned 58,000 acres of land on the top of Black Mesa over to the Peabody Coal Company. Peabody supplied the Navajo Power Plant at Page and another at Bullhead City, Nevada, through a slurry pipeline that tapped precious Hopi water. While Boyden was representing the tribal council, one of his law partners was assisting Peabody with its plans to merge with Kennecott Copper, a firm with which the Mormon church had been interlocked for years. When the government refused to permit the merger, Peabody was sold to a consortium that included the Bechtel Corporation.

With the signing of the Peabody lease, WEST Associates' Grand Plan for the development of the Colorado Plateau intersected with the world of the Hopi, triggering yet another controversy over the secretive activities of the BIA, a handful of tribal officials, and the tribe's attorney. In his efforts to form a tribal government sympathetic to his plans for Hopi resources, Boyden went so far as to have the tribal council hire a Salt Lake City public-relations firm to write speeches for the tribal chairman and to tell the world that "the Mormon religion is the predominate Hopi religion." When BIA trust official David Harrison was asked about possible conflicts of interest involving Boyden's work for the Hopi and his firms' work for Peabody, he dismissed them as "not any worse than the oil companies."

Although at first the BIA and tribal attorneys had little trouble getting Indian tribes to lease their resources, getting them to relinquish their water rights was a more complicated matter. Indian water rights are governed by the Winters Doctrine, which grew out of a dispute between white settlers and the Gros Ventre and Assiniboine Indians confined on the Fort Belknap reservation in northern Montana. Both parties drew their water from the Milk River. As the number of white settlers grew, the amount of water left by the white ranchers for Indian farming dwindled to a point at which the Indians faced starvation. The dispute reached the courts, and the Supreme Court ruled in 1908 that Indian water rights were special reserved rights created at the time the reservation was established. This meant those rights did not depend on the canons of western water doctrine, such as the concept of prior appropriation. Although the courts have never made it clear whether the Indians reserved their right to the water or the federal government reserved the right for them, the Winters Doctrine gave the Indians a powerful claim, at least on paper, to much of the water in the arid West. Theoretically, they could base their claims on both present use and future needs rather than being bound by the "use it or lose it" doctrine.

The realities of Indian water development were, of course, quite different. When the Reclamation Act of 1902 brought federally subsidized irrigation to the Uintah basin home of the Ute tribe, the Ute opposed the new irrigation project as the height of white chicanery. First they had had their lands stolen from them. Now they were being told to pay to irrigate the remaining lands with water which they considered theirs from the start. Their fears were confirmed when most of the water developed was directed to Mormon ranches or to lands leased from Indians by Mormon settlers.

The Indian New Deal brought small-scale irrigation projects to the reservations, but in the era of massive projects like the Hoover Dam, which were built with future population in mind, the government did not fund large-scale irrigation projects for the existing Indian population. One of the principal reasons for pushing Collier's disastrous soil-conservation program on the Navajo reservation was that fully one-third of the silt that plugged the Colorado River could be traced to overgrazing of Navajo lands.

When the Bureau of Reclamation after World War II planned massive water projects for Arizona and the Interior West, the Navajo put pressure on the Bureau of Reclamation to build a Navajo irrigation project on Fruitland Mesa. As a result, the Bureau of Reclamation, working with the BIA, proposed a storage facility and irrigation project on the San Juan River, a tributary of the upper Colorado. Even though the Indians had a major claim to the river, they were excluded from the bargaining over allocation of the Colorado.

The deal for water projects in the upper basin, which led to the passage of the Colorado River Storage Project Act in 1956, did not include the Navajo Indian Irrigation Project (NIIP). NIIP had been opposed by Colorado's Representative Wayne Aspinall because it could affect his state's projects. New Mexico at first also opposed NIIP because the Navajo claim to the San Juan River could limit the amount of water that New Mexico could divert into the Rio Grande Valley. Once again the Indians were at the end of the line when water projects were handed out.

In 1957 the Navajo tribal council was pressured into waiving its priority claim to the San Juan River. At the same time, the tribal council accepted New Mexico's plan to link authorization of the NIIP to a project known as the San Juan–Chama Diversion, which would carry the waters of the San Juan out of the Colorado basin into the Rio Grande Valley. The Navajo, in the process, compromised their rights to the San Juan under the Winters Doctrine. In 1962, Congress authorized the two projects, but authorization proved to be an elusive victory for the Navajo.

The Navajo project, according to Congress, was to receive 508,000 acre-feet and to be built at the same time as the San Juan–Chama Diversion. In 1966, Secretary Udall asked the Bureau of Reclamation to reevaluate the project. The Navajo, who reportedly heard about the reevaluation from newspaper accounts, were dead set against it, since Udall was proposing a smaller project with an emphasis on corporate, rather than family, farming, despite the law passed by Congress. While the NIIP was being reevaluated—without Navajo participation, because the Navajo had declined to place a representative on the reevaluation task force—construction of the San Juan–Chama Diversion proceeded on schedule. By 1970, the diversion was completed, but NIIP was still only partially constructed. In addition, the NIIP facilities that had been completed, including the main intake for the entire project, had been scaled down to a project that would use only 330,000 acre-feet. In effect, the Interior Department had stolen 178,000 acre-feet from the Navajo even after the Navajo gave up claims to additional water.

When the Carter administration took office, Interior hired Harris Arthur, one of the principal Navajo critics of the Bureau of Reclamation's handling of NIIP, to deal with NIIP. After two years, Arthur succeeded in getting an opinion from Interior's solicitor that NIIP was entitled to its full 508,000 acre-feet. When Arthur returned to the reservation from Washington, he found that the OMB was recommending that future construction on the less than half-finished NIIP be postponed. "I honestly believe," stated Arthur, "that much of BuRec's planning was influenced by outside forces." The principal enemies of the project, Arthur concluded, were still the lower-basin states and the energy companies.

From the very moment that the Navajo proposed a large irrigation project, Arizona, a lower-basin state, joined the opposition, fearing those plans would interfere with the construction of the Central Arizona Project. As a result, the promoters of that project used their own duplicitous approach to Indian water rights to limit the Navajo's potentially huge claims on the Colorado. After the federal government committed itself to pushing for the Central Arizona Project in 1952, supporters were horrified when they learned that the government described Indian rights to the lower Colorado as "prior and superior" to the rights of the project promoters. A meeting was called in Washington to discuss Indian water rights. In attendance were Attorney General Herbert Brownell; Northcutt Ely, special counsel for California; and the governors of Arizona, California, and New Mexico. According to Ely's account, Brownell quickly agreed to remove the offensive statement from the government's petition in *Arizona* vs. *California*. There was a problem, however. By procedural rules, the original copies of pleadings could not be withdrawn by the litigants. In order to get around the rules, the reasons for changing the petition would have to be explained to the court. The Justice Department hit on a simple solution. The document was removed from the clerk's office without permission of the court and a new page was substituted for the original.

Norman Littell, the Navajo's attorney, tried to get government permission for the Navajo to hire a special attorney to plead their case before the special water master appointed to handle the dispute between Arizona and California. The repeated pleas of the Navajo fell on deaf ears. In the end, the United States, having barred the Navajo from presenting their own case, did not include the Navajo in its plea for Indian water rights on the lower Colorado.

Arizona was also concerned about the water situation on the upper Colorado, particularly when a coal-fired power plant at Page, Arizona, was deemed necessary to provide power for the project's pumps. When the waters of the upper Colorado were allocated in 1948, Arizona received 50,000 acre-feet because part of the San Juan, north of Lee's Ferry, passed through Arizona. Since this part of Arizona was within the Navajo reservation, the Navajo had rights to the water. Once Udall and WEST Associates reached an agreement over joint control of the new power plant and the use of Indian coal, all that was needed was water for the plant. Getting the Navajo to give up their water rights became necessary. Above all, it was important to avoid a situation in which the Navajo might go to court and open the whole question of Indian water rights.

In 1968, under pressure from Udall and the Bureau of Reclamation, the tribe agreed not to challenge the allocation of 50,000 acre-feet to Arizona. Instead discussions focused on the compensation the tribe would receive for waiving its rights—for example, financial donations by the Salt River Project, one of the participants in the project, to the Navajo Community College. Dependent on the bureau and the utilities for its information, the tribe never really discussed the question of its rights to the upper Colorado. Once the massive plans for energy development on and around the Navajo reservation were under way, the Department of the Interior, the utilities, the energy companies, and the states of the Colorado basin worked together effectively to limit the Navajo's water rights on the Colorado River.

In the 1980s the Secretary of the Interior has ultimate control over allocations on the San Juan, with the power of approval over any new allocation. While numerous energy companies continue to pressure Interior for water rights for coal-gasification plants and other projects, only Utah International has a clear title, established in the 1950s, to San Juan water with rights to 44,000 acre-feet—a situation allowing Utah International to continue to play a central role in energy development in Indian country.

In Utah, the Ute have also been persuaded to defer their claims to Colorado water. In 1965 the Ute were approached by state water officials who were seeking new sources of water for the Central Utah Project. Their plan called for tapping the Uinta basin water by means of tunnels that would divert water through the mountains to the Wasatch Front. A significant part of the water rights in the Uinta basin were still held by the Ute. A project official proposed that the Ute agree to support the project by deferring their rights to some of the water until the year 2005. In exchange, project backers agreed not to engage in costly litigation with the tribe over the validity of its water rights and to develop some irrigation and water facilities on the reservation.

The Ute paused to consider this offer. Many of them had opposed reclamation from the start. Finally, at the urging of their tribal attorney, the ubiquitous John Boyden, the Ute signed the deferral agreement. The agreement proved to be the beginning, not the end, of the problem. "That was fifteen years ago," explained tribal chairman Ruby Black. "In fifteen years, they haven't done anything." In fact, the units that would bring water to Indian lands were the last scheduled for construction and neither have been funded.

While the alliance between the Department of the Interior, the utilities, the energy companies, and the Colorado basin states succeeded in reducing Indian claims to vital water resources, the development of mineral resources on the reservation gave Indian affairs an entirely new significance. Utah International's lease with the Navajo in 1957 proved to be the first in a long succession of leases signed by major energy and mining companies with the Indian tribes of the West. The Navajo's leases were negotiated by their tribal attorney, Norman Littell, a Washington lawyer who had served as assistant attorney general under Roosevelt. Littell at first turned down the tribe's job offer, but as he later explained, "I was so appalled with the domination of the BIA and the total absence of representative government in any realistic sense among the Indians that I weakened and said yes." When Littell went to work for the tribe, he found that its oil and gas leases were let on a negotiated, rather than competitive, basis. By accepting competitive bids, Littell built up the Navajo treasury to $100 million.

The mineral leases were a turning point, but neither Littell nor the BIA was aware of the future value of Navajo resources. The energy companies, with their global perspective, were becoming increasingly aware of the importance of coal in the future energy economy. The BIA, despite its trust responsibility for its Indian wards, showed little interest in the future of coal and was easily rolled over by the corporations.

When Stewart Udall was appointed Secretary of the Interior, many people, including the aging John Collier, looked forward to a new era in Indian affairs or at least a return to the policies of the New Deal. At first, Udall and Littell got along well. Littell had pushed for increased revenues from mineral leases and had been an advocate of industrial development on the reservation. Udall also made industrial and Indian-resource development the central concerns of his Indian policy.

Littell's problems began with Raymond Nakai's election as tribal chairman in 1963. Nakai had run on a platform that called for the firing of Littell. In the election, Nakai charged that the tribal council ran the tribe, and Littell ran the tribal council. After his election, Nakai went immediately to Washington. With the assistance of attorneys close to Udall and President Johnson, he pressed Udall to get rid of Littell. Udall soon fired Littell, despite an opinion by the solicitor general that only the tribal council could dismiss their attorney.

Littell's dismissal meant the end to competitive bidding for Navajo resources. Kerr-McGee, for instance, had been trying through its attorney, Clark Clifford, to get oil leases on the reservation without submitting to competitive bidding, and Littell had blocked them. With Littell gone, the tribe signed a lease without competitive bidding for the first large oil field in Arizona. President Johnson, a close friend of Senator Robert Kerr, later sent the Navajo a personal telegram of congratulations when the tribe received a check for a Kerr-McGee uranium deal. With Littell gone, Udall was also able to get the tribe to go along with plans to use water from the San Juan for the Page power plant.

THE RISE OF INDIAN ACTIVISM

In 1966, Udall forced the resignation of Indian Commissioner Phileo Nash and got President Johnson to appoint Robert Bennett, an Oneida with twenty-nine years in the BIA. Udall felt that Nash was too slow in pushing for industrial development. He particularly resented Nash's shelving the BVD company's plans for a garment factory on the Navajo reservation. Nash had apparently given in to pressure from New York unions which were concerned about runaway shops using cheap Indian labor.

With Bennett's appointment, Udall announced that he would reorganize the BIA and propose new programs, but his new direction got off to a rocky start. When Bennett called a meeting of BIA employees in Albuquerque to discuss reorganization, the National Congress of American Indians, headed by Vine Deloria, Jr., called on the tribes to send representatives.

Indian activism, inspired anew by the tactics of the civil rights movement, had been growing steadily since a fight to secure fishing rights in the Pacific Northwest erupted in the mid-1960s. Many World War II veterans had carried on the lonely fight against termination. Now a new generation of activists—some college educated and others, like some of the founders of the American Indian Movement, graduates of prisons and urban ghettos—had come to the fore. The War on Poverty also contributed to the renewal of Indian resistance by giving young Indians an opportunity to tackle tribal problems outside the stifling influence of the BIA. Fear of a return to termination continued to run high, especially after Senator Henry Jackson, who had the support of Senators Frank Church and Clinton Anderson, called for an end to federal trusteeship at Bennett's confirmation hearing. According to Deloria, the Indians who went to Albuquerque were particularly irked when they heard that Udall was proposing that tribes be disqualified as sponsoring agencies in the War on Poverty and that community action funds be turned over to the BIA.

At the Albuquerque meeting, Indians representing sixty tribes were barred from the reorganization meeting. When Bennett finally met with his Indian charges, he explained that there had not been an open meeting between the BIA and representative Indians in thirty years. After the Albuquerque meeting, the Johnson administration proposed an Indian resources and development bill, the new departure promised by Udall.

Sounding very much like a McGeorge Bundy–Walt Rostow program for an underdeveloped country, the bill called for $20 million a year in loan guarantees and an insurance fund for industrial, commercial, and agricultural development. Indians were to be given access to private money markets through mortgages on their land and the issuance of bonds by Indian corporations. A number of Indians regarded Udall's program as termination in a new form. This time financial institutions were to be allowed to gain a new foothold on reservations through mortgage arrangements. Senator Ernest Gruening pointed out that the bill "strengthens and perpetuates the authority of the Secretary to regulate and dominate the life of the Indian." The bill was ultimately defeated.

While John Collier brought the wage system to the reservation through public-works programs, Udall brought corporate America to Indian country. In the early 1960s a hundred plants were built on Indian reservations by companies such as General Dynamics and Fairchild Camera and Instruments. Twenty-six plants were built in 1966 alone. In this way Udall hoped to improve the lot of the Indians. The corporations, as always, were looking for cheap labor. As the *New York Times* put it, "Unusual dexterity and an infinite capacity for tedious and exacting work—such as tying flies on fish-hooks—make the Indians adaptable to certain light industries."

In July 1969, Robert Bennett resigned his post as Indian commissioner, charging that the Nixon administration ignored the plight of Indians. Nixon then appointed Louis R. Bruce, Jr., to take his place. Half Mohawk and half Sioux, Bruce was a lifelong Republican who had participated in the fight to grant Indians citizenship in the 1920s and was active in the National Congress of American Indians. His family owned a 400-acre dairy farm in New York. Bruce, a former football star, was most at home, according to newspaper accounts, in a three-piece suit sporting a fraternity pin in his lapel. In an era of increasing militancy on the part of Indians, Bruce said that he felt young Indians needed to express themselves and that he was going to set up a youth advisory committee in the BIA. His biggest problem, he said, was finding Republican Indians to staff the heavily Democratic BIA.

In the fall of 1969, Bruce accompanied his boss, Secretary of the Interior Walter Hickel, and Vice-President Spiro Agnew, to address the National Congress of American Indians in Albuquerque. At the meeting Hickel was roundly booed, called a honky, and told to go home. Indian activists considered the appointment of Hickel a particularly dangerous insult. They charged that as governor of Alaska, he had participated in "high-handed, inconsiderate, illegal theft of native Alaskan, Eskimo, and Indian tribal lands." Once in the cabinet, Hickel further antagonized Indians by making vague statements about "cutting the cord" of federal dependency.

Within a month of the meeting, a group of Indians seized Alcatraz Island in San Francisco Bay. This act was one of a series of escalating confrontations, which started with the fish-ins in Puget Sound and culminated in the armed occupation of the village of Wounded Knee, South Dakota. The Nixon administration, preoccupied with the opposition to its policies in Vietnam, was actually attempting to change things in the BIA. Commissioner Bruce had transferred a number of tribal superintendents and appointed fifteen young Indians to BIA posts. In July 1970, Nixon made a major speech on Indian affairs in which he denounced termination and called for self-determination. Blue Lake was then restored to the Taos Pueblo.

The Nixon administration was particularly concerned with the situation in Alaska, where the oil companies could not proceed with their plans for the trans-Alaska pipeline without a final solution to Indian land claims. With the growing emphasis on domestic energy sources, the oil companies dropped their strategy of covert assaults on Indian resources. With the assistance of the BIA, they became more sophisticated in dealing with Indian matters than the federal government. The companies worked closely with native Alaskan leaders to set up regional corporations with a voice in land selections. The Interior Department asked a group of native leaders operating out of oil company offices in Washington to help draft the land-claims bill. Some 43 million acres were ultimately transferred to village and corporate control and payments of close to a billion dollars were made to the native corporations for various leases, royalties, and bonuses.

The corporate approach to a settlement of Alaskan land claims did not lessen the growing tension in the Lower Forty-eight. If anything, the manner in which the oil companies and the Department of the Interior placated the Alaska natives stood in marked contrast to what was being discovered about the earlier dealings of Interior, the BIA, and the energy companies with the energy-rich tribes of the West. The exact nature of the Peabody leases for Black Mesa, for example, was a well-kept secret. After pursuing officials from Peabody, the BIA, and the Hopi tribal government for months, anthropologist Richard Clemmer (as well as individual Hopis) was still unable to get a copy of the lease. In a similar situation, most of the residents of the Northern Cheyenne reservation in Montana did not find out that Peabody and a number of other companies had leased more than half of the reservation for coal exploration until the exploration crews showed up and started drilling in Indian burial grounds and generally disrupting life on the reservation.

The gradual revelations about the extent and nature of the deals worked out between the BIA and the energy companies in the 1950s and 1960s triggered a wave of law suits challenging the leases on Indian lands. Many of the suits were brought before the courts by the Native American Rights Fund, an Indian legal-defense organization funded by the Ford Foundation, the federal government, and others. Indian activists were futher incensed when Rogers Morton, after replacing Hickel as Secretary of the Interior, appointed John Crow, an old-line BIA bureaucrat, to the position of deputy commissioner. Word got out that Crow's job was "to keep the lid on" the activist BIA "faction," made up of Bruce's young recruits, known as Bruce's Troops or the Dirty Dozen.

In this atmosphere, hundreds of Indian activists converged on the BIA offices in Washington in late 1972 from all across the country in a campaign called the Trail of Broken Treaties. Their twenty-point program called for the restoration of a treaty relationship between the United States government and the sovereign Indian tribes, giving the tribes what Deloria called a "quasi-protectorate status." Their program also called for a review of treaty violations and procedures for ending chronic violations of Indians' treaty rights.

Once in Washington, an ugly confrontation developed over the use of BIA facilities, which culminated in the activists' seizure of BIA headquarters. In the process, considerable damage was done to the building and numerous files were either destroyed or spirited out of Washington. Some files that gave the public a view of the deals that had been made by the BIA behind the tribes' backs reached columnist Jack Anderson. Having wreaked a measure of vengeance on the BIA, a number of the activists under the leadership of the American Indian Movement returned to the Sioux reservation in South Dakota where they carried out the seizure of the village of Wounded Knee. After an armed confrontation that lasted for months, they withdrew from Wounded Knee when the federal government promised to renegotiate the controversial treaty of 1868. The promise was never kept.

By 1974 the legal actions initiated by the Native American Rights Fund and the environmental organizations had brought the federal coal-leasing program to a halt. Secretary Morton was forced to impose serious restrictions on the leasing of coal on public property. Various law suits challenging Indian leases forced the BIA to call for the renegotiation of these leases. The administration worked with the oil companies to reach an accommodation in Alaska, but the tremendous outpouring of hostility from native Americans seriously delayed the plans of the energy and utility companies to turn the interior West into a massive energy colony.

THE CARTER ADMINISTRATION IN INDIAN COUNTRY

The Carter administration inherited the impasse in Indian affairs caused by the escalating confrontation between Indian activists and the energy companies and the BIA over the development of Indian resources and the historical failure of the government to respect its treaty agreements with the Indian people. The administration also inherited a BIA that was demoralized by internal factionalism and discredited by revelations about its role in the giveaway of Indian resources.

During the transition, Carter turned for advice to a group of young Indian professionals, many of whom worked in Washington and had one foot in the world of activism and another in the halls of Congress and the bureaucracy. After his appointment, Secretary Andrus took the initiative by establishing the position of Assistant Secretary of Indian Affairs, to elevate the status of Indian issues in the Department of the Interior. As with several other Carter innovations, the idea of creating an assistant secretary originated with the Nixon administration, when the new position was discussed at the time of Nixon's Indian speech in 1970.

Andrus appointed Forrest Gerard the new assistant secretary and then brought other critics of Indian policy into Interior. Gerard became an aide to Senator Henry Jackson when Jackson tried to undercut criticism of his support for termination. Among the new appointees were Harris Arthur, a Navajo who helped found the Shiprock Institute, a research organization that was challenging energy and water plans for the Navajo reservation; Tom Fredericks, director of the Native American Rights Fund; and George Crossland, an Osage who was working with the Northern Cheyenne to assert tribal control over coal development.

Interior then set out to help renegotiate the leases that had been a major cause of the Indian uprisings in the early 1970s. In 1970 the Navajo had elected Peter MacDonald as tribal chairman. MacDonald, who was committed to the development of Navajo resources, made renegotiation of the tribe's big coal leases one of his highest priorities. MacDonald's first opportunity occurred when Consolidation Coal Company (a subsidiary of Continental Oil) and El Paso Natural Gas asked for an extension of a lease signed in 1968 for a strip mine to provide coal for a gasification plant. Although the companies had no firm commitments to purchase the coal, since plans for their gasification plant were far from complete, the two companies threatened to go ahead and mine without a a new lease.

After a period of negotiations, MacDonald and tribal attorney Vlassis got the companies to agree to new terms: 55 cents a ton, or 8 percent of the coal's selling price. At this point, the BIA entered the picture in its role as final arbiter of Indian affairs. Since a new law boosting the rate on coal from public lands to 12.5 percent had just been passed, the BIA was convinced that the Navajo could get more for their coal. "The El Paso lease was ridiculous," said Richard Hughes, an attorney who ultimately challenged the new leases in court on behalf of Navajo living in the Burnham, New Mexico, area, where the mine is located. "They were already in breach of contract. It was a giveaway with minimum environmental controls. It was also solely speculative since El Paso had no market." Although MacDonald was afraid that the BIA's interference would somehow undermine the tribe's earlier negotiations, once the BIA entered the picture, a new lease was quickly drawn up along the lines suggested by the BIA. Despite his problems with the El Paso lease, MacDonald was in the process of devising an entirely new strategy for Indian energy development.

MacDonald played a central role in the founding of the Council of Energy Resource Tribes (CERT) in 1975 to gain a greater voice for Indians in the development of their resources. With the heads of twenty-five tribal governments backing the council, MacDonald presented the organization's demands to the Federal Energy Office. They included money for a resource inventory, voiding of all existing mineral leases, greater responsiveness in Washington to Indian demands, and funding for the new organization.

At first, CERT was branded an Indian OPEC. There were fears in Washington that "the Indians might unite in opposition to the government, follow OPEC's lead, and collectively turn the screw on the society that had exploited them for centuries," Christopher McLeod wrote. Gradually MacDonald's strategy began to mesh with the more sophisticated approach being used by the energy companies after their experience with the Alaskan natives.

MacDonald was particularly eager to get out of the clutches of the BIA, which demonstrated limited ability in dealing with the problems of tribal energy resources; restrictive leasing procedures; and a habit of making deals without informing the tribes. MacDonald was considering, in place of leases, joint ventures that would give the tribes part ownership of new energy projects after the tribes developed their own ability to evaluate their resources and control development.

To avoid the BIA, MacDonald and other CERT leaders worked closely with the new Department of Energy. In this way, MacDonald revived the strategy employed by Indian activists in the 1960s of playing one part of the bureaucracy off against another. The Department of Energy was responsive to CERT's efforts, since in the Great Washington Bureaucratic Wars it was competing with Interior for influence over the country's energy policy. After the Energy Department formed, George Crossland, the energy adviser to the Northern Cheyenne, became the first director of the department's Office of Indian Affairs, and Ed Gabriel left its Office of Consumer Affairs to become director of CERT. The conflict between the BIA and the Energy Department for influence in Indian energy affairs finally led to a turf fight over which agency would take the lead in dealing with CERT. "Interior had gotten to the White House," said an Energy Department employee, "and said our Indian is Gerard and Interior will be the lead agency." The fight was resolved by making the Energy Department the lead agency in dealing with CERT. Interior retained control of leasing.

Despite this resolution, Interior continued to feud with the Department of Energy over the role of CERT and influence in Indian affairs. The CERT-DOE connection worked to the advantage of the energy companies, which had staked out their own sphere of influence within DOE, but were less influential in Interior.

Although Andrus had tried to reform the BIA, the Department of the Interior was still unable to overcome its historical inadequacies in dealing with energy matters, its legacy of paternalistic control, and its alliance with tribal governments, many of which had originally been BIA fabrications. Thus, when the Shoshone pressed their claim to their lands in Nevada, Andrus at first appeared to be trying to meet their demands. Tampering with the claims process proved to be too politically sensitive a matter for Andrus, particularly since many western politicians were already denouncing Interior because of the Carter hit list.

Andrus did try to move ahead in the area of Indian water rights in Arizona. He made the resolution of the Indian-allocation question a precondition for making the final allocations to Central Arizona Project water users. In December 1980, Andrus announced that the first allocations of a little more than 300,000 acre-feet were going to twelve Arizona tribes. Project supporters were outraged by Andrus' allocations and immediately took the decision to court. The supporters were critical because the Indians did not have to shoulder the burden of shortages in drought years and because Andrus refused to force the tribes to accept treated effluent (that is, sewage) to be used for irrigation in exchange for some of their project allocation.

"The Indians are going to be growing cotton while the cities and industries are shutting down for lack of water," claimed Governor Bruce Babbitt with considerable exaggeration. Babbitt, who served as Indian liaison for the Western Governors' Policy Office, bemoaned the fact that the Indians already living in Arizona were going to get enough water for eight hundred thousand future Arizonans.

Despite Andrus' effort at reform, the Department of the Interior was still locked into the historical relationship between colonial master and subjects. By the 1980s the BIA was still a powerful force on the reservation. The Secretary of the Interior still enjoyed a wide range of powers over Indian affairs, which flew in the face of all the rhetoric about self-determination. The department continued to be caught in a classical and inescapable conflict between its obligations to the Indian people as defined by the trust relationship and its obligations to the non-Indian public because of its control of public lands and resources. The Indians, for instance, enjoyed, through the Winters Doctrine, an impressive claim to the dwindling water supply in the arid West. In reality, the future of Indian life on the reservation was seriously threatened by the way in which the white world, with the assistance of the Department of the Interior, was grabbing the remaining water supplies before the Indians could assert their rights. Andrus slowed the pace at which outside forces, led by the energy companies, were overwhelming the Indians' last reservation strongholds in their quest for domestic energy supplies. By the end of Andrus' term, the administration was once again bending to the pressures of the companies that wanted what the Indians had, in the name of high profits and the public welfare.

During the energy crisis of the 1970s, much public attention was focused on the question of Indian resources. Once again the myth of the rich Indian, which began with the discovery of oil on Indian lands in Oklahoma in the 1920s, gained credibility. Indians actually remained the poorest of the country's minorities. At least half the Indian population did not live on reservations that covered rich mineral deposits but in the worst urban ghettos. Disease, alcoholism, suicide, unemployment, lack of education, and much shorter life expectancy than whites still were prevalent. Even among the energy-rich Navajo per capita income hovered around $1,000 a year. By official estimates, 31 percent of the work force was unemployed and less than 2 percent of young Navajo completed college. Even if Indian resources were developed under tribal control and for the benefit of tribal members, only a small percentage of the country's Indians would benefit.

In the Southwest the struggle for Indian sovereignty presented a new problem for the federal government. The border states of Arizona and New Mexico have large Indian populations that still retain nominal control over extensive parts of these two states. When the Mexican-American population is added to the political equation, the region is seen to be increasingly threatened by political fragmentation. If Indian activists are able to push their quest for sovereignty, the reservations could develop the characteristics of little nation-states dependent on the federal government but with a measure of autonomy. As more Mexicans move into the Southwest, the region could be further torn between the forces of homogeneity and balkanization.

10 The Mexican Factor

The squeeze was on. Carter administration officials pressured, cajoled, pleaded with, and threatened their would-be Chicano allies to give support to, or at least remain neutral on, the Carter plan dealing with the border. Inflamed by nativist attacks, rising unemployment, and a growing fear of a "Quebec syndrome" in the southwest, the issue had built up during the 1970s before Carter took office. Former CIA Director William Colby warned that the immigration issue was more than just a domestic problem. Relations with Mexico, he declared, potentially posed a bigger foreign-policy threat than even Russia or China. "Without the safety valve," Ronald Reagan also warned, "some very disruptive things could occur south of the border."

When Jimmy Carter came to power, there was a great deal of talk in the capital about the "Mexican issue." The Carter people knew that the border between Mexico and the southwestern United States had never been a fixed point in political space or time. The border had represented both barrier and opportunity: a barrier to the free movement of labor and the opportunity to open the gates for that labor and to allow the flow of capital to enter a shifting and expanding market. The border signified an artificial construct counter to the great Chicano cultural myth of Aztlán. The border was also a setting for western business' hopes for that last big deal, a deal involving the exchange of resources, labor, markets, and investment capital on a scale to rival the deal that gave rise to a budding western U.S. capitalism.

The president, despite his farmer's appreciation of the need for cheap labor, leaned toward a hard line on restricting migration. The Carter plan, announced in August 1977, consisted of limited amnesty for Mexicans residing in the United States for more than seven years. The plan called for identification cards to distinguish between citizens and "aliens" in an attempt to stop the migration flow northward and to establish sanctions against employers who knowingly hired the "noncitizen" and undocumented workers.

The Carter people, led by domestic-affairs adviser Stuart Eisenstadt, were lobbying heavily for their position, leaning on their onetime Chicano supporters

245

to break ranks with more militant groups in the community who took the position "Somos Todos Indocumentados" ("We Are All Undocumenteds"). Liberal Congressional figures and Chicano administration officials were enlisted to create a break in the ranks, any break that would allow the Carter people to declare that on this issue they faced a divided, rather than united, community.

The pressure had come too late. Demonstrations were sweeping southwestern metropolises from Los Angeles to San Antonio, although most of them were not reported in the Anglo media. It was a tremendous outpouring of anger against the attitudes of Anglo politicians and the actions of the Immigration Service. These actions included the proposing of electrification of the border area near San Diego, sweeps through the barrios to round up undocumented Mexicans, and increasing collusion between employers and Immigration Service officials to keep a Mexican labor force in the cities docile and underpaid. That kind of collusion led to the angry demonstration at the El Paso border by Mexican maids and house workers who were being deported across the border after having failed to receive their paychecks. The big demonstrations made even the most conservative of Mexican-American organizations hard-nosed and resistant to the Carter pressure. The response was a resolute and defiant no to any conditions save amnesty.

By the fall of 1977, as the Carter administration tried to hold together a proposal already unraveling at the edges, all the different components of a complex of issues had begun to coalesce: issues of labor and capital flow, the rise of Chicano politics, the reemergence of Mexico as a major resource producer and a critical economic entity, and the ever-present, volatile issue of the border. The Mexican factor had become the link for a range of issues, all keyed to the future of the Southwest.

CREATING THE BORDER

The history of the Southwest is a history of conquest and resistance. Prior to the triumph of the Spanish conquistadores, the lands of the great southwestern desert stretching from Colorado to the northern Mexican states of Sonora, Baja California, and Sinaloa, were inhabited by more than three dozen Indian tribes which raised corn, beans, chile, and cacao along the area's river banks and practiced a communal form of agriculture. The Spanish conquest was a bloody affair. Resistance by the Sinaloa, the Yaqui, and other tribes continued well into the nineteenth century. The Mexican war of independence in 1810 consolidated the power of a new class of Mexican-born Spaniards and Spanish-Indian mestizos. Much of the area's arable land fell into the hands of the church, a new merchant class, and various civil and military authorities.

Upsetting that balance of power, the United States war against Mexico in 1846 created a new dynamic that ultimately led to what historian Mario Barrera called a "colonial labor system in the Southwest." The annexation of Mexican Territory sanctioned by the Treaty of Guadalupe Hidalgo in 1848 and the Gadsden Purchase of 1853 lopped off nearly half of Mexico's land base as well as one hundred thousand Mexican citizens ranging from the poor Indian farmers to the large Spanish landowners of the new territories of California, New Mexico, and Arizona. Soon after, the new border states on the Mexican side became potential locations for United States investments in land, mining, oil, and agriculture.

As the Southwest began to develop economically, during the latter half of the nineteenth century, the Mexican landowning class began to be displaced from its economic base of power. Anglo capitalists, primarily cattlemen, farmers, land speculators, and the federal government, through such agencies as the National Forest Service, were able to dispossess the Mexicans from the land. Consequently, the source of Mexican political power and class standing in the area was undermined. A southwestern economy based primarily on mining, agriculture, and cattle emerged in the new territory. The beginnings of an industrial and manufacturing structure were made possible by the advent of the railroad in the last two decades of the nineteenth century.

From the outset, a critical factor in the development of southwestern economic forces was the availability of a pool of cheap labor that could provide a dual wage structure for the railroad operators, mine owners, and cotton growers. The use of foreign labor in the building of the West linked the successive waves of Chinese, Japanese, Filipino, black, and Mexican labor to the rapid development and eventual settlement of the new southwestern states.

Mexican labor came from two sources: residents who had been displaced from their land following the conquest and annexation, and imported Mexican workers, primarily from the northern Mexican states. As early as the 1880s, southwestern farmers, such as Arizona's cotton growers, dispatched labor recruiters across the border into northern Mexico. When the railroad in the Southwest extended itself south of the border, whole families were brought across the border by special trains paid for by the growers. By 1911 recruitment of Mexican labor began to expand rapidly. That year the Dillingham Commission on Immigration issued a report on immigration that singled out Mexican recruitment as beneficial because of the proximity of the source. "Because of their strong attachment to their native land, low intelligence, illiteracy, migratory life, and the possibility of their residence here being discontinued, few become citizens of the United States. . . . Thus it is evident," the report concluded, "that in the case of the Mexican he is less desirable as a citizen than as a laborer."

At the time the Dillingham Commission was preparing its report Mexican laborers had already been heavily recruited by the railroads, providing upward of 17 percent of the total maintenance force on western United States railroads. Mining interests soon after joined the railroads in sending labor recruiters south, sometimes as far as central Mexico, to spread the word about work in the mines. At times free transportation across the border was provided to workers. World War I greatly increased the recruitment drives by stimulating growing new markets. Texas and Arizona cotton growers, Imperial Valley farmers, Colorado sugar-beet growers, the rubber companies in California and Arizona, the hard-rock mining companies throughout the West, and even a sprinkling of industrial employers from the Midwest joined the list of those interested in this new source of labor. This additional labor supply was used in part to replace or supplant the poor white and black laborers who had been drafted.

By 1920 Mexican labor had become a critical component in the structure of the Southwest's economy, allowing employers, particularly in agriculture, to establish profit margins on the basis of the lower wage rates. A spokesman for the Arizona Cotton Growers Association commented in 1920 that the cotton growers of the Salt River valley were able to maintain, despite the high demand for labor and an upswing in the economy, "as perfectly an elastic supply of labor as the world has ever seen and . . . an even low level of prices for wages throughout its territory." The cotton, mining, railroad, agricultural, and industrial interests had advocates in Congress, such as Arizona's Representative (later, Senator) Carl Hayden and Texas' Representative (later, Vice-President) John Nance Garner, who worked closely with high government officials to support the migration from Mexico and to establish crucial exemptions to keep the program functioning smoothly.

In 1924, as a result of nativist sentiment aimed particularly at Japanese migration, an immigration law was passed that established the Immigration and Naturalization Service (INS) and the United States–Mexico Border Patrol. The southwestern growers and other employers were able to use influence to exempt western-hemisphere nations from the quota systems set up by the legislation. Literacy requirements governing the "legality" of migration made many of the more than half a million Mexican migrants who had already entered the United States "illegals" or "undocumenteds." That condition of illegality justified the first Border Patrol raids in 1924 in California's Imperial Valley. The growers, with the assistance of local business groups, immediately pressured the Department of Labor to force the new INS to work out an understanding with the growers. A short time after the first raids, the INS reversed itself and established a new procedure to regularize the availability of undocumented Mexicans working north of the border.

By the late 1920s United States employer interests had carefully orchestrated the migration and displacement of Mexican labor. Mexican labor was clearly favored over the traditional immigrant who settled in the country initially as part of an organized labor pool but then became assimilated by the second or third generation. The Mexicans were favored as migrant workers or "commodity migrants," as Mexican sociologist Jorge Bustamante called them, rather than potential citizens. With accessible transportation to and from the border and the existence of seasonal employment patterns in several of the jobs involved, Mexican labor became a permanent circulating pool from which employers could draw.

Much of the analysis of the origins and growth of Mexican labor migration equates these "pull" factors of United States employers encouraging migration northward with "push" factors within Mexico precipitating the move north-ward. The "push" factors had been significant even prior to the Mexican revolutionary period of 1910-1919. The Mexican government of Porfirio Diaz (1876-1911) had encouraged the displacement of rural agricultural labor by favoring concentration of land ownership. The followers of Diaz had hoped that large-scale landholding might hasten the modernization of agriculture and undermine the long-standing subsistence agriculture of the Indians. Under the Diaz government, major land grants had been seized or acquired by a number of foreign businessmen, including western entrepreneurs William Randolph Hearst and Harry Chandler. These land grabs and subsequent displacement of the peasants were resisted throughout this period.

The events of the Mexican revolution continued the conflict over control of the countryside and also demonstrated the political character and fluidity of the border. The revolutionary movement of the socialist-oriented Liberal party, headed by Enrique and Ricardo Flores Magón, advocated a distribution of the large landholdings. The party recruited a binational army of exiled Mexicans, United States Wobblies, and Mexican and Indian peasants to implement their revolutionary program. When clashes on both sides of the border occurred, the United States government intervened to protect its property interests as well as to indict the Flores Magón brothers on charges of violating the Neutrality Act.

The cataclysmic events of the Mexican revolution and the conflicts in the countryside were enough to cause Mexican peasants and landless rural workers to migrate to the north. But the impulse northward was strengthened by the carefully formed pull-induced migration routes created by United States employers. The transient nature of this labor force lent itself to the development of periodic mass "repatriation" campaigns, particularly in periods of economic recession. The first large-scale repatriations, initiated in part by vigilante groups, took place during the 1920–1921 economic decline, which hit the West particularly hard. The initially weak resistance to repatriation encouraged employer interests to assume that they had found in Mexicans an ideal work force: "less quarrelsome and less troublemaking than any other labor that comes into America," Harry Chandler declared before a congressional committee. The situation in the late 1920s began to alter that employer view, as large numbers of Mexican workers began to organize into trade unions, many of them inspired by the revolutionary events south of the border.

Prior to the 1920s, United States trade unions largely ignored Mexican workers and only organized them in the railroad and miners' unions. A number of Anglo trade unions resented the use of "cheap Mexican labor" to undercut organizing efforts but did nothing to change the situation. By the late 1920s, organizing efforts by Mexican trade unionists began to have an impact, even in the dual-wage agricultural system.

Deportations in the attempt to break up labor and radical organizations among Mexican migrant workers became widespread during the Great Depression. Deportees included the New Mexico organizer of the Liga Obrera de Habla Español, the head of the Colorado beet-workers union, leaders and key members of the United Cannery, Agricultural, Packing, and Allied Workers of America (CIO), and leaders of the El Paso smelter workers. The INS, which played an active role in breaking strikes and deporting union leaders, became an adjunct of antiunion employer groups, such as California's Associated Farmers, and antiradical government investigatory groups, such as the House Un-American Activities Committee. The INS participated in Colorado border blockades against Mexican laborers in 1935 and 1936 and other massive repatriation campaigns.

By the mid-1930s the formerly docile Mexican migrant worker was perceived as a leading participant in radical movements. The San Francisco Chamber of Commerce, in a gesture of xenophobia typical of the period, established the Committee to Combat Communism, which urged the Department of Labor to deport the "alien Communists" because of the "rapidly growing menace of alien radicals which is sweeping the industrial and agricultural areas of the Pacific Coast."

The deportation sentiment soon mushroomed into a widespread repatriation policy implemented on the local, rather than national, level. Antiradicalism campaigns inspired by business and grower interests fed on depression fears of unemployment and increased welfare rolls. The campaigns created an impetus toward large-scale deportation efforts. Mexican migrants were summarily dismissed from the welfare lists. Local and state governments passed laws forbidding migrants from working on relief-type government-funded projects. A second cycle of repatriation, far greater than the deportations of the 1920–1921 period, sent hundreds of thousands of "legal" and "illegal" Mexican migrants back south of the border. By the end of the decade, the number of repatriated Mexicans nearly equaled the number of migrants entering the country.

While growers continued to rely on Mexican workers and sent their "emissaries" to Mexico to recruit workers on a seasonal basis, the large-scale immigration of displaced poor white farmers into the West—victims of the Dust Bowl—had created a new supply of seasonal labor, which lessened the need for a high volume of Mexican labor. The Great Depression ultimately institutionalized the recruitment-deportation cycle, or what Carey McWilliams called "entry, work, and repatriation," to be followed by reentry with each new work season.

While the flow of Mexican labor slowed down during the depression years, the flow of capital sent south by United States business interests also diminished. Despite the nationalist upheaval of 1910–1919, Mexico was subject to a high level of foreign investment and control prior to the late 1930s. In his autobiography, Charles Jones of Richfield Oil described just such an example. In the mid-1920s Jones had wanted to hire former Mexican President Álvaro Obregón as a Richfield representative to help secure oil concessions for the company in Baja California. Jones wined and dined Obregón and offered the Mexican leader a large retainer and a number of other substantial perks. Confident of success, Jones discovered to his dismay the next day that the chairman of Standard Oil of California had also come to town to woo the former president. Within hours after Jones's own meetings with the Mexican leader, Obregón announced that he would represent the California oil company for purposes of obtaining concessions throughout the entire country.

"All problems are simplified when there is land enough and the people know how to cultivate it, but the simplest questions become complicated as soon as people are torn away from the soil," B. Traven wrote in his classic novel The White Rose, describing the destruction of a Mexican Indian hacienda and rural Indian culture by the actions of a United States oil company. Reacting against their continuing displacement from the land, landless Baja tenant farmers, in what became known as the Assault on the Land, invaded and occupied the lands of foreign landowners and investors in 1937. They planted the national flag and refused to leave until their demands were met. Their actions paralleled the rise of urban and rural movements throughout Mexico. The new Mexican government of Lázaro Cárdenas enacted a series of sweeping measures, including the nationalization of the oil industry and railroads and an extensive redistribution of the land. The land program attempted to enlarge and to collectivize the *ejido* (communal plots of small farmers) to build upon traditional farming methods in an effort to improve the varieties of the Mexican staples of wheat and corn, and to try to make the units economically viable through new irrigation and financial assistance from newly created state institutions, such as the Ejido Credit Bank.

Whatever the limits of the Cárdenas reforms, they incurred the active hostility of United States business interests. "Mexico brought the wrath of the world down upon itself for being the 'wild-eyed revolutionary' that dared nationalize huge foreign-owned enterprises, including railroads and oil fields," wrote Business International, an organization of United States multinationals, more than forty years after the Cárdenas actions. "The country was ostracized by the community of nations, particularly by the United States," Business International went on, "and forced into a period of isolation, in which it had to look inward to its own resources to meet its needs."

BRACEROS AND "WETBACKS"

By the attack on Pearl Harbor, a shift in attitudes had already begun. Discussions between the new Mexican government of Ávila Camacho and the Roosevelt administration on ways to "win the war" refocused the question of the border and the role of United States investment capital and the Mexican migrant. Ávila Camacho wanted to end the divisiveness of the Cárdenas period and reintegrate the Mexican economy into United States–dominated industry, trade, and labor systems.

With American blessing, Ávila Camacho devised a new agricultural program, which emphasized the way agriculture might serve as a basis for the "founding of industrial greatness" for Mexico, which in turn could help the United States–linked war effort. As opposed to the self-contained system that kept the food supplies and labor force within the rural countryside, the Ávila Camacho program favored producing food for the cities and for the export market. As part of the effort, Ávila Camacho invited the Rockefeller Foundation into Mexico to organize an agricultural research program. The foundation's field director for Mexico quickly became head of a new office established within the Mexican Agriculture Ministry designed to oversee the changes in agriculture. The Rockefeller Foundation efforts, wrote Frances Moore Lappé and Joseph Collins, "systematically discarded research alternatives oriented towards the non-irrigated subsistence sector of Mexican agriculture," favoring instead the big irrigation projects of the Mexican northwest. "The focus was on how to make seeds, not people more productive," declared Lappé and Collins. "Agricultural modernization came to substitute for rural development."

The emphasis on agricultural modernization coincided with the expected investments of several new United States, and particularly southwestern, agricultural companies who created joint ventures with large Mexican land-holders who had benefited from the Rockefeller program. Unlike the earlier, more speculative foreign land operations, such as Harry Chandler's 830,000-acre Baja ranch, medium-sized companies, such as Santiago-Wilson, American Fruit, and Deardoff-Jackson, were interested both in joint production and in financing Mexican growers to produce such export crops as tomatoes, peas, bell peppers, and melons. The United States companies and their Mexican partners set up packing sheds in the coastal areas of Sinaloa and Sonora. They provided the capital for fertilizer, storage facilities and transportation to the southwestern United States export markets. The postwar Miguel Alemán government aided this development by pumping government money into construction of huge dams for irrigation projects in the Mexican northwest. Much of the building was controlled by the friends and families of government leaders. The heavily populated central mesa regions of Mexico, where most of the ejidatorios and owners of small plots were located, were ignored.

As this new, integrated agricultural system began to take shape, the Mexican government pressed the Roosevelt administration to settle the long-standing dispute over the disposition of the Colorado River water. The construction of the All-American Canal in the 1930s was accurately perceived by the Mexicans as an attempt to divert and control the flow of Colorado waters on the California side of the border, water that ordinarily would have flowed directly into Mexico. The Roosevelt administration, as part of its overall foreign-policy objectives, wanted to settle that dispute as well as long-standing differences over the Rio Grande, which had divided Texas and Mexico. Negotiations between the Mexicans, the federal government, and representatives from the different Colorado basin states produced a compromise in early 1944 that guaranteed a delivery of 1.5 million acre-feet to Mexico except in the case of drought on the American side of the border. The treaty was ratified the following year despite California's opposition.

While negotiations proceeded over disposition of the Colorado, a crucial accommodation was reached between the Mexican and American governments that regulated the flow of Mexican labor to the United States. Although the agricultural policies of the Ávila Camacho government had been earmarked to free up rural labor and food supplies for the beginnings of an urban-based industrialization program, pressures north of the border for an increase in migrant labor postponed that industrial development. Furthermore, northwestern Mexican agriculture, which was gradually becoming oriented toward the United States export market, had increasingly displaced rural farm labor, providing a ready-made migratory labor pool.

Within the United States, the need for a new, regulated labor supply had increased by 1941. Much of the existing non-Mexican labor force in the Southwest had been either called into military service or drifted from the lower-paying rural agricultural, mining, or unskilled industrial work toward the better-paying, urban-based manufacturing jobs geared toward war production.

By the 1940s southwestern agriculture had become thoroughly dependent on a surplus labor supply made up of "highly mobile, unsophisticated migrant populations," as authors Harland Padfield and William Martin put it in their seminal 1965 study of Arizona agriculture. "The whole cost structure of Southwestern agriculture in general," Padfield and Martin wrote, "is based upon this structure." This "labor-obsessed" industry, "in the midst of labor surpluses created by automation in other industries, [still] fears a shortage of labor."

On July 23, 1942, an extensive agreement covering the recruitment and importation of Mexican laborers ("braceros") for southwestern agricultural fields and western railroads was signed between the two governments. The main provisions of the program, entitled the Mexican Farm Labor Supply (or Bracero) Program, provided a formal labor-recruitment program to be administered by federal agencies. Provisions designed to safeguard the rights of the farm laborers included antidiscrimination clauses, written contracts, adequate housing and sanitary conditions, and, most important, a prevailing wage structure and a determination that a "labor shortage" existed prior to importing braceros. On September 29, 1942, with both sides heralding the agreement as a way to help the war effort, the first trainloads of braceros arrived in Stockton, California.

Throughout the war, the formal provisions of the agreement were violated and undermined. Growers attacked the New Deal agencies for their minimal implementation of migrant rights, claiming they exacerbated relations between employers and braceros. After the war, with the New Deal in retreat and the labor movement in disarray, the program was extended far beyond its original intention as a war-related manpower program. The role of the federal government was reduced, and contracts were now to be negotiated directly between the employers and the Mexican government, without any direct guarantees of the provisions by the United States government. When the Korean War mobilization provided the new justification for institutionalizing the program, the program received a statutory basis as Public Law 78. Public Law 78 was extended several times before it expired in December 1964.

From the late 1940s on, the Bracero Program was controlled by grower interests. Even during the war, growers had hired braceros directly, to avoid written contracts and government guarantees. The key prevailing-wage and certified labor-shortage procedures were interpreted in favor of the growers by the Farm Placement Service, which administered the program and was explicitly tied into agricultural interests. For example, Edward Hayes, while chief of the California service, counseled growers on the side. When Hayes resigned his Farm Service post in 1959, he immediately became manager of the Imperial Valley Farmers Association, which also served as the labor agent for the Di Giorgio Fruit Corporation.

The bracero system also became an effective device in undercutting any attempts at unionization of farm labor. Throughout the life of the program, and particularly in the period 1948–1951, when serious attempts at organizing were made, growers effectively intimidated braceros and even used them as strikebreakers. When representatives of the National Farm Workers Union succeeded in interesting braceros and other uncertified Mexican migrant workers in union efforts, the growers deported the "troublemakers," frequently enlisting the aid of the INS.

Along with the bracero, the uncertified *mojado*, or "wetback," became a central ingredient in regulating the flow of labor in the 1940s and 1950s, as well as a key to the union-busting strategy of the growers. The pejorative term *wetback* dated from the period following the creation of the Border Patrol in 1924 when thousands of Mexican migrants entered the country illegally by wading across the Rio Grande. The wetback, like the bracero, was essentially defined by his or her economic role. "The border, more or less open to provide an escape hatch for millions of utterly poor Mexicans, is like a cunningly designed filter that separates the economic utility of the Mexican illegal entrant from the rest of his cultural makeup," wrote Ernesto Galarza, the National Farm Workers Union organizer and brilliant chronicler of Mexican migrant labor. "Never a participating member of the community or society," Galarza concluded, "the wetback lives anthropologically in no-man's-land."

From the very first days of the Bracero Program, the grower recognized the utility of the undocumented worker in maintaining and controlling a stable and high-volume labor supply. The Bracero Program provided only for a given number of laborers and relatively short-term contracts (usually four months).

Despite the fact that more than 4.5 million braceros entered the country during the life of the program, many of them were "repeaters," who had come back a second, third, or fourth time. Many braceros also returned as "wetbacks," knowing in advance that their employer would rehire them on their return.

Employers, frequently in conjunction with the Border Patrol, engaged in the practice of "drying out" the undocumented workers: growers would hire large numbers of undocumenteds who, after their work had been done in the fields, would be "apprehended," and at the border, the undocumented workers, with the INS looking on, would have the tip of their toe placed on the Mexican side of the border to then be declared eligible to return to the American side legally as braceros. "What we want of the Border Patrol," a border inspector said of the growers' instructions to their INS allies, "is to let in enough wetbacks for us to get our crops harvested and to keep the others out."

During the recessionary period of 1953–1954 there emerged new pressures for a large-scale repatriation effort. Under INS Commissioner General Joseph Swing, a West Point classmate of President Eisenhower, a xenophobic campaign called Operation Wetback was initiated. Special INS patrols swept urban barrios and farm labor camps in western Arizona and southern California. As the supply of wetbacks decreased in 1953–1954, growers substantially increased their bracero supply and waited out Operation Wetback, with their overall labor supply source still secure. By the end of 1954, more than a million wetbacks had been apprehended and deported. As the recession faded, turning into an economic upswing over the next eighteen months, the number of deportations declined dramatically to less than seventy-five thousand in 1956. The Mexican-American community in the Southwest had been ill-prepared to resist the onslaught of Operation Wetback. Community organizations such as the League of United Latin American Citizens (LULAC) and the American G.I. Forum had long promoted the idea that their constituency, the scattered and minuscule Mexican-American middle class, identified with its American citizenship. In a cautious, conservative reaction to the racist sentiment at the time, the American G.I. Forum even gave support to the Operation Wetback campaign in an attempt to distinguish between its constituency and the apparently unwanted undocumented worker.

Groups such as LULAC and the G.I. Forum did maintain, nevertheless, identification with their Mexican origins. During the war, tensions between Anglos and Mexican-Americans flared up, resulting in the dramatic "Zoot Suit Riots" in the Los Angeles barrios. The attempt by young Mexicans to define their cultural identity in the form of the *pachuco*, a figure of rebellion, was the subject of inflammatory attacks in the pages of the Los Angeles newspapers. The attacks fed on racism spawned by the repatriation and antiradical, antiunion campaigns of the 1930s. The Zoot Suit Riots involved drunken Anglo servicemen who systematically swept through the barrios to beat up Mexican residents, particularly the young pachucos, with the cooperation of the local police. The community was deeply affected. Early civil rights organizing surfaced in this period.

Through the 1940s and 1950s, the Mexican communities of the urban barrios and rural farm camps still suffered from a lack of a clear political and social purpose. The social barriers between the "wetback" and the urban Mexican-American, the bracero and the disaffected young Chicano or the returning Mexican-American veteran, hampered efforts to create a coherent community response to the racial dynamics in the Southwest, dynamics that stemmed from the long-standing migrant-labor policies.

In the early 1960s a culture of resistance grew around the efforts to organize a new farm workers' union headed by Cesar Chavez, a young Mexican-American who had learned politics through community organizing activities in Los Angeles. With a more liberal Democratic administration in Washington and a more sympathetic Congress, the organizing of the farm workers placed the Bracero Program in serious jeopardy for the first time in its more than twenty years of operation. For the first time, the Department of Labor, under farm worker pressure, began to enforce regulations such as the availability of hot water and the requirement of beds with springs and mattresses.

Growers began to have second thoughts about the necessity of the program. Some of the large agricultural interests, particularly the cotton growers of California and Arizona, had already begun to turn to mechanized harvesting, which resulted in a decline in the number of braceros needed for production. With a decline in the number of laborers and the rise of farm-worker organizing efforts growers realized they could maintain their system relying exclusively on undocumented workers. The growers reluctantly gave in to congressional efforts to end the program. In December 1964 the last bracero crossed the border, but the flow of labor would remain as critical to the region as ever.

MAQUILADORAS, UNDOCUMENTEDS, AND THE RISE OF THE CHICANO

After the termination of the Bracero Program, attention turned south of the border. During the early 1960s Mexico's northern region "was a powder keg ready to ignite," as Peter Baird and Ed McCaughan put it in their study of United States–Mexican relations. Unemployment in the border cities ran as high as 50 percent, a situation compounded by the termination of the Bracero Program, which had acted like a magnet in drawing Mexicans northward toward the border.

As social and economic conditions deteriorated, radical political trade-union and peasant organizations began to grow, winning victories in local Baja elections. The radicals organized squatter brigades that invaded the big cattle ranches in Chihuahua along its border with New Mexico and Texas. An independent radical peasant organization, the Central Campesina Independiente (CCI), was created to challenge the government-controlled peasant organization. Within a matter of months CCI attracted fifty thousand members. The organization quickly became embroiled in contesting the growing power of a developing Mexican agribusiness in the northwest, which was tied to United States agricultural processing and distribution firms.

Mexican agribusiness had grown significantly by means of government investments in irrigation and fertilizer and a policy favoring reconcentration of landholdings in the northwest. The termination of the Bracero Program provided a further boost. During the 1960s, the large Mexican groups, often aligned with United States companies, particularly California-based processors, increased their exports to United States markets. That policy, strongly encouraged by the Mexican government, also brought into question the continuing problem of the use and status of the Colorado River. More than any other single factor, the Colorado had come to symbolize the unequal relations between northwestern Mexico and the southwestern United States.

After the United States–Mexico Colorado River treaty was ratified in 1945, the question of the water quality of the river took center stage. In 1952 the Mexican secretary of resources revealed that 31 percent of the Mexican agricultural land irrigated by the Colorado waters had become useless because of the high salt content generated by uses north of the border. The remaining 69 percent of the land was also affected to some extent. In October 1961 the problem was exacerbated by the completion of Arizona's Wellton-Mohawk irrigation project, which covered 65,000 acres in southern Arizona near the border. The project allowed Arizona farmers to pump highly alkaline water from an underground reservoir in the Wellton-Mohawk Valley into the Colorado just above the border as it entered Mexico. Arizona engineers predicted that it could take forty years before the underground salt water had been completely pumped. In the process, the river was becoming a cesspool, directly affecting any possible agricultural development on the southern side of the border. The Bureau of Reclamation claimed the quality of water delivered was irrelevant to the 1944 treaty. "We could deliver sewage to Mexico," Commissioner Floyd Dominy proclaimed to congressional allies.

The Wellton-bypass situation had an immediate effect on the increasingly volatile peasant politics of Baja. A majority of Baja's communal farmers rallied together under the leadership of Alfonso Garzon Santibañez, who attacked the Arizona farmers, the United States government, and a hesitant Mexican government, which had held back from taking any direct action. Garzon and his organization demonstrated against United States companies active in Mexico, such as cotton-seed producer Anderson-Clayton, which had close ties to the Baja and central Mexican power structure. The Garzonista forces, along with the northern Mexico radical political movements, which capitalized on the discontent raised by high unemployment, threw a bad scare into both the Mexican and United States governments and eventually pushed both sides to the negotiating table.

The salinity issue also threatened to disturb the fragile alliance of Colorado basin states. Barry Goldwater, for example, in attemping to protect his Arizona agribusiness constituents, blamed California irrigation projects as the real source of Mexico's problems. Arizona Senator Carl Hayden in turn blamed Mexican farmers for irrigating too much land with insufficient water, thereby allowing salts to accumulate in the soil. California officials blamed both Mexican and Arizona growers for the problem.

By the end of the decade it had become clear to all the basin states and the federal government that some sort of cleanup of the water had to be done in the interests of maintaining Mexican stability and friendly relations. Instead of cutting back on their own projects or instituting conservation measures, the basin states, partly as a means of maintaining their own fragile unity, turned to the federal government to provide an expensive bail-out. The Colorado River Basin Salinity Act was signed and ratified in 1974. The new treaty provided for the construction of several multimillion-dollar desalinization plants and salinity control projects, the largest to be built at Yuma, Arizona.

The unemployment factor, heightened by the termination of the Bracero Program, generated the strongest fears among United States and Mexican officials about possible political consequences. The Mexican government of Gustav Díaz Ordaz in the early 1960s decided to establish industrial-type parks in border areas. Within the parks, factories were to be set up for the assembling and processing of products for export to the United States and other countries. These plants, or *maquiladoras*, would in turn be eligible for duty-free importation of any raw material, machinery, parts, or tools needed for the manufacturing and exporting of the products assembled.

Pressures for this type of program were also based on the economic needs of certain labor-intensive industries in the United States. Since World War II a number of these industries had created "runaway shops," transplanting whole manufacturing and assembly operations to such places as Taiwan, Hong Kong, the Philippines, and South Korea, where a large pool of low-wage labor existed. Many of the high-tech industries that had been so influential in postwar California now had their eye on Mexico with its buildup of a low-wage labor pool and its more favorable geographical position in relation to transportation costs and the availability of technical and managerial personnel, due to its proximity to United States markets and company headquarters. "Our idea is to offer an alternative to Hong Kong, Japan, and Puerto Rico for free enterprise," the Mexican minister of commerce told the *Wall Street Journal* in 1967.

The new Border Industrialization Program went into operation in 1966. One of the first companies to shift production was Motorola, which conveniently moved its Phoenix assembly plant two hundred miles south to the Mexican border city of Nogales. The company estimated that the move would generate an annual savings of at least $4 million since Nogales wages averaged $1,060 a year compared to $5,350 for the Phoenix electronic assemblers.

The program grew rapidly. The *maquiladoras* expanded from 20 plants in 1966 to 476 in 1974. Employment grew from twenty thousand to more than fifty-three thousand. Many of the electronics companies shifted production not only from United States plants but from overseas operations in Europe, Korea, and Japan. These were some of the largest companies in the United States— RCA, Fairchild, Litton, Zenith, Motorola, Texas Instruments, General Electric, and Bendix, among others.

Complementing the shift of the electronics plants was the growing garment trade south of the border. The garment industry had a long history of runaway production to escape wage demands, unionization efforts, and organizing against the conditions of the sweatshops. By the 1930s, a number of garment companies had moved operations to southern California and the Southwest to tap into the growing Mexican urban labor pool. In the early 1970s several garment companies made their way to Mexico, encouraged by the Border Industrialization Program. By 1973 some 108 garment plants had been set up along the border, most of them fly-by-night sweatshops that had fled previous locations, although a few big companies such as Levi Strauss and Gulf and Western's Kayser-Roth company also established operations in the border region.

The conditions of work at the *maquiladoras* left a great deal to be desired, even in comparison with equivalent low-wage operations on the United States side of the border. Hours were long, and the work tedious. The organization of work was controlled by United States quality engineers, who tried to implement "no-talk, no-movement" procedures. The intricate assembly line work did not benefit workers in terms of developing skills, one of the main rationales for the program.

The employment of large numbers of women in the *maquiladoras*, along with the growing undocumented migrations of the late 1960s and early 1970s, reinforced the continuing decline of the traditional Mexican family, which had been based on rural community structures. In their place arose a culture of immigration, along with an entirely new and garish border culture exported from the United States. Gambling, the heroin trade, and increased tourism complemented the extraordinary explosion in population in the border region. The growth rate at each of the main border cities was phenomenal. From 1950 to 1980 Tijuana's population jumped from 62,00 to 566,000; Mexicali's from 69,000 to 478,000; Nogales' from 24,000 to 75,000; Ciudad Juarez from 126,000 to 667,000; Nuevo Laredo's from 58,000 to 238,000; Reynosa's from 42,000 to 347,000; and Matamoros' from 51,000 to 229,000.

This heavily populated border area, wrote Mexican critic Carlos Monsiváis, was "not only exploited but overexploited. Places piously called 'vice towns' are really places where intense economic and social exploitation takes place." The border cities, as Oscar Lewis pointed out, suffered not only from the "culture of poverty," as did other areas throughout Mexico, but from the equally debilitating culture spawned by the extensive penetration of United States mass media.

American media-inspired consumerist expectations conflicted with the social and economic realities of the overcrowded, garish, and dirty border cities with their poor housing, lack of transportation, and the raffish honky-tonk flavor of a vice den catering to the North American tourists. Nevertheless, there were several counterinfluences that tended to complicate and modify the American media-inspired mass culture of the border towns. A complex border culture began to emerge that was based on a mix of popular singers, ranchera music, and the more commercial "nortena music" with traditional rural folk music.

By the early 1970s, the idea of the consumer-oriented "good life" north of the border complemented the ever-increasing demand by United States employers for Mexican workers in the Southwest. The termination of the Bracero Program, the rise of mechanization, and the conversion of agricultural land in such places as central Arizona's Maricopa County meant a consequent drop in the overall percentage of Mexican migrant labor in agricultural employment. According to figures compiled by a Massachusetts Institute of Technology (MIT) research team headed by Wayne Cornelius, the employment patterns of Mexican migrant workers shifted from a breakdown of 81.4 percent in agriculture and only 7.4 percent in industry shortly after the end of the bracero employment to 45 percent in agriculture and 20.8 percent in industry, with significant increases in commerce (14 percent), construction (10.6 percent), and service work (8.6 percent) in the mid-1970s.

With the shift in employment patterns, the profile of the migrant worker began to change accordingly. The undocumented, or "illegal alien," as he was dubbed in the press, had become as much an urban as a rural figure employed in a range of jobs, almost all dead-end work. The undocumented workers found jobs as janitors, garbage collectors, dishwashers, busboys, maintenance workers, unskilled construction workers or laborers, itinerant gardeners, or unskilled nursery workers. Whole industries such as southern California's garment, hotel, and restaurant trade became heavily dependent on these inexpensive, unskilled workers who, by the nature of their "undocumented" status, had little inclination toward protesting long hours, poor pay scales, or lack of advancement.

The growing number of undocumented workers in the cities of the Southwest also created a range of "hidden" economic benefits to employers and the regional economy as a whole. A study prepared for the Department of Labor in 1976 pointed out that about three-quarters of the undocumented work force paid Social Security and federal income taxes on their wages, while in contrast, less than 4 percent had children in United States public schools and only one half of 1 percent had received welfare benefits. Those findings were borne out by several other studies, including a mammoth research project by Bustamante that indicated that while 74.4 percent paid taxes, less than 1 percent had children in school and only 7.8 percent received any form of free medical benefits. Bustamante also discovered that 6.3 percent of those he interviewed had been apprehended before they had collected their wages, a situation often the result of employer–INS collusion. "Mexican labor is not cheap by nature," Bustamante declared, "but is cheap because of the immigration laws. It is a labor source not paid for its real economic value." The hidden benefits help explain the continuing economic viability of the Southwest, especially its urban centers, during periods of economic recession.

By the late 1960s local Chicano communities had developed distinct concerns, many of them separate from the questions concerning the illegal migration. The terms *Chicano* and *Aztlán* reflected a growing cultural awareness and identification with the civil rights and Third World nationalist movements of the 1960s. The term *Chicano*, a truncated form of the word *Mexicano* signifying the Mexican who lived north of the border, indicated a new self-awareness that linked the community's "North American" identity as "minority group" with its Mexican heritage. Aztlán, the mythical land of the Aztec Indians who had migrated from these northern lands to what is today Mexico City, was an equally powerful symbol. The idea of Aztlán defined the historical migratory movements as being deeply rooted in the Mexican past and as reflecting a return to the area of origins for *La Raza*, the great people of the Southwest. Through the 1960s a new kind of Chicano leader emerged, with one foot in the civil rights movement and War on Poverty organizations and the other foot in a growing nationalist politics embodied in the compelling symbol of Aztlán.

One of the most important groups to generate a new kind of Chicano consciousness was the César Chávez–led United Farm Workers. The union's effective "movement-oriented" tactics, such as its famous grape boycott in the late 1960s and its attempt to organize the most exploited of the Mexican workers, the farm laborer, captured the imagination of the urban-based Chicano community and helped unify the rural Mexican laborers. While the United Farm Workers attempted to mobilize in the countryside, a number of urban Chicano groups took root. Corky González' Denver-based Crusade for Justice grew initially out of González' work in Denver's Neighborhood Youth Corps and local Democratic party politics. By 1966 and 1967, after the Crusade for Justice had been officially launched, González and his group moved quickly away from traditional civil rights organizing and electoral politics toward a mixture of socialist and nationalist politics. They turned to a strong practical emphasis on economically and socially self-contained institutions in the community.

Similarly, northern New Mexico's Reies López Tijerina and his Alianza organization combined long-standing resentments against the Anglo land grabs, going back to the days of the treaty of Guadalupe-Hidalgo and the Santa Fe Ring in the nineteenth century, with organizing and political techniques derived from the more nationalist-oriented Black Power movements.

The difficulties of organizing and translating programs based on this new Chicano politics were enormous. The rise of Chicano militancy led to repressive countermeasures by the police and other law-enforcement organizations similar to their attacks on groups like the Black Panther party or the American Indian Movement. In 1970 local Chicano organizers in southern California issued a call for a Chicano Mobilization against the war in Vietnam pointing to the high participation and death rates of Hispanic servicemen. The demonstration symbolized the potential unity of moderate and militant organizations.

The turnout for the demonstration—twenty thousand people from all over the Southwest—was an unqualified success. A confrontation at the rally site between police and a few participants transformed a peaceful mobilization into a violent riot. Three people, including newsman Rubén Salazar, were killed by Los Angeles County sheriff's deputies, and among the hundred arrested was Corky González, who was accused of suspicion of robbery because he was carrying $300, money that was being used to pay for the Crusade for Justice members' stay in Los Angeles.

By 1972, many of the Chicano groups had reached the peak of their growth. The inability to integrate civil rights and nationalist perspectives hampered the young and relatively fragile Chicano movement. A pivotal conference in El Paso, Texas, aimed at creating a nationwide La Raza Unida party broke down into serious divisions between a militant, "nationalist" left wing headed by Corky González, and a moderate, electoral-oriented right wing, headed by José Angel Gutiérrez and his Texas-based Raza Unida party. The presence of groups led by Reies Tijerina and César Chávez' United Farm Workers supporters factionalized the conference even further. The conference failed to establish any significant unity among the disparate groups and interests.

The end of the highly visible Bracero Program and the continuing shift from agricultural to urban-based employment caused the undocumenteds issue to fade from the public eye in the late 1960s, particularly as attention focused on the rise of a more vocal Mexican-American, who, as a Chicano, asserted his or her Mexican identity with the militant minority-bloc politics of the period. Repressive actions against undocumenteds in the barrios, such as the police shooting of two Mexican nationals in a much-publicized case in Los Angeles in 1970 or the continuing state of siege in East Los Angeles by sheriff's deputies in the early 1970s were perceived as attacks against the whole community.

By 1973, that focus had begun to change as the fourth large emigration-repatriation cycle emerged with the advent of the 1974–1975 recession. The new head of the INS, former Marine Corps commandant Leonard Chapman, launched a vigorous militaristic-sounding campaign against the "illegals." In speeches, interviews, and testimony in Congress, Chapman declared the existence of a "silent invasion" of between 8 million and 12 million illegal aliens costing the American taxpayers $13 billion. The United States was being overrun by illegal aliens, Chapman told his audiences, asserting that the undocumenteds were occupying jobs needed by the unemployed and not paying their share of taxes while collecting welfare checks and unemployment payments. Appearing before Congress to try to beef up INS funding and manpower, Chapman termed the situation a "national crisis" and urged Congress to pass legislation to make it unlawful for an employer to hire illegals. "Give me a thousand more [Border Patrol] men," stormed Chapman, "and I'll liberate a million jobs for U.S. citizens."

The press had a field day with the issue. Each new speech of Chapman, Attorney General William Saxbe, or other high government officials and each new government-sponsored study designed to back up their assertions turned into headlines warning that "invasions" were imminent and that "floods" were becoming "torrents," in language reminiscent of the worst jingoistic descriptions of the Japanese, Chinese, and Koreans during recent wars.

These scare tactics also turned into a war of statistics as INS supporters marshaled figures almost exclusively based on a private research effort called the Lesko Study. The Lesko numbers, as revealed by several later studies, including those of the Bureau of the Census and the Research Service of the Library of Congress, were far off the mark and at best represented extremely inflated "guesstimates" without any scientific sample. In 1981, Jorge Bustamante, using the largest sample of undocumented migrants ever studied, estimated the range of Mexican migrants to be between 400,000 and 1.5 million.

By the 1976 election, the issue of the "illegal alien," as the press continued to identify the undocumented Mexican workers, had become the dominant issue for the Chicano community as well as a critical question for the southwest as a whole. Shortly after Jimmy Carter took office in the United States and José Lopez Portillo assumed the presidency in Mexico, the issue took on national and international dimensions as the interplay between the flow of labor north and the flow of capital south once again took center stage.

OIL, POLITICS, AND THE NORTH AMERICAN COMMON MARKET

"The immigration of Mexican labor to the United States has not been an isolated event," wrote Chicano activist Magdalena Mora at the height of the Chapman-inspired crisis. "It has been and continues to be an essential factor in the building of the economic empire of the Southwest. The borders have always been open borders. It may be said that these borders have been a rather permeable entity, a membrane that joins rather than separates. Exceptions occur only when the doors are closed to the passage of labor, but never to capital."

A *Los Angeles Times* editorial in December 1978 put it succinctly: "Mexico—A Three-Letter Word." Oil. Oil dominated the headlines, sent a horde of bankers and entrepreneurs rushing to Mexico's door, preoccupied economic planners on both sides of the border, and transformed the fear of Third World revolution into the corporate and political clamor for a North American Common Market.

The new factor of Mexican oil burst on the scene unexpectedly in the spring of 1977, when the nationalized oil organization Petroleós Mexicanos, or Pemex, announced that a major new find of oil and gas reserves in the Campeche area in southeastern Mexico gave Mexico potential reserves of the magnitude of the great Arabian finds in the Mideast. But oil had long been a factor in the turbulent history of United States–Mexican relations. The nationalization of the industry in 1938 had turned the United States-based multinational oil companies into a hostile force. Along with United States government personnel, the oil companies attempted to sabotage the budding Mexican oil industry, making it nearly impossible for Pemex to replace simple parts and keep up with the technology of the industry. Through the 1940s and 1950s negotiations between the United States and Mexico over potential export of Mexican gas had broken down. Pemex officials suspected that the United States oil companies contributed to these strained relations. In the early 1970s the Mexican government of Luis Echeverría, which had made the initial discoveries of new sources of Mexican oil and gas, quietly passed that information to the Ford White House. The Ford administration realized that the new Mexican discoveries could undercut OPEC prices and pressured the Echeverría government to increase its oil production substantially. The Mexican government resisted, fearful of the consequences of a too rapid rise in production and a potential dependence on the United States market. The Echeverría government kept a low profile on the oil issue, downplayed the discoveries, and denied it would export Mexican oil to undermine OPEC.

With the oil factor hovering in the background, the 1973–1975 recession hit Mexico particularly hard. The *maquiladoras* programs were severely disrupted by the economic downswing as more than thirty thousand jobs were lost when plants shut down or shifted operations. That loss of jobs in turn had a negative effect on other parts of the border economy, including social-service budgets already strained by the economic and social problems of the area. The downturn also affected the economy of the United States border cities, where up to 65 percent of *maquiladoras* wages were spent on sales purchases by Mexicans crossing over for the day.

The rapid decline of the *maquiladoras* in the 1974–1975 period could be traced to employer reaction against an increased radical and trade-union consciousness among the workers in the border plants. In the early 1970s, unions had been organized at several border plants. The threat of strikes in a number of instances had forced wages up for the first time. When the recession hit, the recently organized workers attempted to protect their newly won gains.

Using the recession as a cover, a number of the *maquiladoras* companies, led by the powerful American Chamber of Commerce of Mexico, warned the Echeverría government to intervene on the side of the employers or face relocation. "The *maquiladora* operations are tightly tied into integrated processes of production and foreign market conditions over which the Mexican government has no control," the chamber's business journal warned in 1975. "If the *maquiladoras* should disappear from the border area, the parks in which they are located would become industrial ghost towns." With 98 percent of all raw materials, energy inputs, and packaging in the border plants coming from abroad (mostly from American and Japanese sources), nearly all the cargo carried to and from the border by United States air and ground transport, and nearly 100 percent of the *maquiladora* production exported to United States markets, the warning had a great deal of credibility.

The Echeverría government was caught in a squeeze. When political unrest continued to grow through 1975 and 1976, land seizures swept through northwestern Mexico and other parts of the country, where the landless rural labor force felt the impact of the economic downturn. Echeverría tried to control the social movements by evoking the rhetoric of the Cárdenas period, a rhetoric that frightened a number of United States corporate executives and financiers.

On November 1, 1976, in the last weeks of the Echeverría government, the Mexican president, in order to refinance loans that had come due, agreed to terms of the International Monetary Fund (IMF) and World Bank. The IMF terms had a profound impact on the country. They included devaluation of the peso, cuts in social services, a limit to net foreign borrowing, curbs on the government deficit and expansion of the money supply, all in return for a $960 million loan and an extension of previous credits. Most important, the Mexican government agreed to generate a new oil-export program that would dramatically shift the emphasis from Echeverría's low-profile approach to the highly visible oil-production program begun by the new government of José Lopez Portillo.

The advent of the Lopez Portillo administration had an immediate soothing effect on United States governmental and corporate fears. The son of a Mexico City professor of military engineering, Lopez Portillo, having received his training in economics, had become Echeverría's Secretary of the Treasury and a close adviser of the president. Lopez Portillo continued the trend toward the growth of Mexico's capital-intensive industries, such as the steel and chemical industries, to the detriment of such labor-intensive sectors as food and beverage production. "The growth of capital-intensive manufacturing," a Business International publication pointed out, "has had the side effect of increasing the concentration of economic power in the hands of a relative few," referring to the twenty to thirty key "family" groups that controlled a range of Mexican industries and financial institutions.

In Echeverría's last years the government's populist rhetorical reaction to attacks from the Left became identified in the minds of United States and Mexican businessmen with the protracted crisis that culminated in the IMF agreements. The powerful Monterrey business elite had actively conspired against Echeverría in his government's waning days. Fears of coups and countercoups had paralyzed the country. An expectation arose, according to Business International, that by simply assuming office, Lopez Portillo would solve the crisis. Under the campaign slogan "La Solución Somos Todos" ("We Are All the Solution"), Lopez Portillo immediately adopted the pose of the compromiser, the negotiator who spoke the language of reconciliation. Within weeks after Lopez Portillo took office, the Pemex oil find was announced and the country immediately began to increase its production of oil.

The impact of the new administration and the transformation of Mexico into a visible oil power produced instant euphoria in Washington and among United States businessmen. United States companies eagerly anticipated an even more lucrative market, aided by oil income and a growing focus on the capital-intensive petro-based industries of chemicals and agribusiness. All kinds of energy-related corporate executives quickly made the trek to Mexico City, followed by international banks, chemical companies, and utility groups. A consortium led by the Bank of America arranged a $1.5 billion loan to Pemex in 1978, one of the biggest commercial loans on record. The loan, coming only two years after the IMF actions, reflected the bankers' confidence in Mexican repayments based on the new government. Similarly, although the IMF had complained of Mexico's growing debt and had encouraged prepayment of certain loans, the chairman of Morgan Guaranty flew to Mexico City especially to offer a new series of loans when the Lopez Portillo government threatened to pay out the original Morgan loan. The effect of this new round of loan activities was to narrow Mexico's options concerning resource development by locking it into foreign, primarily American, financing mechanisms and corporate activities. United States banks were mortgaging Mexico's future.

By the late 1970s, Mexico had become a major stopover not only for the banks but for multinational executives in general. Occidental Petroleum's chairman, Armand Hammer, even brought his collection of Rembrandts and other Renaissance masters to Mexico City, donated some works of art to Mrs. Lopez Portillo, and spoke of "art as an emissary." At the same time, Hammer explicitly linked his art gifts to Occidental's commercial ties to Mexico. The Occidental Petroleum chairman hoped for joint ventures in chemicals and fertilizers, the sale of the company's technological expertise, and the ability to market the Pemex oil in the United States market.

The IMF devaluations and the new Lopez Portillo policies helped revive the sluggish *maquiladora* operations. The IMF-forced devaluation of the peso had meant nearly a 50 percent cut in salary for *maquiladora* workers and a doubling of the profits for the plant owners. By 1978 the *maquiladoras* began to have a healthy and revived look. Fears about political instability in Asia as well as concern over rising Asian labor costs, tied to the value of the rising yen (as opposed to the Mexican peso's dependence on the falling dollar), made the *maquiladoras* an attractive site. Lopez Portillo, who spoke of extending the *maquiladora* concept to the Mexican interior through a special package of wage concessions, justified the program by its creation of new jobs and an increase of exports to help the balance of trade. The *maquiladora* strategy, as Jorge Bustamante pointed out, constituted a highly unstable contribution to Mexico's balance of payments because of its complete dependence on external, United States–related factors, such as economic downturns and political decisions made north of the border. The new jobs, Bustamante argued, were far fewer than the number of people thrown into the labor pool by the Lopez Portillo agricultural policies, which continued to favor large-scale production of export crops such as tomatoes in favor of the more labor-intensive small-scale farming of staple crops such as corn and wheat. The large-scale farming relied on United States investment capital, packaging, distribution, and warehousing efforts and United States import regulations that frequently undercut Mexican products. Pesticides produced by United States petrochemical companies such as Union Carbide were widely used. Some of those pesticides, as a *Los Angeles Times* investigation pointed out, had been banned in the United States because of their harmful health effects.

The key to it all remained oil. Mexico had plenty of it, although estimates of actual, probable, and potential reserves varied widely. All estimates placed Mexico among the world's most important sources of petroleum. The estimates ranged from Pemex chairman Díaz Serrano's pronouncement that reserves might outstrip Saudi Arabia's reserves, placing Mexico number one among producers, to a more modest 1980 Rand Corporation analysis that placed Mexico's reserves somewhere between fifth and seventh, trailing only Saudi Arabia, the United States, the Soviet Union, Iran, and possibly Iraq and Kuwait. Even the lowest estimates were of sufficient magnitude to convince United States governmental and corporate figures that Mexico, the oil power, had become an undeniable force in global energy politics.

The new Carter administration, following its predecessor's lead, began to picture Mexico as a savior from OPEC. Under the leadership of Energy Secretary James Schlesinger, government officials anticipated that Mexican oil production would increase to as much as 4 million to 5 million barrels per day by 1985, twice the amount projected by Pemex. One CIA study even estimated that the Mexicans had the capability of producing more than 10 million barrels per day by 1990. Schlesinger and other United States officials hoped that Mexico's widespread dependence on the American market for oil and gas exports—about 80 percent in the late 1970s—would remain high and favorably influence United States dealings with OPEC.

The Mexican government realized that such heavy dependence placed pressures not only on the volume of production but the price of the exports. That fear was intensified by the 1976–1977 negotiations over the sale price of Mexican natural gas to the United States market. After Pemex and the United States transmission companies agreed to an initial price, Secretary of Energy Schlesinger (called a "gringo idiot" by former U.S. ambassador to Mexico Julian Nava), tore up the agreement, claiming the agreed-upon price was too high and should instead be keyed to a lower figure paid to Canadian suppliers. Schlesinger's intervention deeply embarrassed the Mexican government, already subject to pressure from renewed anti-American feelings.

Mexican officials also resented American pressure on the volume of production. Pemex initially planned to increase production from an average of 1.5 million barrels a day to 2.25 million barrels per day by 1980, of which about half would go for export. That figure was to rise gradually during the next decade as Mexico attempted to diversify its market sources, shifting from an 80 percent to 60 percent market dependency on the United States.

One goal of the production strategy was to resist, especially in the wake of the fall of the Shah of Iran, a too rapid economic development financed by quick oil revenues. "We want to avoid the mistakes of Venezuela and other oil exporters. We mustn't use our oil to import food and luxury goods. We must build renewable wealth before our non-renewable wealth runs out," a senior government official told the *New York Times*.

A debate began to shape up between factions of the Left that wanted to slow down oil production and use oil revenues in labor-intensive industrial and agricultural sectors and factions of the Right that advocated a rise in oil production to help finance Mexico's long-standing quest for the creation of a capital-intensive industrial and technological economy. Although Lopez Portillo continued to give lip service to the fears of the Left about United States domination, by 1980 he had clearly chosen the ruling elite's long-standing policy of government stimulation of industrial development. The Right believed this policy would generate more wealth and would create a managerial class and a larger professional and service-oriented middle-class sector.

Under the government slogan of "Alliance for Production," the Lopez

Portillo administration initiated policies favoring the growth of private investment and trade through fiscal incentives, credits, and the clearing away of
government regulations. Those policies gave an enormous boost to the large
Mexican conglomerates, such as Monterrey's Valores Industriales S.A. and
Grupo Alfa, whose wide range of ventures included steel and beer making,
electrical-equipment manufacturing, big tourist developments, and joint fishing
ventures with Japanese and European companies. The Lopez Portillo government relaxed the restrictions on foreign ownership, giving foreign companies up
to five years to find Mexican partners who, by law, had to own 51 percent of any
joint venture.

As a result of the Lopez Portillo policies, net capital flow into the country
rose dramatically in the late 1970s from such sources as United States and
German auto makers, consumer goods manufacturers, and numerous companies involved in the production of capital equipment for the oil sector and
other industries. Despite the rapidly expanding flow of capital into Mexico, the
country's social and economic problems continued to increase. Population
growth had spiraled after the war from 26 million in 1950 to 49 million in
1970. Even after the Echeverría government began to favor a government-
sponsored birth-control program (often using American birth-control technology, some of which had been discredited in the United States), the population
continued to grow dramatically. It reached nearly 70 million in 1980, with
predictions of a population of 110 million by the year 2010, although the
growth rate had declined from 5 percent to 2.8 percent by 1980.

An extraordinarily high level of unemployment was the most serious problem
for the Mexican economy. "Until this decade," Business International wrote in
1978, "the cultural backwardness that went along with economic deprivation
meant that the country could sustain 20 percent to 30 percent unemployment
(including subemployment) levels without extraordinary social problems as a
result. But mass media and mass education have combined to make growing
unemployment into a possible social and political nightmare in the near
future."

The Lopez Portillo policies favored the agribusiness, tourist, and capital-
intensive petro-based industrial sector, which all actively sought out university
graduates for their skilled and higher-paid work force. The small growth of a
middle-class and managerial sector did little to offset the massive unemployment stemming from population growth and from policies resulting in the
displacement of poor farmers from the countryside.

By 1980 at least half of the 18 million Mexican work force were unemployed
or underemployed and less than 40 percent received the legal minimum wage.
With unemployment estimated at anywhere between 20 percent and 45
percent, the problem only seemed to be getting worse because more than eight
hundred thousand people entered the work force each year. Under increasing
pressure to expand the country's economic growth rate, Lopez Portillo, citing
the unemployment problem to offset criticism from the Left, decided in 1980 to
increase oil production to 2.7 million barrels per day, up nearly 20 percent from
earlier Pemex goals. "Mexico talks leftist but pumps up oil production," a
Business Week headline declared, in commenting on Lopez Portillo's rhetorical
juggling act.

Despite the continuing problem of unemployment, the increased oil production, along with the massive increase in investment, began to have a hothouse effect on the Mexican economy. Ironically, in the midst of high unemployment, labor shortages began to occur in skilled positions at several industrial centers as well as in mining, fishing, and even at some unskilled jobs in a variety of areas. By 1981, shortages had been experienced in Mexico City, Guadalajara, and—significantly—Monterrey, one of the states which has traditionally provided a steady stream of undocumented migration.

The growth of an oil-based economy also began to give Mexico some leverage on the international scene, particularly in relation to its giant neighbor to the north. For more than a decade, Mexico had maintained economic designs on the markets of Central America. With its own rapidly growing economy and desire for new markets, the Lopez Portillo government began to articulate a position favored by the Left. "The government would rather see stable left-wing governments rather than unstable military dictatorships," one Mexican economist pointed out, a position that placed the Mexicans in conflict with stated U.S. policy objectives in Central America.

By the late 1970s it had become clear to United States policy planners that an unstable and possibly hostile Mexico presented even more of a threat than a Mexico unreceptive to United States pressure on its oil-export program. In 1978 a National Security Council draft study entitled "Presidential Review Memorandum 41" suggested that the issue of Mexican oil and gas supplies could no longer be viewed in isolation from other factors. To establish import levels favorable for United States needs, the study suggested lowering tariffs and other trade barriers to Mexican exports and a new immigration policy, including a new bracero-like "guest worker" program or an expanded H-2 (contract worker) program.

Two years later a Rand Corporation study on Mexico's petroleum and United States policy went a step further than the National Security Council's assumptions. "The path of Mexico's petroleum development," the Rand analysts argued, "will affect trade and investment, immigration and employment, and border relations. These areas are so interrelated and crucial to the United States that it is not reasonable to argue that any one should dominate U.S. interests and objectives over the long term."

By 1980 this idea of linkage had begun to be carefully and cautiously explored by United States corporate executives interested in Mexico as an area for investment and potential market for American goods. The notion of a tradeoff between the flow of labor and oil north and the flow of capital south had been raised as early as 1977 by Felix Rohatyn of the investment firm of Lazard Frères, who had commented that "the logical thing to do is to come to some arrangements with Mexico whereby there would be a free interchange not just of labor but of goods and materials."

Anaconda's Ralph Cox, speaking before the annual meeting of Western Regional Council corporate executives in December 1979, spoke enthusiastically of the linkage notion. "We need to find ways to enhance relations other than through dollars," Cox told the western businessmen. "Mexico has needs; they have, for example, all that population growth. For their stability they need more employment outlets or else you can have revolutionary turbulence over there, with Communist tendencies developing out of the situation. And yet here in the United States we'll have a labor shortage in the next two decades, so maybe what we need to do is legitimize the movement of Mexicans here to provide our labor needs." Although Cox, in a later interview, indicated that the importance of a labor-capital tradeoff was not yet widely understood by the western business community, several corporate executives had begun to give strong support to the linkage idea.

One linkage supporter, Richard Mallery of the Arizona law firm of Snell and Wilmer, saw the possibility that Arizona could become a "gateway to Mexico" in terms of trade, investment opportunities, and political and cultural links. Mallery, whose law firm represented the Valley National Bank and other clients doing business in Mexico, defined the border as a "political boundary that has nothing to do with the cultural and historical relationships between the Southwest and Mexico which have existed for centuries." Border crossings, according to the Phoenix lawyer, should not be interpreted as "illegal" acts but as people "simply coming home." Mallery's border analysis was framed by his attempt to create a Phoenix-based Pacific Basin Institute. Mexican businessmen would play a central role in the institute, which would provide a context in which Arizona businessmen—namely, Mallery's Valley Bank clients—could pursue relations with their potential Mexican partners.

The linkage issue was also raised by United States politicians and government officials, particularly in the West. California's Jerry Brown, Arizona's Bruce Babbitt, and California's Ronald Reagan all spoke in the late 1970s of the possible tradeoff. In 1978, Brown's chief of staff, former San Diego business-man Richard Silberman, spoke of the "common heritage" rather than a divisive border separating the two countries. Babbitt projected "an enormous market for Mexican labor in the United States." Reagan and Brown, along with Texas' John Connally, all raised the idea, during the early stages of the 1980 presidential campaign, of a North American Common Market embodying the free flow of goods and possibly the free flow of labor between Canada, the United States, and Mexico. After his election, Reagan continued to promote the Common Market idea.

Unlike the cautious, frequently off-the-record statements by corporate executives regarding linkage, the politicians' advocacy of the North American Common Market was widely publicized and ultimately produced a reaction in both Canada and Mexico. The notion was perceived as favoring United States interests by creating a lopsided trade pattern whereby United States exports north and south would expand most significantly under a duty-free customs union. "For many Canadian and Mexican businesses," *Fortune* magazine pointed out, "the removal of tariff walls would surely lead to some unpleasant consequences."

While United States businessmen kept a low profile on the issues of capital and trade flows, the question of the labor migration continued to dominate the headlines and generate controversy. Most corporate executives steered clear of the issue, basically content with existing policy, which continued to allow a substantial migration northward, although it failed to deal with severe civil rights and discrimination issues for the undocumented labor force. The labor movement through the late 1970s maintained its traditional opposition to the border crossings, despite changes in several member unions which confronted a growing Mexican work force in their industry. Unions such as the International Ladies Garment Workers (ILGWU) and the Laborers International Union had the choice of incorporating the undocumented workers into their ranks or maintaining a continued hostility in the face of overwhelming numbers of Mexican workers in unskilled garment and construction work.

The unions' problems were compounded by the use of undocumented and other immigrant workers, such as Vietnamese, as strikebreakers while the INS looked the other way, regardless of union complaints. When the unions began to organize undocumented workers as the ILGWU began to do in 1976 and 1977, the situation was immediately reversed. In numerous instances, the INS responded directly to employer calls and raided plants in the midst of organizing drives. The ILGWU leadership, under pressure from its growing Mexican membership, continued to recruit undocumented workers despite the employer-INS collusion. The possibility of a contract with an "immigration clause" that would forbid INS raids on plant property and provide legal help in the case of deportation proceedings was considered. At the 1980 national AFL-CIO convention, the ILGWU attempted to reverse long-standing AFL-CIO positions on the migrant work force but backed down in the face of a solid federation leadership advocacy of a restrictive border policy. Joining the labor federation in extensive lobbying efforts in Washington were population-control groups, such as Zero Population Growth and the Federation of American Immigration Reform. By the late 1970s these groups had become the leading edge of the restrictive border movement. They backed legislative efforts such as employer sanctions and beefed-up security patrols.

In June 1977, with great fanfare, the Carter administration responded to the various pressures by announcing a major overhaul of border policy. The Carter program included a general amnesty for undocumented Mexicans who had lived in the United States for more than seven years and a "temporary alien resident" status of a five-year duration for all other undocumented migrants. The Carter plan also called for sanctions against employers who hired undocumented workers, an identification card to distinguish "legitimate" residents from undocumented workers, and a beefed-up Border Patrol to attempt to shut off future migration.

The Carter people immediately began to mobilize support for their plan, while attempting to isolate "moderate" Chicano leaders and groups from their more radical counterparts. "There was enormous pressure on us," recalled Vilma Martinez, director of the Mexican-American Legal Defense and Educational Fund, of the Carter efforts. "First Stuart Eisenstadt [presidential domestic adviser] called us, and then they got our friends in the administration—all the liberals and the Chicano government officials—to follow up, continuing the pressure. They would say we have *got* to support the plan. If we didn't, things would get worse, we'd get a Rodino Bill or Eastland's plan. The Carter plan, they insisted, was the best we could get."

Even the Chicano moderates, however, had misgivings about the Carter package. Employer sanctions were perceived as a discriminatory measure against all people of Mexican descent, since employers might naturally shy away from hiring any brown-skinned employee for fear of later penalties. Similarly, the identification card increased the possibility that Mexicans as a whole would be treated in a demeaning manner.

Some Chicano groups felt some sort of compromise might be necessary. "A few argued that a tradeoff—a better amnesty provision for the employer sanctions—might be the price we'd have to pay," Martinez recalled. "But then came those big demonstrations in support of the rights for undocumented workers and against the Carter plan. That clinched it. Once we saw those demonstrations, we knew it would be easier for all of us to simply oppose the entire package. The Carter people tried their best to get *any* Chicano organization to break ranks, but none did. It was a great moment for all of us."

The organization most responsible for the outpouring of support for the undocumented migrants in that summer of 1977 was a Los Angeles group called the Center for Autonomous Social Action (CASA). Through the late 1960s and early 1970s, CASA, headed by longtime activist Bert Corona, had based itself "on the concept that the immigrant worker is an integral aspect of the U.S. working class," as CASA member Magdalena Mora put it. That policy was reflected in attempts to obtain health care, educational and amnesty rights for their undocumented constituents, a decent wage, and the right to organize into unions.

CASA's efforts were hampered by divisions between moderate and radical Chicano groups and the shifting position of the crucial Farm Workers Union. The union changed from support of amnesty to calls for a more restrictive border because of the increasing use of undocumenteds as strikebreakers. The emergence of the INS-inspired anti-Mexican campaigns in the mid-1970s and a general repressive mood against the illegals placed CASA in a pivotal role within the Chicano community. The organization had grown rapidly between the period of the first large-scale barrio sweeps by the INS in 1975 and the unfolding of the Carter plan two years later, because of the group's ability to attract undocumented migrants by providing a range of services, including legal help around deportation proceedings. That effort culminated in the mass outpourings throughout the Southwest in the spring and summer of 1977. Under CASA's leadership, the Chicano community had become united in the notion that the rights of the undocumented migrants reflected the rights of the entire community. The concept "We Are All Undocumenteds" had become by the late 1970s a political strategy as well as a symbol of the mood in the community.

By the late 1970s the immigration issue had come to a head. Overt racism and more subtle pleas to shut down the border were resisted by a unified and angry Chicano community. The harassment ranged from individual acts of terrorism against undocumenteds to the Border Patrol's increased use of military technology left over from the Vietnam War. The Ku Klux Klan set up its own border patrol in California. In southern Arizona three undocumented Mexicans were robbed, stripped of their clothing, hog-tied, and then, for three hours, stabbed, beaten, and threatened with castration and hanging. Three Anglo cattlemen were arrested for those acts but were later acquitted by a local jury, which, in the words of one of the undocumenteds, "perhaps did not like Mexicans."

Ultimately, the Carter plan, attacked on the left by the unified Chicano community and on the right by some restrictive border advocates who wanted even tighter controls, failed to mobilize necessary support. By the 1980s, the issue remained unresolved, as the different constituencies regrouped, anticipating new battles around what had become the pivotal issue in a complex of factors that affected not only the future of the Southwest but future relations between nations and their powerful private sectors.

THE POLITICAL BORDER

The Mexican factor, at the outset of a new decade, remained a disjointed, unresolved set of interrelated issues. The question of the Colorado River, for example, despite two treaties and several multimillion-dollar projects, continued to hamper United States-Mexican relations. A spring 1979 GAO report questioned the economic feasibility of the desalinization plants then under construction as costs skyrocketed during the late 1970s and completion dates got postponed. The GAO advised scrapping the plants and instituting increased conservation instead. The suggestion that unnecessary water development projects be eliminated frightened upper-basin interests. Those interests made certain that efforts to clean up the increasingly saline Colorado remained the federal government's responsibility, no matter how costly or problematic such efforts might be. Meanwhile, the river, overbooked and overutilized, trickled into Mexico resembling more a waste water drainage system than a mighty river flowing to the sea.

In like manner, the energy issue complicated, rather than simplified, Mexican options and United States governmental and corporate responses. The giant energy corporations, chemical companies, banks and insurance companies, and agribusiness concerns continued to line up at Mexico's door along with their Japanese and European counterparts. The California Business Roundtable set up its own Mexican Factor Task Force, initially headed by the Bank of America's A. W. Clausen and designed to deal with these economic issues and the impact of the growing Mexican constituencies of California and the Southwest. Several corporate organizations, such as Arco and the Southern California Gas Company, established special "Hispanic outreach" committees to keep abreast of political changes in the Chicano communities as well as establish a modicum of "goodwill" with moderate Chicano leadership.

The growing awareness of the Chicano constituency placed renewed emphasis on the question of migration. Migration policy had passed through several phases since the first recruiters for the railroads and the cotton growers had swept through the state of Sinaloa at the turn of the century. The complementary system of braceros and undocumented workers had been instrumental in the labor-intensive phase of irrigated southwestern agriculture. The growing number of undocumented workers in the cities of the Southwest in the 1970s had provided a critical supply of labor for a range of service-oriented and light-manufacturing industries that depended on a low-paid work force.

Several generations of migration northward had created a complex class and cultural dynamic in the Southwest. Chicano and undocumented workers continued to serve as a "reserve" or secondary labor supply in low-wage industries. Many had become "marginalized," as economist Mario Barrera defined it, similar to their unemployed and underemployed black urban counterparts who survived on the edges of the urban economy. A small but important Chicano middle class that held jobs generated primarily by the public sector, had also grown, represented by the range of "moderate" political and social organizations in the Chicano community.

Although the CASA organization fell apart from internal factional divisions a couple of years after the large-scale mobilizations of 1977, the political thrust of organizing undocumented workers at the work place and around their civil rights had spread to other groups and coalitions throughout the Southwest. Former CASA leaders joined existing unions or set up independent labor organizations to organize undocumented workers in the countryside, such as the campaign of the Arizona-based Maricopa County Organizing Project. Organizational work remained difficult, and its continuity limited. The power of the community remained a potential power, heavily dependent on the integration of the undocumented migrant into the larger urban community.

In the wake of the debacle of the 1977 Carter plan, migration policy through 1980 continued business as usual—that is, as former INS head Leonel Castillo put it, a system that allowed and yet contained the flow of migration. The notion of a guest-worker program began to surface, more diverse than the grower-controlled Bracero Program but one that would reinstitute the "commodity migrant" aspects of an earlier period.

The renewed deliberations on the migrant issue continued to point out the central component of the Mexican factor—the border as a political, rather than a geographic, boundary. Circulating between their definition as an instrument of economic utility and their potential role as a political force, the undocumented workers of the cities of the Southwest had become a critical constituency in the makeup and direction of the region.

11   Citizen Armies

One of the most persistent and inaccurate western myths is that the frontier was peopled by Americans of European descent, moving ever westward from the Atlantic seaboard. In fact, for centuries, people have been converging on the West along time-worn land and sea routes from all parts of the world. Ever since the massive gold and land-inspired American migrations of the nineteenth century, western leaders, plagued by a fear of labor shortages, have sought to increase the flow of people migrating to the region. Many settlers came, but the instability of frontier life and the promises of land and mineral riches meant continued problems with a stable work force. After 1847, San Francisco swarmed with young, able-bodied men, but employers found their number insufficient to build the railroads, construct irrigation systems, and work in the fields.

Beginning with the use of Chinese labor on the railroads, southwestern employers as diverse as cotton growers, hard-rock mining operators, textile manufacturers, and electronics companies have sought to import a cheap and docile labor force to offset the perceived problem of labor scarcity. The steady importation of cheap labor since the middle of the nineteenth century has had a decidedly international flavor. First came the Chinese, then Japanese, Filipinos, and Mexicans, followed by the arrival of Okies, Arkies, and black workers from the South in the 1930s, 1940s, and 1950s.

The dynamics of scarcity and surplus, union labor and cheap labor, have been central to the southwestern economy and labor market, which has a history filled with conflict and violent class confrontation, but also accommodation and strikebreaking. Southwestern trade unionism has a colorful and complex history, dating back to the days of the gold rush when San Francisco's carpenters went out on strike to raise their daily wage from $12 to $16. In the West, much of the early union organizing took place among hard-rock miners, railroad workers, lumbermen, agricultural workers, sailors, dockworkers, and trade and service workers, whereas East Coast unionism had been manufacturing-based.

Prior to the Great Depression, western unionism was militant, radical, and subject to the direct, often brutal, opposition of the employers, many of whom were absentee owners. The story of the conflicts in the mines became an essential part of western folklore, from the Ludlow massacre at the Rockefeller-owned coal mines in Colorado to the bitter conflicts between the Wobblies and the Guggenheims in the gold mines at Tonopah, Nevada. The interior West was peopled with martyrs and heroes who championed the cause of the organization of the working class, heroes such as the balladeer and organizer Joe Hill, who was executed in Mormon Utah, and the fiery, charismatic leader of the Western Federation of Miners (WFM) and the IWW, Big Bill Haywood.

From its earliest conflicts in the 1890s, Haywood's WFM embodied much of the excitement, militancy, and limitations of western trade unionism. The WFM, the largest union in the IWW in its formative days, represented a cross section of the mining work force and was an early advocate of an industrial form of organization. Soon after the launching of the IWW, the WFM reversed itself, bitterly attacking the Wobblies and former WFM leader Haywood, while retreating to a more conservative craft orientation.

During the 1920s and early 1930s, the Mine, Mill and Smelter Workers' Union (the new name for the WFM) was relatively inactive. Resting on past gains, the union was primarily concerned with employer attempts to chip away at its various strongholds. During the Great Depression, and especially after the passage of the National Labor Relations Act, the union reactivated, and became one of the most democratic and politically oriented of the new CIO unions.

Through the war years, the rejuvenated miners' union actively fought racial discrimination in the Southwest. Ultimately, the combination of the anti-Communist and antiradical campaigns directed against the more militant CIO unions and the decline of the domestic mining industry put enormous strains on the union. The union's membership initially rallied around its leadership, whose defiance of the Taft-Hartley Act's ban on Communists led to the union's expulsion from the CIO. The union, obliged to end its forced isolation, reentered the mainstream of a relatively depoliticized labor movement in 1967 by merging with the United Steelworkers. By the late 1970s, when mining operations expanded once again in the wake of the western energy and mineral boom, the Mine, Mill and Smelter Workers' Union had become at best a memory for western hard-rock miners. To most of the organized trade unionists of the interior West, the long tradition of militancy and conflict running through the WFM, the IWW, and the Mine, Mill and Smelter Workers' Union was a thing of the past.

The traditions of militancy and conflict had also been present in the organization of workers in California, although such traditions were tempered by a racially divided work force and an equally powerful tradition of business unionism. Some of the earliest organizing efforts in San Francisco grew out of attempts by white workers, many of them Irish, to exclude Chinese workers. Thus, when the Italian fishermen struck and then later organized a cooperative sales society, they did so as part of an effort to drive out Chinese peddlers and maintain control of fish prices. In classifying the early California labor movement, labor historian Irving Bernstein described "the San Francisco pattern of organization and bargaining" as emphasizing the unionization of such areas as trade, retail, shipping, and construction and the eventual organization of industrywide employer associations to counteract the power of the unions.

By the turn of the century, San Francisco was a fully organized "union town," with the Union Labor Party holding power in the city for more than a decade. Los Angeles, on the other hand, was an open-shop town that made a bid for new industry and business operations on the basis of its nonunion and lower-salaried work force. A bitter feud between the business leadership of Los Angeles, led by *Los Angeles Times* publisher Harrison Gray Otis, and the San Francisco unionists, led by Mayor P. H. McCarthy, wracked California through the first decade of the new century.

Ultimately, the conservative Los Angeles business leadership resisted the attempts to organize the city along the "San Francisco pattern," despite the statewide gains for working-class rights and organization won under Governor Hiram Johnson (1911–1917). During the 1920s and 1930s, the Los Angeles business groups were the main proponents of antiunionism. Organizations such as the Better America Federation were created to undercut union organization and political influence. These organizations were particularly successful in pushing the state legislature in an antiunion direction.

Even the San Francisco unions in this period were in retreat, trying to rebuff attacks from statewide employer groups and overcome the bitter aftereffects of a corrupt union leadership. The 1930s revived the San Francisco movement and brought to the forefront a new radical, politically-oriented work force, particularly in the shipping and maritime trades. More narrow and apolitical, yet still militant, trade unions such as the powerful Teamsters emerged to emphasize industrywide bargaining and "stability" with uniform wage rates. Both wings in this revived and growing union movement were successful in northern California, which witnessed the Longshoremen-inspired San Francisco general strike in 1934 and the creation of the Teamsters Western Conference organization in 1937. The insurgent working-class movements also penetrated southern California with a series of bitter strikes in the garment trades, the interurbans, and the agricultural fields.

World War II had a dramatic impact on the structure of California industry, the state's work force, and the changing fortunes of the trade-union movement. A factory-based industrial takeoff had occurred, centered on the aircraft and shipbuilding industries but including the growth of a diversified manufacturing base of auto, rubber, food-processing, and steel. Wartime employment increased rapidly, particularly in southern California, as more than 1.2 million workers entered the work force between April 1940 and July 1945. These changes had a complex impact on California trade unions. There had existed in California a "dual labor market," consisting of a large pool of cheap immigrant labor, and a smaller supply of highly paid Anglo skilled workers. Labor scarcity in northern California led to successful trade-union activity and a higher wage scale than the rest of the country, while certain industries, such as agriculture, survived and prospered through their poorly paid nonunion work force.

The rapid creation of an industrial base in southern California during the war dramatically increased the number of organized workers within the work force. Arrangements were made between the federal government; national unions such as the autoworkers, steelworkers, and machinists; and western employers such as Kaiser and Lockheed to facilitate the rapid organization of trade unions, in exchange for the famous "no-strike" pledge and a moderation of wage demands. Union membership rose to such an extent in southern California that by the end of the war the Los Angeles area had actually surpassed San Francisco in the overall number of trade unionists.

Not all employer and employee forces went along with the wartime accommodation. A bitter strike at North American Aviation in 1941 and disputes at a number of other large industrial plants threatened to undercut the fragile "labor peace" and the imposition of what was later called "top-down" unionization. Recalcitrant business figures, such as Southern Pacific's Paul Shoup and the ever-vigilant antiunion Merchants and Manufacturers Association, opposed the labor accords and attempted to pass a right-to-work initiative on the California ballot in 1944. The right-to-work measure, which had also been placed on ballots in Florida and Arkansas, was designed to prevent union-shop or closed-shop agreements, then prevalent in several of the new industrial developments on the coast. The mood in the state had become decidedly hostile to the old conservative business alliances that had once been so powerful. Even the San Francisco Chamber of Commerce and Governor Earl Warren, who had come to power two years earlier strongly hostile to the labor movement, broke with their southern California allies to oppose the measure. The right-to-work initiative went down to defeat by a three–two margin.

After the war, the trends toward a more diversified employment base continued. The percentage of population employed in the agriculture, service, trade, mining, and transportation sectors decreased while increasing in heavy manufacturing and light industry. A new electronics and high-technology industry grew in northern California's Silicon Valley and the southern California basin. The instant creation of a heavy-industrial sector caused problems during conversion to a peacetime economy and increased the dependence of the California economy on the military, particularly in such sectors as aviation. With the Korean War and the large increases in cold-war military expenditures the California industrial base and work force stabilized.

The shift in employment during and after the war strengthened California trade unions. Strikes, particularly during the 1950s, decreased in intensity and size as unions sought accommodation with employer groups. Even some of the most militant and politically conscious unions, such as the Longshoremen, shifted from attempting to maintain the maximum employment to accepting modern techniques, such as containerization, which dramatically reduced the labor force on the docks. Nevertheless, political divisions between the labor movement and the more conservative California business leaders continued to surface. Although such groups as the Merchants and Manufacturers Association had changed orientation from antiunionism to accommodationist "labor relations," a residue of strong right-wing antiunionism had survived in California.

Led by California Senator William Knowland, a second campaign to pass a right-to-work initiative was launched in 1957 despite the opposition of a number of key corporate figures, including J. Paul St. Sure, an establishment lawyer who headed the Pacific Maritime Association. Mustering their strongest rhetoric about "compulsory unionism," "freedom of choice," and the "Communist menace," the 1958 right-to-work campaign resembled a last hurrah for the once-powerful antiunion leadership bloc. With the opposition mobilized under the banner of Democratic gubernatorial candidate Pat Brown, the right-to-work forces once again went down to a resounding defeat. The defeat restructured relations between the labor movement and the private sector in California. An ideological framework was created for a more fully integrated role for the trade unions in the growth-oriented politics of California during the next two decades.

While the unions gained acceptance in California after the war, business leaders in other southwestern states moved toward antiunionism. The campaigns against unions made these states particularly attractive to new industries interested in relocation. In 1946, Arizona—despite a rich, long-standing militant labor tradition—became the third state in the country to pass a right-to-work initiative. In the period prior to Arizona statehood, the mining unions were a powerful presence, influencing the state Democratic party and sustaining a prolabor radical sentiment.

During the Great Depression, conflict between labor and management became intense, particularly in the fields. In 1938, following labor conflicts at sheep-shearing camps and lettuce fields, Arizona agribusiness leaders, including cattleman Kemper Marley (forty years later a suspect in the Don Bolles murder), created the Associated Farmers of Arizona. The Associated Farmers, modeled after the California organization of the same name, combined antiunion activities in the political arena with repressive strikebreaking activities in collusion with law-enforcement agencies.

In 1945 the Arizona Associated Farmers launched a major drive for a right-to-work bill in the state legislature. Under the sponsorship of the Veteran's Right-to-Work Committee, a united business community launched an initiative drive for the 1946 election with an effective campaign pitch that linked the antiunion initiative to the availability of jobs for returning veterans. Drawing on a large financial war chest, the right-to-work forces won by a surprisingly large margin. After passage of the right-to-work measure, Arizona's surviving unions became relatively "passive" organizations, making only modest wage demands.

Nevada and Utah also passed right-to-work laws. The fate of right-to-work and other antiunion measures in Utah was strongly linked to the position of the Mormon church. In the first several decades of Mormon settlement, the church leadership cooperated with unions, many of whom were led by gentiles. The unions' efforts were almost entirely directed against gentile businesses, whereas Mormon laborers felt protected by the church's cooperative system of production and distribution and saw their work as part of the effort of "building up Zion."

When that cooperative system collapsed in the 1890s, the unions shifted their attention to Mormon, as well as gentile, operations. Church leaders quickly changed their policy and began to attack unions as a "rebellion against duly constituted authorities." As early as 1896, the church first-presidency issued a statement advocating the right-to-work principle. The right-to-work cause, which included Marriner Eccles as one of its leaders, became a central feature of the overall economic strategy uniting the church and individual businessmen, both Mormon and gentile.

The church was a leader in the right-to-work campaigns in Utah, Arizona, and Nevada. During the 1946 Arizona campaign, the church helped swing the election in favor of the right to work by means of statements by President Heber Grant and Council of Twelve member Joseph Merrill although young Mormon politicians like Stewart Udall opposed the law.

In June 1965 the church First Presidency issued a dramatic letter to all Mormon congressmen in an attempt to undercut congressional efforts to repeal the anti–closed shop provisions of the Taft-Hartley Act. One member of the Council of Twelve wrote to a Mormon congressman that he should "stand up and be counted," since his loyalty to the church would be judged on the issue. David King, a representative from Salt Lake City, did defy the church directive and was subsequently defeated for reelection because of the issue.

The Mormon church today continues to maintain its strong support of the right to work. When officials of the Utah Federation of Labor met with church lawyer James McConkie in the late 1970s, McConkie declared right to work one of three issues (along with ERA and abortion) with "moral import." The church still employs its considerable resources to maintain open-shop conditions in its geographic sphere of influence.

Mormon businessmen in Utah, such as entertainment-industry figures like the Osmond family and Sunn Classics' Charles Sellier, have used the state's open-shop provisions to their advantage in attempting to establish a new, nonunion film center outside Hollywood. Escaping the highly unionized work force in Hollywood, Sunn Classics shifted its operations from Los Angeles to Park City, Utah, in the mid-1970s to take advantage of Utah's nonunion labor market. Similarly, the Osmond family, in establishing its multifaceted studio operation in Provo, Utah, highlighted its cheap, nonunion labor force.

With increasing talk about the attractiveness of the Sun Belt market, Utah, Arizona, and Nevada businessmen, along with officials in state government, promoted their state's right-to-work provisions as a lure to incoming industries. The Utah Development Division, a state agency influenced by local businessmen, issued brochures aimed at attracting new industry. The brochure heralded the state's right-to-work law and linked it to the high productivity of "hardworking Utahans," the labor force's lower wage scales, and the ability to recruit a nonunion work force.

Aside from the Mormon influence, the right-to-work laws in Arizona, Nevada, and Utah were a result of rapid population growth and economic expansion that resulted from new energy and mining developments and the growth of electronics, light machinery, garment, and service-related industries. The tendency of the interior West, especially prevalent in the right-to-work states, was toward lower wages, particularly in relation to California and the Northeast. The one major exception was the large energy projects, where the scarcity of skilled workers led to significantly higher wages. The overall lower wage scale outweighed such problems as the lack of skilled labor and the distance from large markets and allowed Phoenix, Salt Lake City, Las Vegas and other locations to maintain a competitive edge in attracting certain kinds of new businesses while placing the labor movement at a disadvantage. The fate of that labor movement became particularly acute with the advent of the large-scale energy and mining booms of the 1970s.

LABOR IN THE MINES

Joe ("Moose") Martinez lived and breathed western mining. Born at a coal camp owned by Colorado Fuel and Iron, the site of the 1914 Ludlow massacre, Martinez grew up in the mines. Five of his uncles had been killed in mine accidents. A third-generation Mexican-American, Martinez worked twenty-three years in the mines, contracted black-lung disease from repeated exposure to coal dust, suffered three smashed vertebrae in a fall from a roof, and lost a finger in a cave-in.

In 1970, Martinez became an organizer for the United Mine Workers in the western region. Each year he traveled thirty thousand miles through Colorado, Utah, and New Mexico, facing constant harassment, which included threats on his life, in his attempts to organize the wayward western mining work force. "Moose is the kind of person who just keeps going all the time," UMW western regional head Steve Galati told the *Wall Street Journal* in the fall of 1979. "He never tires."

Martinez and the UMW's task force became crucially important by the 1980s when the westward shift of the coal companies and the energy multinationals locked up western coal. The West's big new strip mines with low-sulfur coal were, in the 1970s, almost all nonunion operations, for the energy companies had carefully constructed a strategy aimed at keeping the unions out.

By devising a nonunion strategy, the companies hoped to minimize the number of workdays lost to strikes, the number of which had increased substantially in the East during the 1970s. Since skilled western miners were a scarce commodity, a high wage scale (by East Coast standards) was paid to western miners. The extraordinary productivity of strip mines meant that western coal and energy operators were able to pay higher than union wages. In this way they undercut the union's basic appeal.

Finally, by shifting operations westward while keeping the unions out, the coal operators and energy companies seriously weakened the national power of the UMW. By reducing the UMW share of coal production to below 50 percent nationally, the companies hoped that the union would remain a weak regional union whose strength would be centered in such states as West Virginia, Ohio, Pennsylvania, and Illinois.

The industry's strategy appeared to be paying off by the end of the decade. In 1979, mine workers at the nation's largest coal mine—an Amax mine in Gillette, Wyoming—rejected the UMW. That same year the UMW lost nine of the thirteen elections held in western mines. The union was further hampered by attempts of other unions, particularly the conservative business-union–oriented Operating Engineers, to organize the mine workers and raid UMW shops.

Part of the UMW's difficulty concerned the nature of the work force. Unlike their eastern counterparts, the western miners tended to be transient workers, without deep-rooted family or community ties. The western miner, wrote

Stephen Voynick, who described his experiences in *The Making of a Hardrock Miner*, is "basically a restless person, one who can feel something closing in on him when he stays in one place too long, a person who thrives on and is refreshed by changes in climate, surroundings, customs and people. . . . For many it is an endless march, simultaneously sad and happy, a compulsive journey to someplace different, yet to the same thing they have just left."

The western mining work force has little sense of its own violent history, which includes the bitter and bloody confrontations of the Wobblies and Western Federation of Miners. The Wobblies had capitalized on the transient nature of the western work force and had turned it to their own advantage by creating a culture of resistance around the figures of the tramp and the hobo shifting from mining camp to mining camp or logging operation to logging operation. The eastern-dominated companies were able to undermine that culture of resistance, using police and vigilante repression and nonwhite workers. Furthermore, the Wobblies, precisely because of the transient nature of their membership, were never able to build a stable union organization at a particular location.

The push for a nonunion western work force in the mines paralleled moves in the late 1970s to develop a nonunion work force in heavy construction at the big energy and power plant projects. The national Business Roundtable, as part of its general offensive against the construction trades, had begun to encourage many of its energy company members to use nonunion contractors for their new projects in the West. The energy companies wanted large contractors such as Bechtel and Fluor to function as project brokers, subcontracting out as the jobs became larger and more complex. The development of subcontracting, according to Max Warren, the western regional head of the Laborers Union, undercut any jobwide union agreement, since the work itself was given out piecemeal. In addition, the absence of unions allowed many of the companies to forego the payment of costly fringe benefits. The largest nonunion contractor, Texas-based Brown and Root, was called in to oversee substantial contracts involving some of the largest energy players. In 1980, Arco's Anaconda hired Brown and Root to do a nonunion construction job for its new $20 million molybdenum mine near Tonopah, Nevada, with Bechtel as the overall management engineer. Even a union contractor like the southern California-based Fluor Corporation explored ways to enter the nonunion area by acquiring a nonunion contractor and shifting work to this subsidiary.

Just the threat of bringing in nonunion people like Brown and Root had an impact on union strength and negotiating tactics. In Arizona, any time there were work stoppages on Arizona Public Service's Palo Verde Nuclear Plant, the largest construction job in the state, the project manager, Bechtel, would threaten to bring in Brown and Root unless disputes were settled and workers immediately went back to work. The threat usually worked.

Despite the antiunion thrust of the big companies, many of the large construction projects, particularly those with federal government participation, still relied on union labor. Both the proposed MX and oil-shale projects, for example, initially appeared slated for union contracting arrangements, a situation that helped lock the unions into early support for both those controversial projects. The situation, however, continued to point toward an antiunion offensive.

Many of the big uranium projects in the Southwest, for example, were nonunion. Some of the big companies, such as Arco and Union Oil, maintained a policy that prevented union people from entering company property to talk to the miners. "I'm afraid," Laborer's official Warren lamented, "that the energy companies are more and more moving toward a point of full exclusion of unions on their western operations."

To offset the corporate counteroffensive, some union organizers turned to their most potent issue—health and safety. During the 1970s, "the most effective man in union health," according to occupational health professor Dr. Samuel Epstein, was Anthony Mazzochi of the Oil, Chemical and Atomic Workers (OCAW) union. Based in Denver, Mazzochi raised issues of low-level radiation, the effects of various chemicals (such as pesticides) on production workers, and a series of related health concerns involving western energy and petrochemical operations.

Mazzochi and his associates had worked closely with Karen Silkwood, the Kerr-McGee nuclear worker who was killed on her way to meet a *New York Times* reporter and an OCAW official in order to expose possible nuclear safety problems where Silkwood worked in Oklahoma. "We organized her effort in my offices," Mazzochi told the *Straight Creek Journal* several years after her death. "She was killed on her way to meet my associate. Feminists and antinuclear people have laid hold of her since then, but she was a trade-union woman on a trade-union case."

Arguing that the health issue was most directly felt "at the point of production," Mazzochi tried to fashion a coalition of rank-and-file union members, health workers, professionals, and environmentalists concerned with the issue of industrial health, and minority groups, such as Navajo Indians or Mexican miners, most directly affected by poor health conditions. Of all the health hazards for working miners in the West, none were greater than the effects on workers of conditions in the uranium strip mines that dotted New Mexico, Arizona, Utah, Colorado, and Wyoming. From the advent of the Manhattan Project in the 1940s, much of the uranium mining was located on Indian lands and frequently used Indian miners and millworkers. These workers had little concern with health issues. Radiation questions were summarily dismissed or ignored by mine owners as well as by the AEC.

Questions of mining safety and health hazards and radiation effects leading to such diseases as silicosis or lung cancer surfaced as early as 1949, when an industrial hygienist from the United States Public Health Service wrote a memo on toxic chemicals found in the air at uranium mills. The memo was published in the *Denver Post*, but action was never taken on the problem. Although mills at the time were surveyed by the federal officials, the mine operators, according to a study by Marjane Ambler, had been assured that the information would not be released to the newspapers, nor would the actual names of the operators appear in government files. This action greatly limited any use of the information for potential litigation. The attitude of the AEC and mine operators had contributed substantially to severe exposure and numerous health hazards.

When congressional hearings on health hazards in uranium mining took place in 1979, several witnesses talked of the terrible conditions in the "dog holes," the poorly ventilated and uranium-dust–filled mines of the first decade of uranium mining. Victim after victim of lung cancer and radiation-related diseases were cited. Dr. Leon Gottlieb, a Navajo Health Service physician testified, "We are witnessing a tragedy, an epidemic of lung cancer among former uranium miners." From a "zero-cancer death rate" among Indians, a significant number of former Navajo miners had, by 1980, died of cancer.

By 1980 attention concerning the uranium and radiation health hazards began to grow. Former Interior Secretary Stewart Udall, for example, became involved in litigation for southwestern victims of uranium and nuclear-related radiation, but the efforts of people like Tony Mazzochi had still not generated a substantial coalition or opposition movement. The western labor movement continued to follow a contradictory set of impulses that tended to pit trade unionists, environmentalists, populists, Indians, and Mexicans against each other rather than move them toward a common strategy. Despite the potential of a powerful issue, the idea of a united opposition force in the West remained, at best, a hope.

DUAL LABOR

The single most divisive factor preventing coalition is the issue of race. Throughout the twentieth century, the western labor movement opposed various attempts to import a cheap foreign (primarily Mexican) work force whether by legislation or through encouragement of illegal migration. The labor movement felt that operations like the Bracero Program or illegal immigration undercut unionizing efforts, especially in the agricultural area, and that the existence of a large-scale cheap labor force depressed wages in particular industries.

The rise of the United Farm Workers in the 1960s tended to overcome, in its early years, the division between undocumented workers and a unionized work force, in part because of the strong movement orientation of the largely Chicano UFW. "La Causa" in the 1960s—for documented and undocumented alike—was everybody's cause. The UFW-inspired union drives were perceived by the entire rural work force as a movement incorporating traditional union demands with nationalist and civil rights aspirations.

By the early 1970s, however, California growers began systematically to employ undocumented workers as a device to hamper UFW attempts to unionize the agricultural work force. When the UFW in 1973–1974 began to demand that the INS prevent strikebreaking activity by deporting undocumented workers, the INS largely ignored the union request and continued its policy of responding exclusively to employers.

The UFW's call to the INS, and subsequent actions, such as a UFW-inspired Arizona border blockade, caused tensions between the union and its backers in the Chicano community who opposed any recourse to the INS. The UFW shifted back and forth during the 1970s, attempting to reconcile its movement aspirations with union policies that frequently caused antagonistic actions toward undocumented workers. This ambivalence led to attempts, particularly in Arizona and Texas, to organize an alternative farm-worker union specifically geared to organize the dispossessed undocumented work force. Those attempts, along with similar efforts by alternative and established unions to organize in the southwestern urban centers, led to some tentative first steps toward developing alliances with Mexican unions to unionize migrant workers.

The lower wage scales were perceived by Chicano labor organizers as an effect, rather than the cause, of a cheap-labor system. Several of the urban-based industries that relied on undocumented workers—textiles, light industry, electronics—were structured around the need for cheap labor. Eliminating the undocumented work force would not produce higher wages, the Chicano organizers argued, but would likely lead instead to relocation—very possibly abroad to the cheap-labor centers like the *maquiladoras* or Pacific basin countries. Much of the mainstream labor movement opposed the thrust of the Chicano organizers and supported instead a "closed border" with "employer sanctions." "We have a responsibility for our constituency, to protect our union members," declared Los Angeles County Federation of Labor President William Robertson. "We have to have some control of people coming across the border."

Robertson's attitude was disputed even within the ranks of key AFL-CIO organizations, an indication that the solid front of the labor movement had begun to weaken. "I have great sympathy for people crossing the border," stated Darwin Aycock, secretary-treasurer of the Arizona Federation of Labor. "They are workers in the same light as I am. They get mistreated by employers."

The growing attempt to organize undocumented workers had in fact met severe resistance from southwestern employers. In one of the more curious efforts, agricultural employers in Phoenix tried to use Navajo workers as a nonunion work force to hinder attempts by union organizers to sign up undocumented Mexican workers, an attempt ultimately rebuffed by agreements between the Navajo tribe and the union organizers. This agreement marked a significant change in the Navajo position toward unions. In the 1950s and 1960s the tribal government had opposed efforts to organize the numerous Navajo workers employed in the coal and uranium mines and the power plants dispersed throughout Navajo territory. The Navajo tribal council opposed the union efforts. As in the case of the 1961 attempt to unionize the Texas-Zinc Mineral Corporation uranium mine on the Navajo reservation near Mexican Hat, Utah, the Navajo had actually contested the right of the unions to hold an election on its territory. Fundamentally, the Navajo leaders, according to a research study by Lynn Robbins concerning Navajo participation in labor unions, were "reluctant to permit unions to operate on the Navajo reservation for fear the unions would exert unwanted political influence on the Navajo Tribal Government."

This position was complicated by the agreements between the tribes and energy companies that involved a trade-off between energy developments on tribal lands (frequently at minimum lease terms) in exchange for preferential hiring clauses. By the early 1970s, serious questions arose concerning the value of the preferential hiring clause for Navajo miners. For example, Navajo workers in 1970–1971 complained that the Bechtel Corporation, construction manager for the Navajo Generating Station, had a strong bias that favored replacing Navajo workers originally hired under the preferential clause with Anglo Bechtel workers from the Mojave plant, which was then nearing completion. Bechtel also placed a number of Anglos with strong anti-Navajo prejudices in key positions at the plant, which simply accelerated the Navajo dismissal rate and greatly increased Indian dissatisfaction with the job.

The discontent with Bechtel at the Page plant led to the organization of the Navajo Construction Workers Association in the spring of 1971. This organization began to link up with newly created Indian-rights organizations. Because of the pressure of this new coalition, the Navajo tribal council recognized worker grievances and accepted the move toward unionization by creating the office of Navajo Labor Relations.

The emergence of civil rights and the issue of control of energy developments on Navajo lands raised once again the overall question of energy developments in the Southwest. During the 1970s the western labor movement, similar to the earlier Interior Department–supported actions of the Navajo tribal government, had strongly backed energy developments on the grounds that the large projects meant a greater number of jobs. Some Indian groups became disillusioned with the promise of jobs. At times they joined with environmentalists in such efforts as the Black Mesa Defense Fund. The labor movement, on the other hand, continued to buy the jobs argument and to remain antagonistic to the environmental groups.

The split between labor and environmentalists had been carefully nurtured by such groups as the California Council for Environmental and Economic Balance (CEEB), the state's main prodevelopment lobbying group, spawned by former Governor Pat Brown and some corporate officials in energy and development-oriented companies such as Southern California Edison. Construction unions had also joined with their corporate antagonists in a coalition supporting nuclear power—even at the moment those very same corporations were beginning to reveal their union-busting efforts on the large western construction projects.

By 1980 antinuclear activists and their environmental allies had begun to explore the possibility of alliances with workers and trade unions around the issue of health hazards in nuclear plants and other energy projects. Some unions, such as the International Association of Machinists, even raised the possibility that new jobs could be created through alternative, labor-intensive energy routes and conservation programs rather than the big, capital-intensive nuclear and coal-fired plants. But deeply rooted suspicions and antagonisms, fueled by effective corporate-dominated efforts like CEEB, continued to divide the western labor movement from its potential allies among the environmental groups. Such an alliance was also hampered by the tendency of some environmental groups to define their interests in protecting the land as a "scenic resource," disregarding class, national, and ethnic issues. Ultimately, the contradictions between constituencies still overwhelmed the possibility of coalition and alliance.

To Eddie Mayne, everything seemed possible. The burly thirty-five-year-old labor leader was a union man from a union family. Mayne's father had worked at Kennecott's Bingham Canyon mine in Utah near his birthplace. His grandfather had been the first president of Local 485 of the Mine, Mill and Smelter Workers Union representing the Kennecott workers in Utah.

Young Mayne had been a practicing Mormon as a teenager, but it turned out his union traditions had a stronger pull than the church. One summer the eighteen-year-old Mayne took a temporary job at the Bingham mine, as so many relatives had done before. Three weeks later Mayne's local was out on strike and the young miner received his initiation rites on the picket lines. The strike lasted ten weeks, and the summer job later turned into full-time permanent work on the track gangs railroading the copper from the mines.

Three years later Mayne's union merged with the giant United Steel Workers of America, and many of the old-time leadership retired or faded from the scene, saying they had no desire to kiss and make up with their longtime rivals in the Steel Workers. Eddie Mayne was one of those who went on to fill the leadership void. Within weeks another strike hit the Kennecott workers. This one would last more than eight months. "That strike was my real education," Mayne recalled. "I saw how Kennecott was able to manipulate us, through their stockpiling and their attempt to break the union. And I saw who was hurting and how other working people helped out. It taught me what the labor movement was all about."

Mayne became a union leader and within a few years assumed the presidency of Local 485. He was a different breed of western labor leader, ready to go on the offensive rather than simply react to the company's actions and sit idly by while businesses used the courts, the press, and the political arena to accomplish their objectives. Mayne saw an opportunity on the statewide level. When some of the industrial unions in Utah, dissatisfied with the parochial and isolated federation leadership, asked Mayne to run for president of the Utah AFL-CIO, Mayne agreed. In a strongly contested election that pitted Mayne and his industrial-union backers against the candidate of the construction trades, Mayne squeaked through and became the labor federation's youngest state president ever.

Mayne immediately moved to change the labor group's image and overall orientation toward other constituencies. "We needed to have a sense of unity, a sense of movement," Mayne declared. "We needed to go back to basics, to the origins of the labor movement. We needed to create a progressive thrust that allowed us to talk to others in figuring out what's been happening to our communities."

The state labor leader began to take up a number of community and political causes, ranging from support for the ERA (a decisive step in Mormon Utah) to the advocacy of social programs for the poor. Mayne's efforts soon paid off. Although Mayne moved gingerly on such issues as the MX system and the big energy projects, limited by the powerful construction trades who backed those projects, he still declared a strong admiration for the Machinists' support of alternative energy policies and sought out information on how to link the question of energy alternatives to the issue of jobs.

Eddie Mayne became a coalition builder. He saw the labor movement as an essential link between constituencies as diverse as minorities, environmentalists, and social activists. Despite his limited success, he symbolized the possibility of new western alliances. Like Tony Mazzochi, the Navajo construction workers, and the organizers of undocumented workers, Mayne and the others cautiously explored a potentially new version of the age-old southwestern dream of control of the land and the land's resources.

BOHEMIAN CLUB ENVIRONMENTALISM

The 275 delegates from a variety of environmental organizations had gathered to take stock of their situation and their movement, ten years after Earth Day and the media's discovery of environmentalism. Many of those attending the Environmental Decade conference at Estes Park in the Rocky Mountains of northern Colorado had become prominent participants in national resource and development decisions. These delegates constituted the official environmental movement, belonging to the largest and best-publicized organizations tackling environmental issues. Many of them had easily shifted between their organizations and positions in the federal, state, and local bureaucracies. They were the people who had helped draft the legislation that had so concerned and antagonized western corporate power and then moved into the public sector to implement the laws they had helped draft.

Yet, despite what Conservation Foundation president William Reilly called the "astonishingly successful" record of environmental legislation passed in the 1970s, the mood of the delegates at Estes Park was pessimistic. The synfuels-related Energy Security Corporation was making its way through Congress and the Clean Air and Clean Water acts were under severe attack by an aggressive corporate counteroffensive that had gained access to the White House, Congress, and the state governments. The prospects for the 1980 election, pitting a resurgent Ronald Reagan against a retreating Jimmy Carter, cast a pall over the conference. At the last session, former Oregon Governor Tom McCall, summing up the bleak assessment, indicated that the environmental movement would have to send out emissaries to "establish diplomatic relations" with Reagan and learn to live with newly consolidated and aggressive corporate forces.

Yet all did not remain bleak. Some, if not most, of the delegates had become well-established figures in the newly created regulatory bureaucracy. Most considered the 1980s a time for a holding action. A few of the delegates had already begun to open relations with some of the more sophisticated business types who saw environmentalism as a movement to be tamed and integrated into the system's dominant structures. Some of the delegates were local activists who had fought protracted battles on local and statewide levels. They were the unsung heroes of a movement that continued to suffer from the telling criticism that it was elitist, its value system and constituency limited to what its right-wing counterparts derisively called "the new class" of young professionals, bureaucrats, and skilled technical workers who occupied an important role in the high-technology and resource-based industries of the western Sun Belt.

What emerged most clearly from the conference was a sense of contradiction: of opposition and containment; of alternative visions and resource-management expertise; of ambitious lawyers and radical ecoactivists; of an upper middle-class Anglo movement and a political approach that derived its perspective from such different sources as Indians and New Leftists. The environmental movement, like the labor movement, entered the new decade not only facing "challenges," but the question of self-definition.

*   *   *

Environmentalism is largely a western phenomenon. The emergence of the environmental decade in the 1970s represented a third wave of a movement with origins dating back to the frontier raids on western resources. The first wave of that movement centered on the fight for the establishment of a national parks system. The conflict developed between two wings of the movement, one rallied around the scenic preservation of undeveloped areas and the other around the rational management and use of resources. The second wave had its origins in the policies of the New Deal, which combined the preservationist stance embodied in such programs as the Soil Conservation Service and the Taylor Grazing Act with the use-oriented policies of the dam builders of the Bureau of Reclamation. The third wave emerged in the 1950s with the fight over the big dam projects on the Colorado and eventually touched every issue of resource development in the contemporary West.

John Muir and Gifford Pinchot were two of the most prominent early environmentalists. They were leading proponents of two different approaches—preservationist and conservationist—and eventually locked horns in one of the West's crucial water battles. Muir, the son of a Scottish merchant, arrived in San Francisco at the age of twenty-nine. He sought out the California wilderness, scaling the Sierra Nevada and becoming the foremost champion of preserving the Yosemite Valley. On June 4, 1892, in the offices of San Francisco attorney Warren Olney, Muir and twenty-six others formed a new organization called the Sierra Club and dedicated it to "exploring, enjoying, and rendering accessible the mountain ranges of the Pacific Coast." The organization consisted primarily of businessmen and professionals who sought to preserve the rich mountain areas and timberlands that stretched across California and the intermountain West. The club quickly became engrossed in a series of campaigns to establish national parks, set aside forest preserves, and keep the mountain areas and valleys such as Yosemite safe from resource development.

Gifford Pinchot, although an occasional ally of Muir and the Sierra Club, had a different attitude toward the issues of western development. The son of a wealthy dry-goods merchant, young Pinchot went from Yale to the profession of forestry. Pinchot believed that the unregulated practices of the timber merchants in the West were essentially unproductive and that a planned sustained-yield management of the forests allowed a more profitable development. Pinchot's career took off after Theodore Roosevelt became president. Along with his counterparts in the Interior Department and the newly established Reclamation Service, Pinchot quickly became a part of Roosevelt's inner circle, helping to formulate much of Roosevelt's political approach to resource development.

Pinchot's conservationist concept of use, or planned resource development, easily meshed with Roosevelt's progressive politics, which called for government intervention in certain areas of the economy in order to function as a planning body in shaping the overall interests of the private sector. The Roosevelt-Pinchot policy came fully into play over the issue of water and land development. Pinchot defined their water program as putting to use every part of the land and its resources in order to serve the greatest number of people possible. In the Owens Valley situation, Roosevelt and Pinchot sided with Los

Angeles development interests against the farmers and ranchers of Inyo County on the grounds that by providing water for urban development, the project served the most people for the most good.

When an attempt was made to build a dam in the Hetch Hetchy Valley in the Sierra Nevada with an aqueduct to San Francisco, Pinchot broke with John Muir in a bitter battle that thoroughly divided conservationists and preservationists and split the Sierra Club over the issue. The preservationists were attacked as "misinformed nature lovers" in their attempt to save the valley as well as unwitting tools of the private power companies, led by Pacific Gas and Electric, which opposed the public-power component of the project. After Hetch Hetchy, the preservationist-conservationist conflict was muted by the new issues that evolved during the New Deal period. Under Harold Ickes, the Bureau of Reclamation emerged as the main advocate of public planning and resource development for shaping the West and subsidizing certain western industries such as agriculture, while conservationist efforts were encouraged through such projects as the Soil Conservation Service.

A powerful national-parks bureaucracy also developed during the Ickes period that worked closely with conservationist groups. After the New Deal, two distinct tendencies emerged within the Sierra Club and the larger environmental movement. One tendency, dating back to John Muir and Hetch Hetchy, was the tradition of active public opposition on issues such as keeping wilderness areas intact. The other tendency was defined by what one Sierra Club leader called the "Bohemian Club tradition." Under that tradition, environmental leaders operated quietly, in discreet places like the Bohemian Club, in order to influence political or business leaders around policy issues.

Ever since its founding in 1892 the Sierra Club had been a self-constituted elite organization, most of whose members tended to be wealthy, conservative Republicans. As late as 1945 the southern California chapter of this exclusive club had refused admittance to a black man. During the early days of Joe McCarthy, the Sierra Club had engaged in its own modest version of Red-baiting. Club leaders were most comfortable in the surroundings of the businessman's private club rather than on the public stump. Their relationship with the bureaucracies of the Interior Department, such as the Park Service and the Forest Service was more one of accommodation than conflict.

When, in the late 1940s, the Bureau of Reclamation began to project a master plan for water development on the Colorado River, much of the club leadership was inclined to compromise, accepting some of the terms of Colorado development. But the club leadership, under prodding from some of the young Turks on the board such as David Brower and Richard Leonard, decided to oppose the part of the bureau's plans that would create a dam in Dinosaur National Monument in the tristate area of Colorado, Utah, and Wyoming. By 1953 an environmental coalition had emerged to fight this proposed Echo Park Dam. In 1952 the coalition was aided by the creation of the position of executive director of the Sierra Club, a position filled by former book editor David Brower.

Brower clearly belonged to the patrician tradition of environmentalism. A conservative Californian whose great love was mountain climbing, Brower had never voted for that other patrician Franklin Roosevelt, although he and other Sierra Club members had gone along with New Deal "environmental policy."

Brower and other club members saw dam building as the epitome of good conservation practice. The opposition to Echo Park and the bureaucratic disputes between the Bureau of Reclamation and the Park Service—disputes in which the club had participated as an extension of the government bureaucracy—had caused the club and its allies to turn toward its forlorn tradition of public opposition.

With Brower as the coalition's full-time organizer and publicist, the campaign to save Dinosaur National Monument became an effective and inspirational affair. Brower organized raft trips down the Yampa River through the area and used films, brochures, special bulletins on the latest events, letter writing campaigns, advertisements in newspapers, articles in national magazines, and even a book on the area edited by Wallace Stegner, all to mobilize support.

The conservationists took the position that the Echo Park Dam idea had to be separated from the overall Colorado River Storage Project proposal for tactical and strategic reasons. By arguing for separate authorization for each component of the project, including Echo Park Dam, the conservationists felt they could block Echo Park Dam's authorization. Thus, Brower argued, they could oppose Echo Park Dam without opposing the entire project with its strong bloc of upper-basin supporters. Sensitive to the charge that they were "just aginners," the coalition's efforts were geared toward opposition to Echo Park Dam in the context of support for water development in the West. "The Club does not oppose a sound upper Colorado project that does not adversely affect Parks, Monuments, or Dedicated Wilderness," Brower wrote.

Despite their tactical accommodation, the conservationist campaign was a major breakthrough for the conservationists. It was aided by California water-development interests who feared that the upper-basin projects would ultimately cut into California's supply of the Colorado. The two groupings held secret meetings to plot out joint strategy. These meetings brought out a long-standing fear of California that existed throughout the southwestern and intermountain states. Advocates of the project were quick to see Brower and the conservationists as an extension of the California bloc. The Salt Lake City and Denver newspapers, for example, identified the Sierra Club as the "Sierra Club of California" in an effort "to link the club with their favorite whipping boy," as Brower put it in a letter to a club member.

The California connection did aid the conservationist coalition's efforts when California congressmen held up the necessary legislation. By the winter of 1955 it was able to eliminate Echo Park Dam by a compromise with the project's advocates arranged through a series of meetings between the conservation leaders, the project's supporters in the Senate, and Interior Department officials. The compromise allowed other parts of the project, including a high dam at Glen Canyon, to go through in exchange for a pledge that no dam "would invade a park or monument." Brower and most of the other conservationists had never seen the extraordinarily majestic Glen Canyon, but since it had never been designated a national-park area, they failed to oppose the construction at Glen Canyon.

When the Sierra Club and the conservationist coalition dropped their opposition, the project—with Glen Canyon—sailed through Congress despite the efforts of some senators who unsuccessfully attempted to enlist conservationist help in killing the entire package. It was a decision that Brower, among others, would live to regret. Brower's regret eventually turned into self-criticism, when he and the club arranged to tell the story of Glen Canyon in a photo-essay entitled *Glen Canyon: The Place No One Knew.* "Glen Canyon died in 1963 and I was partly responsible for its needless death," Brower wrote in the foreword to the book. "So were you. Neither you nor I, nor anyone else, knew it well enough to insist that at all costs it should endure. When we began to find out, it was too late."

Brower blamed the Glen Canyon project on the Bureau of Reclamation's need to generate revenues to disguise a massive subsidy involved in the Colorado River projects, a criticism he had made privately, but never publicly during the Dinosaur National Monument fight. "The inability to finance reasonable development of the West by means that financed it elsewhere," Brower wrote, "has cost all men, for all time, the miracle of an unspoiled Glen Canyon."

Despite the conservationists' anguish over Glen Canyon, their mobilization around Echo Park Dam had generated tremendous interest in the movement. It demonstrated the capacity of the conservationist groups, and the Sierra Club in particular, to mobilize large numbers of people and effectively exert pressure on a national scale. But the coalition's opposition to Echo Park Dam had failed to raise either the issue of subsidies or overall development. Its alternative scenarios focused on what the coalition considered to be the more economical and less scenically destructive coal-fired and nuclear power plants.

The loss of Glen Canyon did serve the purpose of highlighting the differences between the behind-the-scenes Bohemian Club traditions and the newly revived method of public mobilization and pressure. While Brower and some of his new supporters vowed never again to allow private negotiations to circumvent a public campaign to save a scenic resource, some of the conservative Sierra Club directors fretted over the increasingly public nature of the club director's criticisms and appeals for mass support. In 1959, after some private lobbying of club directors by the Forest Service, the Sierra Club board passed a resolution calling for limiting the public attacks to what it called "objective and constructive criticisms" in which the "motives, integrity or competence of any [government] official or bureau" would not be questioned—a resolution that acted as a direct slap in the face of the club's executive director. Brower's position, however, was strong enough to force the board by the early 1960s to question any large-scale dam construction on the Colorado River. This position placed the conservationists directly in opposition to the Bureau of Reclamation and its overall approach to the West, which spoke of "conquering the wilderness" and "subduing the earth," as one bureau publication put it.

The bureau was led by a cigar-chomping no-nonsense bureaucrat named Floyd Dominy, who had become particularly adept at creating congressional alliances and utilizing the enormous power of his most important allies, Carl Hayden in the Senate and Wayne Aspinall in the House. Along with Secretary of the Interior Stewart Udall, the bureau was the prime advocate of the largest and most significant water-development project on the Colorado—the Central Arizona Project.

The Arizona plan called for two dams adjacent to the Grand Canyon area to serve as major generators of electrical power. The Grand Canyon dams immediately became a red flag for the Sierra Club and conservationist groups, particularly after the Glen Canyon loss. Once again a major coalition was created, with Brower and the Sierra Club resources at its disposal.

The Grand Canyon campaigns were even more substantial and vociferous than the earlier Echo Park Dam actions. The conservation groups had improved their ability to mobilize people and generate public concern. After one of Brower's more imaginative tactics—a full-page ad that included a photo of the Sistine Chapel and a text that asked, "Should we also flood the Sistine Chapel so tourists can get nearer the ceiling?"—the Internal Revenue Service decided to revoke the club's tax-exempt status, an action that immediately backfired as thousands more joined the club and its campaign.

As the conservationist campaign gained strength, Udall and project backers decided to compromise on the dam issue in order to save the overall project. Udall was aware that though Brower and the Sierra Club were now adamantly opposed to the big dams, they still accepted coal-fired and nuclear power plants as positive alternatives to the Grand Canyon dam sites. At congressional hearings, Brower specifically testified that he would happily accept a coal-fired plant as the lesser of two evils despite the problems of strip mining. "We thought that strip mines were not of scenic importance as opposed to the Grand Canyon," Brower later commented. Brower and the club had neither supported nor opposed the Page and Mojave projects of the Grand Plan. When Udall and the WEST utilities worked out their deal to enlarge the Page plant with the Bureau of Reclamation providing additional front-end capital and receiving revenues from power generation, the conservationists once again went along, dropping their opposition to the Arizona project with the elimination of the Grand Canyon dam sites.

By 1968, at the conclusion of the Central Arizona Project fight, Brower and the club had emerged as a potent force. The conservation issue had been broadened from a concern for scenic resources and wilderness to the new environmental issues of air and water pollution, energy, and rapid development. The movement had developed a militant and conservative wing. On the one side were Brower and his allies, who increasingly relied on public campaigns and were suspicious of the development plans of the government and private sector. On the other side were some of the Sierra Club directors, who feared what they perceived as militancy and stridency in Brower's tactics. That division turned into a confrontation over the Diablo Canyon nuclear plant, which ultimately resulted in Brower's expulsion from the club and the emergence of several new-wave environmental groups.

Diablo Canyon was the proposed site for a nuclear plant to be built by Pacific Gas and Electric in the Nipomo Dunes area south of Diablo and just north of the city of Santa Barbara. When Nipomo Dunes was first suggested, Sierra Club directors, including Brower, opposed the location, although not the concept of a nuclear plant. Brower and several of the club leaders argued for a location in a more developed area such as Bodega Head or Morro Bay, as opposed to a wilderness site like Nipomo Dunes, on the grounds that an additional plant in an already developed area would not interfere with a scenic resource. By the late 1960s Pacific Gas and Electric knew that the creation of a nuclear plant in a more heavily populated area was an impossibility, since the utility was under increasing pressure from the AEC to come up with adequate evacuation plans in case of an accident. Many, although not all, of the Sierra Club people were ignorant of the accident and evacuation problem and were unaware that the utility was itself in search of a spot even more isolated than Nipomo.

Pacific Gas and Electric had, like the Forest Service several years earlier, become adept at influencing and lobbying certain Sierra Club board members. The utility and several of those board members had become quite friendly during the Nipomo negotiations. One key board member, Richard Leonard, had developed a "Dear Sherm" relationship with Sherman Sibley, the chairman of the big San Francisco utility.

Together these board members and the utility people came up with the Diablo site about a hundred miles north of Nipomo. At a carefully staged board meeting the Diablo site was accepted, but the conflict had just begun. Brower and several of his allies on the board, already suspicious about the issue of site selection, began to campaign to overturn the board's decision after they discovered that Diablo was indeed more of a wilderness site than they had at first been led to believe. Although Brower himself began to harbor doubts about the nuclear alternative, the issue evolved not around nuclear power per se but the questions of location and, more important, the imposition of the Bohemian Club tradition of cozying up to the government or private sector. In a series of tense meetings in the winter of 1968, the Sierra Club reversed itself twice on the issue, changing from support to opposition and then back to support of the Diablo site.

The division between the two wings and their two respective approaches was coming to a head. In April 1968 Brower had solidified his position with the election of a slate of directors called the ABC group ("Aggressive Brower-type Conservationists"), who were opposed to Diablo and in agreement with the stronger, more public approach of the executive director. Brower's group was strongly opposed by board members such as attorney Leonard (whose wife would eventually become a member of Pacific Gas and Electric's board of directors and executive committee) and real estate developer Maynard Munger, who liked to say that his Sierra Club ties enhanced his image as a realtor.

The anti-Brower slate was especially horrified at the initial Diablo reversal in terms of club "credibility" and had little stomach for strong tactics or confrontational approaches. By 1969 the traditionalist anti-Brower directors had regrouped and had their nemesis on the defensive. They won a referendum on the Diablo site (emphasizing the credibility issue) and defeated a Brower slate in the 1969 board elections. At a famous June 1969 board meeting, the traditionalists succeeded in ousting Brower from the director's post, an action that Brower and some of his allies were convinced had a relationship to Pacific Gas and Electric's lobbying efforts. Brower's firing closed out an era that had been fraught with conflict since the post had first been created in 1952. The onetime discreet and patrician-like environmental movement would never again be the same.

ECOACTIVISTS AND ENVIROCRATS

In early 1970 a new environmental movement appeared on the scene. Organizations proliferated, ranging from traditionalist groups, such as the Audubon Society and the Conservation Foundation, to single-issue protest groups, such as the one formed around the Santa Barbara oil spill, to the newly formed, more professionalized groups such as Brower's Friends of the Earth. The perspective of such groups spanned a radical critique of the environmental implications of corporate power to traditional notions of wilderness preservation. The new concept of ecology, popularized by such writers as Murray Bookchin and Barry Commoner, began to attract many of the young students, professionals, and dropouts who constituted the sizable New Left, antiwar, and counterculture movements of the late 1960s. California activists were the cutting edge of this new movement.

A number of these different groups came together to participate in the Earth Day ceremonies of April 1970, which became the touchstone event for the new environmentalism. Earth Day had been given an almost official sanction with the blessings of some members of the Nixon administration, the media, and a number of the large multinational corporations, such as Procter and Gamble, General Electric, Arco, Chevron, Standard Oil of New Jersey (Exxon), General Motors, Du Pont, and Goodrich, all of whom advertised in environmental publications or bought prime-time television ads supporting Earth Day. Despite the semiofficial embrace, many of the people who turned out for Earth Day rallies had a greater affinity for their New Left and counterculture counterparts than their would-be government and business allies. At Michigan State University, Stewart Udall was heckled by an angry crowd even after he agreed to donate his $1,000 fee to an environmental action group. Interior Secretary Walter Hickel outraged many Earth Day activists when he gave a speech at the University of Alaska on Earth Day entitled "Be Part of the Solution, Not the Problem" and then went on to endorse the construction of the Alaska pipeline, which had begun to emerge as a key issue for the new environmentalists.

The Nixon administration felt particularly uncomfortable with this new movement. Senator Edmund Muskie of Maine emerged as the main champion of the environmental cause in the Senate and Nixon's potential challenger in 1972. The new environmentalists, imbued with the activism of the 1960s and having an access to power, were able immediately to effect a number of changes through legislative and administrative actions. A large new bureaucracy consisting of such agencies as the Environmental Protection Agency and a number of new administrative staff positions were established to implement several new laws concerning air and water pollution, land use, and wilderness areas. The Udall policy of bridging, through certain projects and compromises, the interests of the government, the resource companies and utilities, Indians, and the conservationists collapsed in the Nixon-Ford era despite the successful passage of major environmental legislation. Instead, a strong adversarial relationship developed in this period. The Kaiparowits battle, for example, was perceived by both sides as an epic fight pitting irreconcilable forces against each other.

The environmentalist victory at Kaiparowits, the favorable media attention, and the creation of a whole new set of laws and bureaucracies, gave the environmental movement a tremendous sense of its own power. Although much of the success of the environmental movement in the early 1970s could be traced to these activist pressures and single-issue movements, the representative environmentalist figure who had emerged by the mid-1970s bore little resemblance to his activist counterparts. Part lawyer, part lobbyist, part troubleshooter, this new environmentalist had helped write the laws of the early 1970s, had helped pressure Congress to enact those laws, had helped elect or defeat a number of those congressional representatives, and had launched law suits against many of the resource and energy companies and other corporate powers.

Several of these new environmental types held staff positions in the many "professional" environmental organizations formed in the Earth Day period such as the Environmental Policy Center, Environmental Defense Fund, Natural Resources Defense Council, or Friends of the Earth. Most of the organizations were heavily oriented toward Washington and the legislative and administrative bureaucracies. The Environmental Policy Center argued for an exclusive focus on Washington and lobbying action.

During the Nixon-Ford years, these "professional" environmental groups functioned through their adversarial role, attempting to force the administration to comply with the recently enacted laws. The Carter presidency changed that situation. Carter had campaigned in 1976 as an environmentalist and had enlisted the aid of environmental organizations and individuals in his campaign. Members of the Environmental Policy Center and other groups were involved in the Carter transitional team and, after the election, held several important secondary posts within the Interior Department and on the president's staff. Environmentalists who became government officials played a role in the hit list; land-use issues; coal, oil, and gas leasing and regulation; and water questions. The Carter administration transformed what had been an adversarial role into direct government participation, a natural progression from the lobbying successes of the early 1970s during the Nixon-Ford years.

The early Carter policy, emphasizing enforcement of environmental laws and a shift away from the big resource projects, helped to generate an equivalent bureaucracy within several of the state governments in the interior West and California. The new staffers, who worked for such governors as Lamm in Colorado, Brown in California, and Babbitt in Arizona, became a new type of bureaucrat—the "envirocrat." They handled such matters as water policies and differed in perspective and policy goals from the old water lobby and its bureaucratic allies. The envirocrat, motivated by environmental and consumerist considerations, was in tune with the rejection of the big resource projects in favor of a conservation-minded approach.

But the envirocrats were hampered by their increasing isolation from any activist movement. They were subject to the powerful corporate counteroffensive that had gained momentum in the late 1970s. Within a couple of years, the Carter administration and the new-style western governors had retreated from their early environmental advocacy. The new envirocrats found themselves in the uncomfortable position of having to resign, to temporize, or to advocate a new round of western resource development.

For one, Carter's Interior Department aide Joseph Browder found himself in an increasingly complex situation. He had headed the task force that selected the new site for the Intermountain Power Project (IPP) and then had been assigned to deal with the Allen–Warner Valley complex. His new responsibilities made him uncomfortable because his former environmental colleagues now questioned his "commitment to the cause."

In early 1980, Browder commented wistfully, "I'd rather be out watching birds than helping the utilities site power plants, but the fact is that it is the responsibility of the Department to help the utilities find sites for their coal-fired plants." By the end of the year, the *Los Angeles Times* was reporting that Utah International was circulating a memo claiming that Browder counseled the company "not to take too seriously" a petition put together by environmentalists and southern Utah ranchers to challenge, before the Office of Surface Mining, the company's plan for a strip mine on the edge of Bryce Canyon National Park. In the Reagan years, Browder was heard from again—as a power company consultant.

Other envirocrats left office to work directly for their onetime corporate adversaries. For some, the antagonism between environmental group, government office, and corporate board room was replaced by a revolving door relationship.

This shift in orientation offered some heady possibilities for people, like Sierra Club leader Mary Ann Erickson, who were ready to make their move. When Erickson walked through the door into the plush New York offices of the powerful New York Equitable Life Assurance Company in June 1978, she had little idea of what to expect. Equitable had been concerned that environmental opposition to any of the big energy projects which Equitable had helped finance could affect the project's financial status. Legal intervention, Equitable realized, meant delays, which in turn affected capital costs. By the late 1970s, Equitable and other lenders and financial investors from the money centers of New York, Boston, Chicago, and, to a lesser extent, California were ready to hire environmentalists as consultants.

Erickson seemed a reasonable choice for the Equitable people. She was a top coordinator within the Sierra Club, an organization that, despite its more aggressive stance in the 1970s, still maintained what the corporate people saw as a tradition of "responsibility." Most important, Erickson fit the representative mold of the 1970s environmental leader: part lobbyist; effective in handling the media, governmental bureaucrats, and corporate antagonists; and equally at home in Washington, Sacramento, and the lush surroundings of corporate board rooms.

Erickson was hired to alert the insurance company on the plans and activities of the environmental organizations and their attitude toward the different projects then being considered as potential Equitable investments. Erickson focused especially on the problems of nuclear power and its growing costs and helped the company to develop, as she put it, "a more rounded perspective." The Equitable people in turn were happy to receive a great deal of hard information about potential environmental strategies as well as a range of contacts provided by their consultant. When the Council of Energy Resource Tribes (CERT) was set up, Equitable sent Erickson as its representative to discuss with the Indians what CERT wanted and to provide the group with management skills. In many respects, Erickson represented the contemporary version of a similar link set up several decades earlier between the American Petroleum Institute and traditional conservation groups.

The sharpest criticism reserved for the private consultations between environmentalists and industry representatives was the underlying assumption that only two parties were needed to resolve a controversial issue. Constituent groups, such as Indians, farmers, ranchers, and the unions, all directly affected by an issue like strip mining, tended to be excluded. In the area of coal policy, new and powerful coalitions of local environmentalists, farmers, ranchers, and Indians had emerged through such organizations as the resource councils in Montana, Wyoming, and North Dakota. These groups suspected that some of the national professional environmental groups were part of the problem and not the solution.

Some big-city environmentalists, charged with being elitist, explored the possibility of forming coalitions with other groups around particular issues. One group, David Brower's Friends of the Earth, envisioned new alliances involving environmentalists, minorities, unions, and other urban constituencies that would lay the foundation for a new and powerful political movement. Such projected coalitions were at best distant possibilities. Many of the existing western issues and policy positions of the environmentalists had the effect of dividing rather than coalescing constituencies.

The question of population control was a key area of division between some environmentalists and minority organizations. The fear of a growing birthrate and of increasing numbers of poor dark-skinned immigrants overwhelming the wealthier Anglo society was at the root of these environmentalists' growing involvement with the immigration issue. Population-control groups, such as Zero Population Growth, and their allies, such as the Sierra Club, decided immigration control would be a major step toward population control. While the population growth of the Anglo middle class had begun to reach a zero point, these groups feared high levels of illegal and legal migration, especially by Mexicans and others from Third World countries with high birthrates. One leader called such immigration "demographic imperialism," a kind of political weapon undermining the dominant Anglo society.

In 1978 several Zero Population Growth leaders and businessmen coalesced to form the Federation of American Immigration Reform (FAIR), a lobbying group specifically designed to further the efforts of groups oriented to population control. These groups had already played a role in the 1976 immigration legislation that lowered legal Mexican immigration from sixty thousand to twenty thousand and eliminated the exemption that had previously allowed Mexican parents to emigrate if their children had been born in the United States. The FAIR coalition immediately made its presence felt by lobbying for a restrictive border with Mexico. It prepared a bill to make it a crime for employers to hire undocumented workers and brought suit against the Census Bureau to prevent the counting of "illegals" in the 1980 census. The law suit pitted FAIR directly against Chicano groups by attacking the very heart of Chicano political strategy, which relied on the increased census count of Latinos to increase their own power base. Through its suit, FAIR also actively sought to ally with Republican and surburban interests.

By 1980, FAIR had begun to replace organized labor as the most effective organization lobbying for the concept of a restrictive border. Although not all environmental organizations backed FAIR's approach, there were only limited attempts to establish a relationship with Latino constituencies, which were such a crucial force in the Southwest.

While the late 1970s witnessed an increasing separation of the more professional environmental organizations from other constituent groupings in the West, more activist environmental groups succeeded in keeping alive the "public protest" traditions of the conservationists. Aside from the proliferation of envirocrats and professional environmentalists, the Environmental Decade also witnessed the growth of coalition-building on the local level and the mushrooming of single-issue "ecoactivist" groups, particularly in the area of nuclear power.

The "no-nuke" groups were a new breed on the environmental scene. Drawing from the New Left and counterculture movements, the antinuclear protests most resembled those against the war in Vietnam in the late 1960s. The nuclear issue seemed to touch and affect every issue and constituency—health and environment, foreign policy and military questions, conflicting scenarios over future energy development, Indian and worker exploitations, quality of life and consumer economics. Drawing large numbers of protestors and active participants, the no-nukes became the movement's most prominent ecoactivists, utilizing an array of tactics from letter writing to civil disobedience. They were not simply a link between the activist 1960s and the single-issue protests of the 1970s but a continuation of the often disregarded environmentalist tradition of public protest.

POPULISM LEFT AND RIGHT

Freckle-faced, thirty-year-old Jeff Fox does not look like a threat to anybody. His bright red hair and impish smile stand out. Growing up in the small Mormon town of Pleasant Grove, on the road from Salt Lake City to Provo, the grandson of a union organizer at Utah Power and Light and the son of Mormon parents, Fox seemed capable of a bright future when he entered the University of Utah in the late 1960s. But things began to change for Fox. On the campus, students had become increasingly upset with the war in Vietnam. Fox joined the main antiwar group and attempted what to many seemed the impossible: to generate opposition to the war in conservative, patriotic Mormon Utah.

After graduation Fox, with his student activism behind him, found it hard to enter any of the traditional routes to success. Working as a prison guard, he became thoroughly committed to what was vaguely labeled "social justice." He and his former activist friends entered the 1970s with no organization and no program to guide their actions. Many of them had stayed in Salt Lake City or in the state, still tied to some undefined sense of community or roots.

Fox began an organization called Utahans Against Hunger, which linked up with similar efforts throughout the interior West. The group dealt with issues of malnutrition, poverty, unemployment, and a host of other social and economic problems. Almost as a fluke, Fox decided to run for a recently vacated state assembly seat for a low-income district in which Fox and Utahans Against Hunger were located. He won his election and joined a handful of other legislators who were a most unusual lot in the conservative legislature. These maverick legislators opposed the MX and large-scale water and energy developments, and supported the ERA, lifeline utility proposals, and a variety of other social and community-oriented programs. Although a tiny minority in the legislature, Fox and the others were far more effective than their numbers indicated. Their ability to articulate a consistent, principled politics could mobilize rather than manipulate constituencies. Jeff Fox had become a populist and a western progressive, providing continuity with a version of politics that had periodically rekindled western traditions of militancy and conflict.

Forty years earlier, radical politics had been a factor throughout the West, particularly in California, where the Great Depression produced widespread support for radical protests, utopian societies, visionary programs, and cooperative organizations. The most substantial grouping was End Poverty in California (EPIC), the quixotic and nearly successful Democratic gubernatorial campaign of Socialist muckraker Upton Sinclair. Based on the campaign slogan "Production for Use," EPIC raised the issues of control over industrial and agricultural work and transformed the particular California and western sense of rootlessness and lack of history into a radical vision. This vision spoke of constructing something new from scratch, of experimenting with an entirely new social order, since the old one, it seemed, could be so easily scrapped.

Although Sinclair failed in his bid for office, a number of EPIC candidates did get elected, including State Senator Culbert Olson, who ran successfully for governor in the next election. The EPIC legacy turned California politics distinctly to the left during the late 1930s and early 1940s by combining a form of inspirational populism with the social liberalism of the New Deal. EPIC also helped, along with a revived labor movement, break the hold of the antiradical, antilabor business and political groups, such as the Associated Farmers and the Better America Federation, which had dominated the politics of the state in the 1920s and early 1930s.

Although broad-based radical movements like EPIC failed to catch on in the interior West, the region witnessed its fair share of political conflict. New Deal–linked coalitions were able to elect such politicians as Arizona's Sidney Osborn, Utah's Elbert Thomas, and Colorado's Edwin Johnson. Ironically, the New Deal–inspired western economic development of the war years and the economic boom that followed helped undercut that same New Deal coalition. The new aerospace and electronics industries of the Southwest attracted a different kind of labor force, oriented toward middle-class aspirations rather than the long-standing class-oriented traditions of those like the hard-rock miners who had been the central core of the New Deal liberal-left coalition in a state like Arizona. The political collapse of that radical-liberal alliance, particularly with the advent of the cold war, led to the decline of the New Deal coalitions. By 1950 every state in the interior West had shifted considerably to the right.

California experienced a conservative retrenchment in the postwar years. California's large popular social movements, which had provided the base for the successful New Deal resurgence of the state's Democrats in the 1930s and early 1940s, had become largely dispersed by the 1950s. These movements were a casualty of McCarthyite witchhunts, political conflicts within the left-liberal coalition, and a political approach that failed to address the new conditions of the boom and the extraordinary population influx into the state.

The emergence of the California Democratic clubs in the early 1950s was an attempt to recreate the New Deal coalition under California's new conditions. But the Democratic clubs' early successes, particularly in the 1958 election of Pat Brown, had more to do with the debacle in the Republican party than the emergence of a solid constituency. The Pat Brown years were somewhat disorienting for the club activists, who applauded Brown's evocation of big government for the big resource and development projects but worried about Brown's partnership with the private sector. The emergence of the issues of the 1960s—civil rights, the war in Vietnam, student reaction to the multiversity—were at once the clubs' finest moment and the beginning of their decline. The clubs had prefigured several of these campaigns in the late 1950s and early 1960s, particularly in the area of civil rights, and provided a crucial link for some of the New Left activists of the early 1960s. Lyndon Johnson's guns-and-butter liberal politics shattered the clubs' coalition and pitted them directly against its onetime sponsor and father figure, Pat Brown.

The rise of the New Left in the 1960s had its own particular manifestation and consequences in the West, later identified as the "California phenomenon"—an odd mixture of counterculture experimentalism, fascination with life-style, and a class structure heavily influenced by the strong preponderance of students, high-technology industries, and an enlarged, professional-based service sector. This life-style politics became crucial in both Colorado and California in the late 1960s and the 1970s, helping to spin off a variety of movements and social constituencies from Rocky Mountain environmentalists to San Francisco's homosexual community.

The New Left also tied into the development of nationalist or ethnic-based politics, which, in the West, emerged in the Chicano, Native American, Asian, and black movements. The combination of a racially inspired radical politics with the pervasive radical sentiments generated by opposition to the war in Vietnam gave the New Left the appearance of a political movement with a fully developed critique of corporate and governmental policies. But the New Left was never able to sustain the organizational requirements of a permanent political movement. During the 1970s it fragmented into dozens of single-issue protest movements. As the resource issues took center stage, several of these single-issue groups, many of which were led by onetime New Left dissidents, became a part of the western political landscape. These movements, including the antinuclear movement, the fight against the MX, and a variety of coalitions opposing water and energy projects, became particularly adept at influencing the course of an individual project or issue, although they generally tended to form and disband solely around that one issue.

In California, New Left graduates became instrumental in organizing the Campaign for Economic Democracy (CED), which was initially perceived as a late-1970s version of the California Democratic clubs. Led by Tom Hayden, the onetime president of Students for a Democratic Society, the CED groups, unlike their single-issue counterparts, attempted to create a highly centralized multi-issue party infrastructure inside the Democratic party under the central theme of "economic democracy." The group's ultimate purpose was the takeover of the Democratic party and the election to local, state, and national offices of CED leaders. Unlike the California Democratic clubs, the CED groups attempted to develop a strategy around such key issues of the late 1970s and early 1980s as energy and resource and development. Unlike their more radical counterparts in the single-issue movements, the CED groups modified their radical analysis with a guarded, cautious approach in the political arena. CED, in effect, represented an attempt to reconstruct a new political coalition that was neither New Left nor New Deal–linked yet retained elements of both.

The breakdown of the New Deal coalitions in the West, along with the rise of the New Left and its various single-issue counterparts, paralleled the rise of a New Right in the West. The New Right was a product of such phenomena as "Reaganism," with its anti-public-sector rhetoric and the sense of victimization by outside forces, whether Washington or Wall Street. Reaganism also expressed the reaction to the New Left and ethnic-nationalist politics of the 1960s and a projection of the family and religion as core elements of the conservative revival. The New Right drew on long-standing western traditions of racism and religious fundamentalism. Although the New Right did not become a significant constituent force until after Reagan's tenure as governor, its positions foreshadowed the powerful single-issue protests that the New Right learned to exploit.

The 1978 California property-tax initiative, Proposition 13, was a prime example of New Right resurgence. Its initiator, Howard Jarvis, was a Utah-born "jack Mormon" who had shifted from situation to situation throughout the West before settling in Los Angeles to become a lobbyist for the large apartment-house owners. Jarvis liked to project himself as a tax crusader. He used antigovernment rhetoric while disguising his clients' interest in this big across-the-board property-tax cut that primarily benefited landlords as well as industrial and commercial property owners. Jarvis could never quite shake off his right-wing, crackpot, and landlord-lobbyist images. He consistently failed to generate political support, as indicated by his distant last-place finish in the 1977 Los Angeles mayoralty race.

With a strong play in the media highlighting the popular anger against the high property taxes for single-family homes and the increasing rise in public expenditures, Jarvis' Proposition 13 was transformed into a "populist revolt." Proposition 13 was passed by an overwhelming majority, and Howard Jarvis was instantly heralded by the media as a populist hero and celebrity. Yet within two years, Jarvis' star faded as rapidly as it had risen.

Jarvis' 1980 attempt to cut back public expenditures by means of a new proposition involving a 50 percent flat reduction of the state income tax was overwhelmingly defeated. Public awareness had increased that these tax cuts— similar to Proposition 13—favored upper-income, rather than lower-income, brackets.

The transformation of Howard Jarvis the right-wing crackpot into Howard Jarvis the populist celebrity-superstar indicated that widespread discontent existed not simply in California but throughout the interior West, a discontent that the New Right sought to exploit. Groups such as the Salt Lake City–based Freemen Institute had the ability to attract powerful backers such as the Ezra Taft Benson wing of the Mormon church and politicians such as Utah Senator Orrin Hatch. The Freemen Institute tapped into deep-seated, anti-eastern-establishment attitudes in the West by centering its attack on such impeccable eastern establishment targets as the Trilateral Commission, the World Bank, and the International Monetary Fund.

The suspicion of the eastern establishment and the Washington bureaucracy (as well as anti-California sentiments) was picked up by a variety of conservative state legislators and New Right forces who created what came to be called the Sagebrush Rebellion. The Sagebrush Rebellion legislators introduced bills to transfer federal control over the vast public lands throughout the West to the states. That attempt to transfer control went back to the days of Gifford Pinchot and Theodore Roosevelt, when western cattle owners and timber interests (many of whom were eastern-based absentee owners) called for states' rights as a means to open up the public domain.

The leaders of the Sagebrush Rebellion ultimately wanted to revert to the wide-open days of the gold rush. Conservative and prodevelopment western legislators dreamed of unleashing a major land and resource grab with the state government condoning the effort, while reaping new tax revenues from rapid development. The major resource companies, represented by the Western Regional Council, dissociated themselves from the effort by local politicians to use the Sagebrush Rebellion as a cover for a new resource grab. The council had fashioned its lobbying strategy around its image as a reasonable corporate power, not a greedy corporate exploiter, symbolized by the nineteenth-century mining companies like Anaconda. The council also judged the Sagebrush Rebellion on the basis of its effectiveness. Since much of the effort consisted of actions by state legislatures that were not likely to hold up in court, the council focused instead on its primary lobbying constituencies—the western governors (most of whom opposed the Sagebrush Rebellion) and the federal bureaucrats in the Interior Department, who had actual working control over western lands and resources.

By the 1980s, western populism had become a fragmented mix of single-issue protest movements; some remnants of the New Left, such as California's CED; and a growing anti-eastern-establishment and anti-Washington New Right. The issues of the 1970s and 1980s—resource development, control of the flow of labor and the structure of the work force, and development and control of the land—had produced no consensus, no single "western outlook," despite headline proclamations to that effect by eastern publications. The lack of a common strategy among diverse constituencies, such as labor, Indians, and environmentalists, tended to blunt the opposition to the continuing development of western resources. With Ronald Reagan in power and the consolidation of the corporate counteroffensive, there were signs of a renewal of opposition in response. Throughout the West, the 1980s promised a new awakening.

"Only a few benefit from farming around here, and these few spend their money outside Pinal County," Carolina Butler was telling an auditorium full of hostile cotton farmers in her usual no-nonsense manner over a chorus of boos and hissing. The farmers gathered at Casa Grande High School in central Arizona were in an ugly mood—the kind of mood that can only be brought about by a fight over water in an arid climate. The farmers had been campaigning for the Central Arizona Project. They did not want any new groundwater regulations that might prevent them from pumping even deeper than they already had—pumping that had caused the ground to crack and the water table to recede to dangerously low levels.

Now these farmers, who for so long had been used to getting their way, thanks to alliances with Bureau of Reclamation and state government officials, the copper mining companies, and even some urban subdividers, had to listen to her. "Just who the hell is she, that damned Mexican, or is it Indian? Damn it, just what is she," one project supporter from the big utility company sputtered.

Although debates about water were usually conducted in obscure and inaccessible language, Butler went right to the heart of the matter. The big cotton farmers might be doing well, she declared, but retail sales figures showed that the little towns of central Arizona like Picacho, Florence, and Eloy, where the families who pick the cotton lived, were dirt poor.

After the meeting, one of the farmers solicitously approached Butler and warned her of the hostility toward her in the room. She laughed it off and snorted, "They always take me for an outsider. Listen, I used to pick cotton in Pinal County. If anyone wants to make trouble, they'll have to contend with the sheriff. His father worked with my father on the railroad."

It is a long way from the cotton fields of Pinal County to the wealthy Phoenix suburb of Scottsdale, where Carolina Butler lives today with her engineer husband, Walker, and their three children, but she has not forgotten any of her trek. Born at the height of the Great Depression in central Phoenix, literally on the banks of the Salt River, she had moved with her family to Picacho, where she went to grammar and high school and worked in the fields during the harvests like thousands of Mexican-American families.

Carolina Butler's activism began when she learned of the plans of a huge insurance company to transform a horse ranch owned by a wealthy matron and located near her Scottsdale home into a huge subdivided planned community. "One little old lady dies and *bam*—they want forty thousand people out here," she recalled her reaction. So she got involved and plunged into the issue, finding out all she could and building files and information worthy of the best investigator.

She lost that fight but entered the war, soon finding herself face to face with the biggest issue of them all—the Central Arizona Project. She plunged into the world of water politics, mastering terminology that had disenfranchised many people and blowing away the myth that water is the province of a few specialists who shape policies and do the bidding of the powerful water lobby. She was approached by some Yavapai, Indians who lived not far from her Scottsdale home and whose land was to be flooded if the project and its major component, the Orme Dam, went through. The Yavapai told Carolina that they wanted to keep their land despite the large amount of money offered to buy them out.

Issues of land and survival—this was language that Carolina could understand. She immediately became an advocate of the Yavapai, the one non-Indian many of the Yavapai felt they could trust. She met and educated bureaucrats, academics, journalists, and assorted sympathizers, taking them around in her boatlike 1956 Cadillac, spewing out facts and figures. She throve on exposing scams, swindles, subsidies, and environmental rip-offs, badgering reporters, testifying at hearings, enlarging her clipping files.

Although she operated largely on her own, she also joined with groups such as National Land for People, which supported the claims and hopes of small farmers and farm workers, people like Carolina's family and friends in Pinal County. She knew she was fighting against strong odds, since the conservative people of Phoenix did not seem to care for Mexicans, Indians, environmentalists, and other "social disrupters," as the chairman of Arizona Public Service called those who dared to question the plans of developers and the water lobby.

But Carolina Butler does not discourage easily. She remembers her trips to California as a child and recent vacations in southern California. She knew that what she wanted to stop in Arizona had already triumphed in California. "I just have some strong feelings about Arizona being turned over to developers," she says, beginning to get wound up about her favorite subject. "It's just obscene; they don't know a saguaro cactus from a hole in the ground." Then she laughs, knowing how much she relishes the fight. "If it weren't so crazy," she says, "I'd probably feel awful."

12   Conclusion

Election night 1980, 6:40 P.M. Pacific Standard Time. Jimmy Carter, the thirty-ninth president, was about to concede the election. He had wanted to concede an hour earlier but had been talked out of it by Jody Powell, his press secretary. Now Carter could not wait any longer as he strode purposefully into Washington's Mayfair Hotel to attempt a gracious exit.

Three thousand miles away, Ronald Reagan was watching the election returns on television in astonishment at his home in Pacific Palisades near Los Angeles. As Carter began his concession speech, Reagan was not the only one surprised by the timing of Carter's statement. It was still more than an hour before the polls would close in the Pacific time zone, but as far as Carter, the southern candidate who had only won his native Georgia in his own region, was concerned, the fight was over. He had never expected to win the West anyhow.

Western politicians simply could not believe it. There were many other crucial races still to be decided, but Carter, consistent to the end in his blundering insensitivity to western politics, was about to jeopardize these races, which would affect the future of his own party.

With Carter returned to obscurity, the West, particularly California, seemed triumphant. The West was Reagan country, the media proclaimed, a solid base from which he pursued his long quest for the presidency. Even the press recognized that Reagan was much more than just another regional candidate. He was the candidate of the corporate board room, the hero of the Moral Majority, the *gauleiter* of the white middle class, the polished figurehead who preached the religion of free enterprise.

For many, Ronald Reagan represented the triumph of the corporate West, a triumph symbolized by the composition of his Kitchen Cabinet—wealthy California businessmen who had launched Reagan's political career. For Sagebrush Rebels; antigovernment, anti-eastern-establishment New Rightists; and all those who identified with Reagan's vision of simpler, purer times, the election heralded a new era. The Reagan presidency represented for them

304

the triumph of the mythic West of rugged individualism over a decaying East, the ultimate geopolitical transfer of power.

Such a power shift seemed to have taken place in both political and economic terms. The earlier right-wing nativists and isolationist constituencies had come from small-town midwestern America. Their champion was Robert Taft, their religion was mainstream Protestantism, and their economic representative was the small-businessman. But their power base was a region on the decline. The New Right of the 1960s and 1970s reflected the power and optimism of new regions on the rise, like the South and the West. In the West, the new believers hailed from the Anglo suburbs of southern California and the boom cities of the interior West, like Phoenix and Salt Lake City—those areas with the greatest population growth according to the 1980 census. Their religion was Catholic, Mormon, and Jewish as well as reborn Christian, and their economic base was grounded in the managerial, professional, and skilled work force of the high-technology military-oriented industries of the region.

This power shift was augmented by the emergence of the Pacific basin as a new center of economic expansion and the continuing preoccupation in the post-Vietnam era with the countries of the Pacific Rim, including by the 1980s the eastern edge of the basin that stretches from Mexico through Nicaragua and El Salvador. This western capitalism appeared powerful, expansionist and well rooted in a dominant California and the resource-rich interior West. Ronald Reagan, the quintessential California celebrity, indicated the growing power of California, signifying, as lawyer Richard Sherwood had proclaimed, that California no longer felt "second best to anyone, any place."

Reagan's triumph, unlike the Goldwater debacle sixteen years earlier, was a mix of practical politics oriented toward a centrist position with a vague New Right appeal that kept the New Right's shock troops, money, and organizations at his disposal. During the campaign, Reagan sometimes undercut his image as a conservative ideologue, losing any clear-cut political identity in the process—a tactic he had perfected during his campaigns for governor of California. Goldwater, in contrast, had locked himself into the Right, isolating himself at one end of the political spectrum and becoming a captive of his shock troops.

Jockeying between his New Right supporters and his mainstream establishment backers, Reagan ultimately signified the further integration of the new western power centers, especially California, with the older, still-dominant centers of the East. When Bank of America chairman A. W. Clausen was appointed by President Carter to head the World Bank just before the election, Clausen was perceived, despite his West Coast headquarters and his position on Reagan's advisory committee, as an establishment banker, fully representative of the money-center banks doing business abroad—as solid as the purest Rockefeller banker. Reagan's reliance on Bechtel executives George Schultz and Caspar Weinberger was understood to reflect his reliance on corporate, as much as western, appointees.

Reagan the westerner was not the harbinger of a new version of the "new Republican majority." Instead, he sought to share power with his corporate backers from New York, Los Angeles, and San Francisco. Reagan, nonetheless, has access to the kind of western geopolitical thinking that began with Brigham Young, developed out of the western engineering impulse during the New Deal among the Six Companies and the Reclamation Service, and emerged on the world scene in the Pacific Rim strategy of the 1960s and the Nixon Doctrine of the 1970s. In the end, the election of Ronald Reagan signified the ultimate triumph of the corporate counteroffensive that had first taken shape in the dark days following the Vietnam debacle and Watergate and had gained momentum during the aimless political meanderings of Jimmy Carter.

Reagan, the national political figure, presided over the big energy companies' continuing campaign to develop the interior West as a major resource-producing center in the post-OPEC period. "The investment story of the decade [of the 1980s], at least in percentage growth," declared the *Wall Street Journal,* "will be in the Rockies." This energy development, the *Journal* went on, "will make the mountain states awesome magnets for new money."

Reagan's election was particularly appealing to the oil companies, so appealing that they, among others, contributed handsomely to the Kitchen Cabinet's campaign to raise private funds to redecorate the White House. "The oil industry wasn't doing badly under Carter. It will do well under Reagan," a Wall Street analyst said of the Californian's triumph. Reagan, far more than Carter, was unqualifiedly oriented toward domestic production. In his eyes, the oil, gas, coal, uranium, and shale are all there for the taking.

Reagan's enthusiasm, his unreconstructed belief in the power of the corporations if left to their own devices, warmed the hearts of oilmen. What the oil companies especially wanted and what Reagan seemed more than willing to give was less regulation, less control, and more subsidies. A few days after the election, the American Petroleum Institute held its annual meeting. "Like expectant children before Christmas," wrote a *Los Angeles Times* reporter, "oil executives spent most of their time assembling a 'wish-list' for President-elect Reagan." The list included an end to price controls on oil (granted within the first month) and natural gas; easing of regulatory and environmental standards in regard to offshore oil drilling and synfuels; more leasing of offshore oil in California and Alaska and on public lands in the Overthrust Belt in the interior West; and exemptions from the windfall-profits tax. To these, other energy producers added more coal and uranium leasing on public lands; less regulation and delays in the permit process for nuclear power plants; gutting of environmental agencies such as the Council on Environmental Quality and the Environmental Protection Agency; and a modification of key environmental legislation, such as the Clean Air Act.

The key to Reagan's domestic energy policy was the new role of the Interior Department under James Watt. Not since the not-so-distant days of the three Rs—"rape, ruin, and run," as Cecil Andrus liked to call it—had the "ministry of western affairs" been so completely committed to an assault on public resources. Watt, a former aide to Wyoming Senator Milward Simpson and an official in Nixon's Interior Department, was handpicked in 1977 by Joseph Coors, the Colorado beer baron, to run the newly formed Mountain States Legal Foundation. The foundation, like other probusiness "public-interest" legal firms set up by conservative businessmen in this period, was designed to function as a supplemental legal weapon for the energy producers, water lobbyists, ranchers, and agribusiness giants in their efforts to launch a counteroffensive against the federal government, environmentalists, and Indians.

Once in office, Watt moved immediately to implement a proproduction, prodevelopment policy. He purged the Carter appointees in the department and appointed to top posts those with a prodevelopment outlook like the former counsel for the Montana Power Company. To run the Office of Surface Mining, with its responsibility to reclaim strip-mined lands, he appointed an Indiana state senator who had argued that strip-mining legislation was unconstitutional. The Bureau of Land Management, with its responsibility for public lands in the West, was turned over to Robert Burford, a Colorado rancher and former speaker of the Colorado house, who had worked with Watt in a campaign against the EPA.

Watt quickly announced plans to permit offshore oil drilling in California (an ironic move for a native son from the energy colony of Wyoming which was later temporarily rescinded after generating tremendous political opposition); ease federal controls on strip-mining; and change the philosophy and approach toward the development of national parks, wilderness areas, and air-quality control. "Watt's idea of a good time in the West is sitting inside his RV, camping inside a strip mined area," one congressional critic quipped bitterly.

Watt's approach, in fact, extended beyond Interior's usual areas of responsibility, for the new secretary attempted to install himself as the lead cabinet official on natural resources and environmental policy. In particular, Watt moved to bring the EPA under his sway through his influence over its new head, Anne Gorsuch, a former Colorado representative who had participated in an earlier campaign against the EPA with Watt and Burford.

Although Watt, a nominal Sagebrush Rebel, entered office as the candidate of provincial conservatives like Coors and Nevada Senator Paul Laxalt, his appointment did not necessarily indicate the triumph of the Sagebrush Rebels over the more cautious executives of the Western Regional Council. With the appointment of Watt, many of the policy objectives of both the Sagebrush Rebels and the council were on the verge of being realized. The new Interior policies did mean greater leasing and greater development without the massive transfer of federal lands to state control. At the same time, Watt attempted to distance himself from the Sagebrush rebels, telling the western governors that he was a "rebel without a cause" since the rebellion had been won.

The big water projects, such as the Central Arizona Project and the Central Utah Project, were also back on track although Watt was asking water users to pay more for subsidized water. Even the synfuels program—the federal money supermarket, which Reagan had attacked during the campaign because of potential government tampering with the sacrosanct private sector—had been partially resurrected. Less regulation, fewer social programs, but continue the subsidies became the Reagan war cry, proving once again that the western leaders of "free" enterprise were as addicted to government subsidies as any second-generation welfare recipient, the difference being that the corporate leaders would get their subsidies while those for the welfare recipients faced major surgery.

Subsidies without regulation were not a visible component of the new Reagan economics as the supply siders blitzed their way through Congress and the media behind a smokescreen of anti-government rhetoric during Reagan's first one hundred days. Reagan policy, in fact, involved two programs in one. The negative redistribution of income to the investing class through budget cuts and tax breaks reversed two generations of New Deal–inspired social programs, while a massive increase in defense spending became one of the most important subsidies for western businessmen. The rearming of America was being orchestrated by Defense Secretary Weinberger, former vice-president of Bechtel, a company with a long history of feeding at the public trough and with involvements in the Arab world. Weinberger, who referred to the new armaments program as the second part of Reagan's program to reindustrialize America, spoke of building 150 new ships and announced major arms sales to Pakistan and his former business associates in Saudi Arabia.

The projected rise in military spending meant more than ever that California would continue its ascent as a geopolitical center of power with a heavily subsidized economy. The military trouble spots of Central America, Southeast Asia, and the Persian Gulf and the continuing focus on China placed California at the heart of the international situation.

For Denver, the new Reagan economics meant a further growth in the city's role as a new energy capital. The substantial increase in oil and gas drilling and coal production, with the new emphasis on exports to places like Japan, would more than offset whatever reduction in scale the synfuels projects were likely to witness now that the euphoria of the federal money supermarket had passed.

In Salt Lake City, the new administration was welcomed with great hopes by the Mormon church, Utah business leaders, and the mélange of fringe groups like the Freemen Institute. Ezra Taft Benson represented the church at Reagan's inauguration, the opening ceremony of which was directed by the Osmond family. Mormon appointments included T. E. Bell, the new secretary of education; Robert Broadbent, former Las Vegas County Commissioner selected to head the Bureau of Reclamation; and Richard Beal, the director of the Office of Planning and Evaluation for the White House. Reagan's top pollster was Californian Richard Wirthlin, member of an old Mormon family.

In Phoenix, connections to the White House were stronger than at any time since Richard Kleindienst and Robert Mardian played key roles under Nixon. With the Central Arizona Project back on line, Arizona's water lobby focused on overturning Cecil Andrus' last-minute allocations to Arizona's Indian tribes. A receptive James Watt was prepared to intervene. Meanwhile, the state legislature moved to gut the groundwater reforms forced on the state by Andrus.

In Las Vegas, Senator Paul Laxalt basked in his new power as one of Reagan's closest advisers. Laxalt, the former casino operator, prepared to use his position to slow down or even eliminate federal investigations into organized crime as well as the federal role in regulating and protecting Lake Tahoe from further casino development. Meanwhile, Frank Sinatra, his new gaming license procured with the help of Reagan, found himself a welcome guest at the White House and at the Justice Department, where Sinatra's friend William French Smith decided what to do with his department's organized-crime task force.

Yet all was not well in Las Vegas and the West, despite the triumph of the corporate counteroffensive. Las Vegas had experienced its first substantial downswing in the months following the 1979–1980 recession, a downswing that paralleled new problems in such areas as housing in Tucson and Phoenix. The boom, if not over, was at least stalled. At the very moment of triumph, all those who had contributed to the counteroffensive saw themselves—despite the subsidies, despite the modification or elimination of government regulation—facing a heightened period of conflict and turmoil.

For Indians, the battles of the past promised to be even more protracted with the push for greater energy development. At the Mountain States Legal Foundation, Watt had pursued an anti-Indian policy. He challenged the right of Jicarilla Apache to tax commercial enterprises on their reservation and fought to limit Indian water rights at Pyramid Lake in Nevada. Some Indian activists, like La Donna Harris, a Comanche who heads Americans for Indian Opportunity, feared Reagan's ascent would signal a backlash and that Indians would have to fight to keep or restore gains they had won ten years ago.

With Reagan in the White House, the issue of cheap labor dominated discussions with Mexico on border policy. During the campaign and in his first months in office, Reagan remained a champion of the trade-off of more oil and more capital penetration for more immigration from Mexico, a policy partially articulated in his North American Common Market approach. His early foreign policy initiatives, focusing on El Salvador and Nicaragua, not only signaled an anti-Soviet thrust, but a geopolitical shift in emphasis. The eastern rim of the Pacific basin, including Canada and Mexico and extending into Central America, took on primary importance in the new foreign policy. During this time, Weinberger and Secretary of State Alexander Haig appeared to have misunderstood the lessons of the Nixon Doctrine and reverted to a crude interpretation of Russian expansionism reminiscent of the "domino theory," particularly in their explanation for the spread of radical insurgencies in Central America. In 1981, it remained to be seen whether a major figure would emerge within the administration with the sophistication and flexibility of Richard Nixon. If such a figure does emerge, he will have to seek a negotiated settlement to the problem of revolution along the eastern shore of the Pacific basin by way of Mexico, the most important local power, with its own geopolitical designs on the region.

As Reagan moved toward a more aggressive stance in Central America, a resolution of the problem of undocumented migration remained elusive. His immigration program, announced in July 1977, was a more restrictive rehash of the Carter approach, with a modest guest worker program thrown in. Meanwhile the Latino communities of California and the Southwest showed signs of increasing politicalization, a development that could lead to an explosive new situation in the changing region.

The politicalization of the barrios was paralleled by changes within the environmental community. Confronted by Watt at Interior, the era of the envirocrat seemed to be passing with the age of ecoactivism once again ascendant. Thoroughly demoralized by the 1980 elections, environmental groups, after an initial period of shell shock, were forced to question the accommodation and passivity that marked the Carter years. They began to toy with the idea of direct action and mobilization.

Similarly, the labor movement was entering a period of conflict and change, the result of its most bitter defeat in recent history. The corporate counteroffensive had played a central role in weakening the labor movement. The elimination of unions in energy-related construction projects, one of the Business Roundtable's most important aims, was coming close to realization. In Arizona, the building trades began exploring the idea of allying with environmental groups in stopping projects like the Springerville coal-fired power plant if such projects utilized nonunion labor.

The tentative exploration of new alliances seemed to extend throughout the range of citizen groups and single-issue organizations that had sprung up in the West in the late 1960s and 1970s. Coalition became the byword. The issues of the 1980s—resource, development, social-welfare and workplace issues and those related to the racial balkanization of the Southwest—were at the heart of new or revived social movements.

By the 1980s the limits of Southwestern development seemed, on the one hand, to be stretched to the breaking point, particularly in terms of resources and the problems associated with "instant cities." Yet the region's corporate powers, the big eastern investors, and government officials in Washington all continued to talk of big plans, plans essential to the continuing growth of national, as well as regional, economies. These new boomers had visions of projects larger than the pyramids, of trillion-dollar military budgets, of excavations rivaling the Panama Canal. These plans reflected the kind of big western thinking that traced its roots to the engineering mentality of the Six Companies, the big grid notions of WEST Associates, and the fervent western imagination, which "laughed at logic" while driving the West's destiny "over obstacles that rational minds deemed insuperable."

The Great Western Boom, the permanent boom, had by the 1980s reached a crossroads, a point of potential crisis at the very moment of the region's apparent rise to power. Underlying the triumph of the corporate counteroffensive lay conditions generating new points of crisis. Each ostensible solution, each new big project, created greater problems and a larger future crisis. And as the region took center stage, the battle for the future of the West became the key national event. The control over resources, the control over land, the control of the borders, the control over growth, and the control over labor are ultimately becoming a single, integrated conflict. The resolution will tell us much about the future of the country.

Bibliography

A contemporary history of the politics and economics of a region requires a certain flexibility and creativity in research. For example, we relied enormously on interviews and other firsthand accounts of events, people, and institutions that were central to the themes of the book. We also needed to examine rigorously both primary and secondary source material in each of our subject areas. This involved a systematic search through newspaper and magazine clip files such as those of the *Los Angeles Times, San Francisco Chronicle, Sacramento Bee, Arizona Republic, Salt Lake Tribune, Deseret News, Denver Post, Straight Creek Journal, Las Vegas Review-Journal, North Las Vegas Valley Times, Utah Holiday, Dialogue, Sunstone, The Ensign, Uno Mas Uno, Proceso, High Country News, Excelsior, New York Times, Wall Street Journal,* and *Asian Wall Street Journal.* We also went through court records; county recorder records; Securities and Exchange Commission files; utility commission files; congressional hearings; Interior Department and other government agency documents; General Accounting Office reports; environmental impact statements; bank regulatory records; corporation commission records; and several library and archival collections throughout the West, particularly the Bancroft Library at the University of California at Berkeley. The wealth of information available in the stock-ownership directories of the Corporate Data Exchange in New York City, especially Volumes II (agribusiness), III (banking and finance), and IV (energy), were a valuable resource.

The following is an abbreviated description of primary and secondary sources used for each section of the book as well as a partial list of interviews.

PART ONE: SUBSIDIZING THE WEST

The Six Companies: The best description of the Six Companies appeared in a three-part series in *Fortune* (August–November 1943). Material on the companies also includes a collection of newspaper clippings and minutes of board meetings at the Bancroft Library and in-house corporate histories, such as Robert Ingram, *A Builder in His Family* on the Bechtels, and Kaiser Corporation's *The Kaiser Story*. We also relied on Marriner Eccles' autobiography, *Beckoning Frontiers*; Sidney Hyman's two books on the Eccleses and their First Security Corporation, *Marriner S. Eccles: Private Entrepreneur and Public Servant* and *Challenge and Response: The First Security Corporation: First Fifty Years, 1928–1978*; and the excellent authorized history of the Bank of America by Marquis James and Bessie R. James, *Biography of a Bank*.

The West as a Colony: There are several books and articles on this theme dating back to the 1930s and 1940s written by Bernard De Voto, Wallace Stegner, Morris Garnsey, Wendell Berge, Walter Prescott Webb, and Ladd Haystead that are of use in analyzing the period prior to the postwar takeoff. De Voto's two articles in *Harper's* were "The West: A Plundered Province" (August 1934) and "The Anxious West" (December 1946).

Water: A great deal has been written on the Colorado River, but special mention should be made of Philip Fradkin's *A River No More*; Norris Hundley, *Water and the West: The Colorado River Compact in the American West*; T. H. Watkins et al., *The Grand Colorado*; John Terrell, *Water War on the Colorado River*; Dean Peterson and A. Berry Crawford, eds., *Values and Choices in the Development of the Colorado River Basin*; and the bulletins of the Lake Powell Research Project at the University of California at Los Angeles.

Energy: Chris Welles, *The Elusive Bonanza*, and Harry K. Savage, *The Rock That Burns*, are two very different classics on oil shale, while the annual Oil Shale Symposium Proceedings, published since 1964 by the Colorado School of Mines, is a thorough and detailed account of this on-and-off-again industry. Various publications of the Western Governors' Policy Office on the energy situation are quite useful, as are overviews by Barry Commoner, Richard Barnet, and Robert Stobaugh and Daniel Yergin. Suzanne Gordon, *Black Mesa: Angel of Death*, and the Anthropology Resource Center, *Native Americans and Energy Development*, provide excellent material on energy development on Indian lands. Alvin Josephy, Jr., "The Murder of the Southwest," in *Audubon* magazine (July 1971), was part of the process of confronting the energy companies and the Department of the Interior on the Colorado Plateau.

The Department of the Interior: Material on the department and its different secretaries is also extensive but confined largely to press releases, speeches, and official testimony. Particular mention should be made of Elmo Richardson, *Dams, Parks, and Politics: Resource Development in the Truman-Eisenhower Era*; Stewart Udall, *Quiet Crisis*; Richard L. Berkman and W. Kip Viscusi, *Damming the West*; Walter Hickel, *Who Owns America*; William E. Warne, *The Bureau of Reclamation*; and John Whitaker, *Striking a Balance: Environment and Natural Resources in the Nixon-Ford Years*. James Cannon has done a thorough study of the leasing of publicly owned coal in *Leased and Lost* and *Mine Control: Western Coal Leasing and Development*. Daniel Dreyfus in his American University Ph.D. dissertation, "Federal Organization and Energy Policy Formation: Politics and Power in the Sonora Desert," provides a firsthand account of the relations between Interior, particularly the Bureau of Reclamation, and the energy companies. We also relied on the excellent coverage of the department, water issues, and the 160-acre limit by Will Hearst and Lynn Ludlow of the *San Francisco Examiner* and George Baker of the *Sacramento Bee*.

The Pacific Basin: Essential background material on the Pacific Rim strategy can be found in the publications of the Stanford Research Institute and the Pacific Studies Center; Peter Wiley, "Vietnam and the Pacific Rim Strategy," *Leviathan* (June 1969); and Richard Nixon, *Memoirs*. Jimmy Carter's quest for the presidency is covered in Clark R. Mollenhoff, *The President Who Failed: Carter Out of Control*; Robert Shogan, *Promises to Keep: Carter's First Hundred Days*; Jules Witcover, *Marathon: The Pursuit of the Presidency, 1972–1976*; and James Wooten, *Dasher: The Roots and Rising of Jimmy Carter*.

Interviews for Part I: Cecil Andrus, Wayne Aspinall, George Ballis, Brent Blackwelder, Joseph Browder, Peter Carlson, Collis Chandler; William Chappell, Ralph Cox, Hugh Evans, Floyd Goss, Dorothy Green, Sandy Hamilton, Armand Hammer, Myron Holburt, Carolyn Johnson, Ron Knecht, Edmund Wattis Littlefield, Les Ludlum, John Lyon, Sr., Dean Mann, Guy Martin, James Mulloy, Owen Olpin, Edward Osann, Rudolph Peterson, Nathan Snyder, Jack Swenson, Morris Udall, Stewart Udall, James Vanderbeeck, James Watt, Barbara West, Gary Wicks, James Wilson, Mary Patt Wilson.

PART TWO: CENTERS OF POWER

California: California—particularly California "exceptionalism"—is the favorite theme of a wide variety of authors, but none can match Carey McWilliams' rigorous analysis of the politics and economy of the state in the period through World War II. His *California: The Great Exception; Southern California: An Island on the Land; Factories in the Field; Ill Fares the Land*; and *The Education of Carey McWilliams* are only part of this remarkable body of work, which must be the starting point for any understanding of California. On California water issues, the *1980 California Water Atlas* not only provides a useful history but has an extraordinary display of charts and graphs that provide an intelligible method for understanding the state's particular features. Erwin Cooper, *Aqueduct Empire*; Remi Nadeau, *The Water Seekers*; and Robert Boyle, John Graves, and T. H. Watkins, *The Water Hustlers*, are a good introduction to the debate during the 1960s over the State Water Project, and the extensive source materials of the Metropolitan Water District and the UCLA Water Resource Library are also helpful. The study by seven analysts from the Rand Corporation entitled *Efficient Water Use in California* and Michael Storper's monographs on a "Soft Water Path for California" are among the most important recent studies involving the state's water situation.

Extensive material on California's energy situation can be located at the California Energy Commission, whose studies paralleled the Natural Resource Defense Council's study *Moving California Toward a Renewable Energy Future*. There are a number of good, detailed studies of California politics from the EPIC period to Jerry Brown's governorship, including several biographies of Jerry Brown, such as James Lorenz, *Man on a White Horse*. Material on the California Business Roundtable includes the authors' March 1979 article for *Los Angeles* magazine.

Works on the rise and development of Los Angeles include Edwin Cotrell and Helen Jones, *Characteristics of the Metropolis*; Richard Fogelson, *The Fragmented Metropolis*; John and La Rue Caughey, *The Biography of a City*; Robert Gottlieb and Irene Wolt, *Thinking Big: The Story of the Los Angeles Times*; and Bill and Nancy Boyarsky, *Backroom Politics*. Jacqueline Leavitt, *Options Lost, Options Remaining: A Preliminary Study of Water and Land Planning in the Los Angeles Region*, from the School of Architecture and Urban Planning at UCLA, is one of several documents that help situate some of the peculiarities of the Los Angeles boom and its consequences. The stories and television newscasts researched by the Community Information Project, a public-interest research firm, are valuable in helping the researcher locate power and corruption in the region.

Materials for the San Francisco section included William Martin Camp, *San Francisco: Port of Gold*; Felix Riesenberg, Jr., *Golden Gate: The Story of San Francisco Harbor*; John Haskell Kemble, *San Francisco Bay: A Pictorial History*; and Gerald Robert Daw, "Bay Fill," in "San Francisco: A History of Change" (Master's thesis, California State University, San Francisco). Deanna Paoli Gumina, *The Italians of San Francisco*, deals with the early history of this important ethnic group. Walter Blum has written a family biography of Ben Swig, while Frances Moffat, *Dancing on the Brink of the World: The Rise and Fall of San Francisco Society*, provides some important tidbits about San Francisco's society figures. Danny Beagle, Al Haber, and David Wellman, "Turf Power and the Tax Man," in *Leviathan* (April 1969), broke ground in analyzing the ties between corporate and political power, while Kevin Starr, "Business Pioneers Who Built a Far West Metropolis," in the *San Francisco Examiner* (October 19, 1980), gives a sense of the continuity in San Francisco's business community. Chester Hartmann, *Yerba Buena: Land Grab and Community Resistance in San Francisco*, and the *Bay Guardian's* The Ultimate Highrise provide critical accounts of the rise of Manhattan West. George Dorsey, *Christopher of San Francisco*; John B. McGloin, S.J., *San Francisco: The Story of a City*; and Frederick W. Wirt, *Power in the City: Decision Making in San Francisco*, were helpful.

Interviews for the California chapter: Norman Barker, Jr., Danny Beagle, Benjamin Biaggini, James Bonar, Tom Bradley, Jerry Brown, Pat Brown, Lee Buffington, Donald Burns, A. W. Clausen, Richard Cooley, Darryl Cox, Nolan Daines, Justin Dart, Gray Davis, John Elberling, R. Gwin Follis, Richard Goldman, Ann Halstead, Chester Hartmann, Tom Hayden, Walter Hoadley, John Jacobs, Anthony Kline, Frederick Larkin, Donald Livingston, Louis Lundborg, Richard Maullin, Herb Mills, Gladys Moreau, Jack Morrison, David Packard, Bill Press, Tom Quinn, Alan Rothenberg, Richard Sherwood, Rocco Siciliano, Richard Silberman, Angelo Siracusa, Sam Yorty, Paul Ziffren, Ronald Zumbrun.

Denver: There are several histories of Denver and Colorado, including Lyle Dorsett, *The Queen City*, and Marshall Sprague, *Colorado: A Bicentennial History*, as well as histories of the two major newspapers written by Bill Hosokawa, *Thunder in the Rockies: The Incredible Denver Post*, and Robert Perkin, *The First Hundred Years: An Informal History of Denver and the Rocky Mountain News*. Ray B. West, Jr. ed., *Rocky Mountain Cities*, has a seminal essay about Denver by Perkin and Charles Graham, plus an excellent introduction to the development of the urban centers of the interior West by Carey McWilliams.

Materials on energy, water, agriculture, and urban growth include reports produced by the Front Range Project, the Colorado Energy Research Institute (see especially Jerome Morse, *Energy Resources in Colorado: Coal, Oil, Shale, and Uranium*), the Rocky Mountain Oil and Gas Association, the Colorado Water Conservation Board, the Colorado Open Space Council, and the Environmental Defense Fund. Ved P. Nanda, ed., *Water Needs for the Future*, includes several essays by participants in Colorado's water policies. The best discussion of the Western Regional Council can be found in the authors' "The New Power Brokers Who Are Carving Up the West" in the March 20, 1980 issue of the *Straight Creek Journal*.

Interviews for the Denver chapter: Sal Carpio, Michael Howard, Bruce Hulbert, John Love, Stephen McNichols, William McNichols, Ken Miller, James Ogilvie, John Parr, Gerald Phipps, Bruce Rockwell, Donald Seawell, Harris Sherman, A. B. Slaybaugh, Felix Sparks, James Thomas, Robert Tonsing.

Salt Lake City: Some of the best historical analysis of the development of Salt Lake City and the Mormon church was written by Leonard Arrington, the church historian, whose *Great Basin Kingdom* is a major work of political economy. The Mormon church itself is extraordinarily conscious about record-keeping and maintains some of the best archival collections of nineteenth- and early twentieth-century Utah history. Richard D. Poll et al., eds., *Utah's History*, has some useful material on the period from the 1920s through the 1960s. The histories of the city's newspapers, written by Wendell Ashton and O. N. Malmquist, have information on the Mormon-gentile conflicts and accommodation. Books on the Mormon church, such as Klaus Hansen, *Quest for Empire*; James Allen and Glenn Leonard, *The Story of the Latter-Day Saints*; Leonard Arrington, Feramorz Fox and Dean May, *Building the City of God*; Davis Bitton and Leonard Arrington, *The Mormon Experience*; Thomas O'Dea, *The Mormons*; and Wallace Stegner, *Mormon Country*, are useful for their social and cultural analysis and discussion of early Mormon history but provide only a limited perspective on the contemporary political and economic history of church and state. Wallace Turner, *The Mormon Establishment*; Robert Mullen, *The Latter-day Saints: The Mormons Yesterday and Today*; and Marilyn Warenski, *Patriarchs and Politics*, deal with more contemporary themes, including the role of women in the church. The authors' "Static in Zion," in the *Columbia Journalism Review* (July–August 1979), and "Mormonism, Inc.," in the *Nation* (August 16–23, 1980), deal with church-owned media and contemporary politics. Monographs and analyses by Gerald Kinghorn and Thomas Powers are helpful in looking into Utah's water situation. Although little has been written on some of Utah's key contemporary political figures and events, the writings and biographies of J. Bracken Lee, Ezra Taft Benson, and Spencer W. Kimball were helpful. Material in the *Utah Historical Quarterly*, *Dialogue* magazine, *Sunstone*, and *Utah Holiday* is helpful for the researcher looking for clues to go beyond church-approved versions of contemporary events.

Interviews for the Salt Lake City chapter: Wendell Ashton, Lowell Bennion,

J. Allen Blodgett, Harry Blundell, Kent Briggs, Jerry Cahill, Ed Clyde, James Conway, Gene Coyle, Art Deck, Rod Decker, Louise Degn, Frances Farley, Ernie Ford, Jeff Fox, Jack Gallivan, Charles Graves, Steve Holbrooke, Sonia Johnson, Lee Kapaloski, B.Z. Kastler, Spencer Kinard, Gerald Kinghorn, Kay Kosow, J. Bracken Lee, Judith Little, Ron Little, Scott Matheson, Kelley Matthews, Sterling McMurrin, Arch Madsen, William Owens, Gerry Pond, Calvin Rampton, Harold Schindler, J.L. Shoemaker, Roy Simmons, William Smart, Ted Wilson.

Phoenix: Much of the story of Phoenix and Arizona concerns the subjects of water and urban development writ large. Some of the best early overviews of the water situation are Dean Mann, *The Politics of Water in Arizona;* the seminal study by Maurice Kelso, William Martin, and Lawrence Mack, *Water Supplies and Economic Growth in an Arid Environment;* and, from the prowater lobby point of view, Rich Johnson, *The Central Arizona Project.* Helen Ingram's writings also provide an important contribution in analyzing Arizona's supply and water management issues.

The seamier side of development in Arizona is thoroughly explored in the twenty-one-part series by the Investigative Reporters and Editors (IRE) that was published in 1977 in several newspapers, including the *Indianapolis Star,* while Don Devereux's continuing stories in the *Scottsdale Progress* have updated the Don Bolles situation. Two books on the Bolles murder and the IRE project are Michael Wendland, *The Arizona Project,* and Martin Tallberg, *Don Bolles: An Investigation into His Murder.* Robert Gottlieb, "Del Webb's Big Gamble is Paying Off," in the May 1979 issue of *Los Angeles* magazine, discussed that Key Phoenix-based corporation. For a friendlier look into Phoenix' proclivity to grow, see the full Arizona Tomorrow report subtitled *A Precursor of Post-Industrial America,* published by the Hudson Institute. See also Charles S. Sargent, ed., "The Conflict Between Frontier Values and Land Use Control in Greater Phoenix."

There are the standard biographical books on Arizona political figures such as Carl Hayden and Barry Goldwater, including Goldwater's autobiography, *With No Apologies,* and the Rob Wood and Dean Smith biography of Goldwater, *Portrait of an Arizonan,* while studies on the charter government period by Paul Kelso and Robert Wrinkle (editor of *Politics in the Urban Southwest*) provide some preliminary data on Phoenix politics. Broad interpretive histories of the state and region include Edwin Corle, *The Gila;* Lawrence Clark Powell, *Arizona: a Bicentennial History;* and David Lavender, *The Southwest.* A more penetrating look into Arizona politics and the state's power structure can be found in the files of *New Times Weekly,* while the Inside Phoenix series of the *Arizona Republic* has useful statistical information.

Interviews for the Phoenix chapter: Bruce Babbitt, Gil Bradley, Carolina Butler, Ed Carson, Owen Childress, Gary Driggs, Paul Eckstein, Karl Eller, Gordon Evans, Kathy Ferris, Robert Goldwater, Alfredo Gutierrez, Margaret Hance, Charles Homans, Helen Ingram, Rich Johnson, Tom Kuhn, Bob McCain, Richard Mallery, Jonathan Marshall, William Martin, Barbara Marx, William Meek, John Meeker, Bob Moore, Jack Pfister, William Reilly, Harry Rosenzweig, Frank Snell, Wes Steiner, Duke Tulley, Keith Turley, Stan Turley, Nicholas Udall, Robert Weissmann, Frank Welsh.

Las Vegas: Some of the best source material on early Las Vegas and the mob can be found in Estes Kefauver's Senate hearings into organized crime, which took place in 1950 and 1951. A revealing look at Meyer Lansky was written by three Israeli journalists, Uri Dan, Dennis Eisenberg, and Eli Landau, entitled *Meyer Lansky: Mogul of the Mob*, while Wallace Turner's and Hank Messick's detailed studies of organized crime and the gambling industry are still some of the best books written on the subject. Jerome Skolnick, *House of Cards*, is an impressive sociological study of the methods of both organized crime and the regulators in the gambling industry. Donald Barlett and James Steele's thorough biography of Howard Hughes, *Empire: The Life, Legend, and Madness of Howard Hughes*, is extremely valuable for researchers. A word should also be said about the excellent coverage of the ever-present mob by such investigative journalists as Al Delugach of the *Los Angeles Times*, Jim Drinkhall and Stanley Penn of the *Wall Street Journal*, Sandy Smith (formerly of *Time* magazine) and Denny Walsh of the *Sacramento Bee*. Histories and biographies of Nevada and major Las Vegas figures include Hank Greenspun, *Where I Stand: The Record of a Reckless Man*; Paul Lalli, *Nevada Lawyer*; Ed Reid and Ovid Demaris, *Green Felt Jungle*; and works by Oscar Lewis, James Hulse, and Gilman Ostrander. See the authors' "Just Don't Touch the Dice," in *Utah Holiday* (September 1980), for a discussion of the Mormon community in Las Vegas. Stephen Brill's *The Teamsters* provided an important account of this powerful union.

Interviews for the Las Vegas chapter: Robert Broadbent, Bob Brown, Richard Bunker, Shannon Bybee, Jr., Adele Castle, Samuel Davis, Ned Day, Ed Dunn, Anthony Earl, Ed Fronski, James Gibson, Ashley Hall, Devoe Heaton, L. C. Jacobsen, Peter Laxalt, Mike O'Callaghan, Wayne Pearson, Ed Reid, Harry Reid, Conrad Ryan, James Seastrand, Cornelius Smyth, Tom Stephen, Peter Thomas, Reed Whipple.

PART THREE: POINTS OF CONFLICT

The New Indian Wars: John Collier's autobiography, *From Every Zenith*, and Kenneth R. Philp, *John Collier's Crusade for Indian Reform, 1920–1954*, provide insights into this remarkably contemporary figure, while Joseph Jorgensen, "A Century of Political Economic Effects on American Indian Society, 1880–1980," in the *Journal of Ethnic Studies* (1978), provides the best overview of the United States' Indian policy. Jorgensen, *The Sun Dance Religion*, provides useful information on the Ute. Darcy McNickle, *Native American Tribalism: Indian Survivals and Renewals*, was also helpful. The dearth of useful contemporary material on the Navajo, with notable exceptions, is offset by numerous works on all aspects of Hopi life, including Richard O. Clemmer, *Continuities of Hopi Culture Change*; Harry James, *Pages from Hopi History*; *Me and Mine: The Life Story of Helen Sekakquaptewa*, as told to Louise Udall; and Emory Sekakquaptewa, "Preserving the Good Things in Hopi Life," in Edward H. Spicer and Raymond H. Thompson, eds., *Plural Society in the Southwest*. The *Navajo Times* (Window Rock, Arizona) gave a lively sense of the fight within the tribe over energy development after Peter MacDonald became chairman before its editor was removed in 1979.

Kirke Kickingbird and Karen Duchenaux, *One Hundred Million Acres*, provides an overview of the Indian land question, while the Indian Law Resource Center, *Report to the Hopi Kikmongwis and Other Traditional Leaders . . .*, provides the most detailed account of the imposition of "self-government" on an Indian tribe and the link between land claims and energy development. For a discussion of the Mormon's Indian Placement Service and their missionary program, see the authors' "The Kids Go Out Navaho, Come Back Donny and Marie," in *Los Angeles* magazine (December 1979); Spencer W. Kimball's biography by his two sons; and Jon Stewart and Peter Wiley, "Cultural Genocide," in *Penthouse* (June 1981). In addition, the Anthropology Resource Center, *Native Americans and Energy Development: Economic Development in American Indian Reservations*, put out by the Native American Studies Center at the University of New Mexico, was helpful. For an understanding of CERT see Christopher McLeod's writings and Winona LaDuke's *CERT: An Outsider's View*.

Norris Hundley, "The Dark and Bloody Ground of Indian Water Rights," in the *Western Historical Quarterly* (October 1978); Monroe Price and Gary D. Weatherford, "Indian Water Rights in Theory and Practice: Navajo Experience in the Colorado River Basin," in *Law and Contemporary Problems* (Winter 1978); and Eric Swenson's unpublished report "Ripping Off Navajo Water Rights: A Case Study in the Exercise of Political Power," provide detailed studies of the curtailment of Indian water rights. The legal briefs, memoranda, and papers of William Veeder (e.g., "Federal Encroachment on Indian Water Rights and the Impairment of Reservation Development"), the foremost champion of Indian water rights, are a must reading and a fascinating task for those attempting to untangle this complex problem.

Akwesasne Notes, put out by the Mohawk Nation in New York, is indispensable reading for an understanding of contemporary events in Indian country, as is its *Voices from Wounded Knee*. As an antidote to the flood of romantic accounts of Indian life that came out in the wake of Dee Brown's *Bury My Heart at Wounded Knee*, the writings of Vine Deloria, Jr., including *God Is Red* and *Behind the Trail of Broken Treaties*, provide unique and often iconoclastic insights into the Indian struggle, while Robert Burnette (a Sioux tribal chairman) and John Koster, *The Road to Wounded Knee*, shows the continuities in Indian politics from the 1930s on.

Interviews for the Indian chapter: Glenda Ahaitty, William Armstrong, Claudine Arthur, Harris Arthur, Thomas Banyacya, Ruby Black, Stephen Boyden, Tom Chabin, Katherine Collard, Colleen Colson, Tim Coulter, Loren Crank, Ron Faich, Joe Gmuca, La Donna Harris, David Harrison, Richard Hughes, Dennis Irving, Wayne Jordan, Joseph Jorgensen, Cyrus Josytewa, Jerry Kammer, Kirke Kickingbird, Hayes Lewis, Robert Lewis, Winona La Duke, Norman Littell, Tom Luebben, Peter MacDonald, Maxine Natchess, Parker Nielson, John O'Connell, Otis Paleoloma, Emory Sekakquaptewa, Wayne Sekakquaptewa, Martin Seneca, Dave Smith, Robert Sundance, Eric Swenson, Katharyn Harris Tijerina, Martin Topper, Steve Tullberg, William Veeder, George Vlassis, Gerald Wilkinson, Beth Wood, Gary Weatherford, Mabel Yazzie.

Mexico: On the border situation and the role of Mexican labor in the Southwest, Ernesto Galarza's writings, such as *Merchants of Labor* (on the Bracero Program), *Barrio Boy*, and *Spiders in the House and Workers in the*

Field, are invaluable for both their rigorous analysis and their ability to help us understand the Mexican experience in the Southwest. The pivotal work of Jorge Bustamante remains the single largest contribution toward an understanding of the situation of the undocumented Mexican workers, while the work of Wayne Cornelius on the same issue is also of tremendous value. Carey McWilliams, *North from Mexico,* is an important historical work, while Mario Barrera, *Race and Class in the Southwest,* is a major help in developing an analysis of the migration factor in historical terms.

The materials put out by the North American Congress on Latin America, including its excellent study *Beyond the Border,* cover a range of subjects, including the Border Industrial Program and the penetration of United States capital into Mexico. The BIP is also thoroughly analyzed by Carolyn Howe in her University of Oregon master's thesis, "The Border Industry Program and the Industrialization of Production on the United States-Mexico Border," as well as *Maquiladoras,* published by the Centro de Estudios Economicos y Sociales del Tercer Mundo. Norris Hundley, *Dividing the Waters,* as well as Louis Soleno Benavente, *Estudio General sobre el Aprovechamiento de las Aguas del Rio Colorado, en el Valle de Mexicali, Baja California y San Luis, R.C. Sonoro,* helped situate the water controversies between Mexico and the United States.

Materials on the Mexican economy and the role of the United States can be found in publications put out by Business International Corporation, including *Mexico: New Look at a Maturing Market,* as well as studies by Judith Adler Hellerman *(Mexico in Crisis)* and Roger D. Hansen *(The Politics of Mexican Development).* Frances Moore Lappé and Joseph Collins, *Food First,* has some useful information on the Mexican agricultural situation. The oil issue is thoroughly detailed in George W. Grayson, *The Politics of Mexican Oil,* while David Ronfeldt, Richard Nehring, and Arturo Gandara, *Mexican Petroleum and U.S. Policy: Implications for the 1980's,* written for the Rand Corporation, was useful.

Several anthologies of the University of New Mexico Press, including *Views from Across the Border* and *Mexican Workers in the United States,* have helpful essays on the culture of immigration and the border, while the series of documents and conference material put out by the UCLA Chicano Studies Center covers a wide range of subjects touching on the border. Note should also be made of the November 1980 issue of *Town and Country* and the critical response in the Mexican magazine *Proceso* on December 15, 1980, which provided a view of the Mexican elite from the point of view of wealthy Americans.

Interviews for the Mexico chapter: Jorge Bustamante, Gloria Chavez, Jessie de la Cruz, Barbara Hoenig, Joaquin Linton, Lydia Lopez, Vilma Martinez, José Medina, Julian Nava, Adolfo Aguilar Zinser.

Citizen Armies: Materials on the labor movement include the works of Irving Bernstein, especially the *Turbulent Years,* as well as those of Len De Caux and Philip Taft. Stephen Voynick's classic, *The Making of a Hard-Rock Miner,* plus Joseph Finley, *Corrupt Kingdom,* explore the United Mine Workers and the mining industry. Deborah Silverton Rosenfelt's essay on the Mine, Mill, and Smelter Workers in *Salt of the Earth* is helpful in situating this key union in the Southwest, as does Kent Hudson's master's thesis "Mine-Mill: The Voices from the Mountains," which covers the Mine, Mill, and Smelter Workers from the point of view of its leaders by way of interviews. Michael Wade, *The Bitter Issue: The Right to Work in Arizona*, helped situate that key issue of the postwar period as did Paul Sultan's study of the California right-to-work law. Lynn Robbin's analysis *Navajo Participation in Labor Unions* from the Lake Powell Bulletins series is the best discussion of that particular issue.

The oral history program and the Sierra Club files located at the Bancroft Library are invaluable source material for the environmental movement. David Brower's own oral history complements John McPhee, *Conversations with the Archdruid*. Wallace Stegner, *Beyond the Hundredth Meridian*, is a classic study of John Wesley Powell's exploration of the Grand Canyon and the Colorado River as well as an account of his struggle in the Washington bureaucracy. Peter Wild, *Pioneer Conservationists of Western America*, provides biographies of a range of environmentalists from Powell and John Muir to Edward Abbey. Elmo Richardson, *The Politics of the Conservation Issue in the Far West*, details some of the early environmental conflicts, while Roderick Nash, *Wilderness and the American Mind*, provides an analysis of some of the ideological and political underpinnings of environmentalism prior to Earth Day. James Ridgeway, *The Politics of Ecology*, is a more radical analysis of the post–Earth Day phenomenon. Massimo Teodoro, ed., *The New Left: An Anthology*, is an essential compilation of New Left thinking, while Michael Miles, *The Odyssey of the American Right*, provides an important historical overview of the New Right. W. Cleon Skousen, *The Naked Capitalist*, demonstrates the Far Right's hostility toward the eastern establishment and international Communism.

Interviews for the Citizen Armies chapter: Darwin Aycock, Brent Blackwelder, David Brower, Peter Carlson, Louise Dunlap, Mary Ann Erickson, John McComb, David Masselli, Ed Mayne, Edward Osann, Paula Phillips, William Robertson, Ron Rudolph, Greg Smith, Earl Warner, Max Warren, Gary Weatherford.

Conclusion: The contemporary study of the shift in political and economic power from the East to the West includes Alfred Watkins and David Perry, *The Rise of the Sunbelt Cities*; Kirkpatrick Sale, *Power Shift: The Rise of the Southern Rim and Its Challenge to the Eastern Establishment*; Carl Oglesby, *Yankee and Cowboy War*; Bernard Weinstein and Robert Firestone, *Regional Growth and Decline in the United States*; Robert Goodman, *The Last Entrepreneurs*; and Roger Alcaly and David Mermelstein, eds., *The Fiscal Crisis of American Cities*. Finally, Kevin Phillips drew important political lessons from this shift in his *The Emerging Republican Majority*, written during the Nixon years, but abandoned his analysis by 1978 in his "Balkanization of America" essay in *Harper's*.

Index